PENGUIN BO[illegible]

SIKHISM

W. H. McLeod is a New Zealander. He took an MA from the University of Otago in Dunedin, New Zealand, and a Ph.D. from the School of Oriental and African Studies in London. In 1990 he also received a D.Lit. from the University of London. For nine years he taught in the Punjab. In 1971 he returned to teach history at the University of Otago, where he has remained ever since, although he pays frequent visits to the Punjab. All of his books and most of his published articles concern Sikh history, religion and society. His books include *Guru Nanak and the Sikh Religion* (Clarendon Press, 1968), *The Evolution of the Sikh Community* (Clarendon Press, 1976), *Early Sikh Tradition* (Clarendon Press, 1980), *Who is a Sikh?* (Clarendon Press, 1989), *The Sikhs: History, Religion and Society* (Columbia University Press, 1989), *Popular Sikh Art* (Oxford University Press, Delhi, 1991), *Textural Sources for the Study of Sikhism* (University of Chicago Press, 1990) and *Historical Dictionary of Sikhism* (Scarecrow Press, 1995).

SIKHISM

Hew McLeod

PENGUIN BOOKS

PENGUIN BOOKS

Published by the Penguin Group
Penguin Books Ltd, 27 Wrights Lane, London W8 5TZ, England
Penguin Putnam Inc., 375 Hudson Street, New York, New York 10014, USA
Penguin Books Australia Ltd, Ringwood, Victoria, Australia
Penguin Books Canada Ltd, 10 Alcorn Avenue, Toronto, Ontario, Canada M4V 3B2
Penguin Books (NZ) Ltd, 182–190 Wairau Road, Auckland 10, New Zealand

Penguin Books Ltd, Registered Offices: Harmondsworth, Middlesex, England

First published 1997
3 5 7 9 10 8 6 4 2

Set in 10/12 pt Monotype Baskerville
Typeset by Rowland Phototypesetting Ltd, Bury St Edmunds, Suffolk
Printed in England by Clays Ltd, St Ives plc

For

Harjot Oberoi
Pashaura Singh
Gurinder Singh Mann
Lou Fenech

who keep the flag flying

CONTENTS

LIST OF TEXT FIGURES

ACKNOWLEDGEMENTS

The following have given advice and help in the preparation of this book, directly or through their various writings: Jerry Barrier, Owen Cole, Lou Fenech, Jagtar Singh Grewal, Mark Juergensmeyer, Khushwant Singh, Gurinder Singh Mann, Eleanor Nesbitt, Harjot Oberoi, Mohinder Singh, Pashaura Singh and John Webster. With much gratitude their assistance is warmly acknowledged. They are, however, freed from all responsibility for what the book contains. I alone am to blame. For her perseverance and continued help in the book's preparation I should also like to thank my secretary Paula Waby. Unfailingly accurate is her style and exceedingly patient her ways. Finally, beyond all hope of adequate expression I owe to my wife Margaret gratitude for her sustained interest and constant encouragement.

GLOSSARY

Ādi Granth: The Guru Granth Sahib (q.v.), the sacred scripture of the Sikhs recorded by Guru Arjan in 1603–4.
Āhlūvālīā: Sikh caste of the Punjab, by origin distillers but successful in acquiring a greatly elevated status.
Akālī: Follower of Akal Purakh (q.v.); member of the Akali Dal (Akali Party).
Akāl Purakh: 'The One beyond Time', God.
Akāl Takhat: The principal *takhat* (q.v.), located immediately adjacent to Harimandir Sahib (q.v., the Golden Temple).
akhaṇḍ pāṭh: Unbroken reading of the Guru Granth Sahib (q.v.).
akhāṛā: 'Wrestling-pit'; an Udasi or Nirmala (qq.v.) centre.
amrit: 'Nectar of immortality'; sweetened initiation water used in *amrit saṅskār* (q.v.).
amrit chhakṇā: 'To partake of *amrit*' (q.v.), to undergo initiation into the Khalsa (q.v.). cf. *khaṇḍe dī pāhul*, *pāhul*.
Amrit-dhārī: A Sikh who has 'taken *amrit*', viz. an initiated member of the Khalsa (q.v.).
amrit saṅskār: The initiation ceremony of the Khalsa (q.v.).
Anand Kāraj: The Sikh marriage ceremony.
Ardās: The Khalsa Prayer, a formal prayer recited at the conclusion of most Sikh rituals.
Aroṛā: A mercantile caste of the Punjab.
Ārya Samāj: Hindu reform movement of the late nineteenth and twentieth centuries (particularly strong in the Punjab), at first sympathetic to the Singh Sabha (q.v.) but soon shifting to hostility.
aṣhṭapadī: An Adi Granth *śhabad* (qq.v.) of eight verses with refrain.
Bābā: 'Father', a term of respect applied to holy men. Used in other Indian traditions.
Baisākhī Day: New Year's Day in rural Punjab, the first day of the month of Baisakh or Visakh.

Bālā janam-sākhīs: One of the extant collections of janam-sakhi anecdotes (q.v.).
bāṇī: Works of the Gurus and other poets included in the Sikh sacred scriptures.
Beās Rādhāsoāmī: A branch of the Radhasoami Sant movement with its principal centre located beside the Beas river.
Bhagat: A contributor to the Adi Granth (q.v.) who was not one of the Gurus (e.g. Kabir, Namdev, etc.).
Bhāī: 'Brother', title of respect given for piety and/or learning.
Bhāī Bālā: A reputed (almost certainly legendary) companion of Guru Nanak.
Bhakti: Belief in, adoration of, a personal god. Also used by Hindus.
bhog: The ceremony which concludes a complete reading of the Guru Granth Sahib (q.v.).
bhorā: Cave, hole in the ground.
bicholā: A relative who makes inquiries concerning possible spouses for a marriageable daughter or son.
charan amrit: Initiation with water in which the Guru has dipped his toe. Also used by Hindus.
chauṅkī: A division of each day in the larger gurdwaras (q.v.) in which a particular selection of *bāṇī* (q.v.) is sung. There are five *chauṅkīs* each day.
chaupad: An Adi Granth *śhabad* (qq.v.) consisting of four verses with refrain.
chaurī: A fan made from yak hair or peacock feathers which is waved over an open Guru Granth Sahib (q.v.), designating the royal authority of the scripture.
chhant: A lengthy Adi Granth *śhabad* (qq.v.), commonly of four or six verses.
Chief Khalsa Diwan: United body formed in 1902 to conduct the affairs of the Amritsar and Lahore Singh Sabhas (q.v.).
darśhan: Audience; appearance before eminent person, sacred object, etc. Also used by Hindus.
Dasam Granth: The scripture attributed to the authorship or times of Guru Gobind Singh.
deg tegh fateh: 'Cauldron, sword, victory', slogan of the eighteenth-century Khalsa (q.v.).

ḍhaḍhī: Village bard.
dharam (dharma): Panthic duty.
dharamsālā: Place of worship for early Sikh Panth (later gurdwara, qq.v.).
dīvān (diwan, dewan): Court; minister of state; assembly; assembly hall; congregation; collected verse of a poet.
faqīr: Muslim ascetic. Loosely used to designate Sufis (q.v.) and non-Muslim ascetics.
Five Ks: Five items (each beginning with the initial 'k') which Sikhs of the Khalsa (q.v.) must wear. The five are *kes*, *kaṅghā*, *kachh*, *kirpān* and *kaṛā* (qq.v.).
gaddī: 'Cushion'; seat of authority.
got (gotra): Exogamous caste grouping within a *zāt* (q.v.); sub-caste.
Granth: The '[Sacred] Volume', the Adi Granth or Guru Granth Sahib (qq.v.).
granthī: Custodian of a gurdwara (q.v.).
gurbāṇī: Compositions of the Gurus.
Gur-bilās: 'Praise of the Guru'; hagiographic narratives of the lives of the sixth and tenth Gurus, stressing their role as warriors.
gurdwara (gurduārā): Sikh temple.
Gurmat: The teachings of the Gurus; Sikhism.
Gurmukhī: 'From the Guru's mouth', the script in which Punjabi is written.
Gurū: A spiritual preceptor, either a person or the mystical 'voice' of Akal Purakh (q.v.).
Gurū Granth Sāhib: The Adi Granth, specifically in its role as Guru (qq.v.).
Gurū Granth: The Granth in its role as Guru (qq.v.).
Gurū Khālsā: The Khalsa in the role of Guru (qq.v.).
Gurū Panth: The Panth in its role as Guru (qq.v.).
Gur[u]matā: 'The Guru's intention', a resolution passed by the Sarbat Khalsa (q.v.) in the presence of the Guru Granth Sahib (q.v.).
Gurū-vaṅs: Descendants of one of the Gurus.
halāl: Flesh of an animal killed in accordance with Muslim ritual whereby it is bled to death (cf. *jhaṭakā*, *kuṭṭhā*.)
Hari: Name of God. Also used by Hindus.
Harimandir Sāhib: The Golden Temple.

haṭha-yoga: The yogic discipline practised by adherents of the Nath tradition (q.v.).
haumai: Self-centredness.
havan jag: Ritual fire ceremony practised by the Kuka Sikhs (q.v.). Also called a *hom*.
hukam: Divine Order; a passage from the Guru Granth Sahib (q.v.) chosen at random. cf. *vāk*.
hukam-nāmā: 'Letter of command'; document containing a command or a request issued by one of the later Gurus to an individual or a *saṅgat* (qq.v.); a similar document issued to the Panth by the Sarbat Khalsa from Akal Takhat (qq.v.).
Ik-Oaṅkār: The One Being; benedictory formula from the Adi Granth (q.v.).
izzat: Honour, self-respect.
jag (yajnā): A religious ceremony, sacrifice. cf. *havan jag*.
janam-sākhī: Hagiographic narrative of the life of Guru Nanak.
Jaṭ: Punjabi rural caste, numerically dominant in the Panth (q.v.).
jathā: Military detachment; touring parties (commonly for the administration of Khalsa initiation).
jathedār: Commander (normally of a *jathā*, q.v.).
jhaṭakā (jhaṭkā): Flesh of an animal killed with a single blow, approved for consumption by members of the Khalsa (q.v.). cf. *halāl*, *kuṭṭhā*.
jūṛā (joora): Topknot.
kachh: A pair of breeches which must not extend below the knees, worn as one of the Five Ks (q.v.).
kaṅghā: Wooden comb, worn as one the Five Ks (q.v.).
Kānphaṭ yogī: 'Split-ear' yogi; follower of Gorakhnath and adherent of the Nath tradition (q.v.).
kaṛā: Steel wrist-ring, worn as one of the Five Ks (q.v.).
kaṛāh prasād: Sacramental food prepared in a large iron dish (*kaṛāhī*). cf. *prasād*.
karma (karam): The destiny, fate of an individual, generated in accordance with the deeds performed in his/her present and past existences. Also used by Hindus.
kār-sevā: Voluntary assistance, normally with the cleaning of the pool surrounding Harimandir Sahib (q.v.).

kathā: Homily.
kes (kesh): Uncut hair, worn as one of the Five Ks (q.v.).
Kes-dhārī: A Sikh who retains the *kes* (q.v.).
keskī: Small under-turban.
Khālistān: 'Land of the Pure', the name adopted by proponents of an independent homeland for the Sikhs.
Khālistānī: A supporter of the Khalistan movement.
Khālsā: The religious order established by Guru Gobind Singh at the end of the seventeenth century.
khaṇḍā: Two-edged sword; Khalsa symbol comprising a vertical two-edged sword over a quoit with two crossed *kirpān*s (q.v.) below the quoit.
khaṇḍe dī pāhul: 'Initiation with the two-edged sword', the Khalsa (q.v.) initiation ceremony. cf. *amrit chhakṇā*, *pāhul*.
Khatrī: A mercantile caste of the Punjab.
kirpān: Sword or poniard, worn as one of the Five Ks (q.v.).
kīrtan: Singing of hymns.
Kūkā: Member of the Namdhari sect of Sikhs (q.v.).
kurahit: One of the four cardinal infringements of the Rahit (q.v.). The four *kurahit* are: 1. Cutting one's hair. 2. Consuming *kuṭṭhā* meat (q.v.). 3. Extra-marital sexual intercourse. 4. Smoking.
kuṭṭhā: Meat from an animal killed in the Muslim style. cf. *jhaṭakā*, *halāl*.
laṅgar: The kitchen/refectory attached to every gurdwara (q.v.) from which food is served to all regardless of caste or creed; the meal served from such a kitchen.
lāv (pl. lāvān): Circumambulating the Guru Granth Sahib (q.v.) or a sacred fire as part of a marriage ceremony.
mahant: The head of a religious establishment; the proprietor of a historic gurdwara (q.v.) until disestablishment in 1925.
man: The complex of heart, mind and spirit. Common Indian word.
mañjī: Preaching office of the early Panth (q.v.).
mantra: A verse, phrase or syllable of particular religious import. Also used by Hindus.
masand: Administrative deputy acting for the Guru. Inaugurated by Guru Ram Das, they served faithfully for some time, but later became

corrupt and were disestablished by Guru Gobind Singh. See *Pañj Mel.*

Mazhabī: The Sikh section of the Chuhra or sweeper caste; an Outcaste Sikh.

Mīṇā: 'Rascal'; a follower of Prithi Chand, eldest son of Guru Ram Das, and a pretender to the office of Guru. See *Pañj Mel.*

mīrī-pīrī: Doctrine that the Guru possesses temporal (*mīrī*) as well as spiritual authority (*pīrī*).

misl: A military cohort of the mid-eighteenth-century Khalsa (q.v.).

misldār: Commander of a *misl* (q.v.).

mokṣha: Spiritual liberation; liberation from transmigration. Also used by Hindus.

monā: Shaven. Mona Sikh sometimes designates a Sikh who cuts his/her hair.

nām: The divine Name, a summary term expressing the total being of Akal Purakh (q.v.).

Nāmdhārī: Member of the Namdhari Sikh sect (also known as Kuka Sikhs), followers of Balak Singh and Ram Singh.

nām japaṇ: Devoutly repeating the divine Name.

nām simaraṇ: The devotional practice of meditating on the divine Name or *nām* (q.v.).

Nānak-panth: The community of Nanak's followers; the early Sikh community; (later) members of the Sikh community who do not observe the discipline of the Khalsa (q.v.).

Nāth tradition: Yogic sect of considerable influence in the Punjab prior to and during the time of the Sikh Gurus; practitioners of *haṭha-yoga* (q.v.).

Nawab (Navāb): Governor; lord; prince.

Niraṅkār: 'Without Form', a name of Akal Purakh (q.v.) used by Guru Nanak.

Niraṅkārī: Member of the Nirankari Sikh sect, follower of Baba Dayal (1783–1855) and his successors. So-called because the sect emphasized the Nirankar form of Akal Purakh (qq.v.).

nirguṇa: 'Without qualities', formless, non-incarnated. cf. *saguṇa* (q.v.). Also used by Hindus.

Nirmalā: A sect of celibate Sikhs which commanded particular strength in the nineteenth century.

Nit-nem: The Sikh daily liturgy.

pāhul: The administration of *amrit* (q.v.) during the Khalsa initiation ceremony. cf. *amrit chhakṇā, khaṇḍe dī pāhul*.
paṅgat: '[Sitting in] line', the custom whereby equality is maintained in the *laṅgar* (q.v.).
pañj kakke: The Five Ks (q.v.); the five items, each beginning with 'k', which members of the Khalsa (q.v.) must wear. Also called the *pañj kakār*.
Pañj Mel: The Five Reprobate Groups. At the Khalsa initiation all candidates must swear to have no dealings with the Panj Mel. These comprise the followers of Prithi Chand (the Minas, q.v.), Dhir Mal, and Ram Rai, the *masands* (q.v.), and a fifth group which today is usually identified as those who cut their hair. The first three groups were followers of descendants of actual Gurus who were pretenders for the title of Guru.
Pañj Piāre: The 'Cherished Five' or 'Five Beloved'; the first five Sikhs to be initiated as members of the Khalsa (q.v.); five Sikhs in good standing chosen to represent a *saṅgat* (q.v.).
panth: A 'path' or 'way'; system of religious belief or practice; community observing a particular system of belief or practice. Common Indian word.
Panth: The Sikh community (*panth*, q.v., spelt with a capital 'P').
panthic (panthik): Concerning the Panth (q.v.).
pāṭh: A reading from the Sikh scriptures.
Patit: A Kes-dhari (q.v.) who cuts his hair or an Amrit-dhari (q.v.) who commits one of the four cardinal sins (the four *kurahit*, q.v.).
paṭkā: A piece of cloth which fits snugly over the *kes* (q.v.), worn by boys and sportsmen. cf. *rumāl*.
pauṛī: Stanza of a *vār* (q.v.).
pothī: Tome, volume.
prasād: Sacramentally offered food. cf. *kaṛāh prasād*. Also used for ordinary food. Common Indian word.
Purātan: One of the extant collections of janam-sakhi anecdotes (q.v.).
rāg (rāga): Metrical mode.
Rahit: The code of belief and conduct of the Khalsa (q.v.).
rahit-nāmā: A recorded version of the Rahit (q.v.).
rāj karegā khālsā: 'The Khalsa shall rule.'

Rāmdāsiā: The Sikh section of the Chamar or leather-worker caste; an Outcaste Sikh.
Rāmgaṛhīā: A Sikh artisan caste, predominantly drawn from the Tarkhan or carpenter caste, but also including Sikhs from the black-smith, mason and barber castes.
rumāl: A handkerchief; a small piece of cloth used for covering sportsmen's or children's *jūṛā* (q.v.). cf. *paṭkā*.
rumālā (romila): A cloth for covering the Guru Granth Sahib (q.v.).
sabhā: Society, association. Common Indian word.
sach khaṇḍ: The 'Realm of Truth'.
sādhan: Method of spiritual liberation.
saguṇa: 'With qualities', possessing form. cf. *nirguṇa*. Used also by Hindus.
sahaj: 1. Slow, easy, natural; 2. Inexpressible beatitude; the condition of ineffable bliss resulting from the practice of *nām simaraṇ* (q.v.).
Sahaj-dhārī: A non-Khalsa Sikh, one who does not observe the Rahit (q.v.).
sampraday: Doctrine, system of beliefs; group holding particular beliefs; sect. Hindu term.
Sanātan Sikhs: Conservative members of the Singh Sabha (q.v.), opposed to the Tat Khalsa (q.v.).
saṅgat: Congregation, group of devotees.
sant: One who knows the truth; a pious person; an adherent of the Sant tradition (q.v.).
Sant: One renowned as a teacher of Gurmat (q.v.).
sant-sipāhī: A 'sant-soldier', the ideal Sikh; a Sikh who combines the piety of the *sant* (q.v.) with the bravery of a soldier.
Sant tradition: A devotional tradition of north India which stressed the need for interior religion as opposed to external observance.
Sarbat Khālsā: 'The Entire Khalsa'; representative assembly of the Khalsa (q.v.).
sardār: Chieftain; leader of a *misl* (q.v.). 'Sardar' is nowadays used as a title of address for all Kes-dhari (q.v.) Sikh men. The corresponding title for a Sikh woman is *Sardāranī*.
sat: Truth; true. Common Indian word.
sati: The burning of widows or concubines on their husband's or master's funeral-pyre.

sati-nām: '[Your] Name is Truth.'
satsaṅg: An assembly of true believers; congregation.
satyagraha: Gandhian non-violent political protest.
sevā: Service, commonly to a gurdwara (q.v.).
SGPC: See Shiromani Gurdwara Parbandhak Committee.
śhabad (śabda): Word; a hymn of the Adi Granth (q.v.).
śhalok (ślok): A short composition (normally a couplet) from the Adi Granth (q.v.).
Shiromaṇī Akālī Dal: The Akali Party.
Shiromaṇī Gurduārā Parbandhak Committee: The committee that controls the historic gurdwaras (q.v.) of the Punjab and Haryana (commonly referred to as the SGPC).
Shiv, Shiva: The god who in Western usage usually appears with the spelling Siva.
Siddh, Siddha: Eighty-four men believed to have attained immortality through the practice of yoga and to be dwelling deep in the Himalayas. They figure in the janam-sakhis (q.v.), where they are confused with Naths (q.v.).
Siṅgh Sabhā: Reform movement in the Panth (q.v.) initiated in 1873. The Singh Sabha became the arena for a struggle between the conservative Sanatan Sikhs (q.v.) and the radical Tat Khalsa (q.v.).
Sūfī: A member of one of the Muslim mystical orders.
takhat: 'Throne'; one of the five centres of temporal authority in the Panth (q.v.).
tanakhāh: A penance for a violation of the Rahit (q.v.).
tanakhāhīā: A transgressor against the Rahit (q.v.).
Tat Khālsā: The 'true Khalsa' or 'pure Khalsa'. In the early eighteenth century, the immediate followers of Banda Bahadur. In the late nineteenth and twentieth centuries, radical members of the Singh Sabha (q.v.).
tīrath: A place of pilgrimage. Word used by Hindus also.
Udāsī: Adherent of the Udasi *panth* (q.v.), an order of ascetics (normally celibate) who claim as their founder Siri Chand (one of Guru Nanak's sons).
Vāhigurū: 'Praise to the Guru'; the modern Sikh name for God.
Vaishnava: Believer in, practitioner of Bhakti (q.v.), directed to the god Vishnu in one of his incarnations (either Ram or Krishan).

vāk: 'Saying'; a passage from the Guru Granth Sahib (q.v.) chosen at random. cf. *hukam*.
vār: A poetic form; an Adi Granth (q.v.) arrangement consisting of stanzas with preceding *śhaloks* (q.v.).
varṇa: 'Colour'; the classical caste hierarchy or a division of it. The four sections are Brahman, Kshatriya, Vaisha and Shudra, with Outcastes placed outside the hierarchy.
visamād: Wonder, awe.
zāt (jāti): Endogamous caste grouping; caste. cf. *got*.
3HO: Healthy Happy Holy Organization, the name by which the Sikh Dharma of the Western Hemisphere (followers of Yogi Bhajan) is generally known.

For fuller entries, see John R. Hinnells (ed.), *A New Dictionary of Religions*, Blackwell, Oxford, 1995, or W. H. McLeod, *Historical Dictionary of Sikhism*, Scarecrow Press, Lanham, Md, and London, 1995.

The Ten Gurus

1. Guru Nanak (1469–1539)
2. Guru Angad (1504–52)
3. Guru Amar Das (1479–1574)
4. Guru Ram Das (1534–81)
5. Guru Arjan (1563–1606)
6. Guru Hargobind (1595–1644)
7. Guru Hari Rai (1630–61)
8. Guru Hari Krishan (1656–64)
9. Guru Tegh Bahadur (1621–75)
10. Guru Gobind Singh (1666–1708)

INTRODUCTION

What is Sikhism? Assuming it exists, can it be adequately defined or will it defy all such attempts? Surely Sikhism can be defined as a syncretic mixing of Hindu and Muslim beliefs. Is it not a Punjabi version of Hinduism? All Sikhs can be recognized by a refusal to cut their hair. Sikhs are renowned as a militant people.

These are some of the questions and assertions that one commonly hears when discussing the Sikhs and their faith. The general question can be answered in the affirmative. Sikhism does indeed exist and it can be sufficiently defined. The definition will show, however, that our other opening statements must be significantly modified or comprehensively rejected. Sikhism is not a syncretic mixing of Hindu and Muslim beliefs in any meaningful sense. Most Sikhs will reject out of hand any suggestion that their religion is a version of Hinduism, Punjabi or otherwise. Not all Sikhs refrain from cutting their hair. Sikhs have certainly earned a reputation as a militant people, but it is a reputation which applies only to a portion of the community.

Sikhism traces its beginnings to the Punjab, where Guru Nanak was born in 1469 CE. To this day an overwhelming proportion of Sikhs either live in the Punjab or belong to Punjabi families. Their number is not insignificant. Although it is difficult to define the edges of the community, it can be claimed that today approximately 14 million Sikhs live in the Punjab or in the immediately adjacent areas of Rajasthan, Haryana and Himachal Pradesh. Another million are to be found scattered over the rest of India, and a million have settled in other countries. A sizeable group has migrated to the United Kingdom, where their number was estimated to be 269,600 in 1987. Appreciable numbers are found also in Canada and the United States, where the figure is estimated to be roughly 175,000 each.

But the Punjab is the homeland, and it is in the Punjab, on either side of the border between India and Pakistan, that most of their shrines and historic places are to be found. Although many places associated with the Gurus are located on the Pakistan side of the dividing line very few Sikhs actually live there. At the partition of India in 1947 the Sikhs cast in their lot with India and virtually the entire population crossed into Indian territory in the mass migrations that took place at the time.

Most of the migrating Sikhs settled in Indian Punjab, though even then they were not a majority in the province. Not until 1966, when the Indian government decided to grant Punjabi Suba (the state comprising only people who spoke Punjabi), did they actually reach that majority. It is a majority which is concentrated in the rural areas of the Punjab. Comparatively few Sikhs live in towns, which are, for the most part, predominantly Hindu in population. Even Amritsar, the holiest of holies for the Sikhs, contains only a minority of Sikhs. Farming in the rich grain-growing areas of the Punjab has been the traditional occupation of most Sikhs, an occupation which continues to the present day.

In studying the religion of the Sikh people one is inevitably confronted by the same contrast as affects any religious system. To any question, normative Sikhism gives one general answer (at least the orthodox form of Sikhism does). Sikh practice, however, frequently delivers a different one.

Some would hold, of course, that this does not matter when the study concerns the religion of the Sikhs. Just what Sikhs do in practice need not concern us. The religion presents the ideal which all Sikhs should strive to match and there the issue can rest. The failure of many Sikhs to measure up to this ideal is unfortunate (say the defenders of this view) but is scarcely surprising. Every religion has this experience with a large proportion of its nominal adherents, and the fact that Sikhism also has it is entirely predictable. Any study should concern the ideal. An awareness of different social practices by many Sikhs can properly be set aside.

Such an assumption is certainly a practicable possibility, but is it a realistic one? This study is squarely based on the assumption that it would not be realistic, nor would it be worth while. A religion can have meaning only as it is applied in practice, and if we are to understand its practical application we shall inevitably find ourselves dealing directly with a variety of social routines. In other words, a study of religion inevitably involves at least an elementary sociology.

In a study of Sikhism we shall also find ourselves dealing with the historical circumstances which have given rise to the religious system, with the result that History is also involved. Sikhs are strongly conscious of the historical background to their faith and it is very quickly evident that the path leads straight to the historical figure of Guru Nanak. The study soon proves to be sensitive, and it is a sensitivity which continues throughout the period of the ten Gurus and indeed well beyond them.

Three historical problems may be identified. The first is a shortage of trustworthy sources, at least to the professional historian. Whereas the popular view accepts tradition as valid historical evidence, the professional historian regards tradition as an altogether unsatisfactory means of reliably reconstructing the past. In this context 'tradition' means that which is handed down within the community (orally or in writing) without being exposed to rigorous historical scrutiny. We shall have more to say about 'tradition' and 'traditional' shortly.

This leads to the second problem. How is this material (much of it traditional) to be interpreted? Recognition by the strict historian of the importance of tradition for an understanding of the past certainly does nothing to make this problem go away. It is, indeed, a much more difficult problem than might appear at first sight, for the person who upholds the traditional view is not necessarily to be equated with ordinary Sikhs who possess little knowledge of historical procedures. What is proclaimed is not the blind faith of the masses but the views of scholars who have been nurtured in the Sikh tradition or have received their information from such sources. Such scholars find it very difficult to comprehend with sympathy findings or interpretations which seriously contest a traditional view.

The third problem, closely related to the first two, involves material which devout believers (in this case Sikhs) hold to be sacred. One treads here on exceedingly delicate ground. The vast majority of Sikhs are absolutely convinced, for example, that Guru Gobind Singh conferred the role of the Guru on both the Granth (the scripture) and the Panth ('path' or 'way'). To question this is to query a firmly held and deeply revered tradition, and the person who wishes to have it academically examined will protest in vain that the examination is being conducted with due dignity and proper respect. It involves venturing upon sacred territory and the responses generated by such an endeavour should surprise no one.

We must always be aware of this situation, and even if we were tempted to forget it we should very quickly be served an insistent reminder. The danger is that the things we say will be treated as blasphemous and for that reason will not be heeded. There is no easy way out of this particular problem, neither should it cause any surprise. Every religion includes a host of followers for whom the academic analysis of the faith is treated as a heinous crime or something approaching one. We need not be surprised at this and we must take heed of such feelings by expressing ourselves as prudently as possible. Those who were engaged in the controversy concerning the life of Jesus a century ago would have needed no reminder of the reality of this situation.

We return to the two words that underlie much of what has been said of these three problems, the words 'tradition' and 'traditional'. What is tradition and what are traditional sources? The word 'tradition' is used in this work in three different senses. First, it refers to a particular group with common or related beliefs (as, for example, the Hindu tradition or the Sant tradition). Secondly, it denotes the actual faith of any such group, the emphasis being firmly laid on those beliefs and customs which have been handed down from generation to generation without normally being subjected to critical scrutiny. The tradition (or traditions) of the Sikhs would be relevant in this context. Thirdly, the word will be employed to designate particular groups of hagiographic sources concerning the life of Guru Nanak. Most of what these sources contain is legend, but the word 'tradition' does not denote this particular characteristic. A synonym for 'tradition' in this context is actually 'cluster', and it is possible to speak of clusters of hagiographic sources rather than traditions.

It is the second of these meanings which has particular importance for this study. Our attention should be focused on the historical sources, and in this sense a source which has been passed down through the community without being subject to adequate historical scrutiny should be regarded as a tradition or a traditional source. It is important to be aware that in this study, whenever either 'tradition' or 'traditional' is used with reference to a historical source, this is the meaning that is normally attached to it. In such cases the source is one which has not been treated to sufficient historical scrutiny.

Inevitably, as with other religious communities, much Sikh history derives from sources of this nature. For Sikhism particular significance attaches to the process, for Sikhs have attached primary importance to the witness of history (or of tradition) to their faith. The historian who questions such tradition will commonly find that fierce controversy is the result, yet cautiously and respectfully he or she is bound to subject the tradition to strict historical analysis. The task must be undertaken with due concern for the feelings of believers. Little is to be gained from the careless or unconcerned demolition of tradition.

A careful approach is needed for the entire range of all ten Gurus from Nanak to Gobind Singh. Indeed, it is required for much that lies beyond those two centuries, though the need for caution is particularly acute when dealing with the Gurus. The present situation is that a considerable trust is placed in an uncritical acceptance of the available sources and these give rise to the traditional history of the Sikhs. These sources consist of a very small quantity of reliable material from the Adi Granth, from the poetic works of Bhai Gurdas,[1] and from the glimpses afforded by a work called the *Dabistān-i-Mazāhib*. This is substantially filled out by tradition, much of it recorded in the nineteenth century by that most famous of all Sikh hagiographers Santokh Singh. In this respect Santokh Singh has been very influential and many of the accepted 'biographies' of the Gurus derive in large part from his *Nānak Prakāśh* and his *Sūraj Prakāśh*.

There is no way out of this problem. It is a problem from the time of Nanak's birth and even before. It frustrates us in our attempts to analyse the sixteenth century and it is a problem that does not get much better for the seventeenth. Work has been done on the first, third and tenth of the Gurus (on Nanak, Amar Das and Gobind Singh), but for the remaining seven Gurus the return has been distinctly unimpressive. The lives of Gurus Angad, Ram Das, Arjan, Hargobind, Har Rai and Har Krishan rely largely on tradition, and Guru Tegh Bahadur is not much better. This does not mean that nothing can be known about them. Reliable sources do report a small amount, and in limited respects tradition can be a generally sound source (as, for example, in the reporting of family relationships or the dates of deaths). In most respects, however, one must be very wary of trusting tradition.

Although this is loss it is by no means all loss. The extensive hagiographic narratives dealing with Guru Nanak may not provide us with an accurate representation of his life, but they have assuredly provided the Sikh community with a subjective image of him which is still vividly present today. The same feature applies also to his successors. To imagine the community with images based solely on historically tested facts is altogether fanciful. These were their Gurus, and the notion that the impression left by them could be partial or attenuated is quite unthinkable. In studying the history of the Gurus it is vitally important to understand the idea or image of all ten figures conceived by past and present Sikhs. To see them as Sikhs today see them (or at least to make the attempt) illuminates the entire Sikh tradition.

Moreover, it is only the historical figures of the Gurus which we are compelled to view through a misty screen. The same certainly does not apply to their teachings, particularly the teachings of Nanak. Guru Nanak does not present his teachings in the manner of a Western systematic theologian, but his numerous works nevertheless contain a pattern of belief that is complete. From this pattern it is possible to extract a system which is complete and in all respects consistent. Nanak preached a religion of the divine Name, and that religion, present in hymns of superb beauty, has descended through the Sikh community to the present day.

The Sikh religion has, of course, been significantly enlarged since Nanak's day and all subsequent developments are not as easily understood as the crystal-clear teachings of Guru Nanak. On the whole, however, they are intelligible. Issues which can be regarded as religious are not nearly as obscure as those which would be treated as historical. As we have already seen, though, Sikhism is a historical religion and Sikhs insist that a knowledge of their history is essential for a grasp of their religion. And they are right.

Because this study of Sikhism is (like any study of any religious system) built upon a particular range of interpretations, it will be as well if it begins by clearly enunciating certain basic assumptions. It is fully recognized that there will be readers who disagree with these assumptions, and that some will regard them as comprehensively and dangerously wrong. My justification for making them is that I believe them to be true. Other readers, however, will see the matter differently, and it will be only fair if the pattern of my own views is laid out at the very beginning. My basic assumptions are as follows.

1. To categorize religions in any complete sense as separate and independent from one another is clearly impossible. By the standards normally employed, however, Sikhism is today a separate and independent religious system.

2. This was not always the case. The community that gathered around Guru Nanak was in no fundamental way different from other such communities which formed in India before, during and after his time. From the third Guru onwards this community (the Sikh community) acquired features which increasingly imparted distinction, but the significant change did not come until the late nineteenth century. During Singh Sabha times (the late nineteenth and early twentieth centuries) reformers emphasized the distance between the Sikhs and Hindu tradition, with the result that Sikhism emerged as a genuinely separate system.

3. Whether or not Guru Nanak was the founder of Sikhism depends upon how the word 'founder' is employed. Sikhs trace the beginnings of their community back to Nanak, and as the initiator of a new panth ('path') he is clearly to be regarded in this sense as its founder. In the Hindu tradition, however, there have been many new panths and if the line is traced back through ideas rather than through personalities the description is inappropriate.

4. The background of Sikhism was the Sant movement of northern India. Guru Nanak was a representative of the Sant movement and he expresses in his works the characteristic doctrines of the Sants. He was indeed a unique figure in the history of religions, but his uniqueness lies in the clarity and comprehensiveness of his inspired teachings and in the beauty with which they were expressed. These qualities impart supreme excellence to his teachings.

5. The teachings of Nanak cannot reasonably be regarded as a syncretism of Hindu teachings and Islam as so many popular books have suggested. Some of the Sants embodied a limited amount of Islam in their hymns, but the burden of their teachings was weighted heavily towards concepts found in Hindu ideals. This is not to deny that Muslim culture exercised an influence on the development of the Sikh community. It does, however, deny that Islam significantly influenced Guru Nanak.

6. Nanak was followed by nine successors. Under these successors the Sikh community grew in size and experienced important developments. This was particularly the case in the time of the third Guru (a period of administrative developments) and of the sixth Guru (a period of military organization).

7. The tenth Guru, Gobind Singh, founded the order known as the Khalsa at the end of the seventeenth century. The Khalsa has been of absolutely critical importance in the development of Sikhism.

8. Gobind Singh was the last of the personal Gurus. Sikhs came to believe that at his death he decreed that the function of Guru would vest jointly in the sacred scriptures (Guru Granth) and the Sikh community (Guru Panth). The Guru Granth came, in effect, to signify the scripture known as the Adi Granth. Whether the Guru Panth signified the wider Sikh community or the narrower Khalsa is a matter which has caused considerable debate.

9. Following the death of Guru Gobind Singh in 1708, the eighteenth century was a time of great testing for the Sikhs, leading first to the rule of much of the Punjab by Sikh *misl*s (warrior bands) and finally culminating in the creation of a Sikh kingdom under Maharaja Ranjit Singh. Sikhism passed through a period of important development during this century, emerging with a clear doctrine of the Khalsa and its associated duties (the Rahit).

10. Sikhism experienced a major reformation at the end of the nineteenth century and the beginning of the twentieth (the period known as that of the Singh Sabha movement). The direction of the reformation was vigorously contested by two groups, namely the conservative

Sanatan Sikhs and the radical Tat Khalsa. The Tat Khalsa won comprehensively and recast the Sikh community in a way which emphasized its independence and its difference from Hindu tradition.

11. There is a general consistency concerning doctrine in the Sikh community. Some differences do exist, however, and there are recognized sects in Sikhism.

12. Sikhism bestows tremendous reverence upon its sacred scripture. This, in practice, means for most Sikhs the scripture known as the Adi Granth. The scripture known as the Dasam Granth occupies an uncertain position.

13. The Adi Granth is universally termed the Guru Granth Sahib as Sikhs believe that it embodies the actual presence of the mystical Guru. Here too the status of the Dasam Granth is uncertain.

14. The gurdwara (temple) occupies a pivotal position for Sikhism. In the gurdwara devotion centres on the Guru Granth Sahib.

15. Not all Sikhs believe in the religion known as Sikhism. It is quite possible to be born into a Sikh family and maintain the outward appearance of a Sikh without assenting to the religious doctrines of the community.

16. Caste possesses an ambivalent status among Sikhs. Orthodox statements of Sikh belief rule it out completely. The vast majority of Sikhs, however, observe its rules, at least with regard to marriage.

17. The place of women in Sikhism is likewise uncertain. Orthodox statements give them equal status with men. In practice the situation is very different.

Finally, we shall define six key terms that are central to Sikhism and which recur in this study. Although all are Punjabi words they are employed in this study as ordinary English terms.

Akāl Purakh or *Vāhigurū*: In this case there are two terms to be defined, both with the same meaning. Akal Purakh is one of several terms from early Sikh usage for 'God'. It is generally used in this study, partly because it best summarizes the concept employed by Guru Nanak and partly because it is still widely used today. Vahiguru is, however, the preferred modern word among most Sikhs and is sometimes employed in this work. Unfortunately neither term overcomes the problem of gender when using English. To Nanak and all who follow him, Akal Purakh or Vahiguru is without gender and by using the male gender for them we inevitably give either term a false slant.

Gurū: Spiritual preceptor. According to Sikhism the Guru was the 'voice' of Akal Purakh (God), who 'spoke' the Word in the hearts of true believers, thereby revealing the divine Name. Nanak was divinely inspired to perform the same function and so became the first human Guru. The same Guru passed through a succession of nine more persons as a single flame can be transmitted to nine successive torches. The tenth human Guru, Gobind Singh, declared himself to be the last personal Guru and is believed to have transferred the functions of the Guru to the sacred scripture and to the Sikh community.

Gurmat: The teachings of the Guru. The word is used to cover all the teachings of all the Gurus and in general corresponds to the English word 'Sikhism'.

Panth: In Indian tradition a *panth* ('path' or 'way') is a distinctive body of belief or the following attached to a particular religious leader. As such it corresponds to a religious movement, denomination or sect. In this respect the roman convention of small or capital initial letters is a distinct convenience. The word 'panth' with a small initial designates any of these movements or sects. With a capital initial, however, 'Panth' is used for the Sikh community. Sikhs proudly refer to their community as simply the Panth.

Khālsā: The order established by Guru Gobind Singh at the end of the seventeenth century. Not all Sikhs are members of the Khalsa and those who do not belong to it do not observe its code of discipline (its Rahit). The observant Khalsa is, however, the solid core of the Panth.

Rahit: The code of belief and behaviour which all members of the Khalsa must vow to obey. According to tradition, Guru Gobind Singh delivered the Rahit fully formed to his Sikhs when he inaugurated the

Khalsa. Analysis of subsequent Sikh history makes it clear, however, that the Rahit has subsequently changed and developed in accordance with the circumstances of later periods.

A grasp of all these terms is essential for an understanding of the account of Sikhism which now follows.

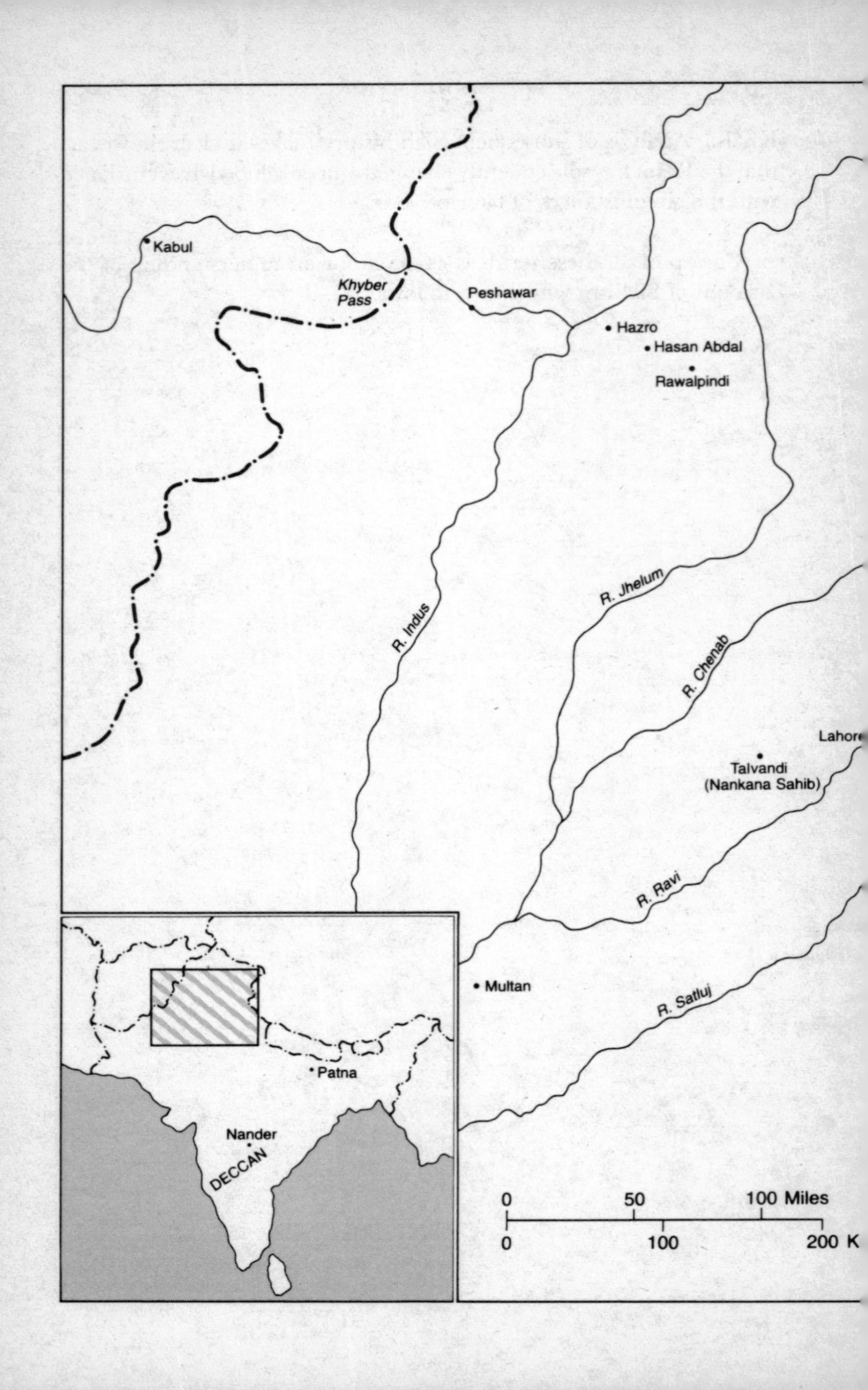

Kabul
Khyber Pass
Peshawar
Hazro
Hasan Abdal
Rawalpindi
R. Jhelum
R. Indus
R. Chenab
Lahore
Talvandi (Nankana Sahib)
R. Ravi
Multan
R. Satluj
Patna
Nander
DECCAN
0
50
100 Miles
0
100
200 K

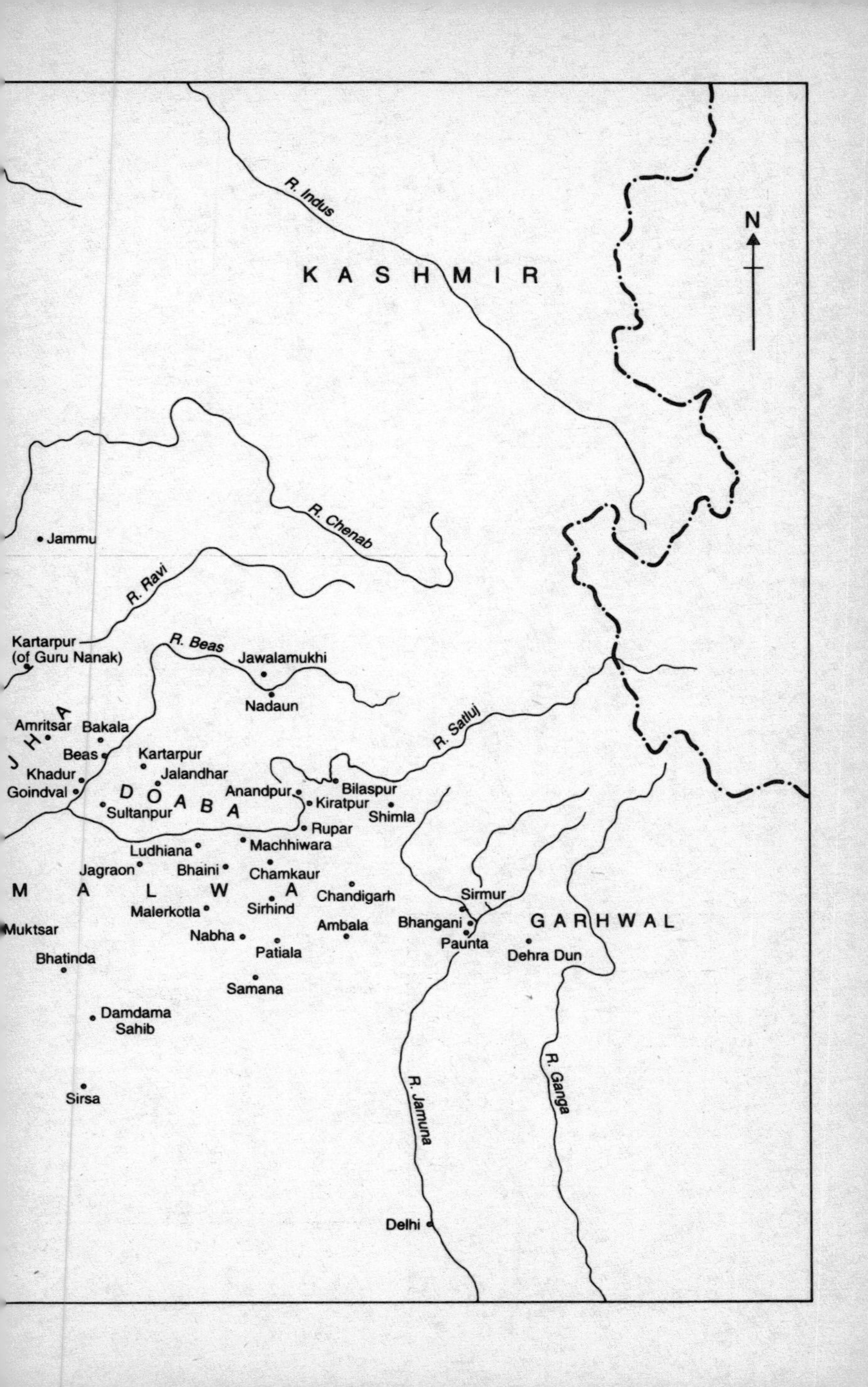

N
KASHMIR
R. Indus
R. Chenab
R. Ravi
R. Beas
R. Satluj
Jammu
Kartarpur
(of Guru Nanak)
Jawalamukhi
Nadaun
Amritsar
Bakala
Beas
Kartarpur
Khadur
Jalandhar
Goindval
DOABA
Anandpur
Bilaspur
Kiratpur
Shimla
Sultanpur
Rupar
Ludhiana
Machhiwara
Jagraon
Bhaini
Chamkaur
MALWA
Chandigarh
Sirmur
Malerkotla
Sirhind
Muktsar
Ambala
Bhangani
GARHWAL
Nabha
Paunta
Patiala
Dehra Dun
Bhatinda
Samana
Damdama
Sahib
Sirsa
R. Jamuna
R. Ganga
Delhi

PART ONE: HISTORY

1

THE EARLY GURUS

Guru Nanak was born in a Punjab village in 1469 and died in the Punjab in 1539. His period is thus clearly established as likewise is the geographical area within which he delivered much of his message. There are in fact lengthy biographies of Nanak which give in great detail accounts of his early life, followed by periods of extensive travels and finally by his settling down in his own village. Unfortunately these accounts cannot be trusted as historical sources, relying as they do for almost all their information on the extensive hagiographies known as *janam-sākhīs* or 'birth evidences'.

Janam-sakhis and the life of Guru Nanak

In his numerous hymns Guru Nanak himself tells us very little concerning the events of his life, and the information which can be ascertained from reliable sources amounts to only the barest outline. This includes the names of his relatives, the village in which he was born, the town where he was employed as a young adult, and the village in which he died. The various janam-sakhis relate lengthy narratives of his journeys in India and beyond, but apart from the fact that he did spend several years travelling, there is virtually nothing that can be affirmed concerning this period of his life.

It would be unfair, however, to disregard the janam-sakhis without at least a brief treatment. The entire corpus has been analysed and very little in them will stand up as historical fact, but simply to ignore them would be to dismiss a sizeable portion of the Sikh tradition and consequently a significant influence on the later development of the community (the Panth). Janam-sakhis consist of collections of anecdotes about Nanak, and although the earliest extant collection is dated 1658 CE, it seems reasonable to suppose that anecdotes had been circulating ever since Nanak's own time. This means that Sikhs of every period since then have been brought up on these popular stories about the first Guru. The anecdotes, moreover, are not tales suitable only for children. Janam-sakhi accounts remain throughout a person's life and any attempt to question them will be met with resolute disapproval.

The anecdotes contained in janam-sakhi collections may be impossible for a historian to accept, but the historian assuredly does not speak for the Panth as a whole. As far as the Panth is concerned, the janam-sakhis are reliable and woe betide the person who dares to question them. These anecdotes, moreover, embody ideals and give expression to approved behaviour. As such they are indeed acceptable to the vast majority of Sikhs and have exercised a marked influence upon successive generations of the Panth.[1]

The janam-sakhis are grouped in several clusters or families, each of which orders its chosen anecdotes in a sequence corresponding to Nanak's life story. Two of these clusters are dominant. Until the late nineteenth century the *Bālā* collection controlled the field, a group of janam-sakhis which had as the Guru's regular travel companion a certain Bhai Bala. During the later nineteenth century the *Bālā* janam-sakhis created growing unease among educated Sikhs, as these collections specialize in jumbled sequences and quaint miracle stories. In 1872, however, another version was discovered which certainly had its fair share of miracles but related them more soberly and did so in the context of a more ordered sequence. This was the *Purātan* tradition. Since its discovery *Purātan* has provided the framework for the more sophisticated biographies of Nanak, leaving *Bālā* in control of the popular market. The story which the janam-sakhis tell is as follows.

Nanak was born a Hindu in the Punjabi village of Talvandi, west of Lahore. His birth and childhood were marked by manifest signs of divine approval, such as the heavenly host which gathered to greet his arrival into the world. When he grew to maturity he was married and had two sons. As a young man he joined his sister's husband in the town of Sultanpur (near the confluence of the Beas and Satluj rivers) and there took employment with the local lord. It was while he was in Sultanpur that he had the religious experience that led him to set out on his journeys to preach his divine message. There is no agreement concerning itinerary in the janam-sakhis, but the modern accounts in English normally follow the *Purātan* pattern, so that is the order followed in the remainder of this summary.

According to the janam-sakhis of the *Purātan* tradition, Nanak made four expeditions outside the Punjab, one to each of the four cardinal points of the compass. On all these journeys he was accompanied by his faithful minstrel, the Muslim Mardana. First he travelled eastward, ending up in what modern commentators identify as Assam. Returning to the Punjab he then visited the south as far as Sri Lanka. Next came a journey to the north that led him through Kashmir and up the slopes of the mythical Mount Sumeru, which the commentators say was Mount Kailash. Finally he travelled westward and visited the Muslim holy cities of Mecca and Medina.

After his four lengthy journeys he settled in the Punjab at a spot on the Ravi river above Lahore. Here the new village of Kartarpur was built. Nanak remained there preaching his message and blessing those who came to visit him. In 1539 (or 1538 if we follow the *Purātan* janam-sakhis) he died in Kartarpur and possession of his body was disputed by Hindu and Muslim devotees. Upon the cloth which covered it being raised, only flowers were discovered. These were divided, the Hindus taking their share for burning and the Muslims theirs for burial.

Within this framework all manner of anecdote is contained, various authors including or withholding them in accordance with the length of their biographies and their susceptibilities concerning the miraculous. One popular anecdote from Nanak's childhood is the story entitled 'The Ruined Crop Restored'.

Like other village boys Baba Nanak[2] went to graze the buffaloes in the morning and having done so he brought them home at dusk. One day he left the buffaloes unattended and fell asleep at the edge of a wheat field. While he slept the buffaloes trampled the crop and ate the wheat.

When the crop of wheat had been demolished its owner appeared and cried, 'Why have you ruined my field? Explain this outrage!'

'Nothing of yours has been ruined, brother,' replied Baba Nanak. 'What harm is there in a buffalo putting down its head to graze? God will make it a blessing.'

The owner was not pacified and began to argue with Baba Nanak. Quarrelling all the way, Baba Nanak and the man who owned the field went together to Rai Bular, who was the headman of Talvandi. When he had heard the owner's complaint the headman commanded that Kalu, Nanak's father, should be brought.

They summoned Kalu and Rai Bular said to him, 'Kalu, rebuke this son of yours, for he has ruined another man's field. You have let him remain simple-minded. Make restitution for this damage to another's property or you will appear before the Turks.'[3]

'What can I do?' replied Kalu. 'He wanders around like a crazed fool.'

'I pardon *your* offence, Kalu,' said Rai Bular, 'but you must make restitution for the damage.'

Then Baba Nanak spoke. 'Nothing has been ruined,' he said. 'He is not telling the truth.'

'*Everything* in my field has been ruined!' exclaimed the owner of the field. 'I have been robbed! Give me justice or else I shall have him summoned before the Turks.'

'Not a blade of grass has been eaten nor even broken,' said Baba Nanak. 'Send your man to see.'

Rai Bular sent his messenger and what should the messenger discover when he went to inspect the field? He found that not one plant had been harmed! He returned and said, 'Nothing has been harmed.' Hearing this, Rai Bular declared the owner of the field to be a liar, and Baba Nanak and Kalu both returned home.[4]

It seems somewhat hard on the unfortunate owner of the crop to be declared a liar, but we miss the point if we focus on details. The anecdote is simply concerned to show the protective hand of Akal Purakh (God) hovering over the child Nanak. Details about other people are unimportant. The same protective hand is also evident in two other anecdotes concerning divine protection for the sleeping child. One of these relates how a tree's shadow remains stationary while Nanak sleeps under it, and in the other a cobra shields him from the sun by distending its hood. The latter example, which is present also in Buddhist tradition, indicates one of the sources from which anecdotes were derived.

Another popular anecdote relates how Nanak, while approaching

Multan on his travels, was greeted by a cup brimful of milk which the local Muslims had sent out to deter him from entering the city. The message was clear. Multan already had all the religious preachers it could hold. Nanak's reply was to lay a jasmine petal on the milk and send it back unspilled, signifying that there was room in the city for the noblest message of all. This anecdote was borrowed from Sufi sources. It was first related concerning 'Abd al-Qadir Jilani's approach to Baghdad and was then repeated twice concerning other Sufis of Multan.

Another anecdote is the story of Lalo and Bhago. On his travels Nanak chose to stay in Eminabad at the humble home of the low-caste Lalo. Word soon spread that he had arrived and a wealthy high-caste person called Bhago demanded to know why Nanak had chosen such a lowly abode when he would have been pleased to offer much grander accommodation. In reply Nanak asked Bhago to send a portion of his rich fare. Taking some of it in one hand and Lalo's vegetable cake in the other, he squeezed both. From Lalo's cake issued milk whereas from Bhago's food there oozed blood.

The story-telling appeal provides one of the two reasons for the immense popularity of these anecdotes and the message communicated by them provides the other. Concern for the sleeping child demonstrates Akal Purakh's care for the chosen messenger. The jasmine petal illustrates the supreme truth and beauty of all that he teaches. And the story of Lalo and Bhago confirms his championing of the low-caste poor against the wealthy and arrogant high caste. The janam-sakhi stories may not have actually happened, but they do serve to enshrine the message that later generations of Sikhs took from the teachings of Nanak.

The janam-sakhis also point to various features of the early Panth. In this respect they testify to later periods than that of Guru Nanak himself, though it is still the early Panth that is represented. One such feature is the Nanak-panthis' somewhat ingenuous understanding of Nanak's key doctrine of the *nām* and of its practical expression in the discipline of *nām simaraṇ*.[5] A common variety of anecdote records how Baba Nanak visited a particular place during his travels, converted the people by means of a miracle or wise pronouncement, and then proceeded on his way. These references make it clear that *nām simaraṇ* was understood as a mechanical repetition of the single word 'Guru'. This, it may be argued, is a part of the total range covered by the concept of *nām simaraṇ*, but plainly it lacks the sophistication of Nanak's own understanding.

Another feature of this standard conclusion to janam-sakhi anecdotes concerns the *dharamsālā*, a room for devotional singing. In every house, we are told, there was established a dharamsala. In other words, each house became a place where devout Sikhs would gather to sing the Guru's hymns. The twin concepts of *saṅgat* (congregation) and *kīrtan* (hymn-singing) are thus emphasized in the janam-sakhis as a regular feature of the corporate life of the Nanak-panth. Elsewhere in the janam-sakhis we encounter a reference to indicate that the dharamsala was one of the features which conferred a distinctive identity on the Nanak-panth. Sikhs of Guru Nanak can be distinguished from adherents of other panths because they possess their own special place of worship.

The janam-sakhis are thus of considerable value. They do not provide much in the way of narrowly historical fact, but they do testify to the impact which Nanak's teachings made upon his early Sikhs and they demonstrate also how some of those teachings were worked out in the life of the early Nanak-panth. When, for example, the Nanak of the janam-sakhis utters the pregnant maxim *nā koī hindū hai nā koī musalmān* ('There is no Hindu; there is no Muslim'), the words may not actually be those of the historic Guru but the interpretation of the saying is consonant with his teachings and has been implicitly believed by generations of Sikhs ever since it was first circulated.[6] Likewise, the description of a childless couple, gathered with a congregation and praying to Baba Nanak for the gift of a son, provides an authentic picture of the Panth at a later stage in its development.[7]

The image of Nanak to emerge from the janam-sakhis is still very much the image which accompanies the Panth to the present day. For ordinary Sikhs calendar art or the bazaar poster is a particularly important decoration for their houses or places of business. No illustration of the Gurus is as popular as the one which shows an elderly Baba Nanak with patchwork garments and a supremely benign expression, eyes half closed in meditation and his hand raised in blessing. This is very much the Nanak that the Sikhs remember.

The early Nanak-panth: a religious community

When Guru Nanak died in 1539 how large was the community of his followers? The traditional accounts of his last years refer to a rapidly growing community of many Sikhs who responded with enthusiasm to his teachings. How do we know that it had become a large one? We may think it quite unbelievable that Guru Nanak could ever have attracted few disciples, but in fact we have little to go on other than the traditional sources. It is true that the janam-sakhis claim that he attracted large crowds from far and near, and that as his fame increased so too did the host of pilgrims coming to his village for his blessing. But that is the way with the hagiographic janam-sakhis, as with all such writings from almost any religious group. Their authors would certainly be unable to imagine one, blessed by Akal Purakh in such a special way, ever attracting only a small number of disciples. It would have to be a very large figure.

We are therefore left with a problem when we are required to estimate the number of disciples Nanak attracted to Kartarpur. That he did attract some is quite beyond question, for otherwise how was Lahina (the future Guru Angad) called to be a Sikh? But was it a large number or was it a small one or was it somewhere in between? We are unable to answer other than on the grounds of assumption. We *assume* that because Nanak's teachings were later seen to be successful among the rural people of the Punjab, it follows that they were successful from the very beginning, and that consequently he attracted many rural people to his centre in Kartarpur during his lifetime.

This would be natural enough. A teacher earns a reputation for great piety and for communicating the message of divine liberation. The word spreads around the neighbouring villages and even those further away, and soon the people are coming for *darśhan*.[8] They come expecting blessing, and having received it they depart. It is all quite natural and believable, and doubtless it is true.

What is not based on assumption is the nature of the Panth that was thus formed. What was the message that Nanak so insistently preached, the doctrine that was at the heart of all he said in the works he has left? The message which Nanak preached, in different styles and in endless variety, was love of the divine Name. The divine Name is the way to spiritual liberation, freely open to all.

> Burn sensual craving, make ink with its ashes; as paper prepare heart and mind.
> Take love as your pen and with reason the scribe enquire of the Guru and list his commands.
> Write on that paper the Name with your praises; write of the infinite power!
>
> *Refrain*: This is the record to learn how to write;
> This is the record by which we are judged.
>
> Where fame is conferred in the presence sublime, where glory and rapture abound,
> They who have treasured your Name in their hearts bear the marks of your grace on their brows.
> For grace is the means to obtaining the Name; all other is bluster and wind.
>
> One may appear and another depart, each with his dignified title and name.
> One may be born to beg food and his clothing, another to rule with renown.
> Each as he passes shall surely discover that lacking the Name he is doomed.
>
> In dread of your majesty, awesomely grand, my body must waste and decay.
> They who were known as the lords of creation have withered and crumbled to dust.
> Our ties with this transient world must dissolve when we rise and proceed on our way.[9]

It was, in other words, an explicitly religious message and the people who acknowledged him as Guru did so for religious reasons. The Panth was therefore a religious organization. Liberated by the divine Name, each person owed the freedom from superstition and empty ritual to the man to whom they now looked up as spiritual guide and leader. Others owed him the same debt and together they formed his body of disciples (or his Sikhs). Whether there were many or few is beside the point. This body of loyal believers constituted his Sikhs, expressing their oneness by gathering as a *satsaṅg* (a congregation or 'fellowship of true believers') for *kīrtan* (hymn-singing). The body constituted the Panth, or (to be more explicit) the Nanak-panth (the society of those who acknowledged the way taught by Nanak as the means of liberation from the spiritual ills that surround us). And it was a *religious* Panth.

This point bears repeating because the Sikhs as we know them today are much more than merely a religious community. The British, in more than two centuries of ruling in India, never knew the Panth as one which was restricted to meditation and devotion. All the writings of British soldiers and administrators have taken for granted that it comprised much more. They had, after all, met this Panth in two hard-fought wars in the middle of the nineteenth century, and the troops who so vigorously opposed them were scarcely moved by the dictates of religion alone.

But we should not exaggerate this point. The Khalsa soldiers were not motivated by religion alone, but it certainly played a part in their sense of common brotherhood. The religion that bound them together was the religion of Guru Nanak, at least in origin and partly at least in substance. It was greatly supplemented by the contribution of his successors (notably by the tenth Guru), but the message of liberation through the divine Name still held sway. Even if not many Sikhs in the mid nineteenth century did anything very practical about the message, it nevertheless commanded the active allegiance of a sufficient number and it was recorded for any who chose to read it in the scriptures which commanded such veneration.

When we go back to the time of Guru Nanak that message is virtually the sole reason for the existence of the Nanak-panth; and the Nanak-panth is, accordingly, a *religious* community which bound together people who affirmed belief in Nanak's conviction of the all-powerful, all-liberating divine Name. This it sustained throughout the sixteenth century; and for most of the seventeenth century it retained the same character. Although it adopted a policy of active defence against adversaries under the sixth Guru, it is only with the execution of Guru Tegh Bahadur in 1675[10] that it begins to emerge as a community with interests which extend further. Only with the lifetime of Guru Gobind Singh does it begin the task of formalizing that change. And only with the chaos and confusion of the eighteenth century does it assume, as the Khalsa, the functions that carry it well beyond the religious definition of a community. By the end of the century the Khalsa is proclaiming the famous words *rāj karegā khālsā*, 'the Khalsa shall rule', and under the leadership of Maharaja Ranjit Singh it assumes the role of a state.

But Nanak, we must repeat, was the Master of a religious community, and it is a strictly religious community which he passed on to his chosen successor. There was nothing surprising in his decision to pass the Panth on to the guidance of a successor. This was, indeed, the regular practice for people who had attracted a body of religious followers in north India. The honour did not necessarily pass to a son, if son there was waiting for the task. Nanak had two sons (Lakhmi Das and Siri Chand), but it was by no means inevitable that they would receive the leadership from their father. As things turned out a different person was chosen.

The janam-sakhis (which disagree concerning who was the older) say or imply that the sons had become rebellious, and while we are not bound to agree with this, we are obviously required to accept that neither was chosen to succeed his father. Instead the choice alighted on Lahina, renamed by Guru Nanak as Angad, or 'the one who is as close as my own limb' (see page 17). Lakhmi Das went on to found the first of the famous *Gurū-vaṅs* families (families in the lineage of a Guru). Some members of this Bedi family achieved considerable importance in the Nanak-panth during the eighteenth and nineteenth centuries as the possessors of influential *gaddīs* (seats of authority). Siri Chand was attracted by the Nath yogis and tradition holds that he was the founder of the Udasi order, which practised religion in the style of the Naths.[11] This, if true, could hardly have been in accordance with his father's wishes and in this sense he may well have been 'rebellious'.

The fellowship or body of disciples which Baba Nanak passed on to his successor obviously consisted of a community that accepted the teaching of liberation by the divine Name. The divine Name lay everywhere around and every man must seek to bring his spirit into harmony with the divine Order which the Name expressed. The same went for every woman, and indeed people of every religion and every caste – and none. In practice the overwhelming majority was from the rural castes of the Hindus, but there was certainly nothing in the teachings to hold back Muslims from becoming devotees. Mardana, Guru Nanak's faithful companion, was one of the few Muslims to be numbered among the early Sikhs.

This practice of *nām simaraṇ* was something which they could do by the repetition of a spiritually charged word or mantra, uttered while engaged in everyday occupations – such terms as *sat-nām* or *vāhigurū*. They were expected to gather with other like-minded people from their village as a *satsaṅg* and sing the hymns composed by the Guru. These works embodied the message he preached, and by singing them together the people would make that message their own. At regular times (which would become more frequent as the person grew towards old age), he or she would be expected to sit and silently meditate, thereby appropriating the power of the divine Name in all its increasing wonder.

Each day the devout Sikh would be expected to visit the place set aside in memory of the Master and there pay respects in whatever manner was approved. These places were originally only the simple rooms known as dharamsalas to the early members of the Nanak-panth. Later the term gurdwara took over, probably towards the end of the eighteenth century.[12] On specific occasions (which would largely depend on the distance at which the believer lived) there would be a visit to the presence of the Master himself. This visit would consist of little more than *darśhan* of the Guru, a passing by him and a display of humble reverence for which the reward would be the conferring of a divine blessing. It might perhaps consist of *kathā* (homily) from the Guru; and if the devotee was particularly fortunate he might be singled out for the Master's direct attention.[13]

Let it be understood that once again we are proceeding on the basis of partial inference, as the life of a believer was so very much taken for granted that it was scarcely worth recording. Our inference is the manner in which people practise *nām simaraṇ* today, and though the practice was probably followed in much the same way four or five hundred years ago, it should remain clear that to some extent inference is our source. This is precisely where the janam-sakhis would be reliable if only they recorded the custom more fully. References in the janam-sakhis are, however, rare and are not always reliable.

This was the kind of community which would have attached itself to Guru Nanak, acknowledging him as guide in all things that involved their spiritual welfare. There is also an opportunity to understand something of the secondary leadership of the early Nanak-panth. Bhai Gurdas, the contemporary poet, lists some of the notable followers of Nanak. Many individuals are identified by caste and predictably the one that stands out is the Khatri caste. This information is predictable because Khatris, although not numerous in the villages of the Punjab, were prominent as leaders in the rural situation.[14]

The ordinary members must be left to the glimpses obtained from the janam-sakhis, supplemented by references in the *Dabistān-i-Mazāhib*. This fragmentary information fits well with the later picture of the Panth, as indeed with the impression which any well-informed person would have concerning village life in the Punjab. A large majority of Sikhs today belong to the Jat caste and it seems reasonable to suppose that the Panth attracted the Jats from the very beginning.[15] The Jats were certainly attracted to the Nanak-panth in large numbers at some stage, and their position in Punjabi rural society makes the process entirely reasonable. On the one hand these were people rated low in the *varṇa* or 'classical' hierarchy because they dirtied their hands by cultivating the soil. On the other, these were also the people who in many instances were the dominant caste in their villages and who would be searching for a legitimizing explanation for their growing power. What could be more welcome than a message informing its hearers that there was no need to show favouritism to the Brahmans for liberation was freely open to all? This would indeed be welcome to the Jats and at some early stage they responded to it.

Apart from these two castes it is difficult to be sure about the constituency of the Panth which gathered around Guru Nanak. It presumably contained a relatively small range of castes, with Khatris elevated in terms of leadership and Jats in terms of numbers. This was the Nanak-panth which passed from its founder on to his successor. Just what numbers belonged to it at this early stage would be impossible to say. In the Punjab of its time it would be regarded as one among many panths, with its founder the focus of devotion for those who chose to make him so. And it would be regarded as a Hindu panth, though this cannot be drawn with any clarity. Lines are never easy to draw clearly in the Punjab villages at this time or for several centuries to come, and the adherence of a small number of Muslims would make the task even more difficult.

Guru Angad

As we step from the time of Nanak to that of his early successors a sense of relative assurance deserts us. There are two general problems which confront us. First, we have nothing like the wealth of source material which confronted us in the case of Nanak. The janam-sakhis may have their considerable problems, but they do at least provide us with something on which to work. Secondly, few scholarly writers have attempted to use what meagre material exists in order to deliver acceptable lives of the successor Gurus. It is true that Macauliffe has provided extended biographies of all the Gurus in his six-volume work entitled *The Sikh Religion: Its Gurus, Sacred Writings and Authors*. In 1893 Max Arthur Macauliffe resigned his appointment with the Indian Civil Service and devoted himself entirely to the literature of the Sikhs, publishing his *magnum opus* in 1909. Ever since its publication this work has retained a pre-eminent reputation among the Sikhs. This, however, is largely because Macauliffe's account is strictly traditional, reflecting faithfully the views of the radical Tat Khalsa section of the Singh Sabha movement.[16] It is not history as a historian would understand the term.

The successor to whom Baba Nanak passed on the Nanak-panth was Lahina, subsequently renamed Angad. It is by the latter name that he is known as the second Guru of the Nanak-panth, occupying the position from the death of the first Master in 1539 until his own death twelve and a half years later in 1552. It is quite clear that he inherited a religious group and it is equally clear that it could be defined as much the same Panth when he passed it on to his successor, Guru Amar Das. Guru Angad lived a relatively quiet life in his chosen village of Khadur. This seems clear enough. What is much harder to determine with any certainty is the manner of life lived by the Guru in his village and the truth of the various incidents related of him during this period.

There are several of these anecdotes, though they are very few when compared with the copious supply regarding his predecessor. One of the janam-sakhi traditions, it is true, shows a particular interest in him and was in fact a tradition which probably took shape in Khadur. This is the *Mahimā Prakāśh* tradition, both in its prose form and in its very different poetic version. Both were composed in the middle of the eighteenth century and for that reason alone are to be trusted only as the voice of tradition. Apart from the fleeting Adi Granth references, with a repetition and slight supplement from Bhai Gurdas, the janam-sakhis (particularly the varying accounts of the two versions of the *Mahimā Prakāśh*) provide us with practically all our information concerning Guru Angad. During the nineteenth century Santokh Singh used these sources, supplemented by oral tradition, to produce in *Sūraj Prakāśh* the standard traditional life of Guru Angad.

As with Guru Nanak's works in the Adi Granth, those of Angad offer little significant comment concerning his life story. One feature which is evident from his compositions is a particular fondness for the early-morning bathe as the prelude to devotion, but the glimpses of his way of life are very difficult to interpret unless we use the janam-sakhis as a guide. This is scarcely surprising. In addition to the nature of these compositions (they too emphasize the religious quality of the Guru's thought), there is the fact that they are brief and very few in number. Some basic detail is, however, available in an Adi Granth panegyric written by two followers of the Gurus. This stresses the choice of Angad as Baba Nanak's successor and the unsuccessful protest directed against his decision by the sons of Guru Nanak.

In other respects the Adi Granth communicates relatively little information concerning the life of Angad. The principal source for his life is in fact the janam-sakhi material which deals with him in conjunction with Baba Nanak. We have already been sufficiently warned of the reliability of the janam-sakhis as sources of biography. With this in mind we shall again approach the janam-sakhis, treating them with due caution. Some elements can be accepted as reliable (such as the details concerning his family relationships), but others must be regarded as at least unproven. On this basis we can extract the following account of the life of Guru Angad.

Lahina (or later Angad) was the son of Pheru, a Khatri of the

Trehan sub-caste. His ancestral home was located near the village of Matte di Sarai in Firozpur District. Later tradition gives his date of birth as corresponding to 31 March 1504. He was married to Khivi, the daughter of a Khatri from Khadur village, and two sons and at least one daughter were born to them. The two sons, Dasu and Data, are represented by the *Mahimā Prakāśh Kavitā* as delinquents, whereas Amro the daughter (in contrast to her brothers) was distinguished by her piety and obedience. According to tradition it was through overhearing her singing a *śhabad* that the third Guru, Amar Das, was led to Guru Angad and so to conversion.

Probably in his late twenties Lahina was converted by the preaching of Guru Nanak, and for the remainder of his Master's lifetime he resided partly in Kartarpur and partly in Khadur. At some stage Guru Nanak bestowed the name Angad on him to signify that the disciple had become as much a part of him as his own limbs (*aṅg*). This implied a special status for Lahina, a position confirmed when he was formally designated successor as Guru shortly before the death of Nanak.

Bhai Lahina thus became Guru Angad when Guru Nanak died in 1539. The succession was evidently disputed by the two sons of Guru Nanak and it was possibly for this reason that Angad abandoned Kartarpur to take up permanent residence in Khadur. For almost the entire period he appears to have remained in Khadur, receiving his Sikhs and imparting instruction to them. A feature of this period was evidently the free distribution of food to people of all castes, and tradition relates that in this respect he was ably assisted by his wife, Khivi. His death took place on a date corresponding to 29 March 1552, Amar Das having been appointed to succeed him as the third Guru of the Nanak-panth.

In these broad terms it is possible to sketch a generally reliable account of the Guru's life, though tradition has to be admitted as the source for several of the items. Tradition becomes the sole source for the various anecdotes which are related by the janam-sakhis concerning Guru Angad. The fact that tradition is by no means necessarily correct is pointed up by the fact that two differing accounts exist for a story so important as Lahina's conversion.

One of them (reported in the *Purātan* tradition) relates that Lahina was the *pujārī* (temple officiant) of Khadur and that as all the people save one were worshippers of the goddess Devi, that was the cult to which Lahina also belonged. On one occasion Lahina overheard the one exception (who was a Sikh) singing a hymn of Guru Nanak. Further conversation with the Sikh convinced Lahina of the truth of the Guru's words, and casting aside the trappings of Durga-worship he too became a Sikh.

The other tradition (related in other janam-sakhis) tells of how Lahina, in common with other pilgrims from the village of Matte di Sarai, made an annual pilgrimage to a 'shrine of Durga', which the *Mahimā Prakāśh Kavitā* later identifies as Jwalamukhi. On one such pilgrimage the party happened to pass by Kartarpur, and hearing that it was the abode of Baba Nanak they decided to visit the village in order to have his *darśhan*. While they were in his presence, Baba Nanak briefly conversed with Lahina, who was instantly converted. In spite of the protests of the pilgrim party which he was leading, he announced that the purpose of the pilgrimage had been fulfilled in Kartarpur and that he would proceed no further.

Here we have two traditions and we must guess which is correct, decide that neither is to be trusted, or conflate the two in the manner of Santokh Singh's *Nānak Prakāśh*. Santokh Singh's version provides the standard modern account, still generally accepted although it did not appear until 1823.

All the other janam-sakhi stories stress the loyal, unquestioning obedience of Lahina to his Master, earning for him the ultimate selection as his Master's successor. Perhaps the most famous anecdote of all is the one which tells how the succession issue was finally settled. In order to test the loyalty of his followers, Baba Nanak once escorted them to a wilderness where he made silver and gold coins appear before them. Many of his Sikhs immediately disqualified themselves by seizing all they could grasp. Further on, most of those who remained eliminated themselves by picking up jewels which in like manner magically appeared on the road before them. Only two Sikhs now remained, one of them Lahina. Guru Nanak led them to a funeral pyre and commanded them to eat the corpse which lay on it, concealed by a shroud. The other Sikh fled but Lahina, obedient to the uttermost, lifted the shroud to do his Master's bidding. Under it he discovered no corpse but Baba Nanak himself. The incident had been devised in order to test his Sikhs and Bhai Lahina alone had passed.

For generations of Sikhs this story has testified to Angad's devoted obedience to Guru Nanak, fulfilling his every wish as a welcome command. The Nanak-panth was a religious community and if its second Guru should have been distinguished for his humility and obedience these are qualities that we should expect to find in it. Unfortunately it is not a meaning that we can draw out of the principal anecdote concerning his time as Guru, related by the *Mahimā Prakāśh* tradition. The second Mughal emperor, Humayun, called on Guru Angad while fleeing northwards from the victorious Afghan, Sher Shah Suri. Guru Angad was playing with children at the time, and continued playing with them, leaving his royal visitor waiting. After an hour the increasingly impatient Humayun laid his hand on his sword, whereupon, as a signal of the Guru's divine power, his hand stuck to the hilt. Angad then turned his attention to him. His hand, he said, would have been better applied to his sword when fighting against Sher Shah Suri than as a means of making a faqir hurry. Humayun apologized and was assured that he would recover his kingdom. Had he not laid his hand on his sword, he was told, he would have received it back immediately. Now, however, he would have to endure an exile before it would be restored to him.

This story no historian could possibly accept, illustrating as it does the powerful hold which the pious imagination exercises. It is absolutely inevitable that such stories should grow and flourish, yet however attractive they may be, the historian will derive no meaning from them other than that future generations regarded the Guru with the profoundest respect and veneration.

There is one last tradition concerning Guru Angad which should be briefly considered. It is commonly believed that Guru Angad invented the Gurmukhi script (the script in which Punjabi is written). This conviction is a comparatively late development, for the earlier sources do not make such a sweeping claim. The script is very like that used by the traders of the Punjab and it would be perfectly natural for Guru Angad (a Khatri by caste) also to write in it. Because it thus communicated the Guru's utterances, it came to be known as Gurmukhi ('from the Guru's mouth').

The Panth which Guru Angad had received from Guru Nanak he passed on to his successor, the third Guru, Amar Das, essentially unchanged. He had received a Panth which consisted of members who were bound directly to their Guru by ties of personal allegiance, and it was such a Panth which he transmitted to Amar Das a dozen years later. It was a religious Panth with a very loose structure holding it together. The headquarters of the Panth travelled with the Guru, and where he was located there was its centre to be found. Each of its members had made a personal decision to belong to it, and this they expressed by a regular visit to their Guru to pay their respects and seek his blessing. He was their Guru and he would still recognize them when they came from neighbouring villages and towns for his *darśhan*.

The Sikhs observed no festivals peculiar to their panthic allegiance, nor did they follow any distinctive practices which marked them off from their fellow Punjabis. In all respects they were the same as people in the same situation in Punjabi society, save only for their chosen allegiance to one who taught them a particular doctrine of liberation from the cycle of transmigration. In pursuing this doctrine they were instructed to meditate on the divine Name, an inward pilgrimage easy to understand, which needed no external assistance. For people with such a belief there was no particular value in attending the village temple, and likewise they could regard the ceremonies of the Brahman as altogether useless. In practice, they presumably still continued to observe these traditional ceremonies, apart from the minority who had made a firm commitment to the new way. They were counselled to rise early and after bathing to meditate on the wonders of the divine Name, for it was by appropriating those wonders that the way of liberation opened before them. This too would be observed with differing degrees of commitment, the truly loyal observing it with rigour and the lax doing so on occasion.

The numbers who belonged to the new Nanak-panth are as impossible to determine as those who belonged to it in Nanak's own day. Probably it would still be fairly small, but there is absolutely no way of telling. That it was still a religious Panth is beyond question. Its members would be seen as people making a personal response to teachings concerning the way of spiritual liberation. Beyond this distinction and the caste distribution in the Panth there would be nothing to separate them from the other Hindu villagers of the Punjab.

2

THE DEVELOPING PANTH

Under the third Guru changes started to occur. The Panth no longer consisted exclusively of those who had made a personal commitment, their place being occupied increasingly by those who had been born into the faith and had known it since infancy. Changes were increasingly needed if the Panth was to retain the freshness and vigour of its founding days. This was the situation which faced the third Sikh Guru, Amar Das.

Guru Amar Das

Amar Das was born in the village of Basarke, near modern Amritsar. His father was Tej Bhan, a Khatri of the Bhalla sub-caste. The daughter of Guru Angad was married into the family of one of his brothers and it was in this manner that Amar Das came to be acquainted with the works of Baba Nanak. Evidently the family lived in Basarke, partly on agriculture and partly on trade in grains. Because his date of birth is disputed, Guru Amar Das's age at his succession to the office of Guru must remain uncertain, but it was obviously an advanced age (probably seventy-three). He held the position for the remarkably long period of twenty-two years, eventually dying in 1574 at the age (probably) of ninety-five.

This sequence enables us to set the third Guru in the context of his family and of his times. The Guru was married and he thus continued the pattern of married Gurus as a feature of the Nanak-panth. It was, in other words, a Panth which taught liberation without going to the extent of demanding asceticism, either from its leaders or from its members. The life of the married householder was affirmed, not that of the celibate ascetic. He had two sons, Mohan and Mohari, whom tradition casts in the usual filial role of opponents of their father's choice of a successor. There was also at least one daughter and probably two. The daughter who is certain, Bibi Bhani, was married to Jetha Sodhi, who as Guru Ram Das became his father-in-law's successor.[1]

Tradition records that Amar Das was instructed by Guru Angad to take up residence in the new village of Goindval, thereby converting it into a place of safety and sanctity. A new village had been founded by a Khatri called Gobind a short distance down the Beas river from Khadur. Gobind was unable to persuade others to stay in it, however, for what was erected each day was mysteriously dismantled that same night. Guru Angad disclaimed the right to have the village named after him and also to go and live there, but he commanded Amar Das to take up residence in it. The building then went ahead steadily and the village was able to progress. Called Gobindval after its founder, the village's name was later shortened to Goindval. The tradition is certainly accurate to the extent that Amar Das took up residence in Goindval and made it the new centre of the Nanak-panth.

This was the period when the Nanak-panth, having passed the first flush of enthusiasm, was in process of consolidation. The earliest Sikhs had been brought into the new Panth by means of a message directly preached and directly accepted. This generation was, however, passing and in its place a new one was growing up, one born into the faith rather than having accepted it personally. It was a generation which required a structure to its faith and it needed certain high points to observe. Some Sikhs will have been converted in the manner of their parents, but others will always have known the Panth as a part of their background and will have grown up accepting it as the path to follow. The informal organization of Nanak-panthis gathering in *saṅgat*s to sing *kīrtan* and coming to visit their Guru was no longer sufficient.

The appearance of later generations owing their adherence to birth rather than to personal choice imposed one variety of strain on a movement of this kind. Growing numbers imposed another, particularly when there was a simultaneous expansion in geographical terms. There is considerable uncertainty with regard to the timing of the measures taken by Nanak's early successors, and indeed the actual measures themselves are not always clear. It seems, however, that significant steps were taken during the period of Guru Amar Das, and that the developments encouraged by these steps established the pattern of panthic organization which was to persist until the founding of the Khalsa at the end of the seventeenth century. The picture is obscure to say the least, but it is to this phase that the indications point, and certainly the period of the third incumbent would be a natural time for panthic organization to take a more definite shape.

The uncertainty associated with these developments should be stressed if we are to appreciate the shadowy nature of much that passes for historical fact during the period of the early Gurus. Measures that are traditionally associated with the period of Guru Amar Das and which are viewed as the product of formal decisions may actually have longer pedigrees and less specific origins. Tradition is, however, reasonably firm on most of these points, and although our detailed understanding may be faulty, the eventual results seem beyond doubt. In these guarded terms we may attribute to Guru Amar Das three distinct varieties of innovation.

One innovation can be regarded as essentially administrative. As the Panth expanded, new *saṅgat*s, or 'congregations', came into existence. Immediate contact with the Guru became increasingly difficult to maintain and it thus became necessary to appoint deputies authorized to act on his behalf as preachers. Guru Amar Das is traditionally credited with having established the *mañjī* system of supervision, and the later *masand* system is believed to have developed from this prototype. The function of the *mañjī*s seems to have been exclusively preaching the message of *nām simaraṇ*.[2]

A second innovation which is usually attributed to the third Guru concerns the institutionalizing of a key doctrine. Guru Nanak had made it abundantly clear that caste status (like all exterior conventions) could have no bearing on access to the divine Name and thus to the means of liberation. It was probably Guru Amar Das who borrowed from the Sufis the practice of compulsory commensality or eating together, thereby giving practical expression to the first Guru's ideal. In the Sikh tradition this inter-dining convention emerged as a specific form of the *laṅgar* (almshouse or public kitchen). In Sikh usage the *laṅgar* comprises the kitchen and refectory attached to every gurdwara in which food is prepared and served to all regardless of caste or creed. This convention requires men and women of all castes to sit in status-free lines (*paṅgat*) and eat together when they assemble on the sacred ground of the dharamsala or gurdwara. Guru Nanak and Guru Angad certainly maintained *laṅgar*s, but the specifically anti-caste character appears to have been an introduction by Guru Amar Das.

The third variety of innovation comprises a cluster of decisions (conscious or implicit) which concerned the developing ritual of the Panth. Whereas the *laṅgar* plainly matched the intention of Guru Nanak, the new practices, together supplying a distinctive panthic ritual, might well seem to be in conflict with it. The first Guru had stressed the interior nature of devotion, dismissing as false and dangerous the kind of external ritual associated with conventional Hindu tradition or orthodox Islam. Decisions attributed to the third Guru may look suspiciously like the kind of thing that Nanak abandoned and roundly condemned. They include the digging of a sacred well (*bāolī*) in the Guru's village of Goindval to serve as a place of pilgrimage for Sikhs. They also include the introduction of particular festival days and the compiling of a collection which was later to become a sacred scripture. Guru Amar Das is also credited with the decision to excavate the sacred pool that marked the founding of Amritsar.

Would Nanak, with his strong emphasis on interiority, have permitted this to occur? There are two answers that can be given to the problem thus presented. The theological answer is that the Guru is one and that decisions made by the third Guru proceed from precisely the same source as attitudes expressed by the first. This answer implies the second response, which is that changed circumstances require fresh decisions. No one is likely to be surprised by this development. A growing and maturing Panth could never have sustained the informality of the first Guru's practice. The formalizing of the tradition occurs in the period when one would expect it and in much the manner that might be anticipated.

A recording of the sacred songs of the Gurus would also have been acceptable in the time of the third Guru. Adherents of the Nanak-panth, as we have already noted, gathered regularly in *saṅgat*s or *satsaṅg*s to sing *kīrtan*, and this was their principal means of learning and reinforcing the Guru's teachings concerning the divine Name. The chances of spurious hymns penetrating such *satsaṅg*s was obviously very considerable and it would have been a natural decision for the third Guru to make, one that produced a manuscript recording only that which was authentic.[3] This would ensure that the *bāṇī* sung by Nanak-panthis would be only *sachhī bāṇī* or 'true' hymns. All possibility of *kachhī bāṇī* ('non-authentic *bāṇī*') would be eliminated. The possibility of *kachhī bāṇī* finding acceptance is illustrated by the janam-sakhi quotations of the works of Baba Nanak. Virtually all their quotations differ in some degree from the text recorded in the Adi Granth. One does not need the presence of rivals to account for misreadings of the sacred text.

The Nanak-panth Guru Amar Das handed on to his successor was therefore the same as he had received, yet there were changes taking place that indicated something of the direction which it would follow. It was still a religious Panth, preaching the message Guru Nanak had taught. Guru Amar Das, through his hymns, repeated the same doctrine of liberation through the divine Name. His followers gathered in *satsaṅg*s to sing the message over and over again in hymns of expanding variety. There is no way of determining the size of his following (no more at this time than there was in the time of Guru Nanak), but it seems safe to assume that it was still the same constituency. Jats dominated it numerically, Khatris were still prominent in positions of leadership. Such at least seems to be a reasonable conclusion. Clearly the Panth was continuing in the manner Guru Nanak had left it and clearly it was the same Nanak-panth.

But it was a Panth that was changing, a Panth that was coming to grips with a later stage in its development. No longer does it consist solely of converts, of those who had made the choice themselves to accept the message preached by Nanak. Now the Sikhs have a pilgrimage centre, and to that centre, Goindval, they are expected to go to have *darśhan* of the Guru. This, for Sikhs, is to be the *tīrath* or place of pilgrimage. Two festival days have been designated for the purpose, and a regular feature of such a visit will be to descend to the well so recently dug. In their dharamsalas, or when visiting Goindval, the Nanak-panthis are not to observe caste. They do, however, preserve caste as a marriage convention and their links with the wider Hindu community are thus preserved unbroken. The Panth is still the fellowship which Guru Nanak had left. The time for radical change has not yet come.

Guru Ram Das

In 1574 Guru Amar Das died, passing the responsibility of leading the Nanak-panth to his son-in-law, Jetha Sodhi, who became the fourth incumbent as Guru Ram Das. Following one who had lived to a very old age, Ram Das was Master of the Panth for only seven years. In his case also most of the information has been passed down by tradition and very little of it can be positively affirmed. There is, however, no question concerning the broad outline. There can be no doubt that Ram Das continued to lead a Panth that was largely rural and which preached liberation through meditation on the divine Name.

Among the traditions concerning Guru Ram Das one thing stands out. Guru Ram Das is very clearly associated with the founding of the new centre of Chak Guru or Ramdaspur, later to be known as Amritsar. The hostility of the sons of Guru Amar Das is said to have been responsible for the move from Goindval. Ram Das established himself in the new location and began excavating the sacred pool. The site thus chosen became the principal centre of the Nanak-panth until the sixth Guru, Hargobind, was compelled to abandon it early in the seventeenth century and move to the safety of the Shivalik hills. Amritsar recovered its prominence during the warfare of the eighteenth century and has ever since remained the chief centre of the Sikhs.

The other feature commonly associated with the fourth Guru is the appointment of *masand*s or vicars who acted on behalf of their Guru in the more dispersed of his *saṅgat*s. The word *masand* evidently means 'throne' or 'raised platform' and is an indication of the status these people were to acquire in the Nanak-panth. These were men who supervised individual *saṅgat*s or clusters of *saṅgat*s on behalf of the Guru, perhaps acting as spiritual guides and certainly empowered to collect the tithes or other contributions which a loyal Sikh might be expected to give to his Master. The Nanak-panth, in other words, had by this time reached the stage where the central organization was to some extent dependent on contributions, and this implies a development in terms of a complex organization.

We have already seen how in the time of the third Guru *mañjīs* were apparently in existence and how their precise nature was exceedingly vague. There can be little doubt, however, concerning the role and authority of the *masands*, or at least a measure of it. The *masand* system presumably did its job reasonably well in the first few decades of its existence and lasted until its decline into semi-independence and corruption produced formal abolition by Guru Gobind Singh at the end of the seventeenth century.

One characteristic of Guru Ram Das deserves particular notice and this is the quality of his works as recorded in the Adi Granth. Kirtan was of the essence of the Nanak-panth and the fourth Guru certainly provided his followers with hymns in praise of the divine Name. The Guru's sense of melody and rhythm place him high according to the exalted standards of the Adi Granth, a feature of considerable importance. The Sikhs of the Nanak-panth appreciated fine singing, and music which matched or exceeded their expectations was bound to have a favourable impact on the growth of the community.

Guru Arjan

In 1581 Guru Ram Das breathed his last. It was still the Nanak-panth which he passed on to his successor and that Panth still upheld the divine Name as the means to liberation. Also, although the appointment of *masands* implied greater numbers and more distant *saṅgats*, we are still quite unable to estimate the numbers who belonged to the Nanak-panth. There was, however, a change of some significance taking place. Guru Ram Das's successor was his son, and from this point onwards the Gurus follow a male line of the Sodhi Khatris, the sub-caste to which Guru Ram Das had belonged. It was not his oldest son, nor even his second son. Arjan, who succeeded his father, was in fact the third and youngest son. But son he was and every Guru who followed him was his direct descendant.

Why was this so? Why, when the first three Gurus had overlooked their sons and appointed other disciples to succeed them, did the fourth Guru choose his son? And why were all future Gurus his direct descendants? There are two answers needed here. The first three Gurus did the natural and sensible thing in appointing loyal disciples to succeed them in the days before the leadership of the Panth had

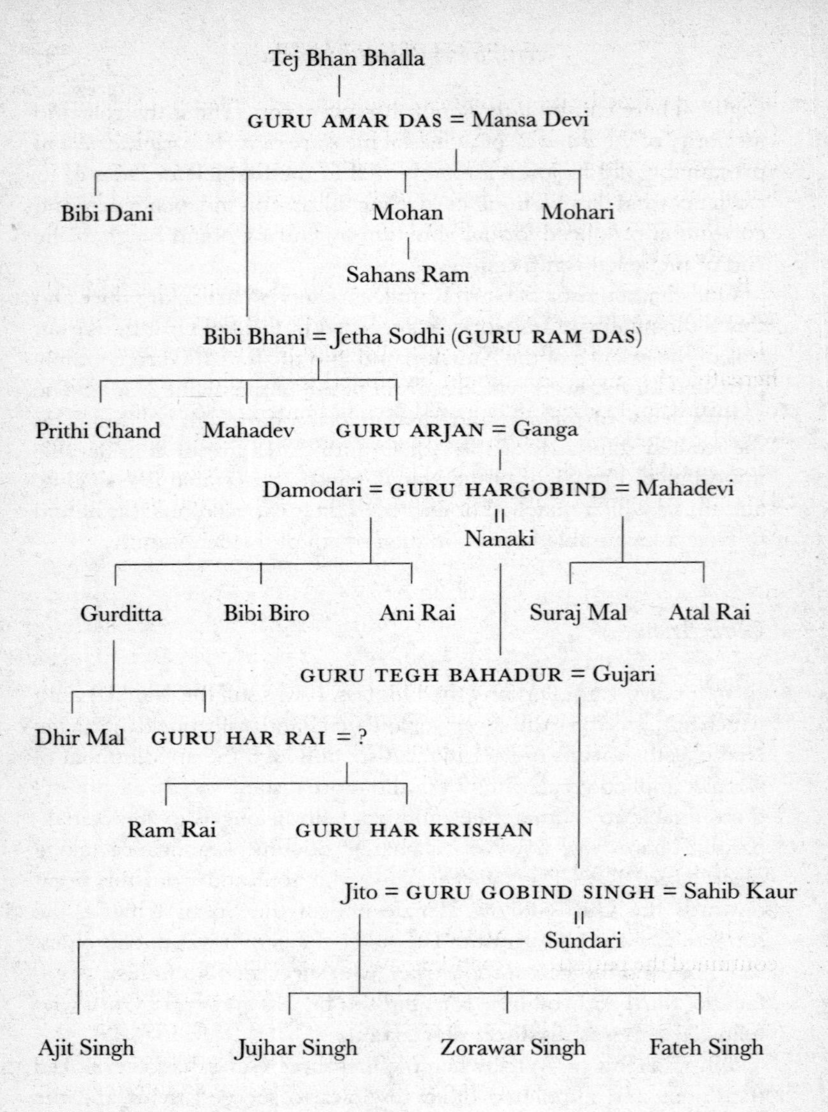

1. A family tree of the descendants of Guru Amar Das and Guru Ram Das

become a target for the ambitious. Tradition casts the sons of all three Gurus as seekers after power, yet it seems most unlikely that the Gurus could raise offspring who would be uniformly hostile to their fathers' intentions. A much more likely explanation is that they would make ideal opponents to confront their fathers' successors and so tradition casts them in that role.

By the time of the fourth Guru, however, the possibility of a disputed succession was real. This may also have played a part in the choice of his son-in-law by the third Guru. Establishing the convention that hereafter the succession should be limited to the direct descendants of Guru Ram Das certainly would not eliminate the possibility, but it would minimize it. Within the Guru's family of Sodhi Khatris the most suitable person should be chosen, and to succeed Guru Ram Das the youngest of his three sons, Arjan, was selected as the fifth Guru.

This theory is not wholly convincing, yet there seems to be no other possible interpretation. As a result Arjan had to face the disappointed and determined enmity of his eldest brother, Prithi Chand, and quarrels over the succession become a feature of the remainder of the Guru period. At least three of these disappointed contenders formed panths of their own, claiming to be the legitimate descendants from Nanak. When Guru Gobind Singh formed the Khalsa at the end of the seventeenth century, the followers of these contenders were singled out as three of the so-called *Pañj Mel* (the Five Reprobate Groups) and members of the Khalsa were forbidden to have any dealings with them.[4] Clearly they had proven a serious danger and to this extent the system of choosing the successive Gurus was only a partial success.

The period of Guru Arjan, which covers the years 1581–1606, continued the pattern of expanding numbers in rural areas. According to tradition these were the years when three towns were established in rural Punjab. Tarn Taran, Kartarpur (a second Kartarpur, not the village of Guru Nanak) and Sri Hargobindpur first appeared at this time. Under the fifth Guru, the Nanak-panth continued to grow and there is strong reason for believing that it grew impressively, particularly in rural areas. The sources are, as usual, slender (largely confined to the Adi Granth and Bhai Gurdas), but the profile certainly matches that of the later Panth.

As we have already noted, Arjan faced a disputed succession when he became Guru. Prithi Chand, his eldest brother, had evidently looked forward to the prestige the office would bring, only to be disappointed by his father's choice of his youngest brother to be the fifth Guru. For several years his opposition proved a great difficulty for Guru Arjan, particularly after Arjan's son was born, when Prithi Chand seems to have attempted something serious in the hope of undermining the child's claims to the succession. There is for this particular episode sound evidence which indicates that Prithi Chand was contemplating serious hurt (possibly actual assassination) to Arjan's only child, the future Guru Hargobind. As proof we have the testimony of both Guru Arjan and Bhai Gurdas. Prithi Chand, having failed in his attempt, set himself up as a rival Guru. To the followers of the legitimate line they were the Minas or 'scoundrels'.

Guru Arjan is important for at least four reasons. First, he it was who completed the excavation of the pool known as Amritsar and built the original gurdwara located in its centre. The eighteenth-century gurdwara that now occupies the site is known as Harimandir Sahib, later to be called by the British the Golden Temple.[5] Secondly, he was the most prolific of the Gurus as a hymn-writer, leaving to the Panth a superb collection of religious songs, with *Sukhmanī Sāhib* at its head. Thirdly, he was largely responsible for compiling the sacred scripture of the Sikhs, the Adi Granth, which was to become the Guru Granth Sahib. And fourthly there was the manner of his death, treated by all Sikh sources as the death of a martyr at the hands of the Mughals. The third and the fourth of these reasons require further treatment.

The Adi Granth is so called to distinguish it from the later Dasam Granth. 'Adi Granth' means 'the First Volume' or 'the Original Volume', separating it from the Dasam Granth, which was compiled during the early eighteenth century.[6] The actual date of beginning the Adi Granth's compilation is not certain, but it is believed it was initiated by Guru Arjan in 1603. The task was certainly completed in 1604. During the past two hundred years it has ascended to a position far beyond that of its only rival. In the eighteenth century the Dasam Granth apparently ranked equal with the Adi Granth, but since that time has dropped away.

The collecting by Guru Arjan of all the hymns of his four

predecessors, together with his own substantial works and those of approved Sant poets, was of critical importance, not necessarily in his own time but certainly in the eighteenth century when the two sacred Granths came to be accepted as the literal embodiment of the eternal Guru after the line of personal Gurus had ceased. Guru Amar Das, as we have seen, had evidently commissioned a preliminary compilation (the so-called Goindval *pothīs* or Mohan *pothīs*) and the fifth Guru is believed to have used this prototype when producing the larger version. In between the two versions came a manuscript prepared on Guru Arjan's instructions that served as a provisional text.[7] The text recorded in Arjan's time was the Kartarpur Bir (or Kartarpur volume).[8] Later in the seventeenth century some compositions by Guru Tegh Bahadur were added and the final result was the Adi Granth. The Adi Granth subsequently played a powerful cohesive role during the later history of the Panth, a role which continues undiminished today.

Guru Arjan apparently planned the enterprise carefully. A camp was set up on the outskirts of Amritsar and there the Guru had a pool excavated. Meanwhile he dictated the contents of the scripture to his amanuensis, the celebrated Bhai Gurdas, or indicated portions which were to be copied from the available prototypes. The pattern of organization is impressive, with the bulk of the scripture divided according to *rāg* (musical mode), type of composition and author.[9] The occasions when the Adi Granth diverges from this pattern are very few indeed.

Tradition relates that the reason for compiling the scripture was that enemies of the Panth (notably the followers of Prithi Chand) were passing out spurious compositions and attributing them to the Guru. The Nanak-panth was still a religious Panth, with singing in *saṅgats* still the primary feature of its life, and it was important for it to have access to reliable hymns in the way that Guru Amar Das had sought to guarantee them. Guru Arjan was fulfilling the same need. The version whose preparation he had supervised would provide an approved text, and anything not contained in it was not sanctioned for use in Nanak-panthi *saṅgats*. His own contribution was the largest of all the authors and is equal in terms of quality. To this day his *Sukhmanī Sāhib* is treasured by many outside the Panth or on its fringes, as well as by those who are firmly located within.

The Nanak-panth was still a religious Panth, a Panth with all the features of developing maturity surrounding it, but still a religious Panth. It was, however, just about to begin the process of change into something more and tradition marks the close of Arjan's life as the hinge of change. Guru Arjan's manner of death in 1606 evidently signifies a determinative turning-point in the development of the Panth. Difficulties had emerged in the Panth's relationship with the local Mughal authorities, and the hostility which fitfully developed during the course of the succeeding century has traditionally been held to account for the significant changes which eventually transformed the Panth.

There can be no doubt that the deteriorating relationship with Mughal authority supplies a large part of the explanation, and that Guru Arjan's death in Mughal custody provides an appropriate symbol for the change taking place. It is not a sudden change, though. The Nanak-panth of the sixteenth century was not instantly transformed into a prototype of the eighteenth-century Khalsa. The continuities remain evident and much that we may affirm concerning the early Panth applies with equal force to its seventeenth-century successor.

The Mughals had entered India in the lifetime of Guru Nanak, their authority established in the north by Babur, who in 1526 won the battle of Panipat against the Lodi dynasty and thereafter ruled as the first emperor. Mughal rule was significantly enlarged by the third emperor, Akbar (1556–1605), and now the fourth emperor was on the throne. This was Jahangir, who ruled from the death of Akbar until his own death in 1627. For most of the period the Sikhs had been too small a group to be worthy of notice, but in the time of Guru Arjan this changed. The Guru was arrested by the Mughal authorities in Lahore and died in their custody. Tradition reports that he perished of extreme torture, and to the Sikhs he is remembered with profound grief as the first martyr Guru.

The death by torture or execution has not been definitively established, but certainly Guru Arjan had attracted the emperor's unfavourable notice and with equal certainty he died in Mughal custody. Jahangir in his *Memoirs* records the episode which angered him. Arjan was said to have applied a saffron mark to the forehead of the rebellious Prince Khusrau, apparently blessing him. Jahangir had earlier heard how the

Guru had attracted many people to his following (Muslim as well as Hindu), and now he determined that either he should put a stop to this 'false traffic' or Arjan should be brought into the fold of Islam.[10]

Sikh tradition relates this directly to the important change which overtook the Panth at the death of the Guru. According to this tradition, Guru Arjan advised his son and successor Hargobind to sit fully armed on his throne; and Hargobind, as sixth Guru, symbolically donned two swords. Whereas one sword represented the continuing spiritual authority of the Guru (*pīrī*), the other signified a newly assumed temporal authority (*mīrī*). Tradition emphatically holds that the Panth was assuming a new militancy and that it was doing so as the Guru's response to the urgency of early seventeenth-century circumstances.

Guru Hargobind

The death of his father must obviously have had an effect on his son and successor Guru Hargobind, but precisely what was that effect? The orthodox view states that Guru Arjan, prior to his death at the hands of the Mughals, sent a message instructing Hargobind that henceforth the Guru must sit fully armed upon his throne. The Panth, in other words, is to assume a dramatically different condition. No longer is it to be a strictly religious group with its members unconcerned about their relations with the ruling power. Instead it is to be a Panth armed to defend itself against a power liable to attack it and persecute its members. As symbols of his altered role the eleven-year-old Hargobind, at his investiture as the new Guru, therefore girded himself with two swords, one representing his *pīrī* or spiritual function; the other his *mīrī* or worldly role.

Mīrī is the power of a *mīr*, an earthly noble or chieftain (a title which the early Sikhs would have associated with the Mughals). *Pīrī*, on the other hand, was the spiritual authority of the *pīr*, strictly a Muslim superior of one of the Sufi orders but generally used of any who had earned a high reputation for piety. Both are in fact terms borrowed from the Muslim culture which extensively influenced the Sikhs in the Punjab. This dual authority was one the Guru now exercised. Seated upon his throne, he exercised a worldly authority in addition to the spiritual powers that were already the right of the Guru. As the commander of an army of men dedicated to the discipline of *nām simaraṇ*, Guru Hargobind was thus the holder of this dual *mīrī-pīrī* authority, which thereafter all the Gurus held as of right. Now the Panth was armed. Now it was in a position to defend itself.

This was the role which, according to tradition, Guru Hargobind assumed at his investiture. The traditional account also includes a number of other features. The woollen rosary which had been worn by his five predecessors was put aside as inappropriate to the new circumstances, and in its place the Guru would wear a sword-belt, weapons and an aigrette. *Masands* were commanded to bring offerings of arms and horses instead of money. Soon afterwards was laid the foundation of Akal Takhat ('the throne of the Timeless One'), facing the chief gurdwara of Harimandir Sahib, and when it was erected he took his seat there. This building was accepted as the seat of *temporal* power in the Panth, as opposed to Harimandir (the later Golden Temple), which represents *spiritual* authority within the Panth. The Panth now faces outward to the world as well as inward to the faithful. And the Panth now faces the outside world armed by command of its martyred Guru and led by his son and successor. According to tradition, the transition from a pacific Panth to a militant Panth, to a Panth that would be prepared to stand and defend itself, was thus made at the beginning of the seventeenth century.

There are two questions to be considered in this connection, each closely related to the other. First, did the Panth undergo the change from the pacific to the militant at the beginning of Guru Hargobind's period? Secondly, if there was such a change (or something like it), how was that change interpreted within the Panth of the time? Was it interpreted along *mīrī-pīrī* lines, with the Guru seen to be assuming specifically temporal powers in addition to the spiritual authority he already possessed? Or was change taking place more gradually, with the shift essentially one of differing personalities? The Guru had changed and Hargobind was a very different person from his father, Arjan. Could these changes in the character of the Panth be later developments (that is, late seventeenth- and eighteenth-century developments), with tradition backdating them to the person of the sixth Guru?

The actual term *mīrī-pīrī* certainly seems to be a later introduction.

The two words constitute the kind of rhyming phrase which exercises considerable appeal, and once it was introduced it would quickly gain currency. This, however, makes no difference to the reality of the situation. Guru Hargobind may not actually have been called *mīrī pīrī dā mālik* (the *mīrī-pīrī* Master), but that still leaves open the question of whether or not he really did occupy the dual role.

Certainly one highly reliable source makes it very clear that Guru Hargobind's way of life was completely different from that of his father, Guru Arjan. This was Bhai Gurdas, a loyal disciple of both. In a famous stanza from his *Vār* 26 he deals directly with the issue.

> The earlier Gurus sat peacefully in dharamsalas; this one roams the land.
> Emperors visited their homes with reverence; this one they cast into gaol.
> No rest for his followers, ever active; their restless Master has fear of none.
> The earlier Gurus sat graciously blessing; this one goes hunting with dogs.
> They had servants who harboured no malice; this one encourages scoundrels.

And having posed the problem as he sees it in the first five lines of the stanza, he provides his own answer in the remaining two:

> Yet none of these changes conceals the truth; the Sikhs are still drawn as bees to the lotus.
> The truth stands firm, eternal, changeless; and pride still lies subdued.

This stanza is worth looking at closely because it casts rather a different light on the subject. It is possible to read it as an expression of genuine questioning on the part of Bhai Gurdas. Indeed, this conclusion is unavoidable. Bhai Gurdas was genuinely perplexed by the behaviour of the sixth Guru, as he surveyed such puzzling features as hunting, gaol-going and even untrustworthy servants in his retinue. The other Gurus were not like this. Why should this one be so different?

And then in his two concluding lines he provides the only answer that seems to him to make sense. The Guru is still the Guru and loyal Sikhs will recognize him as such. This suggests that change had certainly taken place under Guru Hargobind, but that the direction of the change was not yet clear.

Two features probably account for the nature of the change. The first is that the Panth had, in a sense, always been armed. The majority of its members were rural folk, predominantly Jat; and the Jats would be entirely accustomed to bearing arms. This does not mean that they would be accustomed to being organized as an army, but it is difficult to imagine a village Jat without at least a staff in his possession. It is also difficult to envisage an unwillingness to make use of it should need arise. In village society conflict is common – conflict over land, water and women – and when such issues arise they are frequently settled by an appeal to the strong right arm. Being Sikhs and belonging to the Panth would make little difference to this, just as it makes little difference in present times. They would not make a display of bearing arms when they came for *darśhan* with the Guru, but neither would it occur to them to leave them at home.

In this respect the Panth was already armed and the Guru who chose to organize it for defence purposes already had the means at his disposal. It is here that the personality of the sixth Guru is important, and this constitutes the second feature. The first five Gurus had, as Bhai Gurdas reminds us, spent their days teaching their followers and blessing them in their endeavours. This one entered upon his responsibilities at the age of eleven and as such would have been dependent for several years upon Sikhs who were close to the family and could act as teachers and guides. Such people may well have been impressed by the signs of growing hostility on the part of the Mughal authorities and it would be natural for them to take precautionary measures. Even if the impulse came direct from the Guru himself, the result would be the same. He was different from his father and the active life appealed to him. As a result he lived a different life, a life which had him hunting with dogs and a life in which his followers were overtly ready to defend their chosen Panth.

This is the situation which later tradition has invested with a deliberate choice to adopt a more militant posture. The symbols that serve this purpose are the two swords, the aigrette and the building of Akal Takhat; and later generations have been taught to see the transformation in these terms. In practice there is not much difference to observe in the symbolic policy as opposed to the actual. Guru Hargobind was a different man from his father, and living in more hostile circumstances he took appropriate measures to meet them. His Panth readily responded to the situation thus presented to them and adopted a policy which was always defensive and sometimes offensive as well.

The story of Hargobind's period and the history of the Nanak-panth during those years leave, like all these early and middle periods, a confused impression. We do have in the *Dabistān-i-Mazāhib* (written shortly after his time) a very valuable source, but it too leaves an impression of confusion on several points. The *Dabistān* does, however, testify to the imprisonment of Guru Hargobind in Gwalior Fort, there to remain until the fine imposed on Guru Arjan was duly paid. This, it declares, was at the instance of the Emperor Jahangir. It is possible that after the term in gaol was over Jahangir decided to show favour to the Guru and may have engaged him in a series of discourses. This is open to more doubt, although the *Dabistān* does claim that Hargobind entered the service of Jahangir and, after his death, that of Shahjahan. The story of how the Guru received custody of the treacherous Chandu Shah is even more questionable, at least in terms of the punishment said to have been meted out to this unfortunate person following his transfer to the Sikhs.[11] We are in the realm of tradition again, as is so often the case.

Tradition also surrounds the other stories told of Guru Hargobind, but it seems possible to pick out a general picture. That the Guru had infantry and particularly horsemen at his command is attested by the *Dabistān*, the figure for the latter being three hundred. That he travelled across north India, as far east as Pilibhit in the Kumaon hills and up to Kashmir in the north, also seems likely. Likewise, it seems certain that in some manner he acquired land in the Shivalik hills, bordering on the plains, and that there he built the village known as Kiratpur. Baba Gurditta, his eldest son, was traditionally entrusted with the establishment of the new village. The land certainly came into his possession at some stage in his career and it was there that he withdrew following trouble on the plains around Amritsar.

The claim that, following the death of Jahangir, his men came into conflict with Mughal troops a number of times can also be accepted. The *Dabistān* certainly names Guru Hargobind as a servant of Jahangir's successor Shahjahan, but the two versions need not disagree. Horsemen in Hargobind's retinue could easily have had brushes with Mughal troops and the stories of the skirmishes that resulted may be essentially true. The first such instance occurred shortly after Shahjahan's accession in 1628 while the emperor was hunting near Amritsar. A hawk of his happened to be captured by followers of Guru Hargobind, and this led to fighting in which some men were evidently killed. The *Dabistān* reports this encounter and sets it in the context of Guru Hargobind's preparations for his daughter's wedding. Another skirmish is reported to have taken place near Sri Hargobindpur shortly after.

In 1631, following the recapture of two horses which the Mughals had previously taken from the Guru's followers, there was further trouble. The horses are said to have been the gift of Sikhs from Afghanistan and were being taken to the Guru when they were seized by Mughal troops from Lahore. They were retaken by the Guru's servant, Bidhi Chand. Following this incident the Guru decided it would be wiser to retire to the relative security of the wasteland to the south. There he encountered a Mughal force at Gurusar in the area of Nabha and a number of men on each side were killed. Yet another engagement occurred at Kartarpur after Painda Khan, his hitherto trusted Muslim follower, changed sides and was killed in the ensuing fight.

Although these conflicts are depicted in most modern accounts as mighty battles displaying conspicuous bravery, one is entitled to assume that these are cases of exaggeration. A combination of disturbed circumstances in the Punjab together with the accession of growing numbers of typically turbulent Jats to the Guru's Panth provides a sufficient explanation for the conflicts which evidently took place, and there is no need to magnify them into full-scale battles. The impression that the Panth attracted growing numbers of Jats and that many of them brought their unruly ways with them is an assumption, but it seems an eminently reasonable one.

Certainly the few sources available testify to the adherence of Jat followers, and if they were notable more for their steadfast loyalty to their leader and for their capacity to fight rather than for the practice of *nām simaraṇ*, who is to be surprised? Village people in the Punjab have always been like this and it would come as a considerable surprise to learn that the Jats in the early seventeenth century were any different. We can accept therefore that, during the time of Guru Hargobind, the Panth attracted significantly larger numbers; that these people were overwhelmingly from the villages; and that panthic membership was a matter of loyalty to the leader rather than deep awareness of the teachings of the divine Name. In the somewhat disturbed circumstances of the time, the rural people were bound to be involved in conflict with Mughal troops; and if a sizeable number of these rural folk should have been tied to a single leader, that leader would certainly have had his fair share of trouble with the Mughal authorities.

Because this share of trouble was growing increasingly serious, Guru Hargobind abandoned Amritsar and moved to Kiratpur on the edge of the Shivalik hills. There he remained until his death in 1644. Deaths which occurred in his family, compounded by disaffection, created serious problems concerning the next Guru. Hargobind had married three wives and had a family of six children, five of whom were sons. The oldest son, Gurditta – evidently marked out to succeed his father – was by reputation strongly inclined towards the Udasi panth[12] and as such would have introduced the Sikhs to the ways of asceticism. Just what difference this might have made was never to be discovered, for Gurditta predeceased his father in 1638.

His other sons had either similarly predeceased him (as with Atal Rai, whose multi-storeyed memorial stands adjacent to the Golden Temple) or for various reasons were thought unsuitable. Tegh Bahadur was thought to be too withdrawn, or so Sikh tradition reports. (His later selection as the ninth Guru casts some doubt on this tradition.) Dhir Mal, the elder son of Gurditta, was believed to be hostile to the interests of the Panth and so was similarly excluded. As the progenitor of the line of Kartarpur Sodhis,[13] this elder son of Gurditta has also been the object of obscure tradition, but orthodox tradition seems clearly to brand him as unsuited to the rank of Guru. Har Rai (or Hari Rai), the younger son of Gurditta, was deemed the suitable candidate, and so became the seventh Guru at his grandfather's death in 1644.

Guru Har Rai

At Guru Har Rai's succession the Panth retired into obscurity for at least twenty-five years. Official disfavour continued to be shown towards the leader of these worrisome rural folk, and within a year of his succession Har Rai was obliged to leave Kiratpur and withdraw further into the Shivalik hills. The Raja of Bilaspur provided him with shelter, and for much of the remainder of his period as Guru until his death in 1661 he lived in a village near the Shivalik town of Sirmur.

Evidently Guru Har Rai was a person of very gentle disposition, for the Sikh traditions (which, significantly, are considerably fewer concerning him) number two stories that emphasize this feature. One anecdote tells of his distress when, walking in a field, he accidently brushed a flower with his clothing and broke its stem. Full of remorse, he thereafter always walked through fields with his clothing tucked out of the way. The second anecdote tells how the Guru (like his grandfather before him) liked hunting, but never if it involved the death of living creatures. Instead of killing his quarry, he snared them alive and kept them in a large zoo or aviary. This second anecdote is a difficult story to believe, but it does tell us something about the Guru's personality and about the impact he made upon his followers. Guru Har Rai certainly enjoyed the continuing support and reverence of his father's Sikhs, but the life he led was a quiet one and most of the time he gave little trouble to the Mughal authorities on the plains.

Just what happened to the Panth during this period is exceedingly difficult to tell. Guru Har Rai is said to have made periodic tours of the plains and some notable families in the Malwa area date their firm allegiance from this time (as, for example, the family which eventually produced the princely rulers of Patiala, Jind and Nabha). We can cautiously believe that, in the Malwa area at least, the growth in numbers continued. It is possible, however, that in Doaba and particularly in Majha there would have been a decline in support as many of the people, cut off from all effective contact with their Guru, let their allegiance lapse.[14] We just do not know. The history of the Panth during this period is obscure to say the least.

The same must be said for the *masands* during the same period. The *masands*, it will be remembered, were the Guru's representatives in the scattered *saṅgats* or congregations of the Panth. By the time of Guru Gobind Singh they had developed an unhealthy appetite for independence and some were corruptly keeping what they had collected in the Guru's name. Guru Gobind Singh's time is still fifty years away, and approximately sixty years had passed since the *masands* were first instituted. We are, in other words, a little over half-way through their history and we may assume that the tenuous control the Guru could exercise (particularly in the Majha area) would have encouraged them to think in independent terms. This, however, is mere assumption.

One further anecdote is frequently told of Guru Har Rai, one which explains why the position of Guru passed to his infant second son, Har Krishan, instead of to his older first child, Ram Rai. Guru Har Rai, late in his career, developed a friendship with Dara Shikoh, the elder son of the Emperor Shahjahan. If it was not an actual friendship, at least it was a connection of some kind, and one that led Dara Shikoh to appeal for assistance to the Guru when he was defeated by Aurangzeb in the struggle for the throne. When the war of succession was over, the successful Aurangzeb turned his attention to those who had assisted his rival and Guru Har Rai was summoned to Delhi to give an account of himself.

Instead the Guru sent his elder son, Ram Rai, who proved (according to Sikh tradition) to be the perfect sycophant. When challenged by Aurangzeb to explain an Adi Granth reference to *miṭṭī musalmān* ('the earth formed from the bodies of Muslims') which the emperor considered slighting, Ram Rai claimed that the words were really *miṭṭī beīmān* ('the earth formed from the bodies of faithless people').[15] On hearing this, Guru Har Rai declared that Ram Rai should never see his father's face again and should not succeed to the position of Guru. There is no support for this tradition other than tradition itself and it must be assumed that Ram Rai fell out of favour for other reasons. What they may have been are impossible to know with certainty, though it is likely that they involved the Mughals, whose preferred successor was Ram Rai. He received land in Dehra Dun from the

Mughals and evidently attracted a following which regarded him as Guru. Obviously relations with the orthodox line were far from satisfactory, but the actual cause remains hidden.

Guru Har Krishan

With Ram Rai disinherited, the choice of Guru fell upon Har Rai's second son, a child of six at his father's death. Soon after receiving the title in 1661, Guru Har Krishan (or Hari Krishan) was summoned to Delhi and there he lived until his early death in 1664. Just what he was doing in Delhi continues the tale of obscurity which covers most of the mid-seventeenth-century Panth. It is, however, certain that he was in Delhi (there is unanimity on this point) and that he died there from smallpox.

*

In just over a century the Panth of Guru Nanak had travelled a considerable distance. At the death of the second Guru, Angad, in 1552 it was still the loosely organized fellowship of Sikhs which had gathered around Guru Nanak. The third Guru, Amar Das, realized that tighter organization was needed and reintroduced into the Nanak-panth some of the traditional rituals of Hindu tradition. A collection of sacred hymns was compiled at his direction and a rudimentary structure of preachers was established. This pattern was sustained by Guru Ram Das and Guru Arjan, the former adding to it a system of deputies (the *masands*) and the latter a formalized sacred scripture. Under the sixth Guru, Hargobind, the Panth radically shifted direction. The Mughal rulers were proving hostile and in order to protect itself the Panth took up arms under the direct leadership of the Guru. During the time of the seventh and eighth Gurus, the emphasis on armed conflict receded, but the Panth remained aware that danger could recur. With the ninth Guru that danger did indeed reappear.

3

THE LATER GURUS

Tradition takes over again when Guru Har Krishan pronounces who will succeed him as Guru. His dying words were the cryptic *Bābā Bakāle*, and from this pronouncement it was assumed that the ninth Guru would be found in the village of Bakala (between Amritsar and the Beas river).

Guru Tegh Bahadur

Legend has it that twenty-two claimants to the title converged on Bakala, creating a considerable problem for the bewildered Sikhs. Their difficulty was overcome by the merchant Makhan Shah, who during a storm at sea had vowed to give five hundred gold mohurs to the 'true Guru' if his life should be spared. Arriving for this purpose in Bakala, he was confronted by twenty-two claimants to the title of Guru and so decided he would lay one (or two) mohurs before each claimant. The authentic Guru would doubtless request the remainder. Sure enough, Tegh Bahadur asked for the balance of the promised gift and Makhan Shah, rushing up to the rooftop, proclaimed that he had located the true Guru.

This is legend, though a very attractive one. A more likely situation was a contest between the followers of Dhir Mal and those of Tegh Bahadur. It is true that this is more guesswork based upon the nearness of Dhir Mal's abode, his known enmity, and the fact that his descendants acted as Gurus right up to the twentieth century. Dhir Mal could well have attached *masand*s to his cause, and in the absence of the legitimate Guru in Sirmur those *masand*s from the Majha and Doaba regions may have supported him.

It should be clear, however, that this is supposition and not proven fact. Tegh Bahadur was in some way nominated to succeed Guru Har

Krishan and in some way he was able to sustain his claim to be regarded as the legitimate heir. The appointment was presumably disputed by the Minas and by the followers of Dhir Mal and Ram Rai. Tegh Bahadur's supporters were, however, able to sustain his position. Leaving Bakala to escape the hostility of his enemies, he retired to Kiratpur on the edge of the Shivalik hills. Soon afterwards he moved to the village of Makhoval, a short distance along the Shivaliks from Kiratpur.

This was in 1665. In the same year Guru Tegh Bahadur departed for the east on a lengthy tour. Just why he went is another matter of conjecture, although most traditional sources declare it a missionary journey. Some claim that he went to visit Sikh *saṅgat*s and others suggest he left the Punjab to escape the attentions of his disaffected kinsmen. Whatever the reason (and all the reasons may well have applied), he travelled as far as Assam in eastern India before retracing his steps.

On the way out his wife had been left at Patna in Bihar as her pregnancy was too far advanced for her to continue the journey. There in Patna, in December 1666, the future Guru Gobind Singh was born. (Although the actual date in December is disputed, the 22nd seems most likely.) The sequence of Guru Tegh Bahadur's travels is uncertain, but the birth probably took place while he was further east. On his travels he visited several Sikh *saṅgat*s in Assam and Bengal, which had been established by small groups of Punjabi Khatris.

The Guru visited Patna on his return from Assam and remained there for an indeterminate period (anything from one to three years). He then returned to the Punjab where, according to Sikh tradition, Aurangzeb was busy with his policy of persecution. It is very difficult to sort fact from fiction in the situation that now presents itself. Sikh sources say one thing, Muslim sources another. Aurangzeb has been depicted as a vigorous and vicious persecutor, a reputation which shows increasing signs of serious exaggeration as time passes. On the other hand, he seems clearly to have been determined to protect the interests of Sunni orthodoxy and took measures to effect this. The two versions are as follows.

The Muslim view is that the Sikh Guru had gathered around him a large body of men and was moving around the Punjab levying forced exactions from all who opposed him.[1] A direction was sent to the Punjab ordering him to Delhi to answer these charges. He was, however, nowhere to be found, and for this reason a warrant for his arrest was issued. With a body of supporters he was apprehended in Agra, taken to Delhi, and executed there for his misdemeanours. The charge was lawlessness and on this charge he was adjudged guilty.

The Sikh account is very different, or rather the accepted Sikh account is. According to this version, Aurangzeb was determined to convert the Brahmans of Kashmir to Islam and vigorous steps were taken. A deputation consisting of five hundred Brahmans came to Guru Tegh Bahadur and begged him to intervene on their behalf. While the Guru was considering their request, his son spoke up, declaring that such a request needed a person of signal piety. Who could fulfil the task better than his father? Guru Tegh Bahadur accepted this advice and told the Brahmans to communicate a challenge to Aurangzeb. If the emperor could persuade him to become a Muslim, they too would convert to Islam. If, however, he refused, then they should be freed from the obligation to do so.

This challenge was communicated to the emperor and the Guru was invited down to Delhi to put it to the test. He proceeded there by means of a circuitous route, visiting *saṅgat*s along the way. In Delhi he refused to meet the emperor's demand that he should embrace Islam and was accordingly executed in Chandni Chowk.[2] This summary, needless to say, does no justice to the anguish and agony of the incident in Sikh reports. Few, if any, episodes in Sikh history or Sikh tradition have received such graphic and heart-rending treatment. The Sikhs had received their second martyr Guru and the second one, like the first, was a victim of the vicious and heartless Mughals. *Bachitar Nāṭak*, attributed to Guru Gobind Singh himself, expresses the grief of the Sikhs as follows:

> For the cause of truth he performed this deed, giving his head in obedience to his resolve.
> Bogus tricks are for counterfeit conjurors, deceits which God's people must spurn.
> Dashing himself on the ruler of Delhi, he departed for God's abode.

> Such was the achievement of Tegh Bahadur, the feat which he alone could perform.
> At the death of Tegh Bahadur lamentation swept the earth.
> From below came anguished wailing, from heaven triumphant cries!

The two lines which precede this quotation from *Bachitar Nāṭak* could conceivably have given rise to the orthodox Sikh interpretation of the death of Guru Tegh Bahadur.

> For their frontal mark and their sacred thread he wrought a great deed in this Age of Darkness.
> This he did for the sake of the pious, silently giving his head.

These lines make no reference to the Brahmans of Kashmir, but it is easy to see how the connection could be drawn.

There is, however, an alternative Sikh tradition, both old and significant. Chaupa Singh's *Rahit-nāmā*, dated near the middle of the eighteenth century, makes no mention of the Kashmiri Brahmans. According to this source, Guru Tegh Bahadur was summoned to Delhi as a result of complaints laid against him by Dhir Mal. These he succeeded in answering and he was allowed to return to the Punjab. He was, however, recalled to Delhi, and when he did not go his arrest followed. The source (the *Chaupā Siṅgh Rahit-nāmā*) is relatively early, dating from shortly before the middle of the eighteenth century, and is significant because it was written by a Sikh who was also a Brahman. Normally this family of Brahmans lost no opportunity to exalt other members of the same caste.

Whatever the explanation, there can be no doubt concerning the effect of the Guru's death on the Panth. The Mughal administration was identified as the greatest of its enemies. The effect on the Guru's son and successor can also be imagined. With his accession the Panth was destined to undergo the most momentous event in all Sikh history.

Guru Gobind Singh: early life

Sikh tradition reaches a climax in the execution of Guru Tegh Bahadur. A mighty storm swept the city. At its height two low-caste Sikhs stole the body away, one of them burning it by placing the decapitated corpse in his hut and then setting fire to the whole structure. The head was carried up to Makhoval, where it was humbly laid before the new Guru, the child Guru Gobind. Amid many tears, it was cremated on a sandalwood pyre. The new Guru then asked how many Sikhs had given their lives for him and in reply was informed that there were only three. All others were able to conceal their identity because they bore no outward sign of being a Sikh. The Guru then resolved that all should bear obvious symbols such that a single Sikh would stand out in a crowd of thousands.

This is the traditional answer to the most fundamental of Sikh questions, the reason why Guru Gobind Singh summoned his Sikhs on that most fateful day in their history and the cause for those most significant of commandments which he issued to them. The founding of the Khalsa constitutes the most important event in Sikh history and it will later be dealt with in greater detail. First, though, there are the earlier events of Guru Gobind Singh's life, setting the founding of the Khalsa in its appropriate context. What follows is the life of Guru Gobind Singh, much of it as reported in tradition but with important backing in some areas from authentic research. It falls into six periods: as a child and young adult; the Shivalik wars; the founding of the Khalsa; the assault on Anandpur; the escape to southern Punjab; and the final period in association with the Mughal emperor, Bahadur Shah.

Gobind Das was the original name of the tenth Guru, at least so it seems. Muslim sources generally refer to him as Gobind Rai, but documents issued by his father, Guru Tegh Bahadur, give his name as Gobind Das. Gobind Das was the only child of his elderly father, born in Patna while Guru Tegh Bahadur was making his visit to eastern India. According to *Bachitar Nāṭak*, he was summoned to take birth from performing pre-birth austerities on the slopes of Hem Kunt near the mythological Mount Sumeru.

And now my own story I tell,
How from rigorous austerities I was summoned;
Called from the heights of Hem Kunt
Where the seven peaks so grandly pierce the sky. [6:1]

Bachitar Nāṭak was traditionally written by the Guru himself and much effort has gone into the attempt to identify the site of his pre-birth austerities in the Himalayas. The fact that the location is described in purely mythical terms makes this a rather doubtful proposition, but a site was nevertheless discovered in the Garhwal region during the early 1930s and during the summer months it attracts many Sikh pilgrims.

From Patna the child Gobind Das was brought to the Punjab to live in his father's Shivalik hills headquarters of Makhoval. When he received his father's head he was only nine years of age. Those responsible for his guidance apparently took their duties seriously. Chief among his guides was his mother's brother, Kirpal. As the Guru grew to manhood, Kirpal evidently assumed the principal position within the Panth, encouraging his young charge to assume the martial style previously adopted by his grandfather Guru Hargobind. It was Kirpal who selected the site of Anandpur, only a short distance from Makhoval but in strategic terms a much better location.

In this way the Guru grew to manhood. These are actually years of almost total obscurity. Plainly, though, as he grew to manhood the Guru also grew to complete mastery of the Panth he had inherited. Devout Sikhs have represented him in the following terms:

> Every description of Guru Gobind Singh's person delineates him as a very handsome, sharp-featured, tall and wiry man, immaculately and richly dressed as a prince. Decked with a crest upon his lofty, cone-shaped turban with a plume suspended behind from the top, he was ever armed with various weapons, including a bow and a quiver of arrows, a sword, a discus, a shield and a spear. His choice steed was of bluish-grey colour and on his left hand always perched a white hawk when he sat on the throne or went out hunting.[3]

This is the Guru Gobind Singh of popular art and imagination, and a very powerful impression it continues to make, both consciously and unconsciously. It is as Lord of the Khalsa that popular Sikh taste reveres him. He is always young and upright, he always bears various weapons, and he is frequently clothed in the most gorgeous of raiment. A common name for him is Kalgidhar, bearer of the plume which invariably surmounts his royal turban. Baba Nanak fulfils the role of one rapt in the most profound meditation. Guru Gobind Singh, by contrast, depicts he who is strong in battle, ever ready to fight for his people's rights and to resist those who deny justice. He also practised the art of poetry, such works as *Jāp Sāhib* and *Akāl Ustat* dating from this period. Some of the Sikh traditions also credit the Guru with a retelling of the tales from Hindu mythology which appear in the Dasam Granth, stories such as those from the *Chaṇḍī Charitra*, the *Chaṇḍī kī Vār* and the *Chaubīs Avatār*.

In the first decade following the death of his father, Guru Gobind Singh received further training in the use of arms and also in the literary and religious ideals which had such a powerful effect on him. Hunting wild animals was a particular pleasure for the young Guru and the expeditions are graphically described in *Bachitar Nāṭak*. At the annual festivals of Baisakhi and Divali, the Sikhs assembled in large numbers, and as they were commonly armed, their presence gave the impression that the Guru's centre of Makhoval had become a fortified camp.

In 1685 the ruler of Sirmur, one of Makhoval's neighbours, invited the Guru to stay in his territory. This was apparently because Sirmur recognized the growing strength of his young neighbour and wanted his support in a threatened war with another of the hill states, Garhwal. Guru Gobind Singh accepted the invitation and moved to the strategic site of Paunta on the banks of the Jamuna river. This was on the border of Sirmur and Garhwal. A fort was built in Paunta and the Guru continued to strengthen his following. Eventually, in 1688, Garhwal invaded Sirmur with his hill allies and aided by mercenaries. Guru Gobind Singh faced their army at Bhangani.

In the battle of Bhangani, which is vividly described in *Bachitar Nāṭak*, Guru Gobind Singh suffered some losses, but his opponents suffered far more. The result was a victory for the Guru and marked him as the strongest power among the hill chieftains. Sirmur received no thanks for the victory, for Sirmur had left him to fight unaided. The Guru abandoned his fort in Paunta and after returning to

Makhoval moved his capital to Anandpur in 1689. Only those who had fought at the battle of Bhangani were at first permitted to reside in Anandpur, a reward for their services and a message to those who had not joined their Guru.

The Guru's next battle was at Nadaun and again he was victorious. The ruler of Bilaspur sought his help against a Mughal army which had been sent to punish him and other hill chieftains who had refused to pay tribute. The Mughal army commander of Jammu had sent a force and Guru Gobind Singh joined the allies who confronted it at Nadaun. In spite of this victory, the ruler of Bilaspur with his supporters reached a settlement with the Mughals and agreed to pay tribute. Guru Gobind Singh had learnt once again how treacherous the hill chiefs could be.

From the point of view of the Mughals, the Guru was merely one of several hill chieftains, though perhaps rather more dangerous than the rest. The gatherings of armed men at Anandpur caused them some concern and in 1693 this feature was reported to Aurangzeb. A force was dispatched against Guru Gobind Singh, but its approach was reported to the Guru and Anandpur was duly prepared for a siege. The Mughal detachment did not attack and a second one was diverted by a rebellion on the part of other hill chieftains. The Guru supported the rebels, but when Aurangzeb finally sent his son to discipline them in 1696, he remained safely behind the walls he had erected at Anandpur.

The founding of the Khalsa

Meanwhile Guru Gobind Singh was maintaining contact with his Sikhs on the plains, or at least with such of them as remained loyal to him. The growing independence and corruption of several of the *masand*s was a cause for increasing concern. A century earlier the *masand*s had been set up by Guru Ram Das with the intention that they would care for the needs of scattered *saṅgat*s and remit their offerings to the Guru. The situation had been bad enough in the time of his father, Guru Tegh Bahadur, with the *masand*s in control of much of the Majha and the gates of Amritsar closed against the Guru. Now it was considerably worse, with practically the whole of the Majha territory and most of Doaba under these rival authorities.[4] This did not, of course, mean that the *masand*s actually ruled over their respective *saṅgat*s. The Mughal authorities in Lahore and Sirhind would have ensured that this did not happen. Nevertheless each one did control his *saṅgat*'s relations with the Guru and, where the *masand* chose, these could be effectively broken off. The offerings were still collected, but they went no further than the *masand*s, who used them for their own purposes.

The *masand*s seem to have cooperated in many cases with schismatic groups among the Sikhs. An indeterminate number of Sikhs were following members of Guru Ram Das's descendants who had set up rival Guru lineages, notably the descendants of Prithi Chand (the eldest brother of Guru Arjan) and of Dhir Mal (the elder brother of Guru Har Rai). To the Sikhs their followings were known respectively as the Minas and the Dhir-malias. Ram Rai, the elder brother of Guru Har Krishan, had also attracted a following known to the Sikhs as the Ram-raias, but his strength lay in the hills, where Aurangzeb had granted him the territory of Dehra Dun.

Many Sikhs, presumably ignorant of what was at issue, had been persuaded to join either the Minas or the Dhir-malias. The former commanded strength in the Majha region around Amritsar and the latter in Doaba around Kartarpur. A substantial part of each region appears to have been cut off from loyalty to Gobind Singh, whom the legitimate Sikhs regarded as the true Guru. This was either because of their allegiance to one of the pretender's families or because of the following of an independent *masand*.

Tradition (or at least strongly dominant tradition) relates that 1699 was the year in which Guru Gobind Singh took decisive action. In 1699 he announced to his followers the founding of the Khalsa and enjoined its discipline on all who accepted initiation into the order. The year 1699 is not definitively established as the date of foundation, but it is overwhelmingly accepted by Sikhs today.[5] The call went out to be present on Baisakhi Day, the first day of the Indian New Year and a day on which the Sikhs were accustomed to assemble for an annual festival. They were to come to Anandpur for the festival and they were to come armed.

When the festivities were at their height, the Guru suddenly appeared before the vast assembly and in a loud voice demanded the head of a Sikh. A stunned silence greeted this unexpected request and at first no one was willing to oblige. Eventually Daya Singh, a Khatri from Lahore, stood up and declared himself willing to sacrifice his head if that should be the will of the Guru. Daya Singh was led into a tent, the thud of a falling sword was heard and the Guru reappeared carrying a bloodstained weapon. He then demanded a second victim and Dharam Singh, a Jat, eventually agreed to surrender his head if that was what the Guru wished. The procedure was repeated and again the Guru emerged with his sword covered in blood, demanding that a third Sikh give his head. The third one to come forward was Himmat Singh, the fourth one was Sahib Singh, and the fifth one was Muhakam Singh.

Details then vary. One tradition holds that Guru Gobind Singh had actually cut off the five Sikhs' heads, but replaced them when the drama was over. Another maintains that, with the five Sikhs apparently slain, he drew back the side of the tent to reveal all five alive, accompanied by five slaughtered goats. Yet another insists that the Guru could never have slain goats. Whatever was done behind the screen, the five live Sikhs were dressed in appropriate garments and led out of the tent. There is a substantial number of these miscellaneous details which create considerable feeling on the part of some Sikhs who discuss this issue today, but at least the general picture is clear. The five Sikhs who had volunteered to give their heads were thereafter known as the *Pañj Piāre* (the Cherished Five or the Five Beloved).

The next morning the Guru administered the Khalsa initiation to them, the *khaṇḍe dī pāhul* or 'sword ritual'. For this purpose water was stirred in an iron vessel with a double-edged sword and was sweetened with patashas (sweets) which the Guru's second wife, Mata Jito, cast into it. The Guru then dispensed the *amrit* (the 'nectar' or water thus prepared), first letting it run off his sword on to the initiate's face five times. Five times he poured it into the initiate's cupped hands, five times he applied it to his eyes and five times he sprinkled it on his hair. All then had to eat *kaṛāh prasād* from the same iron bowl. Many Sikhs maintain that, when it was over, he instructed the Panj Piare to administer initiation to him. The Guru had brought the Khalsa into being and he then proceeded (so those who accept this tradition believe) to accept his own initiation from the Khalsa.

Next the Guru promulgated the Rahit (the Khalsa code of belief and conduct). All those who accepted initiation into the Khalsa were required as an essential part of the Rahit to wear the Five Ks (the *pañj kakke* or *pañj kakār*), so called because each of the five articles begins with the letter 'k'. These were *kes* (uncut hair), *kaṅghā* (comb), *kaṛā* (iron or steel wrist-ring), *kirpān* (sword) and *kachh* (the pair of breeches which must not come below the knee). Male members were to add the name 'Singh' to their given name and female members were to add 'Kaur'. Finally the Panj Piare administered the rite to all who chose to accept it. Tradition reports that many thousands of those gathered there accepted initiation into the Khalsa. All this took place on the ground now overlooked by Kesgarh Sahib Gurdwara, second only to the Golden Temple in sanctity.

We have here the founding of the Khalsa according to Sikh tradition. It is most unlikely – indeed impossible – that tradition would be seriously astray on an event so critical for the future of the Panth. Equally, however, it would be strange for tradition to get it all right, and in fact there are already questions raised by the details which cause disagreement among the faithful.

The traditional reason for the creation of the Khalsa is to ensure that every Sikh (or at least every grown Sikh male) would be instantly recognizable. In a crowd of thousands he would immediately stand out. Being thus conspicuous, he would be in no temptation to hide himself when danger was abroad. He would stand up for his Guru, and, when standing up meant fighting, then fight he would. The Guru's Sikhs were, moreover, required to stand forth for a purpose. The origin may have been the need to defend the Guru, but the long-term purpose was to smite and destroy the Mughal empire. For this reason they were to be imbued with a new and unique spirit. They were to regard themselves as the chosen messengers of Akal Purakh and for this reason all Mughals were to be seen as the enemy who must be overcome. Later, with the fighting against the Afghans in the middle of the eighteenth century, the role of adversary was extended to all Muslims. All Muslims (not just the Mughals or their servants) thus became the enemies of the Khalsa.

This is the traditional reason for the founding of the Khalsa and certainly it carries much conviction. There is, however, another reason, namely the Guru's determination to terminate the authority of the *masands* and abolish the order. In instructing his Sikhs to join his Khalsa the Guru was, in effect, summoning them to join something which already existed. *Khālsā* was a term employed in Mughal terminology to designate those lands that were under the direct care and supervision of the emperor, separate from those which were entrusted to provincial governors and rent-free landowners. In the same way, the Guru's Khalsa consisted of those Sikhs who were cared for by the Guru personally as opposed to others who were entrusted to the *masands*. In summoning Sikhs to join his Khalsa, the Guru was commanding them to renounce the authority of the *masands* and attach their allegiance direct to the Guru.

This means that he was abolishing the *masand* system, a system that had performed a valuable service on behalf of the early Gurus but which had long outlived its usefulness. Sikhs were commanded to have nothing to do with the *masands* and those who obeyed them. Included in the same condemnation were the Minas, the Dhir-malias and the Ram-raias, who, together with the *masands* and the followers of the *masands* comprised the *Pañj Mel* or the original Five Reprobate Groups.

This explanation cannot stand alone, however, for it would mean that *all* Sikhs were summoned to join the Khalsa, not just those prepared to be prominently visible and to fight for their Guru under any circumstances. It would mean that Sikhs who cut their hair (the Sahaj-dhari Sikhs) would also belong to the Khalsa, though they could hardly have received the Khalsa initiation and certainly would not observe its Rahit.[6] Obviously membership in the Khalsa order involved more than merely renouncing the *masands*. It involved a very conspicuous appearance (for Sikh men at least), and this the Sahaj-dharis were not prepared to accept. The Guru's actions were represented as contrary to the expectations of his Brahman and Khatri followers, with the result that many of them refused initiation. The former disappear almost entirely from the following of the Guru and the Khatris stay on in reduced numbers as mainly Sahaj-dhari Sikhs. In other words, they did not accept initiation and they did not observe the Rahit.

The Panth therefore became, in terms of its caste constituency, even more strongly Jat. Was the Rahit which was delivered to the newly formed Khalsa shaped by their ideals? Two of the items assuredly included in the simple Rahit which was promulgated at this stage were keeping hair uncut and bearing arms. These would certainly have borne a close correspondence to Jat patterns of behaviour and would, at the same time, have had much to do with the reluctance of Khatri and Brahman Sikhs to enlist in the Khalsa. It poses a continuing question for the Panth, one which will be examined in greater detail when dealing specifically with the Rahit.[7]

The institution of the Khalsa, with its conspicuous external symbols, also raises the question of how its creation could possibly be reconciled with Guru Nanak's adamant insistence that external features must necessarily stand squarely in the way of liberation through the divine Name. In this particular case Sikhs have no difficulty in giving a response. The theological answer is the same one as is given for the introduction of changes by Guru Amar Das or of worldly activities by Guru Hargobind. The answer is that there is only one Guru, successively inhabiting ten human bodies, and what Gobind Singh decreed at the end of the seventeenth century was what Nanak would have decreed in the same circumstances more than 150 years earlier.

The assault on Anandpur

The tradition continues with a Mughal decision to destroy this trouble-some person who was making problems for them on the fringe of their empire. Vazir Khan was the Mughal governor of Sirhind (the province immediately adjacent to the Guru's territories), and, aided by the Guru's enemies among the hill rulers, he laid siege to Anandpur. Many are the tales of heroism told of this episode in the Guru's career. The actual siege began in 1701 when an alliance of the jealous hill rajas joined forces to attack the Guru. Their prize weapon was an elephant trained to wield a mighty sword with its trunk. Protected with heavy iron shields and inflamed with intoxicants, the rampaging creature threatened to batter down the gates of Lohgarh, one of the two fortresses within Anandpur. A famous warrior, Bachitra Singh, was dispatched by the Guru to deal with the monster. He thrust his lance with such force that it pierced the elephant's frontal shield and penetrated its forehead. Squealing with pain, the crazed brute turned on its own army and, with threshing sword, ran amok among the besieging troops. The havoc it caused was so serious that (according to tradition) the hill rajas were forced to raise the siege and depart in disarray.

The rajas, however, regrouped their armies and returned again, this time supported by Vazir Khan and a Mughal force from Sirhind. Under the command of Vazir Khan, the alliance laid determined siege to Anandpur in 1704 and by maintaining a tight cordon for several months brought the garrison near to starvation. Many of the Guru's followers, ground down by the privations of the siege, renounced their allegiance to him and departed. Those who remained were ordered to prepare for evacuation.

On the night of 20–21 December 1704 the surviving garrison, led by the Guru, broke out of Anandpur. With a group of those who escaped, the Guru managed to secure a small fort in the village of Chamkaur, several kilometres away. Again they were besieged and this time the attackers were determined to secure their objective. The Guru's two elder sons were killed during the attack and it seemed the same fate must await him also. His surviving followers insisted, however, that he must be preserved, and under cover of darkness he was able to slip through the Mughal cordon.

Travelling alone, the Guru eventually found himself in the Machhiwara wasteland. There he was discovered by Sikhs who had also escaped and was given shelter by the headman of the neighbouring village. After leaving Machhiwara the Guru evaded his Mughal pursuers by disguising himself as a Sufi holy man from the distant town of Uch. Soon after his escape he learnt of Vazir Khan's most despicable act. The Guru's two younger sons, captured with their mother following the evacuation of Anandpur, had been delivered to Vazir Khan. Having offered the two children the usual choice between conversion to Islam or death the governor ordered the defiant children to be bricked up alive in the city wall. This particular incident made a deep and continuing impression on the Panth, as is illustrated by the frequency with which the scene is still a subject for the popular art of the Sikhs.

Moving on to Khidrana in Firozpur district, the Guru gathered his scattered force again and another battle took place. Among the slain were forty Sikhs who had earlier renounced their allegiance to the Guru but who had been shamed by their women when they returned to their homes. Rejoining the Guru's army, they now sealed their restored loyalty by death. Encountering the last dying survivor on the battlefield, the Guru forgave their desertion and acknowledged their renewed allegiance. Ever since they have been remembered as the Forty Liberated (*chālī mukte*), still commemorated in the prayer of the Khalsa known as *Ardās*.[8]

From Khidrana (or Muktsar as it came to be called) the Guru moved on to Talvandi Sabo in Bhatinda district, known to Sikhs as Damdama or 'resting place'. In Damdama Sahib he remained for about one year. Tradition relates that here he occupied himself with converting the villagers of surrounding villages and in recording the sacred scriptures. The manuscript of the Adi Granth was in the hands of the family of Dhir Mal, who refused the Guru's request to hand it over. For this reason the Guru recorded not only large portions of the Dasam Granth but also (from memory) the complete text of the Adi Granth.

It should be emphasized that many of these stories derive from strictly traditional history, not from sources that have been properly researched. This applies to many of the anecdotes related of the period covering the Guru's travels from Anandpur to Damdama Sahib. On one occasion, it is related, the Guru, following his escape from Machhiwara, was given shelter in the village of Jatpura (Ludhiana District) by a Muslim official called Rai Kalha. Before leaving he presented Rai Kalha with a sword, adding that it was never to be used. It was to be retained as an honoured memento. Rai Kalha and his son both respected the Guru's instruction, but his grandson ignored it and used the sword for hunting. The Guru's command cannot thus be mocked. While attempting to slay a stag, the grandson accidentally struck himself with the sword and died of the self-inflicted wound.

On another occasion, shortly after the battle of Muktsar, the Guru is said to have shot a partridge, plucked it and cast it before his falcon.

After some hesitation the falcon began to eat the dead bird. The partridge, explained the Guru, had been a cultivator in his last incarnation and the falcon had been a moneylender. The cultivator, having borrowed funds from the moneylender, had squandered them. When the moneylender demanded his due payment, the cultivator asked for more time, naming the Guru as his surety. The debt remained unpaid and eventually both died. Reincarnated as partridge and falcon, they had been brought together again so the debtor could repay what he owed. The Guru, acting as guarantor, had ensured that this would be done. All who make similar promises in the Guru's name should remember that eventually they will be compelled to pay their debts.

The death of Guru Gobind Singh

During the assault on Anandpur and the retreat to southern Punjab the Mughal emperor had been Aurangzeb. Guru Gobind Singh evidently assisted Aurangzeb's son, Bahadur Shah, in his inevitable war of succession, and once Aurangzeb was dead the Guru travelled down to Agra where Bahadur Shah was now installed. Bahadur Shah received him graciously, but did not do anything about punishing Vazir Khan for the attack on Anandpur. Guru Gobind Singh joined Bahadur Shah with a retinue of troops and travelled down to the Deccan with him. There, in the small town of Nander on the banks of the Godavari, he was stabbed in the abdomen by a Pathan whom tradition firmly attaches to Vazir Khan. The Pathan was dispatched by the Guru and the stab wounds were stitched up. A few days later, however, the stitching broke (one tradition says that the Guru was testing a new bow which had been brought to him) and the end was near. He died shortly after, on 7 October 1708.

Before he died, realizing his end was near, the Guru summoned his Sikhs and declared that the line of personal Gurus was now at an end. Thereafter they should regard the functions of the Guru as vested in the Granth (which became the Guru Granth) and the Panth (the Guru Panth). In this way the Guru will remain ever-present and ever-accessible to his Sikhs. It is not made clear which Granth is referred to (whether the Adi Granth, or both the Adi Granth and the Dasam Granth). Likewise, the definition of the Panth is left uncertain. Is it the wider Nanak-panth or is it the narrower Khalsa Panth? These cause continuing debate, but not so the general intention of the Guru. The line of personal Gurus was at an end and the Guru would thereafter be present in the Granth and the Panth.

This is, of course, the voice of tradition which is speaking. Did Guru Gobind Singh, before he died, actually confer the function of Guru on the scripture (the Guru Granth) and the gathered community (the Guru Panth)? The traditional command was that with his death the line of personal Gurus was to come to an end and thereafter the Sikhs should look to the sacred Book (or Books) and to the community. Did he or did he not so instruct his Sikhs? Or do we not know?

One possibility is that the tradition arose because Guru Gobind Singh had died without a living heir. His two elder sons had been killed at the battle of Chamkaur during the evacuation of Anandpur, and the two younger sons had been captured and executed by Vazir Khan in Sirhind. The Guru's death therefore involved his followers in a problem. Banda, the Guru's successor as military leader, was acknowledged by some as Guru, but as he was not a member of the Guru's family, others withheld their allegiance. Eventually the difficulty was resolved by treating the gathered Panth as the corporate presence of the Guru, its decisions having the same effect as the decisions of the personal Guru himself. Meetings of the Panth would also be conducted in the presence of both sacred scriptures, and so they too came to be regarded as the eternal Guru.

This theory is, however, too neat. The presence of the Adi Granth was already recognized as the Guru even while the personal Guru was still alive, and meetings of a *saṅgat* also involved the Guru, at which he would be mystically present. Clearly the doctrine represents a more complicated situation than the theory allows. There is, moreover, a source that is probably much closer to the death of Guru Gobind Singh and which supports the tradition. *Gur Sobhā* was written by a poet called Sainapati who had elected not to become a member of the Khalsa but who was a loyal follower of Guru Gobind Singh. A strong probability favours 1711 as the year of the completion of *Gur Sobhā*, and in it Sainapati writes as follows:

On an earlier occasion the Guru had been approached by his Sikhs and had been asked what form the [eternal] Guru would assume [after he had departed this earthly life]. He had replied that it would be the Khalsa. 'The Khalsa is now the focus of all my hopes and desires,' he had declared. 'Upon the Khalsa which I have created I shall bestow the succession. The Khalsa is my physical form and I am one with the Khalsa. To all eternity I shall be manifest in the Khalsa. They whose hearts are purged of falsehood will be known as the true Khalsa; and the Khalsa, freed from error and illusion, will be my true Guru.

'And my true Guru, boundless and infinite, is the eternal Word, the Word of wisdom which the devout contemplate in their hearts, the Word which brings ineffable peace to all who utter it, the Word which is wisdom immeasurably unfolded, the Word which none may ever describe. This is the light which is given to you, the refuge of all who inhabit the world, and the abode of all who renounce it.'[9]

If 1711 is the correct date for *Gur Sobhā*, the traditional version receives very strong support. The balance of probability favours the claim that the Guru actually made the crucial pronouncement; and it seems safe to assume that Guru Gobind Singh, in all likelihood, declared that after his death the Khalsa Panth and the scripture would embody the personality and the guidance of the mystical Guru. Note, however, that Sainapati explicitly designates the Khalsa as one of the two recipients, not the wider Sikh Panth. What is not clear is why Sainapati himself declined to join the Khalsa.

This discussion of the final intention of Guru Gobind Singh also carries over to the question of the Dasam Granth, which in the eighteenth century shared with the Adi Granth the status of the eternal Guru. It too was, for a time, a part of the Guru Granth, for accounts of the eighteenth-century meetings of the Sarbat Khalsa (the 'entire Khalsa') explicitly mention that these meetings were held in the presence of the two open scriptures. According to the traditional view, the contents of the Dasam Granth were all written by Guru Gobind Singh himself, much of it during the time he spent at Damdama Sahib following the evacuation of Anandpur. The Sikhs thereafter had two scriptures, the Adi Granth and the Dasam Granth. Detailed consideration of the Dasam Granth must await its treatment in the chapter dealing with Sikh scriptures.[10]

Guru Gobind Singh looms very large indeed in the consciousness of Sikhs and for that reason he figures prominently in the stories of their faith. He shares with Guru Nanak much the greater part of Sikh tradition, attracting accounts of supreme heroism and anecdotes which display his profound wisdom and common sense. Dressed in gorgeous raiment with a plume in his turban, seated on his horse and armed to defend his Panth, his is a regal figure which shines brightly in the memory of his Sikhs and gives rise to noble traditions. These traditions are very important in the continuing growth of the Panth. Their growth tells us much about his followers in the years and the centuries that follow.

4

THE GROWTH AND EXPANSION OF THE PANTH: 1708 TO THE PRESENT DAY

With the death of Guru Gobind Singh in 1708 it might appear that the religion of the Sikhs was now fully developed. There were, however, two critical periods that lay ahead. One was the whole of the remaining eighteenth century, a period obscure yet very important as far as the development of Sikhism is concerned. The discipline of the Khalsa was rudimentary when it began. By the end of the century, it emerges fully fashioned and secure.

The second period is the Singh Sabha reform movement, from its foundation in 1873 until it was eventually overtaken by the Akali political movement in 1920. Within the Singh Sabha movement there opened up a deep division between two groups, leading ultimately to the victory of one of them. The victor was the Tat Khalsa section, and their success led to a highly significant shift in the Sikhs' assessment of their own religion. Before the coming of the Singh Sabha movement, many Sikhs had regarded their religion as a special branch of the Hindu tradition. With the force and persistence of the Tat Khalsa message, however, they were increasingly persuaded that Sikhism is indeed a new religion, wholly separate from both Hindu tradition and Islam.

The Singh Sabha phase is flanked by two other periods which contain much of historical interest to the Sikh people, yet add relatively little to their pattern of beliefs. During the first half of the nineteenth century there was the Sikh kingdom of the Punjab, occupied by four decades of Maharaja Ranjit Singh's stable rule and one decade of rapidly growing confusion and collapse. The state was annexed by the British in 1849, an event that was followed by the years of growing unease which culminated in the founding of the first Singh Sabha in 1873. The period after the half-century of Singh Sabha activity was followed by the Gurdwara Reform Movement of the early 1920s, leading to the passing of the Sikh Gurdwaras Act in 1925. By this time Sikh activity was firmly enmeshed in politics, a stage which has yet to end. The intervening years are marked by events of great importance, but the importance was political and it still continues to be political today.

The uprising led by Banda Bahadur

The death of Guru Gobind Singh in the Deccan town of Nander was followed soon after by a widespread uprising in the Punjab. In Nander the Guru had met an ascetic called Madho Das who came from the Jammu hills, which flank the northern boundary of the Punjab. Tradition relates that Guru Gobind Singh recognized in Madho Das the very person whom he was seeking. Renaming him Banda ('Slave'), he dispatched him to the Punjab, armed with appropriate emblems of authority. There he was to raise rebellion in the Guru's name and in particular was to bring revenge upon the head of Vazir Khan, the treacherous governor of Sirhind.

All this derives from tradition, the actual sources which record it being much later and themselves dependent on traditional information. There are many questions raised by this episode in Sikh history. Why did the Guru choose for such an important assignment someone whom he had known for only a brief period? Were other leaders appointed to stir up the Punjab? Was Banda initiated as a member of the Khalsa? Why did he take so long to reach the Punjab from Nander? These and other questions arise from the lack of source material and the only firm conclusion is that there can be no definitive answers.

When Banda did enter the Punjab, however, this obscurity largely disappears as he now emerges in the Mughal histories. His call to the Panth met with a satisfactory response and at the head of a growing army of peasants he marched up the Punjab. A series of towns fell to him, notably Samana (the home of the executioner of Guru Tegh Bahadur). Eventually, in May 1710, the large force which had gathered around him faced Vazir Khan about sixteen kilometres from Sirhind. Vazir Khan was much better armed than Banda, but, confronted by a determined host, he was overcome. He himself was killed in the battle and many more besides him. Suchanand, his Hindu Dewan who had strongly advised the killing of Guru Gobind Singh's two sons, was taken alive and put to death. Several accounts exist of the battle of Sirhind and the capture of the town, all stressing the terrible destruction that Banda's army wrought upon it.

For five more years Banda's activities kept the Punjab in a state of alarm, sometimes receding as he retired to the hills in temporary defeat, then advancing again as he returned with renewed strength to wage war once more against the Mughal authorities of Sirhind and Lahore. Eventually he made a critical mistake, cutting a canal to surround himself with a protective moat while being besieged. This action also cut him off from all supplies and he was finally compelled to surrender. He was taken to Delhi in chains and there given the usual option of conversion to Islam or death. He steadfastly chose death and was executed in June 1716.

As a mighty hero, a figure of myth and tradition, Banda has continued to play an important part in the moulding of the Khalsa character. He is Banda Bahadur, Banda the Brave. Paradoxically, he is greatly admired yet is also regarded as having tried to lead the Panth astray. The issue concerns the division that opened up between the Bandai Sikhs (the Sikhs following Banda's example) and the group which has come to be known as the original Tat Khalsa. At some stage in the revolt (probably about 1713) Banda is reputed to have abandoned the blue clothes of the Khalsa for red, to have insisted on vegetarianism for his followers and to have changed the Panth's salutation from *Vāhigurūjī kī fateh* ('Hail to the Guru's victory!') to *Fateh darśhan* ('Behold the victory!' or, loosely, 'Press on to victory!'). In so doing he was, it is claimed, setting up a panth of his own, amending practices instituted by Guru Gobind Singh. All this is placed in the context of a dispute with Mata Sundari, one of the widows of Guru Gobind Singh, who took the opposing view to Banda.

For the sources of this episode we are largely dependent upon the nineteenth-century works of Rattan Singh Bhangu, Santokh Singh and Gian Singh. This at once places a question mark upon it, for sources so far removed from an actual event can be little trusted. On the other hand, this particular incident is most unlikely to have found mention in such works unless there were something behind it. Sources which normally regard Banda as the hero of the Khalsa do not lightly introduce an episode of this kind. Probably it is safe to assume that the answer to the problem lies in the factionalism which has been so much a part of life in the Punjab, Banda representing one faction and Mata Sundari acting as at least the figurehead of the other.

What we do not know is whether Banda actually adopted the variant lifestyles with which he was charged or whether he was merely accused of having done so. The opposing faction (those who were identified as the Tat Khalsa) evidently had links with Mata Sundari and may well have conducted the controversy in the standard way. This should come as no surprise, for the Gurus were frequently bothered by challenges to their authority in precisely the way that the rules of factional conflict would lead us to expect. The difference is that whereas the Gurus managed to win such contests, Banda lost this one.

Factional conflict appears to be at least a part of the answer and perhaps it was the whole one. There is, however, another point that needs to be noted. This period was only a short time after the formal founding of the Khalsa. If the story of Banda's actions is true (or substantially so), it may follow that the Khalsa, during the years immediately after the death of Guru Gobind Singh, was still feeling its way with regard to the correct rules to be followed. The apparent failure of Banda to take initiation also fits this situation. The Khalsa knew that it had a certain amount to obey as defined by Rahit, but it was a Rahit which covered only some areas of their lives.

This conclusion amounts to little more than speculation, but it is inference of this kind which makes sense of what was happening to the Khalsa during the course of the eighteenth century. The problems with Banda are numerous and our knowledge of many features of Banda is either limited or totally absent. It is important, however, that the difficulties should not be exaggerated. The early eighteenth century was a period of rapidly growing unrest, extending into a series of destructive attacks on the authority of the Mughals in the Punjab as elsewhere in India. Banda certainly played his part, and so too did other followers of Guru Gobind Singh. Of Banda's brief and turbulent career, of his great daring and of his eventual death at the hands of the Delhi rulers there can be no doubt whatsoever.

The Khalsa's struggle for survival

With Banda dispatched in 1716 something resembling stability returned to the Punjab. The Mughal governor of the Lahore was Abdus Samad Khan, succeeded in 1726 by his son, Zakariya Khan. In 1745 Zakariya Khan was succeeded by his son, Yahya Khan. The ties which bound the Mughal empire were loosening during this period, and although its authority was formally acknowledged, the fact that son succeeded father as governor indicates that the Punjab (like other areas) was moving towards autonomy. Following Banda's execution, efforts were vigorously pursued in the Punjab, seeking out members of the Khalsa and, if they resisted, summarily killing them. Those who were not inclined to bow to the governor's will found it convenient to take refuge in the Shivalik hills or in the desert lands to the south. In this way the bearded Sikh largely if temporarily disappeared from the plains, most of those who remained preferring to remove their beards or to stay shaven.

The campaign to exterminate the Khalsa had a very brief life, if in fact this really was the intention of Abdus Samad Khan. In the early 1720s the situation had eased, though areas of confusion still remained. Law and order were seriously impaired away from the main towns and main lines of communication, and although the lives of Khalsa Sikhs might be threatened, their opportunities for disturbing the peace in rural areas were also greatly increased. Moving rapidly through the remoter areas, they were able to contribute to the disorder. Many were killed. Many were not and were able to maintain a guerrilla existence.

Together with Banda's rebellion, these were the years in which the traditions of the Khalsa were consolidated and the Rahit took firmer shape. As such it is one of the phases which is of crucial importance in the growth of Sikhism. Rather than a narrative of the actual events, it is the *interpretation* of what took place that really matters. Persecution borne triumphantly is a powerful tonic for any community. The blood of the martyrs is indeed the seed of the Khalsa and it makes little difference whether history is adequately or accurately told in the process. Sikh people take great heart from the heroic persecution of this period in their history, and, if need arise, can readily apply its various incidents to their own experience. In recent years they have not been slow to recognize the modern Abdus Samad Khans or Zakariya Khans.

Out of this period in the first half of the eighteenth century come some historical figures vividly remembered as noble heroes in the traditions of the Sikhs. Kapur Singh is one of these. Zakariya Khan was vigorous in his efforts to control the troublesome Sikhs and sent out various expeditions to deal with them. After several years of effective effort, the governor tried to secure even greater peace by the offer in 1733 of valuable land to the leader of the Khalsa. The offer was communicated to the Sikhs in their jungle retreat and, failing to decide who was their undisputed leader, the Khalsa conferred the honour on the man who was waving the fan over their assembly. In this manner the lowly Kapur Singh came to be known as Nawab Kapur Singh. The story may seem difficult for some to believe, and the written sources for it come from the nineteenth century, yet it arises from an actual episode in Punjab history and it concerns a real figure. Kapur Singh rose to undoubted prominence as a leader of the Khalsa during succeeding decades.

Another hero was Mani Singh. In 1738 Mani Singh, who had been the custodian of Harimandir Sahib in Amritsar since 1721, sought permission to hold the Divali fair.[1] This request was granted on condition that he should agree to pay 5,000 rupees to the state after the fair was over. Sikh sources hold that he was unable to pay this amount because a detachment of troops, stationed near Amritsar, kept many of the people away. Mani Singh was arrested, given the choice of Islam or death, and when he refused to renounce his faith was cruelly executed.

And there are many more heroes whom the Panth remembers from this period. Bota Singh is renowned as a brave Sikh who claimed his independence from the government of the Mughals by brazenly levying a toll on all who used a portion of the imperial highway. This he did with the assistance of another Sikh, an Outcaste named Garja Singh. In 1739 a force was dispatched and both men died in resisting it. Another hero is Taru Singh, who in 1745 was executed by having his scalp torn from his head. Sikh tradition remembers such men as martyrs to the faith.

In 1746 disaster overwhelmed a substantial number of Sikhs. With a large force, Lakhpat Rai, the Hindu chief minister of the governor of Lahore, set out in pursuit of a substantial group whose whereabouts had been reported by intelligence. He caught up with them at a place called Kahnuwan and there inflicted a severe defeat on them, remembered by Sikhs as the *Chhoṭā Ghallūghārā* or 'Lesser Holocaust'. In 1762 this was followed by the *Vaḍḍā Ghallūghārā* or 'Greater Holocaust', when an even larger number of Sikhs was destroyed by the invading Afghan army of Ahmad Shah Abdali.

Rise of the Sikh misl*s*

The eighteenth century is certainly not represented as a time when the Khalsa won every battle, and the heroes of this period are commonly men who die as noble martyrs rather than as stalwarts who triumph through the force of arms. By the middle of the century, however, the balance of power was beginning to shift and a new kind of hero was beginning to appear. Jassa Singh Ahluvalia is the best example. Although he commanded a relatively small group of men, he was recognized as the supreme Sikh leader in the middle years of the century. During these years, whenever the dispersed forces of the Khalsa wished to combine their operations, Jassa Singh Ahluvalia was the person to whom they turned as their commander.

This was the period when the ruler of Kabul, Ahmad Shah Abdali, conducted a series of nine invasions from Afghanistan, the first beginning in 1747 and the last petering out in 1769. It was also the period of the Sikh *misl*s, independent armies of Sikhs from a particular area who owed allegiance to their commanding *sardār* or chieftain. There were traditionally twelve of these *misl*s, though there were also other small armies of Sikhs commanded by independent *sardār*s. Each operated within a certain area of the Punjab, and varied in size from a compact unit to the composite groups which in effect formed confederacies. The latter case happened when a deceased *sardār* was succeeded by two or more *sardār*s with close family ties to him. There were two such confederacies. One was the Bhangi *misl*, which operated in western Punjab and included Lahore within its sphere of influence.[2]

The other was the Phulkian *misl* of the Malwa territory, all of its *sardārs* being descendants of a Sikh named Baba Phul who was converted by Guru Har Rai.

The *misls* had begun to emerge earlier in the eighteenth century as groups of horsemen gathered under their chosen *sardār*. During the invasions of Ahmad Shah Abdali, they evolved into more coherent forces and acquired considerable skill in conducting a particular kind of cavalry warfare. They were never strong enough to confront the Afghan army in open battle, but they had the rapid mobility to enable them to harry and disrupt its activities. With their men drawn from the villages of the Punjab, they were fighting on their own ground and could count on support from the remainder of the Punjabi rural population.

On the occasions when they decided to unite for a particular purpose, they constituted the Dal Khalsa or Army of the Khalsa, with Jassa Singh Ahluvalia as its usual head. If conditions were sufficiently settled, the dispersed units of the Khalsa met twice annually before Akal Takhat in Amritsar. These were the occasions when the community was constituted as the Sarbat Khalsa or the 'entire Khalsa'. Both Granths lay open at their gatherings (the Adi Granth and the Dasam Granth), and any decision reached was called a *gurmata* or 'will of the Guru'. Because of the manner in which it was reached, a *gurmata* was binding on all members of the Khalsa, including those who were not present when it was adopted. This gave the fighting force of the Khalsa a considerable advantage, even when it was divided into twelve *misls* and other detachments. It also greatly strengthened the doctrines of Guru Granth and Guru Panth, the belief that the mystical Guru operated through the scriptures and the community.

The Punjab under Maharaja Ranjit Singh

For as long as they were confronted by a common enemy the Khalsa generally remained united. Once Ahmad Shah Abdali was dead, however, the *misls* rapidly became involved in internecine warfare. With Mughal power destroyed and the Afghan now gone, it became a question of which of the *misls* had the power to control the others, so to become the effective ruler of the Punjab. This was the question which was settled during the last decade of the eighteenth century.

The obvious candidate was the extensive Bhangi *misl*, and for a time it seemed it would succeed. The Bhangis were, however, opposed by the more compact Shukerchakia *misl*, centred on the area to the north and west of Lahore. In 1792 the Shukerchakia *sardār* died, leaving control of the *misl* to his young and highly ambitious son, Ranjit Singh. By means of marriages, threats and open warfare, he absorbed all the *misls* to the north and west of the Satluj river. Those to the south and east of the Satluj were protected by the arrival of the British, who in 1809 signed with Ranjit Singh the Treaty of Amritsar, guaranteeing the river as the boundary between the two powers. Ranjit Singh had to abandon his hopes of uniting all the Sikh territories, but he was at least master of the central and western Punjab. To his kingdom he subsequently added Multan, Kashmir and finally Peshawar.

The kingdom of Ranjit Singh ushered in a notable period of Punjab history. This consisted of Ranjit Singh's four decades of rule, terminating with his death in 1839, and a final decade of rapidly growing confusion. In 1845–6 and 1848–9 two Anglo-Sikh wars were fought and the kingdom was finally annexed by the British in 1849. The four decades of Ranjit Singh's rule were marked by conquests in three directions and by the creation of a strong army based on the European model. As such they constitute a period remembered by the Sikhs as truly glorious. The Sikhs were only a small minority of the total population of the Punjab, yet under the effective rule of a Sikh maharaja the achievement had brought great renown to the name of the Khalsa.

Varieties of Sikhs during the nineteenth century

But the half century occupied by the Kingdom of the Punjab produced relatively little of importance concerning the development of the Sikh religion. The only significant exception was the beginning of the Nirankari and Namdhari sectarian movements during Ranjit Singh's latter years. The Nirankaris were dismayed at the neglect of Guru

Nanak's teachings and the Namdharis were alarmed by a failure to live up to the hallowed principles of the Khalsa.[3] Other Sikhs saw no need for concern.

Beyond this there was nothing of great importance. Ranjit Singh was certainly a loyal Sikh and he showed great acumen in having his government referred to as Sarkar Khalsa, the Government of the Khalsa. In terms of religious belief and practice, however, he was certainly not innovative, nor was the period as a whole. Shortly before he died he made lavish contributions to Brahmans; and after his death four of his widows and seven other women described as 'slave girls' cremated themselves on his funeral pyre. These actions certainly did not indicate close adherence to the teachings of the Gurus and for some Sikhs they have left to the memory of Ranjit Singh a divided reputation. He is greatly admired for his conquests and for his civil administration, but those who are particular in their Sikhism regard his religious principles as a reversion to Hindu practice.

In fact there was nothing surprising in the acceptance of Hindu beliefs. This was before the birth of the Singh Sabha reform movement and at the time the attitude among most Sikhs was completely in accord with that of Ranjit Singh. The Khalsa was certainly distinctive in that its members were outwardly recognizable by particular symbols, and each was committed to follow the Rahit, which, it was believed, had been conferred on the Khalsa by the tenth Guru. They were still members of Hindu society, however, and there were plenty of other Sikhs who did not belong to the Khalsa.

These Sikhs who did not belong to the Khalsa adopted a range of different identities. Some were Sahaj-dhari Sikhs who lived as ordinary Hindus but looked to the sacred Adi Granth as the source of all their beliefs. These members of the Panth lived mainly in the towns, or, if dwelling in villages, usually followed such occupations as shopkeeping or money-lending. They had not been initiated into the Khalsa and the Rahit played no part in their personal lives. If they took formal initiation, it was by the rite of *charan amrit*, administered by people whom they acknowledged as religious preceptors. There were many such people within the Panth, who during the eighteenth and nineteenth centuries would, in a variety of non-Khalsa ways, act as spiritual guides. The Khalsa Sikh, on the other hand, took initiation from other

Khalsa Sikhs in the ceremony of *khaṇḍe dī pāhul* (initiation of the two-edged sword).

Others were Udasis, ascetic Sikhs who claimed spiritual descent from Siri Chand, one of Guru Nanak's two sons. The Udasis were celibate and they too refused to acknowledge the Rahit. As such they lived radically different lives from ordinary Sikhs (particularly those of the Khalsa), but they maintained that they were true Sikhs and that their yogic style was in accordance with the Gurus' teaching. Their numbers had multiplied greatly during the reign of Ranjit Singh, their centres generously patronized by the state, which evidently perceived them as supporters of its authority. The same growth patterns also applied to the Nirmala order, yet another variety of Sikhs. Before Sikh rule was established during the late eighteenth century, the Nirmalas received scant attention from the Panth. Sikh rulers paid them due respect, however, and by the end of the Kingdom of the Punjab they too were important as an ascetic Sikh order noted for its emphasis upon traditional learning.[4]

There were several more varieties of Sikh in the middle of the nineteenth century as the Panth emerged from the defeated Kingdom of the Punjab and acknowledged the rule of the British. Khalsa Sikhs were certainly the most prominent among them, a prominence easy to understand when one remembers the conspicuous nature of the appearance of male members of the order. At this time, however, the Khalsa was not by any means the sole variety. The Khalsa has never been identical with the wider Sikh Panth, and even today it does not stand alone. In the middle of the nineteenth century it comprised a smaller proportion than it does today, and there was little to suggest that the Khalsa mode was in any sense the only style for all who aspired to be fully and completely Sikh.

The Singh Sabha movement

All that, however, was to change and the change came about as a result of the Singh Sabha movement. To be more precise, the change occurred because of a fundamental cleavage within the Singh Sabha. It came about because a deep division emerged within the movement and because one of the opposing groups won a convincing victory over the other.

The original founders of the Singh Sabha movement were Sanatan or 'traditional' Sikhs, believing that the Panth certainly consisted of the followers of the Gurus but regarding it as a part of wider Hindu society. For the Sanatan Sikhs there was abundant room for variety within the Panth. Those who were not Khalsa members and who did not regard the Rahit as mandatory were just as entitled to call themselves Sikhs as the Khalsa variety.

The Sanatan Sikhs, who were identified with the original Singh Sabha founded in Amritsar in 1873, were opposed by a much more radical opinion centred on Lahore. The radicals were Sikhs of the Tat Khalsa, the 'True Khalsa'.[5] For the Tat Khalsa it was impossible to be both a Hindu and a Sikh, as those of the Sanatan persuasion maintained. The only correct style for a Sikh was that of the Khalsa, and although they did not actually cast out the non-Khalsa variety, they explicitly adopted the view that these non-Khalsa Sikhs were on their way to becoming Sikhs in the full sense of the term. In other words, they were said to be aspiring to become members of the Khalsa. The term Sahaj-dhari, which had long been applied to those who refrained from accepting the Rahit, was reinterpreted to mean 'slow-adopting'. According to this new interpretation, they were Sahaj-dharis in the sense that they were 'slow' in adopting the Rahit, but eventually they would certainly reach this objective.

During the last two decades of the nineteenth century and the beginning of the twentieth, these two groups vigorously contended for the interpretation of what it meant to be a Sikh. The Sanatan Sikhs maintained that variety was entirely permissible in the Panth and that the Panth merely marked out the Sikhs as a special group in Hindu society. In reply, the Tat Khalsa vigorously upheld the view that Sikhs emphatically were not Hindus. They also insistently asserted that the Khalsa mode was the one mode that all Sikhs either accepted or else made their ultimate objective. Ultimately victory went to the Tat Khalsa, and since the early years of the twentieth century Sikhs have been progressively learning three things. First, Sikhs are not Hindus. Secondly, Khalsa membership should be the objective of all Sikhs. Thirdly, Khalsa membership requires obedience to the Rahit.

When the British annexed the Punjab in 1849, they pushed through radical measures for the economic advancement of the area, concentrating on such things as improvements in communications and the extension of the canal system. They also encouraged education, giving aid to missionary schools set up in the province. A common British view was that Sikhism was bound to 'merge back into Hinduism', for the British could perceive what they interpreted as abundant evidence of Khalsa decay. What this meant was that they were mistaking the more prominent kind of Sikhs for the whole of the Panth. It seemed obvious to them that there were plenty of signs of an indifferent observance of the Khalsa Rahit and many of them drew the conclusion that this must spell the end of Sikhism.

This, however, had always been the case. Around 1860 or 1870, at the time when these observations were being made, many of those who lived in the villages were very relaxed about questions of identity. Muslims might be easier to distinguish, but the difference between Hindu and Sikh was much more difficult to discern. Although this was somewhat simpler in urban areas, the villages were where a large majority of the Sikhs actually lived. It seemed that only in the Indian Army were the Khalsa symbols adequately maintained, the British requiring all Sikh recruits to observe them scrupulously.

Some Sikhs shared this opinion held by the British. Sikhism, they reasoned, had been sufficiently protected under the Sikh Kingdom, but with the annexation of the Punjab in 1849 the Panth had slipped into a condition of indiscipline and negligence. Something must be done. A group of prominent Sikhs convened a meeting in Amritsar in 1873 and after a series of subsequent meetings decided to found a society called the Singh Sabha. The decision was a very important one.

There were two immediate reasons for the action. One was an incident involving the Namdhari sect of Sikhs in 1872 which threatened to damage relations between respectable Sikhs and the British. The other was the news that four Sikh students of the mission school in Amritsar had announced their intention of converting to Christianity. Both were clear indications of the Sikh decline in spirit and devotion, or so it seemed to the Sikhs who participated in these meetings. Among those who attended were members of the old Sikh élite (men such as

Khem Singh Bedi, a direct descendant from Guru Nanak), together with affluent landowners, scholars and religious leaders. These were the founders of the new movement, an association which gave expression to their distinctive ideals.

The founders of the first Singh Sabha were predominantly conservative Sikhs, concerned to sustain and protect the society in which they had been nurtured. This was a society which permitted a variety of Sikh identities, different modes of worship (which included the worship of images), an emphasis upon caste and close ties binding Sikhs and Hindus together. They came, as a result, to be termed Sanatan Sikhs, the 'traditional' Sikhs. In the programme they devised particular emphasis was laid upon the promotion of periodicals and other appropriate literature, their assumption being that those who needed to be influenced would be accessible through the printed word. British officers were invited to associate with the Singh Sabha and matters relating to government were expressly excluded from its range of interests. The first Singh Sabha was an organization of the upper classes, very similar to the urban associations emerging in other parts of India but specifically concerned with issues affecting the Sikh Panth.

Sanatan Sikhs versus Tat Khalsa

The programme of the Amritsar Singh Sabha soon brought considerable opposition within the Panth. In the Punjab, as in much of the remainder of India, the British were producing considerable changes in terms of the economy and of the society affected by those changes. New trading networks arose in response, progressively displacing sectors of the population which had traditionally exercised social leadership and authority. These ascendant classes were the people who were able to benefit from the Western system of economics and also from the variety of education introduced by the British to the Punjab. Education during the nineteenth century was largely in missionary hands, but the new dimension introduced by it was essentially its Western nature.

These classes provided the Tat Khalsa constituency, Sikhs who disagreed strongly with the actions of the Amritsar Singh Sabha.

Those with radical opinions, drawing strength from the educational developments in Lahore, gathered around such people as Gurmukh Singh and Harsha Singh Arora. Jawahir Singh was another of their leaders, and so too was Ditt Singh, a rare instance of an Outcaste Sikh leader who attained prominence in the Panth. These radical Sikhs voiced serious disagreement with what the Amritsar group was doing, attacking what they conceived to be their weaknesses. Eventually this opposition formed another branch of the Singh Sabha in Lahore. This was in 1879, and it too proved to be of crucial importance for the Panth.

This Lahore group came to be known as the Tat Khalsa. Although its charter was very similar to that of the Amritsar association, the Lahore Singh Sabha proved to be much more aggressive. It attracted one prominent member from the landed aristocracy (Attar Singh of Bhadaur), but on the whole its primary membership consisted of intellectuals, men who had gained qualifications through the educational system brought by the British. Among those who achieved significance in the Tat Khalsa were Kahn Singh Nabha (author of a major encyclopaedia of Sikh doctrine and history) and Vir Singh (noted for his many contributions to all manner of Punjabi literature).[6]

Following the foundation of the Lahore Singh Sabha, numerous other Singh Sabhas came into existence. All Punjabi cities had one, most of the towns were also represented, and in a few cases short-lived Singh Sabhas were also located in villages. In almost all cases they took sides with either Amritsar or Lahore, each of the two main Singh Sabhas attracting a constellation formed by these other societies. The Lahore group (in other words, the followers of the Tat Khalsa) was considerably more successful than Amritsar. A third variety of Singh Sabha, dominated by the eccentric Teja Singh Overseer, was begun in the village of Bhasaur. Teja Singh regarded the Tat Khalsa as altogether too conservative, and the Bhasaur Singh Sabha (also known as the Panch Khalsa Diwan) was for several years a definite nuisance. Eventually he was formally banished from the Panth in 1929 and the controversies he had raised died down.

The main intellectual proponent of the Sanatan Sikhs was Avatar Singh Vahiria from Rawalpindi district, a life-long protégé of Khem Singh Bedi. For some years he was the editor of the Sanatan magazine

Srī Gurumat Prakāśhak, which was founded in 1885, and he spent much of his life touring around the Punjab preaching the Sanatan message. The author of eight books, he covered virtually every topic in Sikhism. His most famous work was the bulky *Khālsā Dharam Shāstar*, first issued in 1894 and in a revised edition in 1914.

The Sikhism preached by people such as Khem Singh Bedi and Avatar Singh Vahiria is difficult to envisage today, so comprehensive has been their defeat by the Tat Khalsa. For them Sikhism tolerated variety and upheld the right of Sikhs to participate in folk religion. Caste was maintained and idol worship was tolerated. There were different forms of marriage for different castes and different rituals could be practised by various members of the Panth. All manner of customs, such as those involving astrology, horoscopes and incantation, were acceptable. Visits to the sacred shrines of Hindus and Muslims as well as to those of the Gurus were entirely approved. Sanatan leaders might not follow these customs themselves, but certainly they were prepared to tolerate them in others. They were part of the immense variety which characterized the world they had known and the world they hoped would continue.

All this was anathema to the Tat Khalsa. Sikhism could not possibly be as broad and as tolerant as Sanatan Sikhs believed. Emphatically Sikhs were not Hindus, and Hindu tradition was not what Sikhs should follow. A booklet first published by Kahn Singh Nabha in 1899 summed up this message in its title: *Ham Hindū Nahīn*, 'We are not Hindus'. Sikhs should not observe caste and they could have no time for astrology or other superstitious Hindu customs. They should never visit the shrines of other religions and they should never practise rituals other than those that were strictly Sikh.

But what were Sikh rituals? Here the Tat Khalsa faced a serious problem, for there was no agreement concerning the Sikh method of conducting religious ceremonies. Strenuous disputes ensued with the Sanatan Sikhs, many of them concerning the one rite which would demonstrably show that the Sikhs were indeed not Hindus. This was the marriage order. Marriages had been conducted by the couple (whether Sikh or Hindu) circumambulating a sacred fire. For the Tat Khalsa this was intolerable and represented a reversion to Hindu practice after the introduction of a separate and distinct method in the days of the Gurus. Instead of using a fire, Sikhs should proceed around the sacred Book, the Adi Granth.

This issue was hotly debated by the two branches of the Singh Sabha, eventually leading to the formal adoption of the Anand marriage order. In 1909 the Punjab government passed the Anand Marriage Act, thereby signalling that the Tat Khalsa had definitively won this particular battle. The Sanatan Sikhs insistently pointed out that there was no evidence of the Gurus having followed the Anand order, nor was there any reference to it in classical Sikh texts. Anand marriage, they claimed, had originated in the early nineteenth century with the sectarian Nirankari Sikhs and had been borrowed from them by the Tat Khalsa. They protested strongly, but they protested in vain.

The Tat Khalsa was clearly securing the upper hand, but the task was proving to be exceedingly demanding. Images had been removed from the precincts of Harimandir Sahib (the Golden Temple) in a famous victory of 1905 and the marriage question had been satisfactorily settled in 1909, but what of the other beliefs and rituals that a devout Sikh should practise? One issue was particularly acute. The Tat Khalsa was adamant in its belief that the only proper identity for a loyal Sikh to adopt was that of the Khalsa. In this, as in so much else, they adopted a view diametrically opposed to that of the Sanatan Sikhs. For Sanatan Sikhs the answer was variety of identities. For the Tat Khalsa there could be only one. Others who called themselves Sikhs could still be accepted as members of the Panth, but only on the understanding that they were working their way towards being full members of the Khalsa.

But precisely what was the order of initiation into the Khalsa and what was the Rahit which the Khalsa Sikh should obey? This was by no means clear. There were certainly *rahit-nāmā*s (manuals containing versions of the Rahit), but how reliable were these? Obviously they could not be accepted as reliable, for they contradicted each other and they contained many items that no enlightened Sikh at the turn of the century could possibly accept. They had, in the opinion of the Tat Khalsa, obviously been corrupted. This must certainly be their current condition, but what was the pure form of the Rahit?

The Tat Khalsa laboured hard and long on this problem, but it was not until 1950 that an agreed Rahit was published. This was *Sikh*

Rahit Maryādā, a modern *rahit-nāmā* which has maintained its position in the Panth surprisingly well. By 1950 the Tat Khalsa victory over the Sanatan Sikhs had been largely won, and the Rahit it promulgated at that time was accepted as the only possible version. This meant that to be a Sikh ideally meant being a member of the Khalsa. *Sikh Rahit Maryādā* became the standard statement not just for the Khalsa but for all Sikhs. The Tat Khalsa had triumphed, and references to the Singh Sabha movement normally assume a Tat Khalsa meaning and definition. This, of course, referred to the devout and the educated among the Sikhs. Gradually, however, the interpretation has been trickling down, and the version of Sikhism enunciated by *Sikh Rahit Maryādā* is by far the most significant in the Panth of the late twentieth century.

Before the late twentieth century was reached the Panth had the best part of a century to live through after the principal thrust of the Tat Khalsa had been made, but at least the main lines for the future had been firmly laid down. The period of the Singh Sabha (specifically the Tat Khalsa participation in that period) had set Sikhism in a fresh mould, a mould that it still retains today. The Panth's history continues, but it is now a Panth which has been fashioned in accordance with the Khalsa principles of the Tat Khalsa reformers. Their victory has not been complete, but it has nevertheless given to Sikhism the distinctive impress of their exclusivist Khalsa message.

One other episode deserves mention during the period of controversy between the Sanatan Sikhs and the Tat Khalsa. In 1899 the Sanatan Sikhs had published a booklet by one of their members, Narain Singh, entitled *Sikh Hindū Hain* ('Sikhs are Hindus'). As we have noted, Kahn Singh Nabha had, on behalf of the Tat Khalsa, replied with his *Ham Hindū Nahīn*. The two sides were already engaged in debate and these two publications made it even more spirited. Eventually the Amritsar Singh Sabha realized that such tactics were not going to win them any support, and so in 1901 they convened a meeting of prominent Sikhs with a view to trying to create a single body that would represent them all.

Within a year they had succeeded and the single body, the Chief Khalsa Diwan, came into being in 1902 with the purpose of representing all Sikhs in matters regarding their faith and political position in the province. Amritsar and Lahore had each formed its own *divān* or 'assembly' earlier, drawing together other Singh Sabhas which shared their respective views. Now at last they had one assembly representing them all and this was the Chief Khalsa Diwan.

The Chief Khalsa Diwan thereafter acted for the many branches of the Singh Sabha, accepted for at least ten years as the principal spokesman for the Sikhs until it was eventually overtaken by the more strident voices of the Akali movement. The intellectuals used it as a channel for their interpretations of the Sikh past, and in this respect it served as a vehicle for material which was essentially that of the Tat Khalsa. Politically, however, it proved to be conservative, pleading the case of Sikhs with the British but doing nothing to upset cordial relations with the imperial power.

The Akalis and the Gurdwara Reform Movement

By the time of the First World War the political impulse generated by the Tat Khalsa movement was passing into more radical hands, and after the war was over it produced the Akali movement. The cause that aroused the Akalis was the future of the Sikh gurdwaras or 'temples', a cause that led them to confront the British from 1920 till 1925 in what came to be known as the Gurdwara Reform Movement.

The history of gurdwara development and administration during the eighteenth and nineteenth centuries is an obscure one. During the eighteenth century they were distinct from the smaller dharamsalas. Routine *kīrtan* was conducted in the latter, the term 'gurdwara' being reserved for shrines associated with particular events in the lives of the Gurus. In Amritsar Harimandir Sahib (later known as the Golden Temple) had become the Panth's principal gurdwara during the course of the century. This rank it acquired in intimate association with Akal Takhat, the venue for the biannual gatherings of the Sarbat Khalsa during the eighteenth-century period of loose confederation.

The history of Harimandir Sahib and Akal Takhat is far from clear during this century and the same lack of definite information applies to virtually all the gurdwaras. They were obviously regarded as appropriate destinations for pilgrims, and some attracted pious donations from affluent or influential Sikhs. It is, however, a very uncertain image which they present. Only with the provision of land grants and other privileges do they begin to emerge from obscurity, and they emerge in a form that was later to attract severe disapproval from the reformers of the Singh Sabha.

Most gurdwaras were in the hands of hereditary *mahants* (proprietors) and many of these *mahants* were able to direct gurdwara income to whatever purposes they might choose. These purposes were not necessarily those the devout would condone, and one of the standard complaints of reformers in the years leading up to 1920 concerned misappropriation of gurdwara funds. In some instances the income of a gurdwara was evidently directed to personal enrichment, and a few *mahants* adopted lifestyles which the pious could only regard as grossly immoral. Offerings were appropriated by corrupt *mahants* and it was believed that women were retained on some gurdwara premises for immoral purposes. The incumbent of Nankana Sahib was a conspicuous example of this. Under the British, their position was further reinforced by the granting of actual titles of ownership. In the eyes of the British administration, the *mahants* had become owners of their gurdwaras and as such were entitled to whatever protection the law might provide.

The situation was made all the worse for orthodox Sikhs by the fact that many of the *mahants* declined to accept the Khalsa identity. Many called themselves Udasi Sikhs, a claim that may have had some justification in the eighteenth century but which it had long since lost. They maintained a connection with the Panth, however, and tradition held that in the turbulent early eighteenth century many of the gurdwaras and dharamsalas were entrusted to them. This was because they did not maintain the Khalsa appearance and would therefore be acceptable to the Muslim authorities.

If this tradition is correct, most of the *mahants* had abandoned their previous Udasi ways and taken up living as ordinary Hindus, complete with wives and children. This was a way of life that was offensive to many members of the Singh Sabha, because even if the *mahant* should lead a blameless life he was not observing celibacy. Sikhism embraced family life, but there was a deep-seated feeling that a person in charge of a gurdwara should be not merely a Khalsa but a *celibate* Khalsa.

Within the Singh Sabha opinions were divided on this question. As far as the Tat Khalsa was concerned there was no need for the *mahant*s to remain unmarried, their principal objections to them being rather their Hindu ways and their treating of the gurdwaras as their personal property. Sikhs of a Sanatan persuasion, however, were not so sure.

During most of the Singh Sabha period the reformers, while complaining about gurdwara management, left the *mahant*s alone as they had more pressing causes to occupy them. The claim against the *mahant*s was first tested in 1913, the case being that of Gurdwara Rakab-ganj in New Delhi. The British administration of New Delhi wanted some of the gurdwara's land to align their roading system and the *mahant* was willing to sell the land. The Chief Khalsa Diwan were anxious, as always, to avoid a conflict with the government, but by this time there were militants abroad and the militants were determined that the government should not have its way. Very soon the administration became aware that it rather than the *mahant* had become the target of the objectors. During the First World War the question lay dormant, but after the war was over it was revived. The British could see that the Sikhs were determined and so the land was returned to the gurdwara.

Radical Sikhs were, however, speaking out by this time. In 1916 the Lucknow Pact between Congress and the Muslim League had not included the Sikhs, and in 1917 the Chief Khalsa Diwan, acting under Tat Khalsa pressure, demanded separate electorates for Sikhs. The Punjabi Hindus objected strenuously, whereupon the Tat Khalsa politicians re-emphasized their Sikh identity still further and objected even more strongly to the observance of Hindu practices within the Panth. In such a conflict the gurdwaras were inevitably involved, and progressively the Tat Khalsa moved towards the freeing of gurdwaras from the control of non-Sikh and non-Khalsa *mahant*s as the primary objective of their campaign.

In this controversy the boundary between the Tat Khalsa and the Akali Dal is impossible to draw clearly. The Akalis drew a much greater volume of support from the villages of the Punjab than had ever been seen in Singh Sabha days, but the leadership of the Akali movement went to men who had previously been identified with the Khalsa wing of the Singh Sabha. Although these men had served their apprenticeship in the Tat Khalsa, their flowering of authority comes under the aegis of the Akali movement. For them the term 'Sikh' meant 'Khalsa' and their objective came to be the transfer of control over the gurdwaras into Khalsa hands.

These men also found the Chief Khalsa Diwan far too respectable and much too loyalist for their taste, and it was their initiative which led to the formation of the Central Sikh League in 1919. This in turn resulted in two new organizations being founded in late 1920. One was the organization that was to seize the gurdwaras. This was the Akali Dal. The other was the Shiromani Gurdwara Parbandhak Committee (the SGPC), which was formed to administer the liberated gurdwaras.[7]

The Sikhs waged a campaign against the Punjab government that was spirited but strictly non-violent, these being the days when Gandhi's theory of *satyagraha* was attracting much attention. The British soon realized that control of the gurdwaras would have to be removed from the hereditary *mahant*s and effectively transferred to the Panth, but the problem was how to accomplish this without losing face. Eventually the transfer was accomplished by the passing of the Sikh Gurdwaras Act of 1925. This wrote into law terms which have been held to be highly advantageous to Sikhs of the Khalsa, though it is difficult to perceive them in the wording of the Act. It certainly did distinguish Sikhs from Hindus, introducing the stipulation that a Sikh could have 'no other religion'. The claim that it introduced statutory Khalsa domination of the Panth is, however, scarcely valid. There was still some distance to travel before the Khalsa could assert a clear claim to dominance, though certainly the claim was being made with increasing insistence.

Subsequent Sikh history

Following the successful conclusion of their campaign, the Akalis decided that the body provided by the 1925 Act to manage the historic gurdwaras should be the SGPC (the Shiromani Gurdwara Parbandhak Committee), formed in 1920. Thereafter the SGPC, elected by the Sikhs and endued with legal status, managed almost all the major gurdwaras in undivided Punjab and as a result controlled considerable estates and patronage. The various events and episodes which have occurred since 1925 testify to the developing sense of Khalsa identity and to the considerable influence in the Panth of both the Akali Dal and the SGPC.

The compiling of *Sikh Rahit Maryādā* was merely one incident along the way. In 1947 the partition of India provided another, the Sikhs opting for India and those living in Pakistan crossing as part of a large and bloody migration. The Indian government's granting of Punjabi Suba (Punjabi state) in 1966 was yet another. This involved a reduction of the boundaries of the Punjab, thereby creating a state which contained a majority of Sikhs. The most recent was the difference between the Congress government and the Akali Dal, leading to the Indian Army's traumatic assault on the Golden Temple in 1984. The assault eventually succeeded, but it did so at great cost. Jarnail Singh Bhindranvale, the charismatic leader installed in the Golden Temple, became one of the Panth's martyrs. Later in the same year Mrs Gandhi, the Prime Minister of India, was assassinated by her Sikh bodyguards, leading to a massacre of Sikhs in several parts of the country. A period of armed warfare between government forces and the Sikh Khalistan movement followed and lasted until the army was able to kill or capture most of the important Khalistanis during the latter months of 1992.

Today the Panth occupies a position of uneasy peace. Politics, punctuated by a bout of armed warfare, has been its history for the last three quarters of a century. A few Sikhs have achieved high office (such as Manmohan Singh, who in recent years served as Minister of Finance in the central government), yet the feeling persists that the Sikhs have not received their just dues from the nation. This, however, does not concern their life as a Panth. Throughout this period the Khalsa has ruled Sikhism, its authority largely and increasingly unchallenged. The definition of the Panth is now very much in its keeping.

PART TWO: RELIGION

5

SIKH DOCTRINE

We come now to the content of Sikh teachings and in particular to the teachings of Guru Nanak. The pattern of religious belief taught by Guru Nanak has been enlarged by later Gurus (particularly by Guru Gobind Singh) and subsequent experience has augmented it still further. The period of the Singh Sabha certainly produced this effect. Nanak's system remains, however, a vital part of the total faith and it retains its form essentially unchanged down to the present day. His doctrine of spiritual liberation through the divine Name has ever remained at the heart of Sikh religious belief, still conferring on his devout followers the assurance that the way lies open before them.

The Sant inheritance

The analysis which follows shows that Nanak was unlike most other religious teachers. The normal pattern is for a religious teacher to deliver a system that is silent or obscure in many respects and for his later followers to work out what is needed in order to make the system relatively complete and harmonious. Nanak was an exception to this rule. From his extensive hymns recorded in the primary Sikh scripture, the Adi Granth, it is possible to frame a system which is complete in every respect. It raises, though, an important question. Many of the teachings of Nanak are very familiar to anyone who understands the north Indian religions of the fifteenth and sixteenth centuries. Is it, therefore, possible to speak of Nanak as unique, or must we conclude that he expressed teachings which were already current?

We must acknowledge that, for a devout Sikh, the religion of Guru Nanak is the result of divine revelation. For such a Sikh various strands may be traced to Hindu tradition and Islam, but the actual belief is unique and was delivered directly to Nanak by the eternal Guru. Thus enlightened, he acquired the title of Guru and communicated the way of liberation to all who would hear him. If we try to trace the path that he taught, our quest must lead us straight to Akal Purakh or God.

This comes as no surprise. Ask devout Christians the same question concerning their faith and you will get the same answer. The same response will also come from a devout Muslim. Every system which affirms belief in one God produces this reaction from the body of its believers. God or Allah or Akal Purakh is the sole and immediate source of what one believes; or, if not the immediate source, this is the ultimate source communicated by a mediator.

This belief must be respected. At the same time we are entitled to explore the surrounding religious landscape and the society in which a particular religion was born. Nanak lived in northern India during the late fifteenth century and early sixteenth century. What religious influences were dominant in northern India at that particular time; or, if not actually dominant, possessed the strength to leave their mark? Do they leave their mark upon Nanak or are his teachings properly considered unique? Even if they do leave an important mark, is the system, as shaped by Nanak, nevertheless a unique system?

One line of approach has been that strong elements of Hinduism and Islam are certainly present in the teachings of Nanak, but that his uniqueness lies in his drawing these together in a genuine syncretism or combination of the two. This is a view which, one assumes, derives from a janam-sakhi treatment of Nanak as the supreme unifier of the two traditions. It can hardly have come from a study of his actual works, for these make little use of fundamental Muslim concepts in the numerous hymns he has left us. Plainly the interpretation is misplaced. Nanak was not one who sought a syncretic combination of Hinduism (whatever that may mean) and Islam.

The failure of this approach does, however, persuade us to look more carefully at the wide field of Hindu tradition. The territory is a very wide one indeed, hence the impossibility of speaking of 'Hinduism'. It contains several different systems (what are called 'panths' with a small 'p'), and here we find one which appears to be saying essentially the same thing as Nanak was concerned to communicate, one which was widespread in the north India of Nanak's own time and the immediate past. This is the Sant tradition of north

India, the range of religious understanding that stressed such features as the formless quality of God (*nirguṇa*) and a doctrine of deliverance that attached no significance to caste. This is the tradition which evokes such names as Namdev (1270–1350), Kabir (*c.*1440–1518) and Ravidas (*c.*1500–50). Most Indian scholars outside the Panth include Nanak within the same tradition. Although the first Guru is seldom if ever called Sant Nanak (a title most Sikhs would find exceedingly demeaning), his place within the movement is explicitly affirmed.

Curiously the Sant tradition is little known among Western scholars, although books dealing with it are now beginning to appear. This is largely because it has been assumed to be a part of the Bhakti tradition and generations of Western scholars have insisted upon treating Kabir, for example, as merely a Vaishnava poet, a believer in the god Vishnu. A 'sant' is treated as a holy person, the letter 'i' being added to make the word 'saint'. Sants are therefore saints of Vaishnava Bhakti and are not perceived as belonging to a distinctive movement.

It is indeed correct to treat the Sant movement as a part of the very wide and very general Bhakti movement, for manifestly it does include at its centre a belief in a personal God. The only proper response expected of the believer is a form of devotion and this devotion qualifies us to speak of the Sant movement as a Bhakti movement. But being a part of the Bhakti movement is not the same thing as identity with its principal representatives. Sants are not saints (the word derives from *sat* or 'truth', not from *sanctus* or any of the other Semitic terms meaning 'holiness') and a sant could not possibly be a Vaishnava (at least not according to the standard definition of the term) in that the Supreme Being that he or she worshipped was *nirguṇa* or 'without qualities'. This certainly was not the case with the Vaishnavas who worshipped the god Vishnu in the form of an image. As we proceed to describe Sant belief, it will become clear that the terms Sant and Vaishnava are distinctively different. At the same time it must be acknowledged that they hold a considerable amount in common and that Vaishnava Bhakti is the system with the greatest resemblance to the Sant tradition.

The claim is that Nanak replicated teachings which were already current in north India, that he merely reproduced beliefs or doctrines which were a part of the religious landscape of his time. That he received his doctrines from Kabir (as is claimed by some) is extremely unlikely and of absolutely no consequence. The teachings of the Sants were gaining widespread currency and Nanak could have absorbed their ideals from a variety of possible sources. According to this view, the fact that he so faithfully reproduces these doctrines sets him firmly within the Sant tradition, effectively destroying any claims to significant originality. Even the appointing of a successor does nothing to affect this judgement. Spiritual lineages are forever appearing and if one wants more recent examples with Sikh affiliations the Nirankari, Namdhari and Beas Radhasoami movements will readily oblige.

In stating the issue so frankly one runs a serious risk of causing grave offence and of alienating many readers before the real discussion has begun. It must, however, be clearly stated if we are to grapple adequately and sympathetically with the question of Sikh origins. Was Nanak merely another Sant, or are there distinctive claims which may be entered on his behalf? If we concede that the links with Sant doctrine are altogether too obvious to be ignored, must we then accept that the Sikh movement is a Sant movement, at least in its earlier stages? Should the Nanak-panth be properly regarded as one among many such panths emerging within the larger context of Hindu tradition and still remaining a part of it? The later Sikh Panth in the time of the Khalsa may well diverge, establishing usages and beliefs which are suited to its later circumstances. But what of the Nanak-panth? Is it an expression of the Sant movement?

For some participants in this debate this question normally implies an affirmative answer, and the answer is commonly carried through to the present day. Subsequent developments may have transformed the later Panth, but it has never renounced its direct descent from the teachings of Nanak, nor have its members effectively abandoned their place within the structure of caste society. For all participants the questions are not simply academic. They are firmly upheld by many other Indians and, with forthright directness, they are rejected out of hand by most Sikhs.

In order to attempt an answer we must first ensure that we understand the tradition which allegedly supplies the principal components of Nanak's doctrine. We shall then survey the teachings of Nanak, briefly examining the fundamental features they offer and setting those features within the total system that his works enable us to construct. Finally we shall return to the problem of origins we have just broached and endeavour to find a solution.

Sant doctrine

First, then, let us try to understand Sant doctrine. The Sant tradition of northern India can be viewed both as a *sādhan*, or method of spiritual liberation, and as a form of social protest. Both elements are inextricably linked. Most of the tradition's leading exponents were from lower castes and the theory of spiritual release that they state or assume in their religious songs is one which plainly rejects the relevance of caste status in matters pertaining to the soul's deliverance from the bondage of transmigration. Brahmans are typically scorned, as are all who claim to exercise authority as purveyors of religious merit or as mediators of divine grace. The condemnation was one that the Sants applied to all such authority and its claimants, Muslim as well as Hindu.

As this verdict makes clear, the Sants laid firm and unqualified emphasis on the interior nature of spiritual understanding and on the discipline required in order to secure freedom from the suffering of death and rebirth. Their ultimate goal remained the same as that of the Vaishnava Bhakti with which Sant doctrine has so often been confused, the same indeed as Hindu *sādhan* in general. The objective was *mokṣha*, liberation from the transmigratory cycle and from the suffering that necessarily attends it. There is no denying the reality of karma, nor of the consequences that ineluctably follow the actions which each individual performs. The difference concerns the method whereby one breaks or terminates the cycle, and to some extent the quality of *mokṣha* which the Sants offered to all who followed their devotional discipline.

This discipline was emphatically and exclusively interior, at least as preached by the more significant of the Sants. The objective was a permanent stilling of all emotion and all conflict, peace in an eternal equipoise that could be achieved by the devout Sant while still living out his present existence. This internal nature of Sant devotion should be heavily stressed. The Sants would have nothing to do with incarnations, with what they termed 'idol-worship', with sacred scriptures, temples or pilgrimages, or at least not in the external sense conventionally associated with such beliefs and practices. There was no value in visiting a temple and paying homage to a piece of stone. There was no value in listening to what were alleged to be sacred words read from some allegedly sacred scripture. There was no value in visiting places of pilgrimage and bathing in their waters, imagining that one was thereby cleansed from all impurity. Frogs do that just as effectively, and if covering oneself with ashes produces any effect, the ass which rolls in the dust is headed for instant liberation.

Because these actions were typically performed as exterior acts of piety, they were regarded by the Sants as worthless. Devotion for the Sants was strictly an interior discipline, one that spurned all exterior custom and practice as a means to liberation. In place of outward piety, one must learn to turn one's attention inward, there to focus it entirely upon the *śhabad* or divine Word uttered in the *man* (the 'heart' or 'mind') by the mystical Guru, the 'voice' of the divine Being. By meditating inwardly upon the divine Word, one would be led into a greater and yet greater conformity of one's spirit to the divine spirit; and in achieving that merging of the self with the divine spirit, one would find the bliss that would be final release from the bonds of transmigration.

Of the Sants, the most famous is Kabir (if Nanak is to be excepted), and as we have seen most of the available literature on the Sants concerns his work. By caste Kabir (*c.*1440–1518) was a Julaha or weaver, one which ranked well down the approved scale. As we have already noted, most of the Sants were of low caste (Ravidas was actually an Outcaste), and, according to their teachings, caste could have no bearing on access to liberation. It was merely one of the outward forms Sants were taught to despise. Most Sants had also received little or no education. In both respects Nanak was an exception, for he belonged to the relatively high caste of Khatris and gives the impression of having been soundly educated.

From this brief summary it will be evident that the message preached by the Sants in their religious songs bears obvious resemblances to other traditions familiar in the north Indian experience. It is easy to see why they should have been confused with contemporary Vaishnavas, for both share the same uncompromising insistence on devotion as the way of liberation. The connection is, moreover, a legitimate one to the extent that the Sant tradition plainly derived fundamental features of its doctrine from Vaishnava belief. The Sant emphasis on interiority points to the other principal source of its belief and practice. This was the Nath panth, a contemporary representative of the ancient tantric tradition. Sufi influence may also have contributed to the development of Sant doctrine, though if this is indeed the case its results are much harder to detect in the terminology of the Sants than are features which derive from Vaishnava and Nath sources.

Of these three contributors to Sant doctrine, the least familiar is undoubtedly the Nath tradition. Today it survives as a fading memory rather than as an active system with acknowledged leaders and dedicated practitioners of its yogic theory. During the time of Nanak, however, it commanded a considerable influence in the Punjab and north India generally. The word *nāth* means 'master' and the *Ādināth* or 'Primal Nath' was identified as Shiv (Siva). In addition to the Adinath, there were believed to exist nine other Naths, master yogis who had attained immortality through the practice of hatha-yoga and who were supposed to be living far back in the Himalayas.

Of these nine the principal figure was, by common consent, the semi-legendary Gorakhnath, to whom all adherents of the Nath tradition owed allegiance. Belief in the nine immortal Naths is obviously connected in some way with the eighty-four immortal Siddhs of tantric Buddhism. In Sikh tradition the two terms, Nath and Siddh (or Siddha), are used interchangeably with a strong preference attaching to the latter.

Adherents of the Nath tradition were commonly known as Kanphat or 'Split-ear' yogis, a name that derives from their practice of wearing large ear-rings. Their direct influence on the educated seems to have been limited, but among the people at large they evidently commanded respect for their austerities and a considerable dread for the magical powers they were believed to possess. The songs attributed to Kabir are shot through with Nath concepts and terminology, clearly demonstrating the extent of their influence on a major representative of the Sant tradition. If these songs are the work of a single person called

Kabir, that person (regardless of his Muslim name) must surely have had close personal connections with the Naths. If they are to be regarded as the composite and evolved products of a Kabirian tradition, the tradition itself was presumably subjected to a strong Nath influence. Whatever the route, Nath influences are plainly evident in the works attributed to Kabir and in other products of the Sant tradition. They are also present in the works of Guru Nanak.

The impact of this Nath influence can presumably be observed in the characteristic Sant stress on the irrelevance of caste status as a means to deliverance, the folly of sacred languages and scriptures, the futility of temple worship and pilgrimage, and their general stress on interior devotion. Such features are, as we have seen, of the essence of Sant belief. Their starting-point is a concept of God which insists upon a wholly formless quality. God is *nirguṇa*, as opposed to the *saguṇa* belief which envisages physical incarnations and accepts visible representations in the form of images.

For the Sants all such exterior forms are totally mistaken, as are the associated practices of temple worship and outward ceremony. God (or Akal Purakh) is to be found within each human heart or spirit, and there alone can one practise the loving devotion which will ultimately lead to union with the divine and thus to the eternal bliss of deliverance. The inner path that the devout Sant must follow is not an easy one, but its reward is sure and it is one which can be secured in this present existence. The reward is the bliss of total peace in mystical union. This is the condition of *sahaj*, a word that leads us back to the Naths and beyond them to the earlier tradition of tantric Buddhism.

This stress on Nath antecedents should not imply that the Sants were mere imitators of Nath belief and practice. Such a conclusion would be far from the truth, for the Sants were generally strong critics of the Naths and their doctrine offers much more than Nath borrowings. *Sahaj*, they insist, is not to be attained through the Nath practice of hatha-yoga. It is to be attained through inward devotion and the practice of meditation. If we are looking for the closest relatives of the Sants, we must still acknowledge them to be the Vaishnava bhaktas, for the essence of Sant belief remains loving devotion to a personal deity. The points to be repeatedly stressed are that the object of their devotion is a strictly formless God and that the actual practice of devotion is a strictly inward discipline.

The teachings of Guru Nanak

We turn now to the teachings of Guru Nanak, observing as we sketch an outline of his system how closely its fundamental features match the insistent emphases of the Sants. The teachings of Nanak are easily accessible. Although his approach to the all-important question of spiritual deliverance is not that of a systematic theologian, there can be no doubt that a developed and integrated system was present in his mind and that it informs the many hymns he has left. The hymns were recorded in the Adi Granth half a century after his death, and it appears that Guru Arjan, in compiling the Adi Granth, had access to an earlier collection compiled by the third Guru (the Goindval or Mohan *pothīs*). The source is thus a sound one and analysis will reveal that a coherent system lies behind the hymns it preserves.

But first we should return to a misunderstanding that we have already mentioned briefly. In our survey of Sant origins we noted that Sufi doctrine may have exercised a limited influence on its development. In the case of Nanak, one commonly encounters the insistent claim that he owed much to Islam and specifically to the Sufis. As we have also indicated, some writers have carried this theory to the point of claiming that his religion can be treated as an example of conscious syncretism, one which deliberately tried to blend Hindu and Muslim ideals. Is there any truth in the claim?

The claim can, in large measure, be dismissed. It is true that many features of Nanak's thought have evident Sufi parallels, but these features can be more immediately traced to Bhakti or Nath sources. Nanak certainly chooses Muslim terminology in a few of his hymns, but only because the hymns are evidently addressed to a Muslim audience. The actual content remains that of the Sants. Later in the history of the Panth there are clear signs of Muslim influence, for example in the form of the janam-sakhis and in some of the legends they repeat. Later still, ill-informed British observers thought they could plainly see evidences of Muslim influence in the Adi Granth.

Their theories were mistaken, but the conviction they fostered of a Hindu–Muslim synthesis has taken a long time to die.

Guru Nanak viewed both the Hindu tradition and Islam in a typically Sant manner. In their conventional forms, both offered systems of belief and practice which largely relied on external authorities and outward response. As such both were to be condemned. Only those who perceived the inner reality of truth could achieve deliverance, and this end could be attained regardless of whether one were a Hindu or a Muslim. Those who follow this inner path are the 'true' Hindu and the 'true' Muslim, as opposed to the 'false' believers who continue to put their trust in ritual and pilgrimage, temple and mosque, Brahman and mullah, Shastras and Qur'an.[1]

The Islamic loanwords which appear in the works of Guru Nanak (as elsewhere in the Adi Granth) are normally used to express such themes as the 'true' and the 'false' Muslim. The most famous example occurs in a *śhalok* from *Vār Mājh*:

> Make mercy your mosque and devotion your prayer mat,
> righteousness your Qur'an;
> Meekness your circumcising, goodness your fasting, for thus the
> true Muslim expresses his faith.
> Make good works your Ka'bah, take truth as your *pīr*,
> compassion your creed and your prayer.
> Let service to God be the beads which you tell and God will exalt
> you to glory.[2]

This is the classic Nanak approach, typical both in terms of its insistent interior emphasis and of its striking use of imagery. In this particular instance it supplies a definition of the 'true' Muslim and in so doing illustrates the use which Nanak typically makes of Muslim concepts. The same contrast between the true believer and the false explains the conjoining of Hindu and Muslim names for God, and when Muslim names for God are elsewhere introduced it is commonly for the poetic purpose of achieving assonance or alliteration. The use of Islamic terms certainly does not guarantee an Islamic content.

It is accordingly incorrect to construe the religion of Nanak as a synthesis of Hindu beliefs and Islam. It is indeed a synthesis, but the components almost all come from native Indian sources. Muslim beliefs are unimportant. The pattern Nanak evolved is a reworking of what he imbibed from the Sants. The categories he employs are the categories of the Sants, the terminology he uses is their terminology and the doctrines he affirms are their doctrines.

It must be repeated, however, that the teachings of Nanak were certainly not a precise copy of what the earlier Sants had developed. He inherited the components of his thought from the Sants, but he did not transmit the inheritance unchanged. He did indeed receive a synthesis and he passed it on. It was, however, transmitted in a form that was in some measure amplified and in considerable measure clarified and integrated. It is Sant thought that we find in his works, but it is Sant thought expanded and interpreted. The result is a new synthesis, a synthesis that is cast within the pattern of Sant belief but which nevertheless possesses a significant originality and, in contrast with its Sant background, a unique clarity.

Having thus discarded a mistaken interpretation of the teachings of Nanak, we can proceed to offer a summary of what they actually contain. We begin, as the Adi Granth itself begins, with Nanak's doctrine of God. Many terms, drawn from a variety of traditions, are used to designate God, each of them offering a facet of Nanak's total understanding. The expression that stands at the very beginning of the Adi Granth and at the beginning of the *Mūl Mantra* (the Basic Doctrinal Statement) is one such term. Consisting of the figure 1 and the letter O, *1-Oaṅkār* represents the unity of God and is translated in such ways as 'the One Oankar' or 'the One Being'. 'Oankar' is actually a cognate of 'Om' and can carry the same mystical meaning, though many Sikhs object to any suggestion that it is the same word. For them 'Om' is Hindu, whereas 'Oankar' is Sikh.

1 Oaṅkār is not commonly used except as an invocation. Another term, one which has achieved a particular prominence in Nanak's usage, is Akal Purakh, 'the Person beyond Time' or 'the Eternal One'. As we should expect from the Sant background of Nanak's thought, Akal Purakh is understood as *Niraṅkār*, 'the One without Form', and repeated emphasis is laid on the ineffable quality of Akal Purakh's being.[3] This does not mean, however, that Akal Purakh is inaccessible to the understanding of men and women and beyond the reach of their affections. Akal Purakh is in fact manifested in the created world and they whose eyes are opened to spiritual understanding will perceive the Presence immanent in all creation. Thus perceiving the Presence, they receive the means of approach so to appropriate the freedom and eternal bliss that is proffered for all to grasp.

Mankind, however, is congenitally blind and for most people the vision of the divine, ever present around them, remains forever concealed. The problem lies in the human *man*, that inner faculty which commonly we call our 'heart' but which is better understood as a complex comprising heart, mind and spirit.[4] Within the *man* evil exercises its vicious sway, and, seduced by the passions it generates, most are blind to the spiritual reality that lies within and about them. Driven by their evil impulses, they behave in a manner which, in accordance with the law of karma, earns appropriate penalties. For such people the result can only be the round of death and rebirth, the endless sequence that extends suffering through all eternity. The fundamental problem is *haumai*, or self-centred concern for all that attracts the proud, the sensual and the selfish. As long as the *man* is in the grip of *haumai* there can be no hope of escape. The endless round must continue.

What, then, is the solution? The solution, according to Nanak, is the *nām*, or 'divine Name'. The person who learns how to appropriate the *nām* will be freed from the chains which bind that person to the wheel of transmigration. The term *nām*, as used by Nanak and elsewhere in Sant literature, is a summary expression for the whole nature of Akal Purakh and all that constitutes the divine being. It is, to use another favoured expression, *sat*, or 'truth', and one commonly encounters the combination *sat-nām*, or 'True Name'. Anything that may be affirmed concerning Akal Purakh constitutes an aspect of the divine Name, and a sufficient understanding of the divine Name provides the essential means to deliverance.

Nām is the sure remedy offered by Akal Purakh, the 'Timeless One' who created the universe and lovingly watches over it. Akal Purakh, the Creator and Sustainer, dwells immanent in all creation, and because all that exists is an expression of the divine being this creation represents the supreme manifestation of the *nām*. The *nām* is the ever-present and all-pervading presence of Akal Purakh, and whoever perceives this presence gains access to the means of mystical unity with Akal Purakh. In that condition of supreme peace lies liberation, for the person who attains it thereby achieves release from the dreaded cycle of transmigration.

How is the divine Name to be appropriated? In what manner is it revealed and what must a person do in order to secure the reward it confers? Although the *nām* is thus revealed for all to see and accept, men and women are congenitally blind, unable to perceive the truth that lies around and within each of them. Deceived by the mischievous prompting of their weak and wayward spirits, they are held in permanent subjection to evil passions and false beliefs. Vainly they seek the elusive means of deliverance, foolishly trusting in such external conventions as the temple, the mosque, devout ceremony or pious pilgrimage. None of these practices can achieve the end they seek and those who preach them are agents of doom. Release can be found only by opening one's eyes to the *nām* and by appropriating its wonders within the mind and the heart.

How then is each misguided person to perceive the *nām*, and how is it to be appropriated? A knowledge of the divine Name can be attained because Akal Purakh is a God of grace, speaking the Word of divine understanding to all who are prepared to shed their *haumai* and listen in humility. The Word (*śhabad*) is the message inscribed in creation, and the mystical 'voice' whereby it is 'spoken' is the eternal Guru. Akal Purakh is the eternal Guru, speaking through the creation which constitutes a visible form. The message thus spoken is the Word that reveals the divine Name. It is a simple message. Look around you and look within. Both around and within you will perceive the divine Order (*hukam*), a harmony expressed in the physical and psychical creation, which reflects the divine harmony of Akal Purakh.

In order to secure liberation one must attune one's whole life to that harmony expressed as the divine Name. This purpose one achieves by means of the regular, disciplined practice of *nām simaraṇ* or 'remembrance of the Name'. A simple version of this technique consists of repeating a word or expression that summarizes the meaning of the divine Name and thus of Akal Purakh (terms such as *sat-nām* or *vāhigurū*[5]). *Kīrtan* (the singing of appropriate hymns) is another form of *nām simaraṇ*, for in this manner also devout believers can attune themselves to the divine. A third method (the most sophisticated version) is a technique of meditation that inwardly reflects upon the meaning of the divine Name, with the intention of bringing one's whole being into harmony with the divine harmony of the Name.

The discipline is not an easy task, nor can one expect to secure the ultimate reward without lengthy striving. It is, however, a sure reward for those who sincerely seek it, and it is a reward which does not require withdrawal from one's daily life. All who follow the discipline of *nām simaraṇ* with devout persistence will progressively ascend to levels of spiritual experience which they alone can comprehend. Five levels of progressively elevated attainment and illumination are described by Nanak in the concluding stanzas of *Japjī*.[6] The end is *sach khaṇḍ* or the Realm of Truth, mystical union in the eternal bliss of total serenity. Thus is the cycle of transmigration broken. Thus does one merge in the divine Name.

For those who achieve this objective two results will follow. One is the experience of ever-growing wonder (*visamād*), leading eventually to the rapturous peace of total blending in the divine (the condition Nanak calls *sahaj*). The other is the final ending of the cycle of transmigration with its painful sequence of death and rebirth. Instead of earning the evil karma which follows from corrupt passion and immoral deeds, one achieves that harmony which separates the spirit from all that keeps the cycle in motion. The end is peace, and with passions finally stilled one attains release. It is a condition which can be achieved during the present life, preceding the physical death that is its final seal. It is also a condition which can be achieved only within one's own inner being. External props and practices merely delude. In spiritual terms their effect must be fatal.

One other point deserves to be mentioned, one which relates to the dominance of religious concerns in Nanak's works. The preponderance of religious concerns is overwhelming, as is shown by one of the few comments that he makes on contemporary events. Nanak witnessed at least one of the incursions of the Mughal invader Babur, and his works include four hymns that are collectively known as the *Bābar-vāṇī* ('Utterances about Babur'). Many writers have assumed that these verses demonstrate a political concern on Nanak's part rather than a religious one. This is not so. The purpose of these four hymns is not to provide a description of a Mughal invasion but to illustrate the fate of the unrighteous. The message is essentially religious, not political. The same applies to three sayings that are commonly quoted as evidence that insecurity and decadence were prominent features of the India of his time.[7] These sayings refer to the whole of the present cosmic age, not specifically to conditions in north India at the time when Nanak was alive. They would indeed include that period, but so too would they encompass all times and all places in the whole of Kaliyug, the evil age in which we live at present.

Nanak was certainly concerned with issues involving human suffering, and one can easily sense in his *Bābar-vāṇī* hymns something of the anguish the Mughal invasion must have involved for many of its victims. For him, though, the complete and ultimate answer to all such needs lay in meditating on the divine Name and in experiencing the bliss that awaited the person who faithfully did so. This he repeated in a seemingly endless multitude of different ways.

Guru Nanak and the Sant tradition

We come now to the third question, the one which has been implicit in all we have said when dealing with the first two. Was Nanak a Sant?

Those who know the works attributed to Kabir and other Sants will find in this brief summary of Nanak's theology much that is familiar and nothing that conflicts with any significant feature of Sant doctrine. In Nanak, as in Kabir, there is the same rejection of exterior forms, the same insistence on the need for inward devotion and its sufficiency as the sole means of liberation. And so we return to the problem that has recurred throughout this survey. Must we conclude that Nanak was a Sant?

For most devout Sikhs the answer must be a firm no. For them Nanak received direct enlightenment from Akal Purakh and, as the direct mediator of the divine message of liberation, there can be no possibility of antecedents. The notion that Nanak could ever be regarded as a Sant is entirely out of the question.

Others, however, do not share that commitment and are required to give a different answer. They will in fact have two answers to give, their response depending on the tone and colour of the question. If it is a strictly neutral question of antecedents and influences, the answer must be in the affirmative. Because he represents the essential concerns of the Sants, it follows that Guru Nanak must be located within the Sant tradition. If, however, the question implies a lack of originality on the part of Nanak, the answer must be an emphatic negative. Plainly there is much that is profoundly original in the hymns we find recorded under his distinctive symbol in the Adi Granth. There is in them an integrated and coherent system no other Sant has produced; there is a clarity no other Sant has equalled; and there is a beauty no other Sant has matched.

There is, moreover, the question of permanence. The fact that Nanak appointed a successor to follow him is scarcely unique, as panths are endlessly springing up in India and the original Master commonly nominates the successor who is to take his place after he dies. But the Nanak-panthi or Sikh case is different. Nothing in the Sant experience can remotely compare to the Panth which was eventually to emerge from that decision of Nanak.

Sikh doctrine after Guru Nanak

The successor whom Nanak appointed was, of course, his disciple Lahina, who assumed the name of Angad. During the period of Guru Angad there was no change in the doctrines taught by the first Master, nor were there any during the time of the following three Gurus. All taught that liberation from the transmigratory cycle depended wholly upon disciplined remembrance of the divine Name in accordance with the instruction imparted by the Guru. The content of their instruction was the same, and so too was the method they used for imparting it to all who would listen. Just as Nanak had embodied his teachings in works of supreme beauty, so too did his four successors continue his example of producing hymns that the faithful would sing in *saṅgat*s. The third Guru, Amar Das, certainly introduced changes in the structure, but these were organizational innovations and strictly speaking had nothing to do with the doctrinal basis of the Panth.

It is with the sixth Guru, Hargobind, that the doctrinal base of the Panth is widened by the acknowledgement of physical force as a necessary means of protection. Perhaps it would be fairer to say that tradition attaches to Guru Hargobind the responsibility for this change in the Panth's stance. As we saw when dealing with the history of the Sikh Gurus, tradition has joined to the time of Hargobind a basic feature that was already present in the Panth. The arming of the Panth, firmly associated with him, belongs to an earlier period and is something that occurred naturally.[8]

It was, however, in the time of Hargobind that armed defence came to be seen as necessary, and later generations credited him with the introduction of the doctrine of *mīrī-pīrī*. No longer was the Guru to exercise the *pīrī* role of his five predecessors, whereby they cared for the strictly religious needs of the Panth. The Panth was now dangerously threatened and the urgent need was for the Guru to assume the *mīrī* role also. It had become incumbent on him to adopt worldly leadership as well as the spiritual variety and to act as their supreme chief whenever their condition was physically menaced. The move towards militancy had been clearly initiated.

During the period of Hargobind the threat from Mughal officials continued and the Guru, who was not a person to be intimidated, maintained what amounted to a small standing army. During the period of his two successors, however, the danger receded. Guru Har Rai withdrew further into the Shivalik hills and the members of the Panth were no longer considered by their enemies to be the trouble they had been during the early decades of the seventeenth century. There were certainly Sikhs who would have defended their interests by force, but during the periods of Guru Har Rai and Guru Har Krishan the affairs of the Panth reverted to the earlier essentially devotional mode. The same applied to the greater part of the ninth Guru's period.

Khalsa doctrine

In 1675, however, the execution of Guru Tegh Bahadur by the Mughal Emperor Aurangzeb put an end to all that. In his place the Sikh Panth acquired its tenth and last personal Guru, and with his growth to manhood the doctrinal base underwent another important extension. In fact it underwent the most important of extensions, for it was under the direction of Guru Gobind Singh that the Khalsa was inaugurated.

Following the institution of the Khalsa, Guru Gobind Singh's remaining years were a time of extensive conflict. His fortress of Anandpur was attacked by rival hill chiefs allied with Mughal forces, the climax being the determined assault that took place in 1704. The Guru was compelled to withdraw from Anandpur and to make his escape to southern Punjab. The death of Aurangzeb in 1707 relieved the threat to the Khalsa and Guru Gobind Singh accompanied the new emperor, Bahadur Shah, to the Deccan. There he was assassinated in 1708.

These were stirring times for the Khalsa and they were also times of intermittent danger to the Guru. Such events, and those of the immediately preceding years, had a highly significant effect upon the beliefs of the Panth. They were responsible for the institution of the Khalsa and they also resulted in an extension of the doctrinal basis of the Panth.

The founding of the Khalsa was an event of absolutely primary importance in the life of the Panth, and the changes it introduced will be discussed in the next chapter. Evidences for the other extensions introduced into the Panth's theology at this time are to be found in certain works included in the Dasam Granth.[9] These are *Bachitar Nāṭak*, *Akāl Ustat* and *Zafar-nāmā*, and above all in the *Jāp*. It is true that none of these works can be attributed with certainty to Gobind Singh, yet even if these compositions are by members of his entourage, it still seems safe to read them (with due caution) as genuine evidence of the beliefs of Guru Gobind Singh. If they emerged in the court of the tenth Guru, they can be held to be the doctrines that prevailed there. They represented, in other words, the doctrines the Guru himself accepted and communicated to his Sikhs. These writings, illustrated by the Guru's actions, can be regarded as the system of belief he himself acknowledged. It was a system that certainly upheld the teachings on the divine Name as communicated by Nanak and his successors, but which added a significant appendage to them.

Jāp in particular reveals the belief system of Gobind Singh. It and other works from the Dasam Granth attributed to him show that he believed in Akal Purakh, the One who can be described in an infinity of ways yet possesses an infinity that still awaits description. Akal Purakh is above all one who is supremely just, exalting those who faithfully follow and punishing the wicked. In the everlasting struggle between the powers of evil and the forces of good, Akal Purakh intervenes on occasion to restore the balance in favour of those waging war on behalf of the good. In *Jāp* the Guru (or the follower responsible for actually writing the work) describes Akal Purakh in highly graphic terms, heaping up the descriptions in brief economical verses. It is a militant faith that is projected, one which was graphically put to the test during the career of the Guru.

In so doing he accepted the emphasis on the divine Name which had descended from Nanak, adding to this an expanded doctrine of Akal Purakh. From time to time the forces of good and evil become radically out of balance, the strength of evil increasing alarmingly over good. Akal Purakh then intervenes in human history to set the balance right. Particular individuals are chosen to act as agents of God, combating with physical strength the forces of evil which have acquired too much power. Gobind Singh believed that he was such an agent and that under him the Panth must be prepared to fight for justice.

To wage this battle he needed a committed force, wholly dedicated to act as a power for good even when that battle must involve suffering and death for many. He needed a committed force and he needed one that would retain its commitment by steadfastly refusing the temptation to seek concealment in times of danger. For this reason he created the Khalsa, its members conspicuously arrayed and sworn to obey the Rahit, which was held before them. This force was never to wage war for power, for gain or for personal rancour. The Khalsa was resolutely to uphold justice and to oppose only that which was evil. Overcoming the dispersed nature of the Panth under the *masand*s, the Khalsa would find strength and cohesion in complete dedication and devotion to its Master. In total loyalty to their Guru, the Khalsa would prevail, and once again the forces of good and evil would be brought into an acceptable balance.

Following the death of Guru Gobind Singh, the role of the personal Guru came to an end. Sikh tradition affirms that shortly before he died the Guru conferred the role jointly upon the Guru Granth (the sacred scriptures) and the Guru Panth (the corporate community of his followers which orthodox Sikhs normally interpret as the Khalsa). The historical questions surrounding this issue need not concern us at this point.[10] The inescapable fact is that Sikhs believe the traditional account, and that accordingly the role of the Guru is understood to have been vested jointly in the scripture and the community by the explicit words of the tenth Guru.

Even if the participation of Guru Gobind Singh were to be regarded as doubtful, it would make no difference to the actual doctrine. Sikhs emphatically believe that the Guru's guidance is expressed by the sacred scripture and by the considered voice of the corporate Panth. Prior to Nanak's time, the Guru, the 'voice' of Akal Purakh, was mystically 'spoken' within an individual believer. Nanak, by his teachings, gave direct utterance to the words Akal Purakh was communicating to humankind and thus came to be acknowledged as the first human Guru. Following his death the status of Guru passed to Angad, and from him onwards down the line of the ten personal Gurus. Ten individual human bodies successively held it, but there was only one Guru, passed on to the next as ten torches are lit by a single flame. Finally, with the death of Gobind Singh, the mystical Guru passed into the scripture and the corporate community, there to remain ever accessible to all who seek it.

Eliciting the word of the Guru from the corporate community has proved to be difficult, partly because the nature of the corporate community has been disputed but more particularly because opinion concerning the Guru's intention has been divided. Since the death of the tenth personal Guru there has been no single person entitled to speak as the Guru and it is only on rare occasions that the Panth speaks with general unanimity. What are known as *hukam-nāmā*s are occasionally issued by the Shiromani Gurdwara Parbandhak Committee (the SGPC), claiming to be the voice of the Guru Panth, but such an occasion is a rare event.[11] The Guru's voice is largely confined to the Guru Granth.

The Guru Granth, however, is abundantly consulted, the word of the Guru sought for a multitude of reasons on an infinite number of occasions. Today, as in generations past, the Guru Granth Sahib is venerated beyond all else in Sikhism, and, as we shall see in Chapter 8, it is shown the utmost respect at all times. Non-Sikh observers sometimes suggest that the Sikh attitude really amounts to idolatry. Sikhs are quick to respond to this, agreeing that certainly they pay the sacred volume extreme reverence but emphasizing that this reverence never proceeds to the point of actually worshipping it.

Today there is no problem concerning the identity of the Guru Granth Sahib, but certainly this has been a problem in the past. During the eighteenth century the Khalsa treated both the Adi Granth and the Dasam Granth as the Guru Granth, meetings of the Sarbat Khalsa being held in the presence of both volumes. At the time of the Singh Sabha reform movement, the Sanatan Sikhs saw no objection to maintaining this attitude, but the Tat Khalsa could not agree. There were too many questions associated with the Dasam Granth, and, although it was still to be treated as sacred scripture, it was, in effect, demoted from its rank of Guru Granth. Only the Adi Granth could really serve this purpose and so today the term Guru Granth Sahib means the Adi Granth alone. The Dasam Granth is meanwhile put to one side.

Only Sikhs of the Nihang sect dispute this and insist on giving the Dasam Granth the same status as the Adi Granth. The Nihangs are, however, a very small sect, if a distinctly old-fashioned and colourful one.[12] A few works which seem quite definitely to be by Guru Gobind Singh are given prominence and portions of them are included in *Nit-nem* (the daily devotional liturgy of the Sikhs). Apart from these works, the great bulk of the Dasam Granth is almost completely ignored.

Throughout the eighteenth century and well into the nineteenth the Panth continued its established pattern of belief, providing room both for the Khalsa and for the Sahaj-dhari Sikhs who did not accept its discipline.[13] During this period the principal changes concerned the drawing of Khalsa lines, and these will be considered in the next two chapters. After the annexation of the Punjab by the British in 1849, certain Sikhs became uneasy at where the Panth was heading, and, as we saw in the previous chapter, the Singh Sabha movement was founded in 1873. Sanatan Sikhs, with their base in Amritsar, saw little wrong with the doctrinal base of the Panth. They were concerned that Sikhs should remain loyal to the Panth and that relations with the British should be friendly. They were, however, soon strongly opposed within the Singh Sabha. The Tat Khalsa, based in Lahore, were absolutely insistent that sweeping reform was essential. In place of a corrupted faith, Sikhs should recover the pure message of the Gurus, demonstrating once and for all that Sikhs emphatically were not Hindus.

In the successful Tat Khalsa efforts to reform the Panth we note two fundamental issues. The first is that their reforms certainly concerned doctrine. Sikhs, they held, were the victims of false beliefs, and in restoring what they held to be sound beliefs they were dealing with doctrines. The second issue we have already noted. It is that many of the reforms introduced by the Tat Khalsa were in fact new imports. These are, however, reforms that chiefly concern the Khalsa. The next chapter, which concerns the foundation and growth of the Khalsa, is the appropriate place to deal with them.

6

KHALSA, RAHIT AND THE FIGHT FOR JUSTICE

The inauguration of the Khalsa by Guru Gobind Singh was without doubt the most important event in all Sikh history. Sikhs today resolutely hold that the event took place on the Baisakhi Day of 1699. This date must be open to some doubt, but there can be none concerning the actual event. There can be no question that on a Baisakhi Day towards the end of the seventeenth century Guru Gobind Singh summoned his following to his centre at Anandpur and there promulgated his new order.[1] It was to change the face of Sikhism.

Khalsa and Rahit

It is perhaps misleading to refer to this important incident as the actual foundation of the Khalsa, for in a certain sense the Khalsa was already in existence. Before the Guru promulgated the new order, the Khalsa which already existed (or an organization corresponding to it) consisted only of those Sikhs who were under his direct care, as opposed to the majority, who were guided by those subordinates known as *masand*s. The *masand* system had been established by Guru Ram Das and had for a time worked well as a means of guiding a flock that was greatly increasing in size and location. As the years passed, however, many of the *masand*s had grown corrupt and increasingly independent of the Guru. At the initial ceremony all Sikhs were commanded by the Guru to abandon the authority of the *masand*s and place themselves directly under his control. Those who accepted initiation formally acknowledged this obligation.

In another sense, however, one can certainly refer to the foundation of the Khalsa. The Guru was summoning his Sikhs to join an order with a distinctive appearance or uniform for all its members. In this sense it was indeed new and can certainly justify the use of the term 'inauguration' or 'foundation'. Entry to the Khalsa is obtained by an initiation ceremony known as *amrit saṅskār*. The term *amrit*, '[the nectar of] immortality', designates the sweetened water which is stirred with a two-edged sword and is then given to each of the candidates. The alternative name for the ceremony is *khaṇḍe dī pāhul*, 'initiation with the two-edged sword'. A detailed account of the ritual is given in the next chapter.[2]

All who took *amrit* received from their Master the Rahit, the code of belief and behaviour that every Khalsa Sikh must promise to obey. Most conspicuously it involves today the command to observe the *pañj kakke* or *pañj kakār*, the five items (each beginning with the letter 'k') that the Khalsa Sikh bears on his or her person.[3] These are uncut hair (*kes*), a comb (*kaṅghā*), a sword (*kirpān*), a wrist-ring made of steel (*kaṛā*), and a pair of shorts which must not come below the knee (*kachh*). Collectively these five symbols are invariably called the Five Ks in English usage. In addition to these the Rahit stipulates many more items, both principles of belief (such as the obligation to practise *nām simaraṇ*) and features of behaviour (such as the absolute requirement that all Khalsa Sikhs abstain from smoking). Today the term 'Gursikh' normally designates a Sikh who has been initiated, with the added implication that he or she is also punctilious in obeying the Rahit. The word is actually a more precise term than 'Khalsa Sikh' or 'Sikh of the Khalsa', the latter expressions being commonly used of those who bear the Five Ks without formally undertaking initiation.

These various items of belief and behaviour came to be written down in what were called *rahit-nāmā*s. The older *rahit-nāmā*s claim to record the actual words of Guru Gobind Singh, heard from his lips by the authors of the documents. These claims must be set aside, though predictably the rejecting of their purported dates does not make the actual years any easier to ascertain. The earliest extant version of a *rahit-nāmā* is the *Chaupā Siṅgh Rahit-nāmā*, which dates from the 1740s. That much has been fixed, but there are other early *rahit-nāmā*s and they contain some very important material. Probably they date from the late eighteenth or early nineteenth century. This is an uncertain estimate, though, and until the *rahit-nāmā*s are subjected to determined research the period of their composition can be only imprecisely known.

Why was the Khalsa established?

There are two general questions that arise in connection with the Khalsa. First, why did Guru Gobind Singh regard the Khalsa as necessary? Secondly, why did the Khalsa need a Rahit?

In the sense that all Sikhs were summoned to transfer their allegiance from the *masand*s and so to join the Guru's Khalsa, the decision is easy to understand. The Guru was being served by many corrupt individuals and his determination to disestablish them can be easily justified. But what should be made of the society which was to emerge from this decision? To many Sikhs this is a pointless question, for was the Khalsa not inaugurated by the Guru? One needs no further justification. He surely knew what he was doing and that is sufficient reason.

Other people, however, are not so easily convinced. Of these the majority probably are Hindus, or at least Sahaj-dhari Sikhs (in other words, Sikhs who do not belong to the Khalsa and who cut their hair). The debate this division of opinion raises is the celebrated 'transformation of Sikhism' theme, the question of why a tradition built on Nanak's *interior* practice of *nām simaraṇ* (or meditation on the divine Name) should have become a militant community and proclaimed its identity by means of prominently displayed *exterior* symbols. Nanak certainly emphasized the need to practise religion internally, and exterior symbols are not likely to be found on his immediate followers. The Khalsa, however, is distinguished by precisely these exterior symbols. How did it happen?

There are actually two distinct issues involved in this general question. First, why did a religion of interiority assume such an overtly exterior identity? Secondly, why did the Panth adopt a militant philosophy and develop an appropriately militant tradition? The two issues deserve to be treated together, for they are intimately related in practice and the answers given to one set of questions must largely dictate the response to the other. Together they raise a fundamental question with a significance extending far beyond the bounds of academic debate. Differing answers to the fundamental question reflect differing responses to major issues which Khalsa Sikhs answer in distinctive ways.

For some the fundamental question is posed in the following form: 'Should the transformation have occurred?' Thus expressed, the question commonly implies a negative answer, an answer which many Indians (including many Punjabi Hindus) are strongly inclined to support. The radical argument runs as follows. Nanak conferred great benefit on his own and succeeding generations by preaching the way of deliverance through the practice of *nām simaraṇ*. This is where Gurmat began and that is how it should have remained. The later Gurus may well have been sore provoked by Mughal authorities, but the decision to arm their followers and to redirect their teachings along militant lines was wholly regrettable. Religion should follow the path of peace, not the path of war.

A modified version of the argument accepts that there may have been reasons for the creation of the militant Khalsa order while firmly rejecting the claim that this should necessarily have transformed the Panth as a whole. The Khalsa should exist as a *voluntary* association within the larger Panth, to be joined by those who find value in its discipline but certainly not excluding from the Panth others who prefer to limit their loyalty to the teachings enunciated by Nanak and his early successors. The divine Name teachings of Nanak should be regarded as the essence of Gurmat. The Khalsa mode should be treated as a strictly voluntary extra.

This is the argument spelled out in Gokul Chand Narang's *The Transformation of Sikhism*. The book was aptly titled, though for a later edition the publishers seem to have thought they could better the name and have called it *The Glorious History of Sikhism*. Whatever the title, the book makes its case very specifically and its lengthy life (it was first published in 1914) clearly shows the continuing interest in its message.

The modified version of the argument raises the difficult question of how one should regard those who affirm veneration for Guru Nanak while rejecting the discipline of the Khalsa – in other words, the attitude of the Sahaj-dhari. This is a question which can be postponed until an attempt is made in Chapter 10 to define the nature of Sikh identity more precisely.[4] At this point we can acknowledge that Khalsa doctrine is strongly predominant within the Panth and that for all who accept the Khalsa tradition the question of its necessity simply does not arise. It needs to be recognized only that a significant change did remodel the Panth and the relevant question must therefore be why this happened.

Four distinct answers have been given to this question of why the transformation of the Panth occurred, and two of these answers deserve to be scrutinized. One theory which can be summarily discarded is the claim that credit for Sikh militancy must be bestowed on the nineteenth-century British rulers of the recently annexed Punjab and on élite groups within the Panth itself who subsequently turned the same tradition against its creators. According to this interpretation, there were several Sikh identities available during the period immediately following the 1849 annexation, and one such identity (the militant Khalsa version) was vigorously promoted by the British in order to serve their own military purposes. The same identity was accepted by the Tat Khalsa leaders and became the focus of their reforming activities late in the nineteenth century.

The brief summary of this theory necessarily does it serious injustice, and before passing it by we should acknowledge that it does incorporate important insights. In general terms, however, it can be rejected. It focuses much too narrowly on the condition of the Panth during the mid nineteenth century, failing to take adequate account of the rise to dominance of the Khalsa ideal during the course of the eighteenth century.

A second answer, one with roots in early Sikh tradition, is that it was for the defence of the Panth. Because Nanak and his successors attracted an expanding group of followers, the Mughal authorities in Delhi and Lahore became alarmed. Egged on by bigoted Muslims and a few malicious Hindus, they began to take steps to suppress the movement. Confronted by this threat, the later Gurus had little choice but to arm their followers or face extinction. They chose the former alternative, thereby converting the Panth from a group of unarmed devotees into one which was able to defend itself. This alone proved to be inadequate and eventually the firm discipline of the Khalsa had to be imposed on men who, in times of real danger, proved to be less than totally loyal.

This second theory can be treated summarily, not because it deserves to be rejected but because it is generally incorporated in the remaining theories. Neither of the two remaining theories accepts it as a sufficient answer to the transformation question, but they do accept it as a part of the total explanation. For both it is a subordinate aspect of the answer, a significant feature which should be not be regarded as the core explanation.

We are left with two conflicting interpretations, one of which has long dominated Sikh historiography and still shows little sign of weakening. This theory affirms that the Panth was remoulded by Guru Gobind Singh in order to defend the truth and secure justice for the oppressed. It begins with the insistent claim that the militarizing of the Panth by the sixth Guru and the subsequent creation of the Khalsa by the tenth were strictly in accord with Nanak's own intention. For many the classic statement of this claim is to be found in the stirring words of Joseph Cunningham, first published in 1849:

> It was reserved for *Nanak* to perceive the true principles of reform, and to lay those broad foundations which enabled his successor *Gobind* to fire the minds of his countrymen with a new nationality, and to give practical effect to the doctrine that the lowest is equal with the highest, in race as in creed, in political rights as in religious hopes.[5]

It was, in other words, Nanak's doctrine of equality which supplied the essential basis for later developments. Nanak had signalled the destruction of caste with words of explicit denunciation. Gobind Singh sealed his intention by requiring all Khalsa entrants to drink the same nectar of initiation from a common cup. Nanak had proclaimed that deliverance from suffering and transmigration is available to all, regardless of how lowly or oppressed an individual might be. His successors, notably Guru Gobind Singh, translated this doctrine into militant defence of the rights of all men. In the face of tyranny, justice can be defended and maintained only by the use of force. If all other methods of redress have failed, it is legitimate to draw the sword in the defence of righteousness. The obligation to perform this duty if need should arise must be accepted by every loyal follower of the Guru.

Many see this summons to a new order and discipline as a sudden change, one which the tenth Guru dramatically thrust upon a startled Panth when he announced the inauguration of the Khalsa on that Baisakhi Day. The execution of his father by order of the Emperor Aurangzeb had convinced the youthful Guru that his followers must learn to defend justice with the sword, and that they must adopt an outward identity of a kind which would make craven concealment impossible. The actions of the sixth Guru, Hargobind, are recognized as a significant foreshadowing of the change which was to come, but the actual transformation belongs to the time of Guru Gobind Singh and specifically to the actual founding of the Khalsa.

This was the dominant view of the Singh Sabha period and it has been restated by Khushwant Singh in *A History of the Sikhs*.[6] More recently, Jagjit Singh in *The Sikh Revolution* has developed this interpretation into a detailed theory of revolution, one which maintains that the period of the Gurus must be viewed as a whole and the Panth they led as the progressive development of a single sustained ideal.[7]

The common feature and essence of these related interpretations is that they all attribute the historical development of the Sikh Panth (at least during the first three centuries of its existence) to the explicit intention of the Gurus. They thus represent a strictly ideological view, one which conformed strictly to the purpose of the Gurus. The Gurus envisaged a particular pattern for the Panth they created, and the actual form it assumed corresponded to their intention. It accordingly developed as a militant order with a particular range of external symbols because that is what the fundamental intention required. Guru Gobind Singh may have been responsible for engendering the spirit and proclaiming the actual form the Khalsa was to assume, but he did so only because a basic egalitarian principle had already been enunciated by Guru Nanak. The intervening Gurus likewise contributed to the same process, each advancing the same basic ideal and formulating practical responses as circumstances demanded.

This interpretation has been contested on the grounds that it stresses intention and ideology much too strongly. There has been no suggestion, of course, that the Gurus lacked clear objectives, nor that they were ineffectual in the pursuit of their declared purposes. The point this fourth interpretation seeks to make is that the weight of emphasis is thrown much too strongly on preconceived intention as an explanation for subsequent developments, and that insufficient allowance is made for what may be termed environmental factors. These factors include the social constituency of the developing Panth, the economic context within which it evolved, and the influence of contemporary events such as those produced by local political rivalries and foreign invasion.

This view holds that the traditional interpretation is much too simple and its use of sources too narrowly selective. It also partly derives from a suspicion of any wide-ranging explanation based on the preconceived intentions of individuals, no matter how influential those individuals may be. Within a narrow and immediate range, such explanations can be wholly plausible, but not for a movement as complex and long-lived as the Sikh Panth. The fourth interpretation thus claims that the progressive development of the Panth must be explained not merely in terms of purposeful intention but also (and in significant measure) by the influence of the social, economic and historical environment. This specifically includes such major features as the militant texture of the later Panth and the growth of the Rahit.

Which of these interpretations accounts for the evolution of the Panth? The British can hardly take the credit, but that still leaves three possible explanations. First, was it simply for the defence of the Panth? Secondly, did the Guru fashion a society dedicated to the pursuit of truth and justice, even at the cost of drawing the sword? Or thirdly, was it a more gradual growth, one that allows the intention of the Guru as an important factor but which finds a large measure of the explanation in historical and social developments that exercise their influence over an extended period? The third of these interpretations is the one adopted here, but it must be stressed that many Sikhs are resolute supporters of the second interpretation.

The Rahit and rahit-nāmā*s*

What, then, is to be made of the Rahit, which all initiated members of the Khalsa must vow to obey? At the inauguration of the Khalsa the Guru is said to have delivered a sermon, explaining his reasons for introducing the new order and enunciating the code of conduct its initiated members were to follow. He was, in other words, proclaiming the Rahit, and it is the Rahit that defines in very specific terms the pattern of belief and practice the Khalsa Sikh must observe.

Tradition readily acknowledges that certain features of the Rahit were already a part of the pre-Khalsa pattern of the Panth, and it records that one major addition (the conferring of the Guru's authority on the Granth and the Panth) was made immediately prior to the Guru's death. It clearly implies, however, that the substance of the Rahit had been delivered to the Khalsa by the time the tenth Guru died in 1708. The Rahit remains thereafter the sole and sufficient statement of Khalsa doctrine, ritual and personal behaviour. As such it supplies the standard definition of Sikh orthodoxy and Sikh identity.

Much that is contained in this popular version of the inauguration of the Khalsa is open to serious question, and although certain features receive support from near-contemporary sources, others do not. At this point the only feature which need concern us is the promulgating of the Rahit, a statement that was absolutely central to the life and purpose of the reconstituted Panth. One would expect that it would have been committed to writing at an early stage, at least within the lifetime of Guru Gobind Singh. The Guru did indeed issue *hukam-nāmā*s or 'letters of command' to particular individuals and *saṅgat*s, and the examples which survive incorporate items that would certainly have been included in any systematic statement of the complete Rahit. This, however, was a form of communication which had been used by some of his predecessors, and although the surviving examples provide valuable examples of contemporary practice, they cannot have been intended primarily as vehicles of the Rahit in any full or systematic form.

No such systematic statement survives from the actual period of the Guru's lifetime. At least one writer has assumed that manuals or comprehensive statements would certainly have been prepared for use by the Guru's emissaries in order to instruct scattered *saṅgat*s in their newly established Khalsa faith. These manuals, it is implied, must since have been lost. Other writers have drawn attention to the upheavals of the period immediately following the foundation of the Khalsa, suggesting that the urgency of conflict would leave little time for careful recording of what otherwise could be effectively communicated by word of mouth and visible example.

The fact that a distinctive code of conduct was operative early in the eighteenth century is indicated by references occurring in Sainapati's *Gur Sobhā* ('Radiance of the Guru'). This is a work of very great significance in terms of tracing the development of Sikh ideals, not least because it supplies an early selection of Rahit items. If *Gur Sobhā* was in fact completed in 1711 (and this appears to be the strong likelihood), its importance is indeed significant. A work issued in 1711 is one which has been written very close to the death of Guru Gobind Singh in 1708. Even with its precise date undetermined, however, *Gur Sobhā* remains a work of great significance. There can be no doubt that it belongs to the first half of the eighteenth century, and in terms of the available sources for tracing Khalsa development this makes it very early indeed. Among the Rahit items which it offers are an insistence on the time-honoured practice of *nām simaraṇ* and a categorical denunciation of hookah-smoking and of cutting hair.

Gur Sobhā remains, however, a narrative poem. It makes no effort to enunciate the Rahit in systematic or comprehensive terms and accordingly cannot strictly be regarded as a *rahit-nāmā*. What of those compositions which can be treated as proper *rahit-nāmā*s? Unfortunately works that can legitimately be regarded as *rahit-nāmā*s present an even wider range of problems.

Although it must seem a drastic statement to make, no *rahit-nāmā* actually survives from the lifetime of Guru Gobind Singh. It is true that there are several such works claiming to record instructions that their writers received directly by word of mouth from the Guru before he died. It is also true that several of these compositions form an important segment of the *rahit-nāmā* corpus as it existed prior to the composing of the modern twentieth-century variety. What then are we to make of these works? Do they not rebut the claim that no *rahit-nāmā* can be dated from the lifetime of Guru Gobind Singh?

In no case is it possible to accept a *rahit-nāmā*'s claim that it reports injunctions received directly from the Guru. For reasons that will shortly be made clear, these claims are in all cases spurious. This does not mean, of course, that questions concerning the actual age and provenance of these *rahit-nāmā*s end at this point, for the problems associated with dating them and placing them in their appropriate contexts are far from simple. There is, moreover, no doubt concerning their considerable importance as standards to which later generations have appealed in the ongoing effort to define normative Khalsa practice, nor about their potential value as indicators of Khalsa development.

The nine *rahit-nāmā*s which appear prior to the twentieth century can be divided according to form into three groups. All offer statements, brief or lengthy, of what a Khalsa Sikh is expected to believe and how he or she should act. Four of the *rahit-nāmā*s are brief works expressed in simple Punjabi verse. Three are lengthy prose collections. The remaining two are brief works in prose. All nine claim or clearly imply derivation from the specific words of Guru Gobind Singh, posing as products of his actual intention rather than as responses to any subsequent period of Khalsa experience.

Simple Punjabi verse:
1. Nand Lal's *Praśhan-uttar*.
2. Nand Lal's *Tanakhāh-nāmā*.
3. Prahilad Singh's (or Prahilad Rai's) *Rahit-nāmā*.
4. Desa Singh's *Rahit-nāmā*.

Lengthy Punjabi prose:
5. Chaupa Singh's *Rahit-nāmā*.
6. The *Prem Sumārag* (or the *Param Sumārag*).
7. The *Sau Sākhīān*.

Brief works in Punjabi prose:
8. A *rahit-nāmā* attributed to Nand Lal.
9. Daya Singh's *Rahit-nāmā*.

Of the four verse *rahit-nāmā*s, two are attributed to Nand Lal, the distinguished member of the tenth Guru's retinue whose Persian poetry commands great reverence within the Panth. These two Punjabi works are briefly entitled *Praśhan-uttar* ('Catechism') and *Tanakhāh-nāmā* ('Manual of Penances'). The former (plainly misnamed) is more discursive than the usual *rahit-nāmā*, concentrating on an exposition of the doctrine of the mystical Guru and stressing the believer's obligation to practise *nām simaraṇ*. By contrast, the *Tanakhāh-nāmā* follows the typical format. Having listed various practices to be either spurned or observed, it concludes with a stirring assurance of the future glory awaiting the Khalsa. Its final words continue to exercise an immense influence. This is the couplet beginning with the words *rāj karegā khālsā*, which are recited at the end of the oft-repeated Khalsa prayer of petition called *Ardās*:[8]

> The Khalsa shall rule, no enemy shall remain.
> All who endure suffering and privation shall be brought to the
> safety of the Guru's protection.

The remaining verse *rahit-nāmā*s, attributed respectively to Prahilad Singh (or Prahilad Rai) and Desa Singh, also follow the standard form. Like the two works bearing Nand Lal's name, both claim to record first-hand information. Prahilad Singh is said to have been with Guru Gobind Singh in Abchalnagar (the town of Nander in the Deccan) during the period immediately preceding the Guru's death there. According to the *rahit-nāmā*'s brief prologue, the Guru evidently realized that the Rahit should be recorded in order that the Khalsa might know its duty after he was no longer present in the flesh. He therefore summoned Prahilad Singh for this specific purpose and dictated the Rahit to him. The *rahit-nāmā* attributed to Desa Singh similarly claims to record the Guru's words, supplemented by information received from Nand Lal.

This same claim is made even more insistently by one of the three prose *rahit-nāmā*s which offer detailed statements of the Rahit. Chaupa Singh Chhibbar was closely associated with Guru Gobind Singh, first as his *khiḍāvā* (adult playmate), then as his tutor, and finally as a trusted servant and counsellor. Such a person might well claim intimate knowledge of the Guru's ideals and intentions. The *Chaupā Siṅgh Rahit-nāmā* does indeed make this claim, recording in profuse detail the many injunctions the Guru is said to have issued for the benefit of the Khalsa.

The other two lengthy *rahit-nāmā*s both belong to a much later period than the *Chaupā Siṅgh Rahit-nāmā*, though this does not mean any retreat from the standard claims to authenticity. In their extant form, both belong to the middle portion of the nineteenth century and at least one of them may well have originated at this time. This is the *Prem Sumārag* (or *Param Sumārag*), a work that begins with an announcement of imminent cosmic disaster and then details in an unusually systematic form the way of life the Khalsa should follow. The *Sau Sākhīān* or 'Hundred Anecdotes' is also vitally concerned with the troubles that must afflict the Panth and with prophecies of the rewards which await the faithful.

This leaves the two prose *rahit-nāmā*s, which confine their attention to the Rahit and deal with it briefly. One of the two, a third work attributed to Nand Lal, is always found in association with the *Chaupā Siṅgh Rahit-nāmā.* The few manuscripts which record the *Chaupā Siṅgh Rahit-nāmā* also append this brief fragmentary statement as a supplement.

The final example is the *rahit-nāmā* attributed to Daya Singh, first of the Panj Piare (the Cherished Five) to offer his head at the founding of the Khalsa.[9] Whereas the Nand Lal prose *rahit-nāmā* is certainly an eighteenth-century product, the Daya Singh version seems plainly to date from the nineteenth century. This feature reminds us yet again that claims to represent the direct dictation of the Guru or a first-hand record of his pronouncements must always be rejected. All are removed, to a greater or lesser extent, from the lifetime of Guru Gobind Singh.

The *Chaupā Siṅgh Rahit-nāmā* can be placed in the 1740s and can be cautiously ranked as the oldest extant *rahit-nāmā.* With it can be bracketed the version attributed to Nand Lal which always appears as an appendix to it. But what should be made of the two other *rahit-nāmā*s attributed to Nand Lal or to the version written by Prahilad Singh? The Punjabi is not the Punjabi which would be attached to a writer as distinguished as Bhai Nand Lal (the member of Guru Gobind Singh's retinue famous for his Persian verse) and there are too many other problems associated with these brief works. One is why the real Nand Lal never accepted initiation into the Khalsa if he was prepared to defend its Rahit. Another is the question of the date attached to Prahilad Singh's *rahit-nāmā*, a date which makes no sense of the author's claims to have dictated the Guru's actual words in Abchalnagar. These works appear to be products of the later eighteenth century and may even come from the early nineteenth century.

The quest for an authentic rahit-nāmā

Such issues were a part of the larger problem of authenticity which confronted the more ardent of the Tat Khalsa reformers at the end of the nineteenth century. That Guru Gobind Singh had promulgated the Rahit was a tradition which could and must be accepted without question. But did the extant *rahit-nāmās* fully and faithfully record the Rahit as delivered by the Guru? Plainly, it seemed, they did not offer wholly reliable versions, for some of their injunctions seemed manifestly to be in conflict with enlightened belief.

At first the Tat Khalsa reformers concentrated on single issues, particularly those which might signal a distinctive Sikh identity as opposed to Hindu tradition and practice (issues such as the important marriage question). In 1901 Kahn Singh Nabha moved a step closer to an authorized *rahit-nāmā* when he published *Guramat Sudhākar*, a compendium of works relating to the person and period of Guru Gobind Singh. This included a selection from the existing *rahit-nāmās*, and in editing the materials available to him Kahn Singh implicitly expressed a particular interpretation of them. Although his selections were presented as abridged versions of extant *rahit-nāmās*, they are more accurately described as expurgated versions. In other words, Kahn Singh had cut items that he believed ought not to be there. What this implied was that the pure Rahit enunciated by the tenth Guru had subsequently been corrupted by ignorant or malicious transmitters of the tradition. By eliminating all that conflicted with reason and sound tradition (as understood by such men as Kahn Singh), one might hope to restore the pristine Rahit, the uncorrupted original Rahit as the Guru had delivered it.

This was followed by a comprehensive statement of the Rahit in 1915 by a committee set up by the Chief Khalsa Diwan.[10] The resultant *rahit-nāmā*, termed *Guramat Prakāśh Bhāg Sanskār*, certainly accorded with the views of the Tat Khalsa, but the lengthy formats it laid down for Khalsa rites of passage were altogether too complicated for acceptance by the Panth as a whole. In 1931 the Shiromani Gurdwara Parbandhak Committee (the SGPC) commissioned another committee to continue the search. This committee produced a report within a year, but it took eighteen more years to settle the issue. During this period India was living through clamorous times, climaxed by the granting of independence and the post-partition migrations in 1947–8. The Sikhs were caught up in these events and the SGPC did not publish an approved version until 1950. This approved version was the *Sikh Rahit Maryādā*. At last the Sikhs had an approved *rahit-nāmā*.

Since 1950 very few changes have been made to the text and during the years since its first appearance *Sikh Rahit Maryādā* has established itself as the authoritative guide to the Rahit. The manual certainly has some shortcomings, but in spite of these it has so far stood the test of time remarkably well. It has run through numerous editions, it has admitted very little in the way of amendment, and it has no rivals for an orthodox understanding of the Rahit. The SGPC continues to issue it, both in its original Punjabi and in English translation, and if a Sikh seeks an answer to any problem of personal observance or Khalsa ritual, *Sikh Rahit Maryādā* is the *rahit-nāmā* to which he or she is likely to turn.

Here we must take care not to exaggerate its importance. The answers to such questions will more commonly be sought orally from a Sikh with a reputation for learning or piety. In some circumstances they may be ascertained by opening the Guru Granth Sahib at random and using it as an oracle. If, however, the appeal is to be made to a *rahit-nāmā*, *Sikh Rahit Maryādā* will normally supply the means. In the pages of this brief manual we shall find answers to many of the standard questions, and there can be no doubt that it has significantly contributed to the maintenance of a normative orthodoxy (an orthodoxy which defines what is ideal as opposed to what people actually do). In the next chapter extensive use will be made of it in describing the worship and ritual obligations of the Khalsa Sikh.

The development of the Rahit

The *rahit-nāmā*s have been given comparatively little attention (particularly by authors writing in English), and almost all that they have received has been strictly traditional in its interpretation. Instead of the traditional approach, the *rahit-nāmā*s must be viewed critically, though the critical approach certainly does not mean that an attempt is being made to demolish them. This clearly is not the case. There is much in them that deserves to be retained, most notably the splendid couplet (quoted above) with which *Ardās* concludes.

The principal problem concerns the manner in which the Rahit was conferred on the Panth. Was it all delivered by Guru Gobind Singh? Did some of the Rahit represent practices already current in the Panth? Was a portion of it delivered by the Guru and the remainder evolved during the succeeding decades or centuries? There is general agreement on the second of these questions. In some cases the Rahit does indeed represent practices that were already current in the Panth, everyone agreeing, for example, that the practice of *nām simaraṇ* was carried over from the Panth's early custom. But what of some of the other features, such as the ban on cutting hair? Were these new features which were delivered to the Panth at the foundation of the Khalsa? And were other items conferred by Guru Gobind Singh or did they enter the Rahit after his death?

Those who subscribe to the resolute variety of traditional scholarship will insist that the essence of the Rahit, complete in all its fundamental features, was present in the intention of Guru Gobind Singh, and that it must have been promulgated before his death in 1708. The actual sources, however, make this view very difficult to sustain. The variant versions of the Rahit which appear in the earlier *rahit-nāmā*s clearly indicate that much of the Rahit crystallized during the course of the eighteenth century and that a fully developed version is not available until we move into the nineteenth century. Indeed, a fully fashioned Rahit does not exist until the attentions of Tat Khalsa reformers have been brought to bear on it during the early years of the twentieth century.

A central item of the Rahit which should be examined is the command that all Sikhs of the Khalsa should bear the *pañj kakke* or the Five Ks. These items are so very important to Sikhs that it requires the greatest of care and discretion when raising the issue for discussion. Apart from the role and status of the Guru Granth Sahib, this would surely be the most delicate of all issues to consider in any study of Sikhism. Precisely because it is so central, though, the issue must certainly be raised. This need becomes compelling when the discussion reveals that an analysis of the relevant historical period leads to a serious questioning of the traditional interpretation.

According to the traditional view, the Five Ks were an absolutely central part of the Rahit as delivered by Guru Gobind Singh, and since the founding of the Khalsa they have never been altered or corrupted. Ever since its inauguration in 1699, say the traditional historians, this particular feature has been upheld by all who regard themselves as true Sikhs of the Khalsa. The Guru issued the command to the Khalsa and ever since that command was given the Five Ks have been loyally upheld.

The objection which must be raised against this interpretation arises from the available sources. There exists no eyewitness account of the founding of the Khalsa, and those who come nearest to the occasion make it clear that the Rahit delivered by Guru Gobind Singh at its inauguration was appreciably shorter than that which is current today. Sainapati's *Gur Sobhā* (which, as we have already acknowledged, was probably completed in 1711) informs us that the Guru required his Khalsa to leave their hair uncut and to carry arms. In other words, there is explicit authority for the *kes* and implicit authority for the *kirpān*. The other three Ks are nowhere mentioned.

There is, however, a *hukam-nāmā* (a 'letter of command') allegedly addressed by Guru Gobind Singh to his followers in Kabul. This bears the date 1756 according to the Indian system of dating, which, when converted into Common Era dating, is the very year of the founding of the Khalsa (1699 CE). In this *hukam-nāmā* he refers to the necessity of bearing the Five Ks. This *hukam-nāmā*, though, is most unlikely to be genuine. It lacks the Guru's seal and it is in direct contradiction to other early sources which make it perfectly clear that the Five Ks were not among the Guru's instructions. He may well have commanded his followers to carry five weapons, but these are not the Five Ks.

The *Chaupā Siṅgh Rahit-nāmā* offers further support to this conclusion. In the first version of the *rahit-nāmā*, no reference at all is made to the Five Ks. This version evidently dates from the 1740s. A later version does include five symbols which must be acknowledged by the Khalsa Sikh, and it names three of them as *kachh*, *kirpān* and *kes*. The remaining two, however, are *bāṇī* (sacred scripture) and *sādh saṅgat* (the congregation of the faithful). The fact that the *Chaupā Siṅgh Rahit-nāmā* permits special consideration to be paid to Brahman Sikhs does not weaken its testimony in this regard. The reference in the later version of the *Chaupā Siṅgh Rahit-nāmā* testifies to the fact that the recognition of the Five Ks was under way, but that it had not yet achieved a complete or permanent form.

None of the other early *rahit-nāmā*s refers to the Five Ks and prior to the latter half of the nineteenth century there is no reference to them in any other work. Even Rattan Singh Bhangu, whose celebrated *Prachīn Panth Prakāśh* appeared in 1841, makes no mention of them. There is clear evidence that the early Khalsa observed such features as the uncut hair (*kes*) and wore the breeches (*kachh*); and the early Khalsa certainly carried swords or *kirpān*s. There are also eighteenth-century references to the wearing of a wrist-ring, and it is reasonable to assume that the Khalsa probably carried a comb in their hair. We look in vain, however, if we seek an explicit reference to the Five Ks before the late nineteenth century. This presumably means that they must have been introduced as a formal requirement during early Singh Sabha times.

It should be emphasized that this interpretation will not be accepted by most Sikhs and that it will be treated by a substantial majority with outright condemnation. This should not deter us from setting out the argument if we feel the evidence justifies it.

It will, of course, be answered that this is where the historical method (with its dependence on documentary sources) inevitably leads us. One should trust the word that is passed down through the Panth. That is the authentic voice of tradition, a voice which can be and must be trusted absolutely. We are here at the point of radical disagreement, with the historian saying one thing and the traditional believer another. It has already been made clear which approach lies behind this book and its conclusion must be as follows. Although the evidence may not point to a verdict which is finally and definitively proven, it certainly offers strong support for such a result. The formalizing of the Five Ks as mandatory Khalsa symbols probably belongs to the late nineteenth century.

The second issue to be raised in this analysis of the contents of the Rahit will probably produce a somewhat milder condemnation. This concerns the early Khalsa's relations with Muslims and the portion of the Rahit which relates to the confrontation with them. Many items in the early *rahit-nāmā*s reflect the fact that the Khalsa was fighting with Muslims. There is also the commandment that Khalsa Sikhs should not have dealings with Muslim women. Kahn Singh Nabha was a prominent member of the Tat Khalsa and his interpretation of this particular item was that Khalsa Sikhs were being warned to steer clear of prostitutes, most of whom were Muslims. The interpretation is distinctly strained, but later still the item was reinterpreted to mean that Sikhs should not engage in extra-marital sex. It appears in this form as one of the four cardinal prohibitions (*kurahit*) in the modern *Sikh Rahit Maryādā*.

Another interesting survival of these anti-Muslim items in the modern Rahit concerns meat-eating. It is the instruction that Khalsa Sikhs may eat only *jhaṭakā* meat (that is, the flesh of animals killed with a single blow), never *kuṭṭhā* meat (*halāl* meat, where the animal has bled to death while the Muslim confession of faith is recited). This too is one of the *kurahit*.

Any adequate analysis of the historical Rahit is bound to be an exceedingly complex task and there is still a long way to go in terms of fully explaining it. Another task will be deciding just what influence the customs of the Jats had in determining the content of the Rahit. The possibility of uncut hair being originally a Jat custom is one example. It should be noted, however, that the prohibition of hair-cutting was incorporated in the early Rahit. Then there will be the question of why the ban on smoking the hookah entered the Rahit. Two things are clear in this regard. One is that the prohibition made a very early entry, for *Gur Sobhā* mentions it. The other is that smoking the hookah came to be translated into a ban on all smoking when the Sikhs came in contact with the European styles involving pipe, cigarettes, cigars and cheroots. But why was it introduced in the first place? Was it because the hookah was associated with the Muslims and for that reason was to be spurned by the Sikhs? This seems the most likely theory, but another which should be considered is that the hookah was too cumbersome for the characteristic form of mobile warfare adopted by the Sikhs.

That is one kind of challenge which presents itself in any consideration of the Rahit and of the *rahit-nāmā*s. Various items of the Rahit need to be explained in terms of the reason for their entry. A different kind of task (and a very important one) must be to ascertain just when the various *rahit-nāmās* were first composed, for obviously they will reflect the understanding of their own time. In this regard there is still much research to be done.

The fact that many items entered the Rahit at a later date does not mean that none of the major elements was promulgated prior to the Guru's death, nor that the emergence of a recognizable Rahit was delayed until the end of the eighteenth century. What it does suggest is that a process which was already under way by 1708 continued to operate through succeeding decades, generating in response to eighteenth-century pressures several of the elements that feature prominently in the traditional Khalsa Rahit. These elements were subsequently purged, supplemented and restated as a result of Tat Khalsa influence late in the nineteenth century and early in the twentieth. The reforming process eventually produced the Rahit as we know it today. Having thus evolved over a lengthy period, it continues to develop, responding slowly to contemporary pressures and producing the new emphases which progressively remould it.

The militant ideal and martyrdom

What, then, are we to make of the militant aspect conferred on the faith by those who uphold the Khalsa ideal? This aspect can be viewed from two perspectives. It can be seen as the heroism of the warrior Khalsa, of the Khalsa Sikh as a *sant-sipāhī* (a 'sant-soldier'), with the emphasis squarely upon the soldierly role. Alternatively, it can be observed from the closely related angle of martyrdom.

The first perspective needs little explanation. A survey of Khalsa history, particularly at certain crucial periods, will at once make this clear. The time of persecution during the first half of the eighteenth century, the Gurdwara Reform Movement of the early 1920s or the struggle with the government of India during the period 1984–92 underline (from the Khalsa's point of view) the paramount need of all Sikhs to confront fearlessly the malevolent designs of the evil and the ill-disposed. This leads us on to the willingness of the Khalsa Sikh to be resolute even to the point of martyrdom. Clearly the two perspectives are but two ways of viewing the same obligation to be supremely brave and undaunted, never to yield to an enemy under any circumstances.

This ideal of militant bravery runs through Sikh history from the early seventeenth century and emerges with particular force from the founding of the Khalsa onwards. During the Singh Sabha period, it was a central theme of the Tat Khalsa, and as a result of their preaching it has remained at the heart of orthodox Sikhism. It is a fearlessness constant and unwavering, though death may be its end. From the death of Guru Arjan down to the present day, Sikh history is sprinkled with martyrs, sometimes receding in frequency but at other times (as the recent troubles with the government of India show) returning to bring both suffering and a splendid renown. For the individual they can mean pain and death, steadfastly endured. For the Khalsa they bring triumphant glory.

This martyr ideal lives on in the Panth and provides much inspiration to Sikhs. It is important to realize that it is not a passive ideal. Sikhs are taught, by the many stories of heroism they hear, that whenever evil returns weapons are to be used. They may be employed as a last resort, but emphatically they are to be used. Their use should never be simply for the benefit of the individual. Only in the interests of justice can swords be brandished or guns fired. Needless to say, there are many instances where it may be suspected personal gain is the real motive, but the ideal which the Panth upholds denies this absolutely. When circumstances demand a militant response, some Sikhs will answer the call directly, and all Sikhs should admire and assist their disinterested use of force to combat evil. For justice and the Panth, all Sikhs should be prepared to undergo suffering, even to the point of martyrdom.

This message was clearly spelt out by the Tat Khalsa during the days of the Singh Sabha movement. The message was not new to the Panth, but it received a force and a coherence which previously it had not attained. Those who did not agree with the Tat Khalsa approach might demur, but increasingly their voices became weaker. The Khalsa was created in order to fight injustice, and fighting injustice is still its calling.

The word for a 'martyr' is *śahīd*, an Arabic word brought by

Muslims and originally introduced into Punjabi to express an important feature of Islamic culture. This clearly was the derivation of the Sikh usage, although Punjabi folklore clearly played a significant part in its development. Courage and sacrifice were themes drawn upon by the village bards or *ḍhaḍhīs*, and still to the present day they sing of the same virtues. The difference is that at least since the eighteenth century the songs of the bards have been undergoing a change in one vital respect. Now they sing of the courage and sacrifices of the Sikh martyrs. They sing of the two martyr Gurus, of Baba Dip Singh and a host of other martyrs from the eighteenth century, and of the noble souls who in the early 1920s gave their lives for the freedom of the sacred gurdwaras. In recent times a new chapter has been added and Sikh martyrology now lists the names of Jarnail Singh Bhindranvale and others like him, men who in the late 1980s and early 1990s laid down their lives while defending the Panth against the designs of evil men and women from Delhi.

This must sound like exaggeration, yet emphatically it is not so. Such concepts have an immense hold and the grip is far too secure to be shaken. The simpler forms may be characteristic of the villages, but the essence of this understanding informs the beliefs of the vast majority of Sikhs, regardless of where they live or what they may do. Sikhism – or rather Khalsa Sikhism – is indeed a militant faith.

If anyone should doubt this, he or she should try referring to the deaths of Guru Arjan or Guru Tegh Bahadur simply as killings or as executions. This they certainly were, but they were much more. These two Gurus were martyrs and as martyrs they should always be proclaimed. Or consider *Ardās*, the prayer of the Khalsa. The section beginning 'Those loyal members of the Khalsa' will leave the same impression.[11] A walk around two museums in India will confirm it (the Baba Bhagel Singh Museum adjoining Bangla Sahib Gurdwara in New Delhi and the Central Sikh Museum in the precincts of Harimandir Sahib in Amritsar). The artwork in both instances, together with collections of weapons, convincingly demonstrates the related themes of heroism and martyrdom.

If one considers the evidence provided by the bazaar posters so common in Punjabi shops and homes, there is little doubt about where popular preferences lie. Baba Nanak in old age, his eyes half closed and his hand raised in blessing, is one of three preferences. This is the eirenic aspect of Sikhism, the Guru rapt in devotion to the divine Name and calling all to follow him on the path to personal peace. The second variety is presented in a series of posters depicting a stalwart Guru Gobind Singh, fully armed and arrayed in princely attire. This is the heroic Guru, the theme which he illustrates being the fearlessness of the Khalsa. The third presents the eighteenth-century figure of the headless but still battling Baba Dip Singh. This immensely popular poster represents the theme of martyrdom.

Posters of this kind may not amount to great art, but they do show with uncanny accuracy where the choices of ordinary Sikhs lie with regard to their faith. These three themes dominate popular Sikh art. The first is the doctrine of the divine Name and the serenity that the divine Name alone can bring. The second is the heroism of the Panth and its willingness to stand erect in the fight for justice. The third is martyrdom, the conviction that bravery is not sufficient unless it extends to the ultimate stage of death.

Sikh ethics and morality

We conclude this chapter with a summary treatment of Khalsa ethics and morality. Several relevant issues have already been briefly considered and it remains only to knit them into a single coherent statement. It is the Khalsa which concerns us at this point rather than the Sikh faith that preceded its foundation, particularly that which came before the time of Guru Hargobind. It is, moreover, the Khalsa of the present day rather than that which preceded the Singh Sabha movement. In the latter instance, however, the difference is not marked. The principal distinction concerns the greater clarity which followed the efforts of the Tat Khalsa reformers as opposed to the implied system of the earlier period.

For Sikhs of the Khalsa the dominant ethical duty is the quest for justice. This, as we have seen, was the paramount concern of Guru Gobind Singh.[12] At the end of the seventeenth century the world was seen to be seriously awry, with the powerful assuming more than their share of authority and the weak compelled in consequence to suffer.

For this reason Guru Gobind Singh created the Khalsa, and every Sikh who enlisted as a member was thereafter committed to the public struggle for justice. It was a very high profile which the committed Khalsa Sikh was required to adopt. By adopting the highly visible Five Ks, all Khalsa Sikhs (and particularly the men with turbans and beards) announced, to all who had eyes to see, that they were members of the Khalsa order and that as such they were pledged to fulfil its obligations.

These obligations were summarized for the Khalsa Sikh in the words of the Rahit, and for Sikhs of today they are found in the modern *rahit-nāmā Sikh Rahit Maryādā*. As the Khalsa is viewed as an army the prime obligation required of all its members is discipline. In this respect the Five Ks, the most prominent of all features of the modern Khalsa, can be interpreted as a positive requirement, and at a Khalsa initiation ceremony the candidate is instructed always to observe these symbols of the faith. They must unfailingly be worn and to neglect to do so represents a serious lapse of Khalsa discipline. In the same way the four cardinal prohibitions (*kurahit*) are regarded as serious infringements and must always be avoided.[13] Committing any of these similarly represents a gross breach of discipline.

The banning of tobacco is increasingly recognized as an admirable trait by the rest of society, but two of the other provisions have caused some concern. The first of these is the refusal to cut one's hair and, in consequence, the obligation to wear turbans by at least the male members of the Khalsa. The second is the compulsory wearing of a *kirpān* for all members of the initiated Khalsa. Both issues are covered in Chapter 10.[14]

Other ethical rules are spelt out for the Khalsa Sikh at the time of taking initiation. *Sikh Rahit Maryādā* expresses the obligation as follows:

> You must renounce your former lineage, occupation and religious affiliation. This means that you must put aside all concern for caste status, birth, country and religion, for you are now exclusively a member of the sublime Khalsa. You must worship only Akal Purakh, spurning all other gods, goddesses, incarnations and prophets. You must accept the ten Gurus and their teachings as your only means of deliverance.[15]

The duties of the new initiates are then explicitly named. They must daily observe the Sikh liturgy, and they should also read or hear some additional passages from the Guru Granth Sahib. Initiated Sikhs who cut their hair or Sikhs who smoke are to be avoided, and the Panth is to be sustained by setting aside one tenth of their income for its support. Certain offences are specified as requiring a penance, notably associating with enemies of the Panth and apostate Sikhs. Dyeing one's beard is banned; giving or receiving a cash dowry in exchange for a son's or daughter's hand in marriage is forbidden; and the use of any drugs or intoxicants is prohibited.

These are the obligations specifically laid upon Sikhs who take initiation as members of the Khalsa, and the imposition of the penalty which accompanies any proven violation is entrusted to five worthy Sikhs of the offender's *saṅgat* (the *Pañj Piāre*). The penalty is normally service to the *saṅgat*, particularly the kind which requires manual labour. This, needless to say, describes the ideal and in practice the ideal is all too frequently evaded. It is, however, an ideal which the loyal Sikh tenaciously endeavours to uphold. Of such substance and purport are all ideals, whether religious or otherwise. Sikh ethics and morality are set before the Panth as models to be emulated, and the extent to which they are obeyed is the true test of the Khalsa.

7

WORSHIP, RITUAL AND DISTINCTIVE CUSTOMS

In the late nineteenth and early twentieth centuries the concern of the Tat Khalsa had been greatly exercised by the presence in the Panth of ceremonies that bore a clear Hindu origin and which were (according to the conviction of the Tat Khalsa reformers) quite unacceptable for Sikhs. During the early years of this period the Tat Khalsa searched for an authoritative work that would set out in systematic form the Rahit as it had been delivered to the Panth by Guru Gobind Singh when he inaugurated the Khalsa. None of the extant *rahit-nāmā*s answered this need and it became clear that the Panth would have to compile a new one. The quest finally issued, as we have already seen, in the production of *Sikh Rahit Maryādā*, first published in 1950.

In making use of *Sikh Rahit Maryādā* there are three notes of caution that should be sounded. The first is obvious. It is that the manual offers ideal forms and we should be grossly misled if we believed that every Sikh obeys its injunctions to the letter. *Sikh Rahit Maryādā*, for example, requires every Sikh to arise between the hours of 3 and 6 a.m. and to repeat *Jāpjī Sāhib*, *Jap Sāhib* and the *Ten Savayyās*. It is not realistic to expect every Sikh to observe these instructions fully, and it is likewise naïve to believe that all will heed its banning of alcohol. In other words, *Sikh Rahit Maryādā* represents the Panth's normative pattern, not the actual behaviour of every Sikh.

At the same time, it should be acknowledged that Sikhs obviously do maintain a considerable degree of conformity to its injunctions and some (particularly in old age) are punctilious in discharging them. No one can possibly know the precise extent to which *Sikh Rahit Maryādā* is obeyed, but it is certainly safe to assume that the pattern it stipulates is generally followed. This applies in particular to the various rituals it enumerates.

The second note of caution concerns the existence of Sikh sects, each with its own version of the *rahit-nāmā*. These versions may not have been formally published, but they do exist and in certain significant details they differ from the orthodox *rahit-nāmā* represented by *Sikh Rahit Maryādā*. The Namdharis, for example, conduct their wedding ceremonies around a fire, not around the sacred Granth. These differences (where important) will appear in Chapter 9, dealing with Sikh sects. This present chapter covers the worship and rituals of what may be regarded as the orthodox Sikhs.

The third caution raises the question of just who is a Sikh in the minds of those who were responsible for compiling *Sikh Rahit Maryādā*. It is important to remember that the issue has been vigorously contested in the past and that important remnants of the controversy still remain today.[1] The Rahit which is presented by *Sikh Rahit Maryādā* is, of course, the orthodox Khalsa Rahit and the Sikh ceremonies which are specified are ceremonies approved by the Khalsa. Some of them are acceptable to Sahaj-dhari Sikhs (that is, to Sikhs who do not accept the Rahit), but others are directly formulated for Khalsa Sikhs. For example, the prayer known as *Ardās*, which figures so prominently in Sikh ceremonies, is a Khalsa prayer. Other examples are that children's hair must never be cut, the Five Ks must be intact on a deceased person before cremation, and the ceremony of Khalsa initiation is included in the expectation that it will be observed. In introducing the section on panthic discipline, moreover, it explicitly claims that the Khalsa is the Guru Panth.

From this it follows that *Sikh Rahit Maryādā* is clearly a Khalsa document. The Sikh whom it describes is a Sikh of the Khalsa, whether an Amrit-dhari who has formally taken initiation or a Kes-dhari who keeps the hair uncut without undergoing the initiation ceremony.

Sikh Rahit Maryādā is divided into two parts, with the first portion further subdivided into three. It therefore treats the duty required of Sikhs in four sections. These are:

1. The individual's devotional discipline.
2. Corporate observance.
3. Rituals.
4. Panthic discipline, by which is meant directives which exclusively concern the Khalsa (in particular the rite of Khalsa initiation).

In the treatment which follows, the rite of Khalsa initiation is described with those of the third section. The chapter concludes with two final sections. Gurpurabs and festivals observed by Sikhs is the first of these, and the second describes the principal gurdwaras.

The individual's devotional discipline

For every Sikh there is a personal liturgy that should be observed every day. This is known as the *Nit-nem* or 'Daily Rule' and has three parts. First, he/she should rise between 3 and 6 a.m., bathe, and then chant or sing the following passages from scripture: *Japjī*, *Jāp* and the *Ten Savayyās*. Next, he/she should repeat at sunset the selection known as *Sodar Rahirās*. Finally, he/she should repeat the brief *Sohilā* selection immediately before retiring to bed. At the conclusion of the early-morning and the early-evening orders, the prayer called *Ardās* or 'Petition' is recited.[2] Bathing is essential before the early-morning order, and (if one is strict) hands and feet should be washed before commencing the remaining two orders. For all three orders shoes must be removed and the head covered. *Nit-nem* may be performed as a solitary individual, in a family group or as the member of a gurdwara *saṅgat* (congregation).

Corporate observance

For Sikhs corporate observance centres on the gurdwara, which literally means either 'by means of the Guru's [grace]' or 'the door of the Guru'. A gurdwara is defined as any place which houses the Guru Granth Sahib.[3] If a particular building does not have a copy of the sacred scripture it cannot be a gurdwara. If there is one present, then technically that place is a gurdwara. This may be a room in an ordinary residence, in which case the room is commonly used exclusively as a personal gurdwara. Even where this is not the case, the Guru Granth Sahib must be treated with special consideration. The volume is carefully wrapped in cloth when not in use and is stored in an elevated position.

Gurdwaras range in size from large structures surrounded or beside

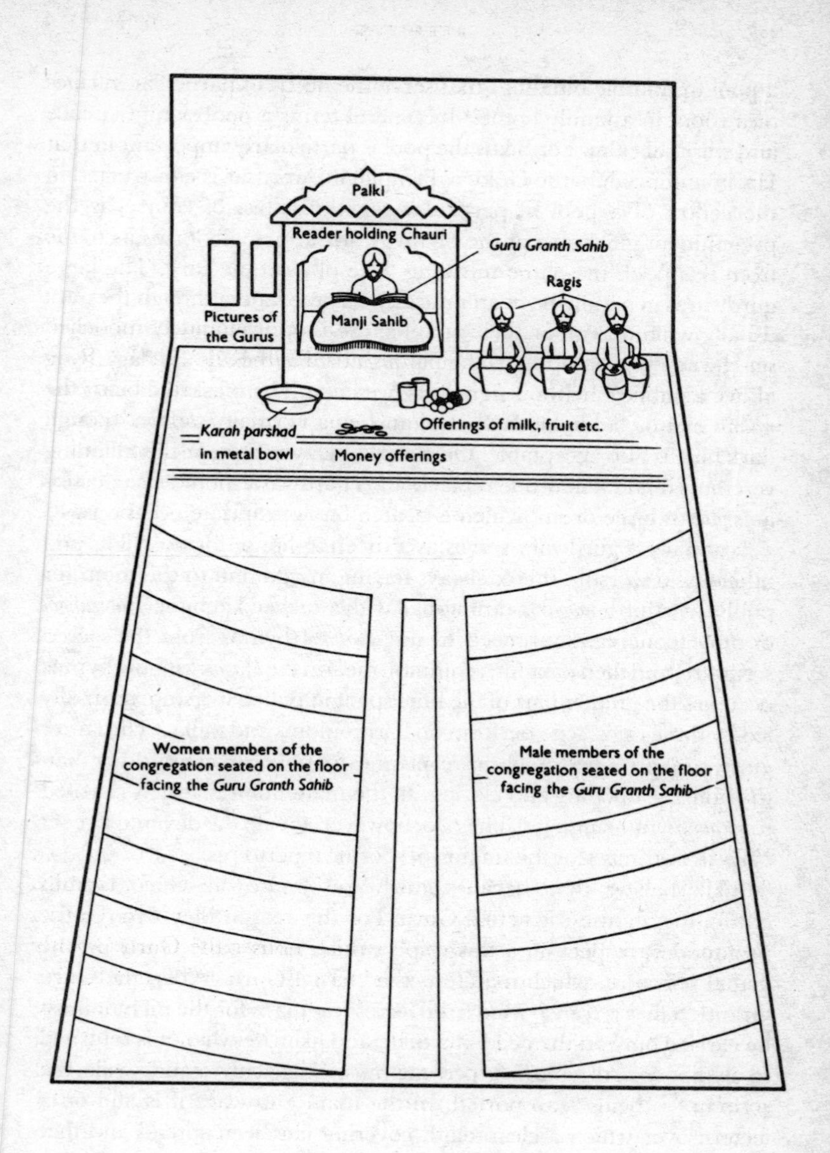

2. Plan of a typical *gurdwara*

a pool to humble buildings that serve the needs of particular villages or a room in a family home.[4] In general terms a pool signifies peace and spiritual calm. For Sikhs the pool is particularly important in that Harimandir Sahib (the Golden Temple) in Amritsar is constructed in the centre of a pool of particular sanctity. This, of course, is the pre-eminent gurdwara of the Sikhs. Amritsar actually takes its name from this pool, the name meaning 'lake of *amrit* (nectar)'. The large gurdwaras generally have an impressive dome, and although they are usually white in colour their architecture is approximately modelled on Harimandir Sahib. A triangular *niśhān sāhib* (the Khalsa flag) flying above a public gurdwara signals its presence. The mast that bears the *niśhān* is also clad in cloth, the colour being normally saffron, though dark blue is also acceptable. On Baisakhi Day each year this cladding is removed and a new one replaces it. A gurdwara should also possess a *nagārā* or large drum, which is beaten on appropriate occasions.

Normally a gurdwara serves as a meeting-house for the Sikhs and others who worship there, always having in addition to the room for public worship a *laṅgar* (a dining-hall with attached kitchen). The *saṅgat* or *divān* (congregation) meets to sing *gurbāṇī* (hymns from the sacred scripture) and then joins for a common meal in the *laṅgar*. Singing hymns occupies the greater part of the time spent in public worship, normally led by three ragis, who perform on harmoniums and tabla.[5] The larger gurdwaras do not normally have set times for public worship, other than the hours of opening and closing. In them attention is largely devoted to *kīrtan* (hymn-singing).[6] They do, however, divide the day into five set *chauṅkīs* ('sittings') for the singing of specific repertoires.

Sikhs believe that, because gurdwaras house the Guru Granth Sahib, they house the actual Guru. For this reason they deserve the profoundest respect, and this respect must focus particularly on the actual scripture, which manifests the eternal Guru. When the Guru Granth Sahib is transported from its resting-place for the night it must be carried only on the head of a Sikh, and likewise when it is returned to its abode. All who are present must reverently stand while the scripture is being transported. In the main gurdwara it is laid on a lectern over which a clean cloth covering has been spread and that has cushions to support it while the bulky volume is opened. Above the lectern is a canopy and the unopened scripture is covered with a mantle. Thus installed, the scripture is then ritually opened. Every moment that it remains open it is attended by a granthi ('reader') or by some member of the *saṅgat*, armed with a *chaurī*.[7] At the conclusion of each day's service the Guru Granth Sahib is reverently closed.

In addition to being a reader of the Guru Granth Sahib the granthi is usually the custodian of the gurdwara which employs him. In the larger gurdwaras there are several other functionaries appointed to assist him. His tasks involve the upkeep of the building, the responsibility for regular services, and respectful attendance on the Guru Granth Sahib. Although these duties will seem in a general sense to be similar to those of a Protestant clergyman, a granthi is not ordained, nor is any other religious functionary of the Sikhs. Sikhism is strictly a lay organization, by which is meant that Sikhs do not believe in ordination and there are no Sikh clergy. References in the popular press to Sikh 'clergy' or 'priests' are mistaken usages.

Granthis are, however, required to undergo training for their position and the SGPC maintains a college for this purpose. Potentially the office is one that calls for dedication by the holder and respect from others, though it would not be correct to assume that all Sikhs have acknowledged this. The position of a granthi is not generally regarded as high-status employment, a situation which reflects popular opinion rather than the dignity of the task. The office is open to women as well as men, though in actual fact practically all granthis are men.

Before entering a gurdwara, everyone (Sikh and non-Sikh) must cover their heads and shoes should be removed. Socks may be worn on condition that they have been used for no purpose other than visiting a gurdwara. Feet, if unclean, should be washed. The first duty of a Sikh upon entering a gurdwara must be to bow before the Guru Granth Sahib, the forehead touching the floor (*mathā ṭekṇā*).[8] The assembled *saṅgat* should then be greeted with palms joined (the customary Indian form of respectful greeting) and with the salutation *Vāhigurūjī kā Khālsā, Vāhigurūjī kī fateh* ('Hail to the Guru's Khalsa! Hail the Guru's victory!').[9] He/she then takes his/her seat, facing the Guru Granth Sahib. In the gurdwara everyone must sit at a lower level than the Guru Granth Sahib, which almost invariably means on the floor, the position of respect in India. Some gurdwaras in Western countries did import chairs (with, of course, an even more elevated position for the scripture), but almost all of these have now reverted to the Punjabi custom of sitting on the floor. There is in most gurdwaras a broad aisle leading from the main entrance to the Guru Granth Sahib at the opposite end of the hall. Men usually sit on the right side and women on the left, though this distinction is not mandatory. Walking around the Guru Granth Sahib or the actual gurdwara should be done in a clockwise direction.

People of any faith, nationality or caste may enter a gurdwara, provided they always show due respect to the Guru Granth Sahib. When they enter they should not bring with them tobacco, alcohol or other intoxicants. The one restriction which is maintained with regard to access is that only Amrit-dhari Sikhs (i.e. initiated Sikhs) are permitted to enter that part of a *takhat* that possesses a particular sanctity.[10] In an ordinary gurdwara no distinction is made between Sikhs and non-Sikhs, nor is any discrimination permitted on grounds of caste or status. A Sikh service of worship cannot, of course, be conducted by a non-Sikh.

The same freedom applies to the *laṅgar*, introduced into Sikh usage to demonstrate that all castes have equal access to liberation. When seated for a meal in the *laṅgar* all must sit in status-free lines (*paṅgat*). High status should not be claimed by sitting forward nor inferior status implied by a position further back. The only qualification is that an Amrit-dhari Sikh who shares a plate *(thālī)* can eat only from one used by another Amrit-dhari. Meat, chicken and fish are never served in a *laṅgar*, not because all Sikhs are vegetarian (many certainly are not), but because those who are may regard the provision of non-vegetarian food as an offensive custom.

Participants in gurdwara worship are free to come and go as they please. A person may stay there for a lengthy period or he/she may simply pay obeisance to the Guru Granth Sahib and depart at once. The usual order of service for gurdwaras which remain open for only a limited period is as follows: ritual opening of the Guru Granth Sahib; extended *kīrtan*; perhaps *kathā* (a hermeneutic or hortative sermon); certain verses from Guru Amar Das's hymn *Anand Sāhib*; *Ardās*; the two salutations;[11] and a final *hukam*. A *hukam* (also called a *vāk*) is taken by opening the Guru Granth Sahib at random and reading the hymn which appears at the head of the left-hand page. If its beginning appears on the preceding page the reader should turn back and start from that point. *Kīrtan* consists of singing passages from the Guru Granth Sahib or from the works of Guru Gobind Singh. The only additional works permitted in a gurdwara are those by Bhai Gurdas and Nand Lal.[12] *Kīrtan* is led by three ragis (hymn-singers), but members of the *saṅgat* are free to join in the singing.

Sikh families are encouraged to maintain a gurdwara in their own houses, a room or a screened portion which is set aside for this exclusive purpose. Each Sikh, in his own gurdwara, is expected to engage in reading the Guru Granth Sahib every day and daily to 'take a *hukam*' in the manner indicated above. A recommended practice is for each Sikh to read right through the entire scripture of 1,430 pages by daily instalments. This should take him/her between four and eight weeks. Other periods are also recommended. It may be only one week (*saptāhak pāṭh*) or it may be as long as a year.

Particular sanctity attaches to an *akhaṇḍ pāṭh* or unbroken reading of the Guru Granth Sahib. This should take approximately forty-eight hours. The *akhaṇḍ pāṭh* is undertaken for some special occasion such as the marriage of a daughter or the opening of a new shop. A team of competent readers is assembled and they prepare for the reading with the following ceremony. *Kaṛāh prasād* is brought into the presence of the Guru Granth Sahib, the six appointed stanzas of *Anand Sāhib* are read, *Ardās* is recited, and a *hukam* is taken. The reading then begins. As it draws to its end, relations and friends are invited to participate in the *bhog* ('consummation') ceremony. This involves the same order as the introduction, consisting of the stanzas from *Anand Sāhib*, *Ardās*, and 'taking a *hukam*'.

One difference from the introductory ceremony involves the distribution to all who have assembled of *kaṛāh prasād*. The *kaṛāh prasād* had been brought into the presence of the Guru Granth Sahib when first the reading was initiated, and now, as a part of the concluding order, it is distributed to all present. *Kaṛāh prasād* means 'sacred food which is prepared in an iron pan'. Its origins in the Panth are not known, nor which Guru introduced it, but presumably it can be directly traced to the Hindu offering of *prasād* in a temple. The practice seems to have been carried over in a modified form from the Hindu custom, with the Guru Granth Sahib, as the divine Word, taking the place of the image wherein divinity is believed to dwell. Its relationship to the Khalsa symbol of iron is, however, firmly maintained.

Kaṛāh prasād is prepared by mixing equal portions by weight of wholemeal flour (*āṭṭā*), sugar and clarified butter (*ghī*). Water equal to the combined weight is added and the preparation is cooked to the accompaniment of the singing or reciting of passages from scripture. When ready it is brought into the presence of the Guru Granth Sahib. The six appointed stanzas from *Anand Sāhib* are read, *Ardās* is recited and the *kaṛāh prasād* is touched with the tip of a *kirpān* to signify that it has been duly sanctified. Portions are then distributed to five worthy Sikhs, representing the Panj Piare. Next comes the person sitting in attendance behind the Guru Granth Sahib, taking care that he/she receives it in a bowl or a cup to ensure that his/her fingers will not soil the scripture. Finally it is distributed among all present, being received in cupped hands and then eaten with the right hand. During this final stage no consideration should be given to differences of caste, nor to those between Sikh and non-Sikh.

Rituals

Sikh rituals were introduced, changed or significantly enlarged during the time of heady controversy at the turn of the twentieth century. The Sanatan Sikhs saw no purpose in initiating a range of new ceremonies which would serve the purpose of distinguishing Sikh from Hindu. Why should the Sikhs not continue to use existing rites? Why, for example, should they not continue to circumambulate the sacred fire when a marriage was being performed? The Tat Khalsa took the opposing view and in the end it was the Tat Khalsa which clearly won. Sikhs were (in their opinion) emphatically not Hindus and a selection of appropriate *rites de passage* would make this clear.

These ceremonies, of course, were not wholly new. The marriage and funeral orders introduced new elements, however, and were given a new direction. *Amrit saṅskār* (Khalsa initiation) certainly retained its existing format, though even here numerous details were added. These ceremonies have now been followed for almost a hundred years and have become firmly established as Sikh practice.

(a) Birth ceremony

The birth of a son is the occasion of much rejoicing, that of a daughter sometimes rather less so. Strict Khalsa members may mark the occasion by a simple ceremony. Soluble sweets (*patāśhā*) or honey are added to water in an iron or steel cup and the water is stirred with a *kirpān* while reciting the prologue and first five stanzas of *Japjī*. A few drops are then administered to the child, the remainder being drunk by the mother. Frequently the mother of the child is kept secluded in her room for thirteen days (a period known as *sūtak* or ritual impurity). *Sūtak*, however, is not approved by normative Sikhism.

(b) Naming ceremony

As soon as the mother is able to rise and bathe she accompanies her family to their gurdwara, taking with them *kaṛāh prasād* or having it prepared on their behalf. If a complete reading of the Guru Granth Sahib has been arranged to celebrate the birth, the visit should be timed to coincide with the *bhog* ceremony.[13] At the gurdwara appropriate passages from the scripture should be sung. The Guru Granth Sahib is then opened at random and a name for the child is chosen, beginning with the same letter as the first composition on the left-hand page. No distinction marks boys' and girls' first names, but to a boy's name 'Singh' must be added and to a girl's name 'Kaur'. The child is thus prepared for eventual entry into the Khalsa. The service concludes with the prescribed six stanzas of *Anand Sāhib* and *Ardās*.

(c) Tying a turban

In many families, when a boy reaches the age of eleven or twelve, he is taken to a gurdwara and there, in the presence of the Guru Granth Sahib and following *Ardās*, his first turban is ceremonially tied on by the granthi or by an elderly Sikh. Two purposes are served by this ceremony. First, it designates the respect with which the turban is regarded. Secondly, it demonstrates the significance of the male line in Sikh families.

(d) *Amrit saṅskār* or *khaṇḍe dī pāhul*: the rite of Khalsa initiation

Khalsa initiation is open to anyone who lives a worthy life and who affirms belief in the principles represented by the Khalsa. It is not limited to Punjabis. At the place of initiation an open copy of the Guru Granth Sahib is required, together with at least seven Amrit-dhari Sikhs, each wearing the Five Ks. One of the seven sits with the Guru Granth Sahib and another stands at the door, while the remaining five (the Panj Piare) administer the actual initiation. Men or women may serve in either capacity, though in fact the responsibility is almost always assumed by males. Prior to the ceremony they should bathe and wash their hair. The five who are to conduct the initiation should be physically sound, possessing both eyes, ears, legs and arms, and they should be free from chronic diseases. No one who has been convicted of transgressing the Rahit should be selected.

Those who are to receive initiation must be old enough to understand the meaning of the ceremony. They too should bathe, wash their hair and appear wearing the Five Ks. No symbols associated with any other religion may be worn, nor are ear-rings and nose ornaments acceptable. Prior to receiving initiation the initiants should stand reverently before the Guru Granth Sahib with palms joined.

One of the five officiants then addresses them on the faith they are to serve, and after an appropriate prayer which looks forward to the preparation of *amrit*[14] a *hukam* is taken. The officiants place a large iron bowl on a pedestal and, pouring in fresh water, they add soluble sweets. They then adopt the 'heroic posture' (*bīr āsan*), kneeling around the bowl with the right knee placed on the ground and the left knee kept upright.

Next the following compositions are recited: *Japjī*, *Jāp*, the *Ten Savayyās*, *Benatī Chaupaī*, and the six prescribed stanzas from *Anand Sāhib*.[15] The person reciting them should do so with his left hand placed on the rim of the bowl, using his right hand to stir the *amrit* with a two-edged sword (*khaṇḍā*). The other four keep both hands on the bowl, with their eyes fixed on the *amrit*. When the appointed passages have been completed, one of the officiants should recite *Ardās*. The candidates should then adopt the 'heroic posture' and each should cup his/her hands, placing the right hand over the left. Five times a handful of *amrit* is given and is drunk by the candidate, the officiant each time calling out, '*Vāhigurūjī kā Khālsā! Vāhigurūjī kī fateh!*'[16] Each time the recipient, after drinking the *amrit*, will reply with the same words. His/her eyes are then touched with the *amrit* five times, and five times it is sprinkled on his/her hair. Each time the officiant repeats the same greeting and each time the candidate replies with the same words. Any *amrit* which is left is consumed by the candidates, all drinking in turn from the same vessel.

After this the five officiants impart the Name of Vahiguru to the initiates by saying in unison the Basic Credal Statement (the *Mūl Mantra*), requiring the initiates to repeat it after them.[17] One of them then expounds to the initiates the meaning of the Rahit, which they are undertaking to obey. Among its several injunctions are a promise always to keep the Five Ks and scrupulously to avoid the four cardinal prohibitions (*kurahit*). The four *kurahit* are:

1. Cutting one's hair or having it cut.
2. Consuming meat which has been slaughtered according to the Muslim rite (*halāl* meat, or *kuṭṭhā*[18]).
3. Extra-marital sexual intercourse.
4. Using tobacco.

The initiants are also urged to have no dealings with other initiated Sikhs who cut their hair, or with Sikhs who smoke. They should regard it as a duty always to support the Panth, setting aside one tenth of their earnings (*das-vaṇḍh*) for the Guru's service. A list of offences against the Rahit which warrant a penance is given. This includes associating with those who can be regarded as belonging to one of the Five Reprobate Groups believed to have been denounced by Guru Gobind Singh.[19] It also specifies eating from the same dish as a person who has not received Khalsa initiation or is an apostate Sikh (*patit*); dyeing one's beard; giving or receiving a cash dowry; and consuming any drug or intoxicant.

At the conclusion of this homily, one of Panj Piare recites *Ardās* and a sixth member, sitting in attendance with the Guru Granth Sahib, takes a *hukam*. Any of the newly initiated who does not have a name chosen from the Guru Granth Sahib is renamed and the ceremony concludes with the distribution of *kaṛāh prasād*, all newly initiated Sikhs receiving it from the same dish.

The ritual of Khalsa initiation demonstrates Tat Khalsa influence at its greatest. In funeral rites, the influence of the Tat Khalsa theorists has been limited, as has that of *Sikh Rahit Maryādā* which is a result of that influence. Ancient Indian customs have proved much stronger. The authority of the Tat Khalsa has, however, been considerably greater as far as the Anand marriage ceremony is concerned; and for the rite of Khalsa initiation (the ritual which concerns the Sikhs alone) it has been complete.

(e) The Anand marriage ceremony

This was the ceremony which generated the fiercest dispute in the days of Singh Sabha controversy. The warmth of the debate was quite understandable, for it is through the celebration of marriage that the Tat Khalsa could most conspicuously declare the separation of the Sikhs from their Hindu neighbours. The Tat Khalsa eventually won and the Anand Marriage Act became law in 1909.

The first step in arranging a marriage is for the parents of a son or (usually) a daughter of marriageable age to ask some relative (known as a *bicholā*) to find a suitable spouse. Working very quietly, the *bicholā* will make inquiries concerning the suitability of various young people, together with details concerning the status and reputation of their families. The *bicholā* will normally only investigate possibilities who match the caste profile of the boy or girl.[20] When a suitable candidate has been located, the girl's parents will ask for a meeting to be arranged at which they can 'see' the boy (*muṇḍā dekhṇā*). The son's family will also view the girl and if either the boy or the girl is not satisfied with the tentative choice it is usually cancelled and another search begun.

If, however, both are agreeable the date of the wedding is fixed. Although a betrothal (*kuṛmāī*) is not essential, it may be arranged if both families are agreeable. For a betrothal the two families should assemble at the groom's residence in the presence of the Guru Granth Sahib or at the local gurdwara. After *Ardās* has been offered, the girl's family should present to the prospective husband a *kirpān*, a steel wrist-ring (*kaṛā*) and some Indian sweets (*miṭhiāī*).

The day before the marriage, the groom proceeds with his *barāt* (wedding party) to the bride's house or the gurdwara where the marriage is to take place, there to be received by the bride's family in the *milṇī* or ritual greeting ceremony. *Ardās* is recited and is followed by the giving of gifts by the bride's family to the groom and his family. The identity of both the givers and the receivers is inscribed in detail by custom, as is the nature of the gifts. Following the *milṇī* ritual the marriage ceremony begins.

Sikh Rahit Maryādā commences its section on the Anand marriage by specifying various conditions. No account should be taken of caste; a Sikh girl should be married only to a Sikh husband; and Sikhs should not be married as children. This is an ideal arrangement. In actual fact the vast majority of Sikh marriages take careful account of the prospective partner's caste, and marriages between Sikhs and Hindus frequently take place in the case of Khatri or Arora families.[21] The manual then states that no account should be taken of auspicious days in arranging the actual date. The consulting of horoscopes should be avoided and such customs as the worship of ancestors or the burning of ritual fires should be spurned. This cluster of objections is aimed squarely at Hindu conventions.

For the marriage, the congregation assembles in the presence of the Guru Granth Sahib.[22] *Kīrtan* is sung either by members of the *saṅgat* or by ragis. The bride and bridegroom should be seated in front of the Guru Granth Sahib, the bride on the groom's left. The person conducting the marriage ceremony instructs the couple to stand, together with their parents or guardians, and begins the service by reciting *Ardās*. He then instructs the couple in the teachings of Gurmat, first jointly and then individually. To signify their assent to the injunctions they both bow before the Guru Granth Sahib.

The bride's father or senior relative then places in her hand the hem of one of the garments worn by the bridegroom (normally a light scarf or sash). This action, known as *palla-phaṛāṇa* or 'giving the hem', is highly emotional for the girl's father, signifying as it does the final surrendering of his daughter (*kaniādān*). Guru Ram Das's *Sūhī Chhant* 2, the *lāvān* hymn, is then sung by the person serving as reader.[23] After each of the four stanzas the couple walk clockwise around the Guru Granth Sahib, the bridegroom followed by the bride, who continues to hold his hem. While they are doing this the *saṅgat* repeats the stanza. After completing the first three rounds the couple prostrate themselves before the Guru Granth Sahib and then stand erect to hear the next stanza. After prostrating themselves again after the final stanza they resume their seats. The hymn-singers follow with the six appointed stanzas from *Anand Sāhib* and the ceremony finally concludes with *Ardās* and the distribution of *kaṛah prasād*.

The wedding-feast then follows, after which the groom and his father proceed to the bride's house and collect all the items of the dowry. The bride changes into clothes which have been brought by the groom's family and she is escorted out of the house, in theory to mount the *ḍolī*. The *ḍolī* is strictly a sedan chair, though nowadays a car will serve the purpose. This symbolizes the final departure from her natal home as she proceeds to join her husband's family. After one night at his residence she returns again to her natal home with her husband. Finally there is the *muklāvā*, the permanent return to the husband's home and the consummation of the marriage. This can vary between a day later and several years, depending on the age at which the marriage took place.[24]

(f) The death ceremony (*antam saṅskār* or *miratak saṅskār*)

Every corpse should be cremated. If this should prove to be impossible it is permissible to dispose of a corpse by casting it into a river or the sea or by some other means. The corpse should be bathed and clad in clean garments, complete with all the Five Ks. After it is laid on a bier, *Ardās* is recited and it is then carried by male relatives to the cremation ground. Women do not enter the cremation ground. *Ardās* is again recited upon arrival and the body is laid on the pyre prepared for the purpose.[25] The pyre is lit by a son, relative or close friend while the *saṅgat* which has accompanied the body sings hymns appropriate to a funeral. When the pyre is well ablaze *Kīrtan Sohilā* is sung, followed by another recitation of *Ardās*. In Western countries the rite has necessarily been adapted to local convention by placing the body in a coffin and transporting it in a hearse to a crematorium. The lighting of the pyre is replaced by the chief mourner pushing the button which consigns the coffin and body to the furnace. Coffins are not a feature of normal Sikh burials and their introduction, though necessary, has caused some dismay among those brought up in India.

After the cremation the ashes of the body should be recovered from the pyre and either cast on running water or buried at the place of cremation. *Sikh Rahit Maryādā* begins and ends the funeral procedure by specifically forbidding practices associated with Hindu custom, once again implicitly making the point that Sikhs are not to be regarded as Hindus. One practice which is sternly forbidden is gathering the residual bones after cremation and depositing them at sacred locations in the Ganga, the Satluj or the Ravi rivers. This too is an injunction largely ignored by Sikhs. Many take the ashes for immersion (with the assistance of Brahmans) in the Ganga at Hardwar, and many more scatter the ashes on the Satluj river near Kiratpur at the place where Guru Hargobind died.

When the cremation is over, a complete reading of the Guru Granth Sahib should be begun, and should (if possible) be finished within ten days. If the deceased was the head of a family a ceremony called *pagarī* ('turban') is performed. The eldest son of the deceased receives from a maternal uncle a turban, symbolizing his assumption of his father's role as head of the family.

Panthic discipline

(a) Panthic injunctions

When *Sikh Rahit Maryādā* speaks of the Panth it means the Guru Panth, one of the two receptacles to receive the function and authority of the Guru when the last personal Guru died in 1708. The other receptacle was the sacred scripture which is construed to mean the Adi Granth and the works of Guru Gobind Singh. This particular receptacle creates the problem of defining just what constitutes the works of Guru Gobind Singh, but at least there is no difficulty with regard to the first one. As far as *Sikh Rahit Maryādā* is concerned, the bounds of the Guru Panth are clearly and distinctly drawn. For *Sikh Rahit Maryādā* the Guru Panth is identified with the Khalsa; and the Khalsa comprises only those Sikhs who have been initiated and who diligently uphold the Rahit. Loyal Amrit-dhari Sikhs constitute the Khalsa and the Khalsa is the Guru Panth.

The Khalsa, defined in this narrow sense, is therefore authorized to pronounce upon matters of fundamental religious importance to Sikhism, and to adopt measures for the proper protection of the Sikh religion. How are these pronouncements made? What Khalsa organization actually makes them? By what authority can it insist that they are obeyed?

A panthic injunction can be promulgated only in connection with issues which concern the fundamental tenets of the Sikh religion. These are defined as the dignity and status of the Gurus and the Guru Granth Sahib, the correctness of the sacred text, the form of the initiation ceremony, the content of the Rahit, the organization of the Panth and matters of like importance. Other lesser issues should be settled by local *saṅgat*s without recourse to religious sanctions.[26] The injunction is known as a *gurmatā* ('the will of the Guru') and is promulgated to the Panth as a *hukam-nāmā*. From the sixth Guru onwards, *hukam-nāmā*s on a wide range of issues were issued to various *saṅgat*s, coming direct from the Guru himself. Today they concern the whole Panth and are used very rarely, though on occasion one has been promulgated. When Teja Singh, the founder of the Bhasaur Singh Sabha, became too extreme for the Khalsa, he was banished from the Panth in 1928 by means of a *hukam-nāmā*. In 1978 serious trouble developed when thirteen Sikhs were shot by Sant Nirankaris at a demonstration in Amritsar, and as a result a *hukam-nāmā* was issued forbidding Sikhs to have any relationships with the perpetrators.

The actual *hukam-nāmā* is delivered from Akal Takhat, having first been resolved as a *gurmatā* by 'the supreme council (*jathā*) of the Guru Panth or by a plenary assembly of the Guru Panth'.[27] In practice this means that today the SGPC decides such issues. The SGPC is chosen by an electorate consisting of all Sikhs in good standing (Amrit-dhari, Kes-dhari and Sahaj-dhari), but its elected membership is exclusively Amrit-dhari. It is, in fact, the ultimate authority in the Sikh religion – at least such is the view expressed by *Sikh Rahit Maryādā*. We shall return to this question of ultimate authority in the final chapter.

(b) The imposing of penances

An offence against the Rahit by an Amrit-dhari Sikh is called a *tanak͟hāh*, and the person guilty of committing one is known as a *tanakhāhīā*. The Amrit-dhari Sikh has promised to obey the Rahit and therefore recognition of the offence is essential whenever the Rahit is violated. Some of these *tanakhāhs* are spelt out explicitly in the order for *amrit saṅskār*. Others are determined by the local *saṅgat* or by the Panth as a whole under the *amrit saṅskār* rubric which reads, 'Neglecting to fulfil any part of the Rahit.'

An Amrit-dhari who is deemed to have committed such an offence is required to appear before the local *saṅgat* and to confess his fault. In the presence of the Guru Granth Sahib the *saṅgat* should choose five worthy representatives (the Panj Piare), who will investigate the nature of the offence and recommend a penance. This should take the form of service to the *saṅgat*, which involves manual labour (such duties as sweeping the gurdwara, cleaning the shoes of worshippers and washing utensils in the *laṅgar*). After a penance is awarded, *Ardās* should be recited.

Any Kes-dhari Sikh who trims or shaves his/her hair, or any Amrit-dhari Sikh who is guilty of one of the four cardinal prohibitions (the *kurahit*[28]) is branded a *patit* or apostate Sikh. (This, at least, is the definition contained in the draft Sikh Gurdwaras Bill of 1986.) A serious view is taken of committing any of the *kurahit* and there are several exclusions levelled against Patit Sikhs in *Sikh Rahit Maryādā*. In fact very few Sikhs are formally branded as Patits, but the category is important as it is a constant reminder of the Panth's view of such grave deeds. A Patit may confess, promise not to continue the deed and receive a penance. After the penance has been awarded the reformed Patit should seek Khalsa initiation again.

Gurpurabs and festivals

Gurpurabs are anniversaries of significant events associated with the Gurus, celebrated on lunar dates of the Indian calendar. Three are of particular importance. These are Guru Nanak's birthday (traditionally observed on a date in November); the birthday of Guru Gobind Singh (late December or early January); and the martyrdom of Guru Arjan (late May or early June). Numerous other gurpurabs are also celebrated, though none with quite the same éclat as these three. Major gurdwaras are festooned and Sikhs flock to them for the festivity or the mourning of the occasion. The practice was greatly encouraged by reformers during the Singh Sabha days, and throughout the twentieth century the gurpurabs have occupied special places in the Sikh calendar.

Festivals are not really different from gurpurabs in the manner in which they are celebrated. They too centre on the gurdwaras, which are arrayed for the occasion, and Sikhs visit them to pay their respects to the Guru Granth Sahib. Two festivals have a particular importance and popularity, both of them celebrated by Hindus but with different reasons offered by the Sikhs for observing them.

One is Baisakhi (or Vaisakhi), the New Year festival held on the first day of the month of Baisakh (March/April). Technically the new year commences a month earlier, but the villagers regard Baisakhi as the appropriate date for the beginning, marking the end of the previous agricultural cycle and the start of a new one. Guru Amar Das took over the existing Baisakhi festival and made it a day for visiting the Guru. Its importance was greatly increased by the fact that Guru Gobind Singh chose this day for the inauguration of the Khalsa, an occasion when large numbers of the Panth would be visiting Anandpur Sahib. As always the festival is marked by visits to gurdwaras and a general rejoicing. Baisakhi is also the occasion for many Sikhs to be initiated into the Khalsa.

The other important festival is Divali, the Festival of Light, held on the day of the new moon in the month of Kattak (October/November). The occasion has long been celebrated by Hindus, with the theme of material wealth. Accounts are closed for the year, houses are cleaned, sweets are distributed and countless lights are lit at night. Sikhs impart a distinctive meaning to it by commemorating the release of Guru Hargobind from Gwalior, where he had been imprisoned by the Mughal emperor Jahangir. Celebrations centre on Harimandir Sahib (the Golden Temple) in Amritsar, which is illuminated for the occasion.

A third festival of some importance, one which is limited to the Sikhs alone, is Hola Mahalla, which takes place on the 1st of Chet (March/April). This is held on the day following the festival of Holi and is said to have been started in order to direct the attention of Sikhs away from what was plainly a Hindu occasion. The instituting of the festival is attributed to Guru Gobind Singh, providing an opportunity for his Sikhs to engage in military exercises. This is possible, though the Sikhs were celebrating Holi into the nineteenth century. Hola Mahalla was evidently elevated to its present status by the reformers of the Tat Khalsa. The festival is still celebrated at Anandpur with martial competitions and a mock battle in which the Nihang Sikhs participate energetically.

Other annual festivals that are observed by Sikhs are Lohri, a festival marking the end of the short winter, held at night on the last day of the month of Poh (January); Basant Panchmi, a spring festival held in the month of Magh (January/February); and Rakhari or Raksha Bandhan, held on the full-moon day of the month of Saun (August), on which a girl ties a ribbon on her brother's wrist, and he promises to defend her honour throughout his life. All three of these festivals are observed by both Sikhs and Hindus.

The Tat Khalsa reformers approved of these festivals, particularly the first three. They were not so pleased about the monthly festivals, however, as these seemed to be examples of Hindu superstition. The fondness for them has nevertheless remained too great and each month Sangrand, Puran-mashi and Amavas are duly celebrated. Sangrand is the first day of the month, observed as highly auspicious by the Panth. Bathing in the pool surrounding Harimandir Sahib is particularly favoured as many Sikhs believe that this confers health and prosperity during the remainder of the month. Puran-mashi is the day of the full moon and marks the end of the lunar month. And Amavas is the night of the new moon, the last night of the 'dark' fortnight when the moon is waning and followed by a 'light' fortnight when the moon is waxing. All three festivals are regularly observed.

The principal gurdwaras

There is an enormous number of public gurdwaras, particularly in the Punjab. Until the eighteenth century the term 'dharamsala' was used for a building or a room where a *saṅgat* gathered for *kīrtan* (hymn-singing), the label 'gurdwara' being reserved for those structures which commemorated some episode from the life of a Guru. Gradually, though, 'gurdwara' supplanted 'dharamsala' and became the general term. Those which commemorate some event in a Guru's life are normally designated now as 'historic' gurdwaras, as opposed to most of the remainder, which provide a meeting-place for a local *saṅgat* or *divān*.

Five of the 'historic' gurdwaras fulfil a special role in the Panth, that of discharging a temporal role as opposed to the spiritual function of all other gurdwaras. These are the *takhat*s, headed by Akal Takhat opposite Harimandir Sahib in Amritsar, where the Sarbat Khalsa would gather for its biannual meetings during the eighteenth century. Akal Takhat is the supreme *takhat* of the Sikh faith and from its balcony all matters of vital importance to the Panth as a whole are promulgated. Each of the remaining four is located at a place important in the life of Guru Gobind Singh. These *takhat*s are Harimandir Sahib in Patna (marking his birthplace), Kesgarh Sahib in Anandpur (overlooking the spot where the Khalsa was inaugurated), Sri Damdama Sahib in the village of Talvandi Sabo (where he rested following his withdrawal to southern Punjab in 1706) and Sri Hazur Sahib in Nander (the place of his assassination). Until recently there were only four recognized *takhat*s, but in 1966 the SGPC raised the central gurdwara in Damdama Sahib to be a fifth.

The other 'historic' gurdwaras are numerous and it would obviously be impossible to describe them all. Only seven have been selected for brief descriptions here. Today many Sikhs undertake a *gurḍuārā yātrā* (a tour of important gurdwaras associated with the Gurus) in the same way that Hindus might undertake a *tīrath yātrā* (a visit to Hindu sacred places). The gurdwaras listed here are among those they would endeavour to include in their tour.

Harimandir Sahib, the famous Golden Temple in Amritsar, is pre-eminent among gurdwaras. The first building on the site was begun by Guru Ram Das and completed by his son Guru Arjan who, following his compilation of the Adi Granth in 1604, lodged the completed volume in it. The sixth Guru, Hargobind, was compelled to leave Amritsar and Harimandir Sahib, withdrawing to the Shivalik hills. For the remainder of the seventeenth century Amritsar remained in the hands of forces hostile to the line of orthodox Gurus. In the eighteenth century it was the scene of frequent fighting between the Sikhs on the one hand and the Mughals or the Afghans on the other,

3. (*opposite*) The Golden Temple and surroundings

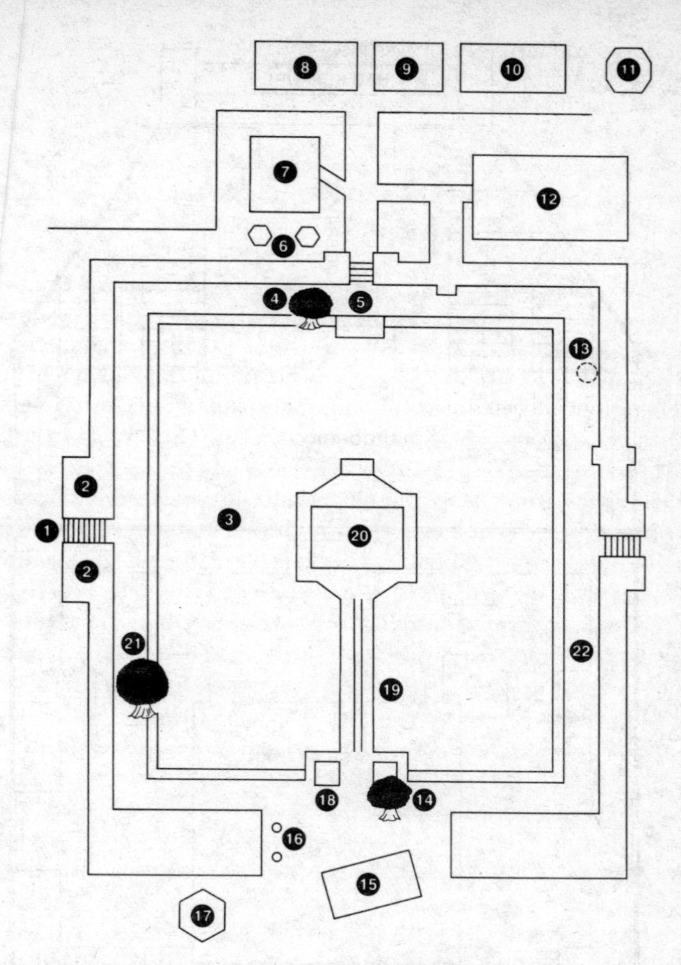

1. *Main entrance and clock tower*
2. *Central Sikh Museum*
3. *Sarovar (pool)*
4. *Dukh Bhanjani Ber (the jujube tree that banishes sorrow)*
5. *Ath Sath Tirath (Shrine of the* 68 *Holy Places)*
6. *Watch towers*
7. *Langar*
8. *Guru Ram Das Serai (guest-house, place of lodging)*
9. *Teja Singh Samundri Hall (SGPC Management Committee Office)*
10. *Guru Nanak Serai*
11. *Baba Atal Gurdwara*
12. *Manji Sahib Diwan (Assembly Hall)*
13. *Baba Dip Singh Shrine*
14. *Lachi Ber (cardamom tree, where a small shrine marks where Guru Arjan is believed to have sat while supervising the digging of the pool)*
15. *Akal Takhat*
16. *Flagstaffs*
17. *Thara Sahib (Shrine of GuruTegh Bahadur)*
18. *Darshani Deorhi (Main Entrance)*
19. *Causeway*
20. *Harimandir Sahib*
21. *Ber Baba Buddha (tree where a marble platform marks where Baba Buddha sat while supervising such tasks as the mixing of mortar during the original building work)*
22. *Parikarama (walk-way around the pool)*

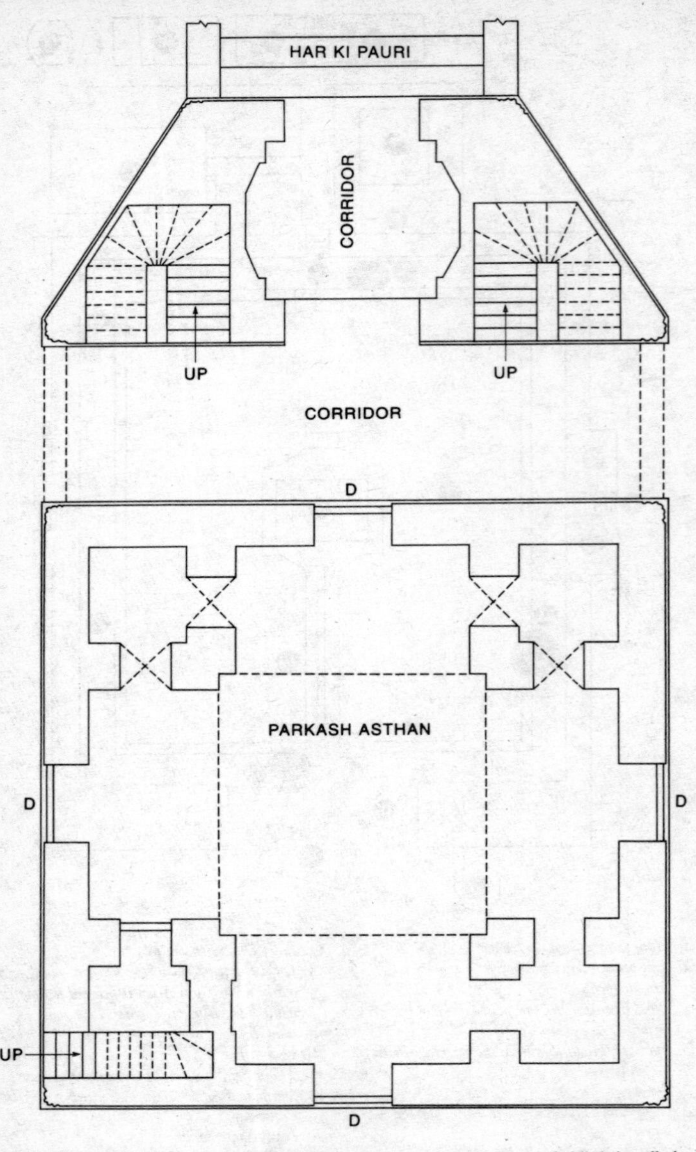

Parkash Asthan: 'The place of light', location where the Guru Granth Sahib is installed.
Har ki Pauri: 'The divine staircase', steps leading down to the pool.

4. Ground plan of the Harimandir Sahib (Golden Temple)

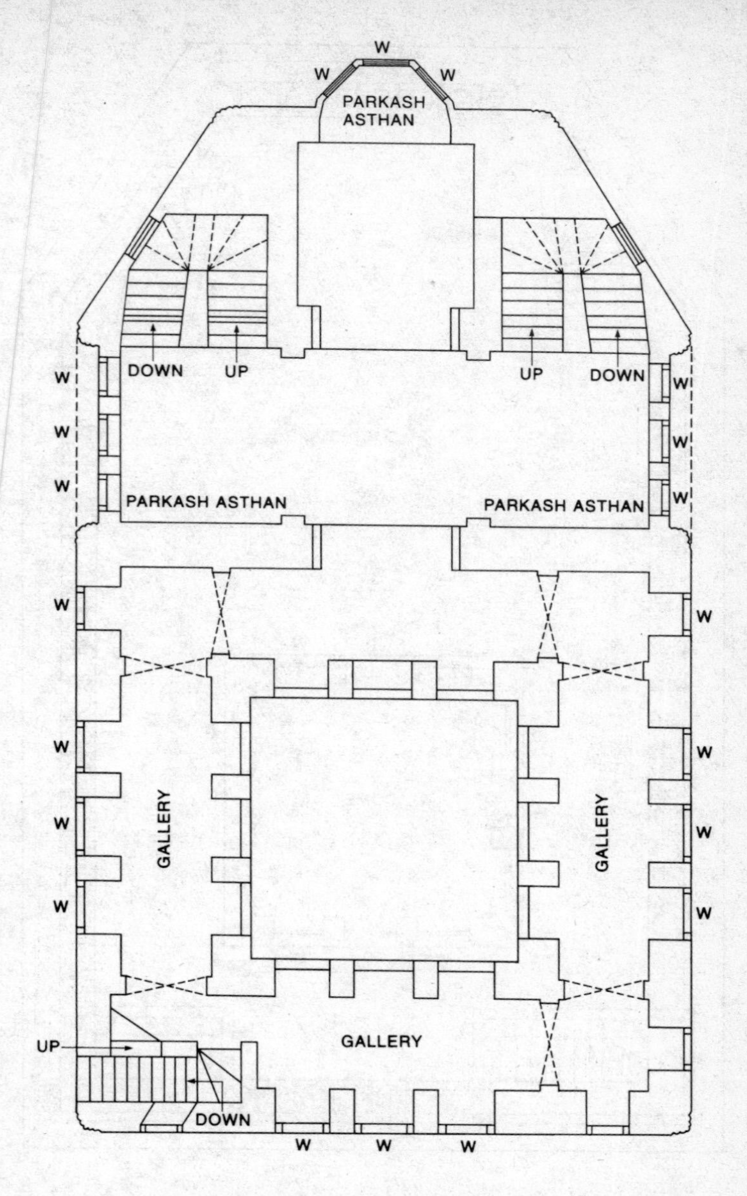

5. Plan of the first floor of the Golden Temple

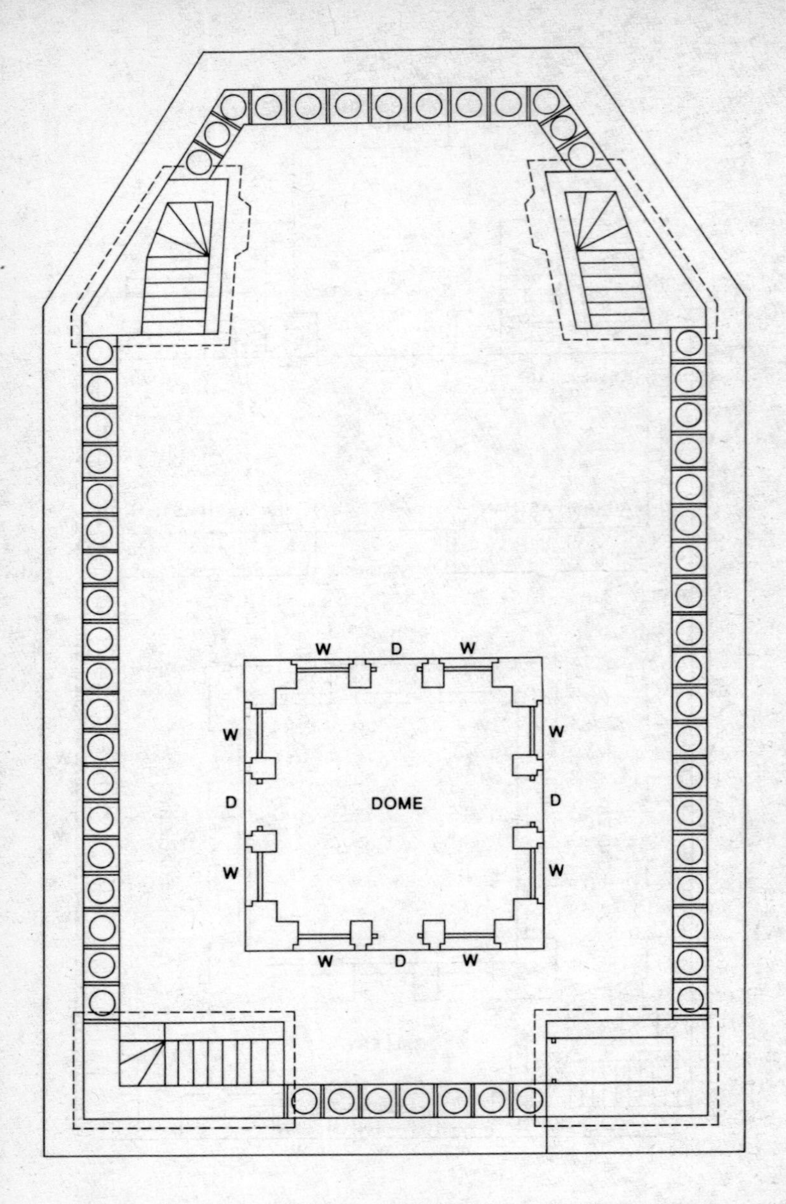

6. Plan of the second floor (terrace) of the Golden Temple

7. Front elevation of the Golden Temple

8. Side elevation of the Golden Temple

and the building housing Harimandir Sahib was periodically damaged.

Eventually peace came to Amritsar. During the early nineteenth century Maharaja Ranjit Singh arranged for gold leaf to be beaten on to its upper two storeys, thereby providing the name (the Golden Temple) by which it is generally known to foreigners. Harimandir Sahib stands in a pool, and opposite the entrance to its causeway is Akal Takhat. As we have already noted, Harimandir Sahib represents the spiritual presence of the Guru while Akal Takhat symbolizes the temporal. The ardour and devotion of the throngs of visitors is exceedingly impressive.

Just as Harimandir Sahib is surrounded by a cluster of smaller gurdwaras, so too is the central shrine in Guru Nanak's birthplace of Talvandi, now called Nankana Sahib. Situated approximately sixty-five kilometres west-south-west of Lahore city, Nankana Sahib is now located in Pakistan. The central shrine is Gurdwara Janam-asthan, reputed to mark the actual spot of Nanak's birth and consequently a place of particular sanctity for Sikhs. Each year the traditional birthday of Nanak is celebrated in Nankana Sahib, with small numbers (being in Pakistan) but with considerable enthusiasm.

Also in Pakistan is the town of Hasan Abdal, on the Grand Trunk Road between Rawalpindi and Peshawar. In Hasan Abdal is located Panja Sahib ('Revered Hand-print'), the gurdwara that commemorates an incident which tradition tells of Guru Nanak's travels. Nanak is said to have stopped with his hand a boulder rolled down the hill by an outraged Muslim dervish who became enraged when Nanak, miraculously opening a spring at the foot of the hill, cut off the dervish's own spring further up the hill. The anecdote is a late entrant into the *Bālā* janam-sakhis, owing its origins to a story which dates from the time of Maharaja Ranjit Singh. Until 1940 the 'impression' of Guru Nanak's palm projected from the rock, and it was evidently only in that year that it was carved into it. The tradition is, however, firmly believed and has produced an impressive gurdwara on the spot. The limpid spring in Hasan Abdal has a pre-Sikh history which has given rise to Buddhist, Hindu and Muslim traditions.

Three gurdwaras particularly merit notice in the Delhi area. Bangla Sahib, near the heart of New Delhi, marks the place where Guru Har Krishan stayed when he visited the Mughal capital in response to a summons from the Emperor Aurangzeb. The gurdwara has been particularly patronized by wealthy Sikhs of the Delhi area and possesses in consequence an impressive group of buildings with the actual gurdwara at the centre. The second of Delhi's gurdwaras is Gurdwara Sis-ganj on Chandni Chowk, near the Old Delhi railway station. This marks the spot where Guru Tegh Bahadur was beheaded by order of Aurangzeb. After the execution the headless body was carried away by a man called Lakkhi Shah to his house in the village of Rakab-ganj (or Rikab-ganj), very near the Houses of Parliament in modern New Delhi. To avoid detection of having taken the body, Lakkhi Shah's whole house, with the body inside, was burnt.

A gurdwara was built on the spot in 1790 by Baghel Singh, one of the raiding chieftains who had briefly taken Delhi, and this was known as Gurdwara Rakab-ganj. In 1913, during the construction of New Delhi, its outer wall was demolished by the government in order to provide a straight road to the Viceregal Lodge. This produced the Rakab-ganj incident in which the government eventually had to give way in response to the widespread protest it raised. The wall was rebuilt in its original position and the road has a permanent bend in it. A handsome modern gurdwara occupies the premises.

The final gurdwara to be described is Kesgarh Sahib in Anandpur, second only in prominence to Harimandir Sahib in Amritsar. It was here, on the edge of the Shivalik hills and overlooking the plains, that Guru Gobind Singh inaugurated the Khalsa. Kesgarh Sahib ranks as one of the five *takhat*s of the Sikhs. Each year it is host to the Hola Mahalla festival, marked by simulated battles and a large procession. It too has numerous subordinate gurdwaras surrounding it.

It should be repeated that this survey covers only seven gurdwaras and that there are many more which might be mentioned. There are, for example, the gurdwaras that house the remaining three *takhat*s, one each in Patna, Damdama and Nander. There are also numerous gurdwaras in the countries to which Sikhs have migrated. Wherever Sikhs go they will endeavour to open a gurdwara as a place where they can gather with others who speak the same language and share the same traditions. The buildings may not be pretentious, but where there are a few Sikhs there one will almost certainly find a gurdwara.

8

SACRED WRITINGS OF THE SIKHS

We have come to a point where we must proceed with particular caution. When the field of study is Religion there is always abundant reason for treading carefully. When it includes a sacred scripture that is profoundly revered, the need becomes pressing. And when that scripture is absolutely central to the belief system in question, the need becomes altogether compelling. Sikhism falls within this latter category. With this caution in mind, the religion of the Sikhs should still be studied and described, though with every care taken to avoid giving needless offence. Every effort must be made to persuade the faithful Sikh that the study is being undertaken with respect, and that even when the results of that research may conflict with the traditional view, those results will be expressed with sensitivity. It is this tone and this intention which must lie behind any examination of the Sikh scriptures.

This caution is particularly necessary in the case of an outsider, though the issue is one that has produced attempts to silence Sikh scholars as well. In recent years charges have been brought against certain Sikhs who have applied the techniques of textual criticism to the Adi Granth and have led to their arraignment before Akal Takhat, the 'Supreme Court' of the Panth. Two who agreed to appear before it were declared *tanakhāhīā*s and were required to undertake the performance of penances. Clearly the field is a very dangerous one in which to work, for Sikhs as well as for others.

The primary issue confronting such a survey is the question of what constitutes a Sikh religious scripture. Everyone agrees that the Adi Granth qualifies handsomely for the title. Substantially compiled by Guru Arjan in 1603–4, the Adi Granth occupies for all Sikhs the absolute centre of their faith, believed to represent the eternal Guru for all time and for that reason known today as the Guru Granth

Sahib (the Granth which is Guru). The Adi Granth can accordingly be accepted as scripture.

So too must the Dasam Granth, although in this case a distinct note of hesitation may be detected. The Dasam Granth was compiled in the early eighteenth century, and although it is traditionally believed to comprise the writings of the tenth Guru, some doubts have obviously made themselves felt. Some of the Dasam Granth seems plainly to be the work of Guru Gobind Singh, but was he responsible for the whole collection? This does not prevent the volume from being scripture and undoubtedly it was accepted in precisely these terms during the eighteenth century. Today, however, it does not rank with the Adi Granth, although the works the Panth universally attributes to Guru Gobind Singh are selectively promoted to this level. The other works in the Dasam Granth are little read and the greater part of the work is largely ignored. It may be scriptural, or it may not be. When pressed for a decision, a Sikh scholar will normally answer that the whole of the Dasam Granth should indeed be regarded as a sacred scripture, yet one has an impression of distinct uneasiness.

At this point we must ask ourselves if we are not creating an unnecessary problem by seeking to fit Sikh writings into a distinctively Western category of scripture. Perhaps the term 'scripture' does not really belong to their religious literature and we are manufacturing a false difficulty by seeking to make it correspond to what is, after all, a Western category. This problem needs only to be raised in order to be set aside. A scripture is a book which is held to be sacred by a particular religion, and if the Adi Granth at least is not held sacred by the Sikhs, the word sacred has no meaning.

The problem is not whether the Sikhs have a scripture or a canon but what deserves to be included in that category. Is it the Adi Granth only, or the Adi Granth plus the works attributed to Guru Gobind Singh, or the addition of the whole of the Dasam Granth? Are the works of Bhai Gurdas and Nand Lal Goya to be included, and if they are, what about the janam-sakhis? And if the janam-sakhis deserve a place, why should the *gur-bilās* literature not find mention? And then there are the *rahit-nāmās*, which deal with that revered subject of religious symbolism, the marks and insignia of the true Khalsa. There is indeed a problem, but it is not one of whether or not the Sikhs have a scripture.

One indicator of what would be regarded as scriptural is perhaps given by the portions of their literature that devout Sikhs learn and recite by heart. This applies to any part of the Adi Granth, though there are some portions which command particular affection in this respect. All Sikhs should, of course, know the *Japjī Sāhib* with which the Adi Granth begins and which is required for early-morning devotions. Not all Sikhs do know it, of course, but a considerable number have learnt it and regularly recite it first thing in the morning after bathing. This they do sitting quietly, preparing breakfast, or on their way to work. A smaller but still considerable number will also know the other passages appointed for devotional purposes, whether for the early-evening prayer (*Sodar Rahirās*) or for the prayer before retiring for the night (*Kīrtan Sohilā*).[1] The devout will also know two lengthy works, *Āsā kī Vār*, which is mainly by Guru Nanak, and Guru Arjan's *Sukhmanī Sāhib*. Beyond these they will know a selection of shorter works, possibly extending to a substantial quantity of the Adi Granth. Clearly the whole of the Adi Granth is regarded as scriptural.

Some of the passages set down for personal devotions, however, come not from the Adi Granth but from the Dasam Granth, all of them works attributed to Guru Gobind Singh. The early-morning order includes his *Jāp Sāhib* and *Ten Savayyās*; and the early-evening order specifies his *Benatī Chaupaī* with *Savayyā* and *Doharā*.[2] This seems to indicate that these works would also be regarded as scriptural. All are from the portions of the Dasam Granth which Sikh opinion generally regards as the work of Guru Gobind Singh, and they are consequently treated as *gurbāṇī* ('compositions of the Guru'). As such they are regarded as scripture, and the same also applies to the other works in the Dasam Granth which are regarded by the overwhelming majority of Sikhs as compositions of Guru Gobind Singh. They are, in other words, those portions of the Dasam Granth which are selectively promoted to equality with the Adi Granth. The remainder of the Dasam Granth is, however, a cause of uncertainty, some affirming that it should definitely be regarded as sacred writ and others adopting a more cautious attitude.

Portions of the Dasam Granth must therefore be regarded with guarded doubt and the same applies even more firmly to the poetic works of Bhai Gurdas and Nand Lal. They may be designated as works suitable for recitation in gurdwaras, but most Sikhs (if confronted with the question of whether or not they are canonical) would feel obliged to answer in the negative. With the janam-sakhis this answer becomes a certainty. The janam-sakhis are hagiographic anecdotes concerning the life of Nanak, and although they are believed to be uplifting, they cannot be classified as scripture. The same applies to the *gur-bilās* works, equally hagiographic in their approach but concentrating on the heroic deeds of the sixth and particularly the tenth Guru. Also outside the boundaries of scripture are the *rahit-nāmā*s.

The Adi Granth

The first of the examples to be considered is the Adi Granth, and this, as we have seen, can firmly and without question be designated a scripture. The primary scripture of the Sikhs is variously referred to as the Granth Sahib, the Adi Granth, the Guru Granth, the Guru Granth Sahib or Adi Sri Guru Granth Sahib. These terms reflect varying attitudes towards the scripture, or at least they do when they are used responsibly. Calling it the Granth Sahib is a term of respect, as the honorific 'Sahib' suggests. 'Sahib' is also attached to important places in Sikh tradition (Amritsar Sahib and Anandpur Sahib, as indeed the locations of all the five *takhat*s) and likewise to gurdwaras of particular sanctity, of which the leading example is Harimandir Sahib or the Golden Temple.

Granth Sahib is therefore a respectful term, but it is not the equivalent of Guru Granth Sahib. The tenth Guru, as we have seen, is believed to have designated the Granth as Guru as well as the Panth, and after his death it was to be the receptacle of the Guru. In calling it the Guru Granth Sahib, the Sikh respectfully acknowledges this status and expresses his belief in an important doctrine of the Panth. It is the 'manifest body of the Guru', the incarnation of the actual presence of the Guru. As such it is treated with the most profound respect.

When, however, the scripture is studied by students rather than by devotees, the title Adi Granth may be preferred. A useful distinction may be invoked here. Whereas Guru Granth Sahib implies (as we have seen) a confession of faith, Adi Granth is a neutral title. *Ādi* means 'first' or 'original' and is used in order to distinguish the volume compiled by Guru Arjan from the later Dasam Granth. The term Adi Granth does not generally appear in common usage by Sikhs. It does, however, appear more frequently as a part of the title by which the printed versions of the scripture are known. The standard title for such versions is the form Adi Sri Guru Granth Sahib.

For historians, philologists and theologians the Adi Granth is a treasure-house which has yet to yield the full store of its riches. In the areas that concern the scholars of these disciplines its resources have been little tapped, a neglect which can be attributed to a variety of reasons. To some extent it may be an ignorance of the richness of its contents. It may also derive from an exaggerated fear of the difficulties which will be encountered, or perhaps from an inadequate recognition of the Panth's importance. There are indeed some major difficulties associated with the text of the Adi Granth, but they are certainly not problems that should inhibit attempts to analyse its language or trace the doctrinal developments it presents.

According to tradition, the Adi Granth was compiled by Guru Arjan during the years 1603–4 CE. To this extent the tradition appears to be well founded. A manuscript bearing the latter date is still in existence and there is no sufficient reason to doubt its authenticity. Tradition also provides an explanation for Guru Arjan's decision to compile this collection of hymns. It is said that his enemies (notably the followers of his eldest brother, Prithi Chand, known as Minas) were circulating spurious works bearing the name of Nanak in order to seduce the Sikhs from their loyalty to the legitimate succession. A group of concerned Sikhs is said to have approached Guru Arjan with this problem, and in order to combat this threat to his authority the Guru decided to prepare an authorized text.

This story may or may not be true. It did not need the intervention of enemies to account for faulty texts (the janam-sakhis abundantly demonstrate this), and if singing the sacred *bāṇī* (hymns) was an important activity for the Nanak-panth (as it certainly was), the Guru who came fifth or thereabouts in the succession would naturally seek to fix the text for his followers to sing. The penalty of failing to do so would be increasing confusion among the ever-widening circle of the

Guru's Sikhs. Arjan was, moreover, bringing an existing collection up to date and substantially increasing it. This collection had been made at the instance of the third Guru, Amar Das, and was contained in the four volumes known as the Goindval or Mohan *pothīs* ('volumes' or 'tomes'). The story of how the Minas were spreading spurious works is possible, but it does not make the most convincing explanation for Arjan's decision to compile a scripture.

For whatever reason, Guru Arjan decided upon a new collection. A first draft was prepared during the years from 1595 onwards, still extant as manuscript 1245 in the Guru Nanak Dev University library. Tradition records that he then established a camp in Ramdaspur (the later Amritsar) in 1603, and to enhance the spiritual peace of the location directed that a pool should be dug. Upon completion it was named Ramsar and beside this pool he supervised the compilation of his authorized version. Just what procedure was followed is not known, but it is evident that the main scribe was the poet and faithful disciple Bhai Gurdas. Hymns included in the Goindval Pothis, together with those of his father and himself, were duly recorded and the bulky manuscript was finally completed in the late summer of 1604. Given the size of the volume (974 large folios), this was no mean task, and one can only assume that the faithful Bhai Gurdas must have been labouring hard. Following its completion, the scripture was then installed in Harimandir, the principal gurdwara of Ramdaspur.

Arjan's principal source was, as we have already seen, a similar collection that tradition ascribes to the third Guru, Amar Das. Although the two extant Goindval Pothis include only the works of the first and third Gurus, it seems reasonable to assume that the compositions of the second Guru were recorded in the missing volume or volumes. This missing portion included the metres in which Guru Angad composed. Also in the extant volumes are the works of other Sants (or, to give them the name by which the Adi Granth knows them, the Bhagats), and it thus provided a substantial nucleus.

The actual copying of the volumes had been done by Amar Das's grandson, Sahans Ram, and at the time when Arjan decided to prepare a second collection they were in the possession of Baba Mohan, the elder son of Amar Das and the father of Sahans Ram. Mohan had, according to tradition, not approved of his father's choice of Ram Das as fourth Guru, and so Arjan, the son of Guru Ram Das, had some difficulty in persuading him to part with the manuscript. His objections were overcome only when Arjan went in person to Goindval and sang a hymn in praise of Mohan outside his window. There is indeed a hymn in the Adi Granth which refers to Mohan, but the context indicates that Akal Purakh is meant.[3] In some way, however, Guru Arjan obtained the manuscript.

This collection, the Goindval Pothis, evidently served as the basis for the new compilation. To these Arjan added his father's works and his own substantial group of compositions. Of the two extant volumes, one is with the family of the late Dalip Chand in Jalandhar City and the other with the family of the late Bhagat Singh in Pinjore (between Chandigarh and Shimla). Both families are Bhallas, the sub-caste to which Guru Amar Das belonged. The text of the Kartarpur version (the version prepared in 1603–4) is very close to that of the Goindval Pothis, particularly the works of the first three Gurus. Arjan is said to have added the works of contemporary Bhagats, although this must have been a very small part of the collection. Almost all of the Adi Granth's *bhagat bāṇī* (hymns of the Bhagats), together with some that are not in the Adi Granth, has been included in the Goindval volumes.

The history of the Adi Granth is reasonably clear as far as its origins are concerned, but unclear with regard to the subsequent history of the original manuscript. During most of the seventeenth and all of the eighteenth centuries the actual location and treatment of the manuscript is obscure. Tradition maintains that it was stolen by Dhir Mal, the grandson of Guru Hargobind and a disappointed candidate for the succession when it went to his brother, Guru Har Rai. Guru Gobind Singh subsequently asked for it to be returned, and when the request was refused he is said to have produced his own copy by dictating the entire contents from memory. To the original text he added compositions by his father, Guru Tegh Bahadur.

If the tradition is to be believed, it means that the later recension containing the works of the ninth Guru was thus created by Guru Gobind Singh. The original version is known as the Kartarpur *bīṛ* (the Kartarpur 'volume' or recension), so-called because Dhir Mal and his successors lived in the small town of Kartarpur near Jalandhar (not the village of Guru Nanak). The version attributed to Guru Gobind Singh is called the Damdama *bīṛ*. A third version is called the Banno *bīṛ*, or rather there exists a version which is traditionally traced to a *bīṛ* called after a person named Banno or Bhai Banno. Tradition also locates it chronologically between the Kartarpur and Damdama *bīṛs*. And tradition stoutly upholds the claims of the concordant Kartarpur and Damdama versions, rejecting Banno with equal firmness. Because of its deviant reputation Banno is also known as the *khārī* ('brackish') *bīṛ*. An alternative explanation derives the name from Khara, the village from which Bhai Banno is said to have come.

There are two accounts available of how the Banno *bīṛ* was produced. One is that Bhai Banno sought permission to take the original scripture to his home village and was granted leave only on condition that he kept it there for only one night. Banno circumvented this provision by stopping frequently on the way to and from his village, making a complete copy, to which he added his extra verses. The other story says that he was commissioned to take the manuscript to Lahore to supervise its binding and did the copying at that time.

Damdama agrees with Kartarpur in all respects, adding only the compositions of Guru Tegh Bahadur and perhaps a couplet that is traditionally regarded as the work of Guru Gobind Singh. As such it is accepted as the 'authorized' version and printed editions reproduce its received text. Banno, diverging from the other two, incorporates a small amount of additional material which the other two versions lack.

The original Damdama version has since been lost, leaving the Kartarpur and Banno versions in disagreement on a few key points. The most important of these led to a lengthy controversy that was only recently settled. A hymn attributed to Guru Arjan appears in full in the Banno version, with only the introductory couplet recorded in the Kartarpur manuscript. In this hymn the author describes the performance of puberty rites for the future Guru Hargobind, and in the course of it he describes the manner in which the child's head was shaved. This challenged a fundamental belief of the strict Khalsa and it was scarcely surprising that the issue should have generated considerable controversy. A careful analysis of the wording and content of the hymn, however, has conclusively demonstrated that it could not have been the work of Guru Arjan and must have been recorded later.[4]

Dhir Mal evidently retained the Kartarpur manuscript in an effort to buttress his claims to the office of Guru, and it must have remained with his family, the Sodhis of Kartarpur, throughout the remainder of the seventeenth century and the whole of the eighteenth. In 1849 it was in the possession of the Lahore court when the annexing British arrived and was restored to Sodhi Sadhu Singh of Kartarpur when he petitioned the British authorities in the Punjab for its return. A copy was respectfully prepared by Sodhi Sadhu Singh and presented to Queen Victoria as a mark of his gratitude.[5]

The real importance attaching to the Adi Granth came with the rise of the Singh Sabha movement in the late nineteenth century and, at almost the same time, the arrival of the printing press. The Singh Sabha reformers laid an insistent emphasis upon the absolute authority of scripture, and the printing press provided them with the means of disseminating it. Copies of the complete volume, with a standard text and pagination, have for many years been available and a large number of Sikh families have at least a *guṭkā* or breviary. A *guṭkā* (or *sundar guṭkā*) contains the complete *Nit-nem* (the Sikh daily liturgy), together with a small selection of other popular works from the Adi Granth.

The place where most observers see a copy of the Adi Granth or the Guru Granth Sahib is in a gurdwara or, to be more precise, in a public gurdwara. When not in use the book is always draped (normally in an expensive *rumālā* or cloth) and lies beneath a canopy. Whenever it is moved it should be carried on the head, and if it is being transported along a road some form of advance warning should be given to ensure that the people who witness its passing may show proper respect. On festival days a copy, mounted on a truck or a bus and properly protected, will figure prominently in the customary procession. The ceremony bears obvious resemblances to the Hindu practice of conducting a procession, the obvious difference being that the Guru Granth Sahib has replaced the Hindu image.

The Adi Granth consists of religious hymns, some of which are classified as *śhabads* and others as *śhaloks*. The *śhabads* are hymns of varying length, a common one being the *chaupad* or hymn of four verses and a refrain. Others have six verses and yet others run to eight. The *śhaloks* are normally couplets, but may run to greater length.

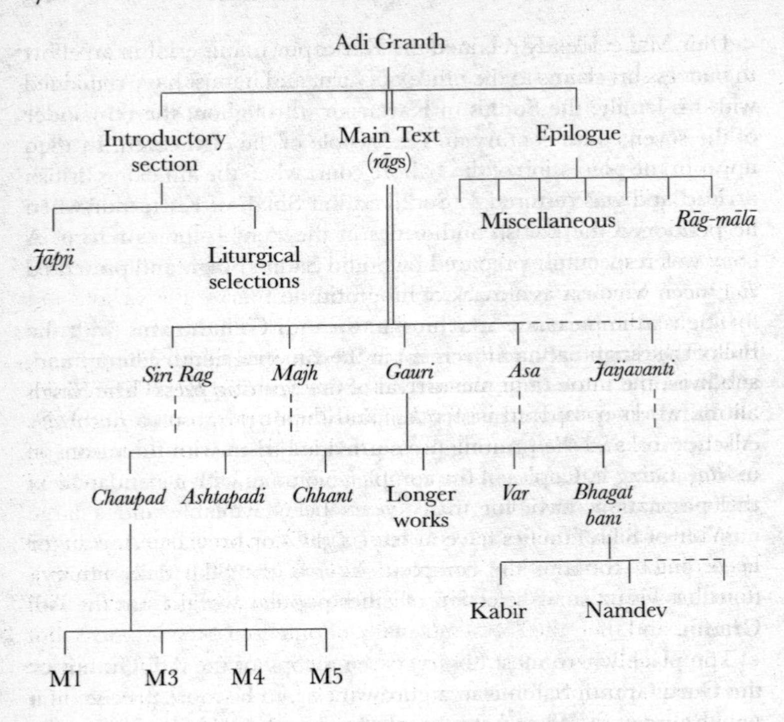

9. The structure of the Adi Granth

Commonly they occur within the *vārs*, which are collections of *pauṛīs* ('steps') or verses (normally by one Guru), each one of which is preceded by two or more *śhaloks*. This covers the greater part of the contents of the Adi Granth, though there are variations on this theme. Only one portion of the entire scripture does not qualify as a hymn, and that is Guru Nanak's chant known as *Japjī* with which the volume begins.

These various works are all organized according to a detailed pattern. First, the scripture is divided into three sections of unequal length. This comprises a brief liturgical section at the beginning, followed by a very lengthy main text and concluding with another brief section, the epilogue. The liturgical section contains the works a devout Sikh will sing or recite on three occasions each day (early morning, sunset and before retiring to bed). These are mingled with works from the Dasam Granth to form *Nit-nem*, the daily discipline Sikhs should observe. Apart from *Japjī*, all are repeated in their appropriate places in the main text.

The epilogue consists of miscellaneous works which could not be accommodated in the second section, for example a portion labelled '*Śhalok*s left over from the *vār*s'. At the very end comes the puzzling *Rāg-mālā*, which is evidently intended to summarize the various *rāg*s (or ragas), the measures used in the main text. That leaves the great bulk of the scripture and this is subdivided several times. The primary subdivision is into *rāg*s or measures, starting with *Sirī Rāg*. This records all the works composed in *Sirī Rāg* and then moves on to *Rāg Mājh*. All the works in *Mājh* are then recorded and the scripture moves on to *Rāg Gauṛī*. After *Gauṛī* comes *Āsā* and so on through a total of thirty-one *rāg*s, concluding with *Jaijavantī rāg*.

Within each *rāg* there is a secondary subdivision, each being arranged according to the length of composition. First come the *chaupad* hymns (four brief stanzas with refrain), then the *aṣhṭapadī* (eight stanzas with refrain), and then the *chhant* (normally of only four or six stanzas, but of appreciably greater length). Next come works by the Gurus that are in the appropriate measure but which by reason of their greater length do not fit the earlier categories. Guru Nanak's *Dakhaṇī Oaṅkār* and his *Sidh Goṣṭ* are examples, both in the *Rāmakalī* measure. Another prominent example is Guru Arjan's *Sukhmanī* in the *Gauṛī* measure. Still within the same *rāg* are the *vār*s we have already mentioned. *Āsā kī Vār* is the best known of the *vār*s and is regularly sung in gurdwaras in the early morning. Finally, at the conclusion of each *rāg*, there is recorded the *Bhagat bāṇī* (works of the Bhagats), the most prolific of whom is of course Kabir.

There then follows a tertiary or third subdivision within each *chaupad*, *aṣhṭapadī* and *chhant*. First come the works of Guru Nanak, then Guru Amar Das, then Guru Ram Das, then Guru Arjan, and (if there happen to be any works by him) Guru Tegh Bahadur. This is in the *chaupad*s. The same process is then repeated with the *aṣhṭapadī*s, and finally with the *chhant*s. Guru Angad is not included as all his compositions are *śhalok*s, with no *śhabad*s by him. All the Gurus merge their identity by signing themselves as Nanak, but the actual author is clearly signalled in the heading of each work by the use of the word *mahalā* and an appropriate figure. A work by Guru Nanak is preceded by the form *Mahalā 1*, by Guru Angad it is *Mahalā 2*, and so on. Sometimes this is abbreviated to M1, M2, etc.

Very few exceptions to these rules of primary, secondary and tertiary subdivision can be found in the Adi Granth. The most famous exception is a verse by Kabir that occurs in a cluster of Guru Arjan's hymns and is headed *Mahalā 5*. This, however, is not really a problem. Guru Arjan is indicating that he agrees with the sentiments of Kabir, who declares that he is neither a Hindu nor a Muslim. As such the hymn is placed in Guru Arjan's selection, but its origins are clearly marked by the retention of Kabir's name in the last couplet.[6]

Just as the organization of the scripture is a model of clarity, so too is the message it communicates wholly consistent throughout the entire work. This presumably is a result of the volume having been almost all assembled by one person at one particular time. The message is the familiar religious one, the message of spiritual liberation through meditation on the divine Name. This is repeated in seemingly endless ways and in a wide variety of idiom, but it all comes down to the same thing. The *nām* lies all around us and within us, the gift of Akal Purakh to all who will but see it. Meditate on this and you shall find liberation.

In terms of language, the Adi Granth presents an interesting variety, one that predictably covers a range of linguistic usage but which nevertheless sustains a sufficient degree of uniformity to justify what has been called the Sacred Language of the Sikhs, or SLS for short.[7] Macauliffe, author of *The Sikh Religion*, is doubtless to blame for the widespread view in Western countries that there is a multitude of languages represented in the Adi Granth. In reality the pattern is quite simple. With a knowledge of Punjabi and Hindi one can easily proceed to a grasp of Sant Bhasha or the Language of the Sants. This was the language employed all over north India during the time when the Adi Granth was composed and compiled, and the person who knows Sant Bhasha and reads the Gurmukhi script should have relatively little difficulty with most of the Adi Granth.

The fact that the Adi Granth is clearly accepted as the primary scripture of the Sikhs does not mean that there are no problems associated with it. Three of these have already been noted. One relates to the sources of the Adi Granth, notably questions arising from the apparent use of the Goindval Pothis; a second arises from the important differences separating the Kartarpur version from that of Bhai Banno; and the third concerns the actual history of the Kartarpur manuscript prior to its discovery in the Lahore treasury in 1849. Another is the manner in which it came to be transmuted into the Guru Granth Sahib in the eighteenth century, a subject that demands particular caution and tact. Yet another concerns issues which derive from the actual text of the Adi Granth. Are the words it records the authentic compositions of the various authors to whom they are attributed or have they been changed in the period of oral transmission that preceded their copying? This problem (which concerns the works of the Bhagats) also raises questions that demand the utmost care. Some of the tasks in the wider area are those that require the skill of a historian, others those of the philologist or textual critic. Commonly they will demand both.

Anyone who is acquainted with the Sikh view of the Adi Granth will at once be aware that this exercise involves research of the most extreme delicacy. Of the issues listed above, the inquiries will be attended by risks of generally ascending uneasiness and the danger of grave offence, particularly the latter two. Great tact is required, for at his or her peril the scholar questions the traditional interpretation of how the Adi Granth came to be the Guru Granth Sahib; and, even more, he or she will create serious disturbance by carelessly broadcasting the view that the text of the Adi Granth may be other than the actual words that were uttered by the Bhagat to whom they are attributed. It will be a very brave or a very rash person who will venture on the last of these.

Some traditional Sikh scholars take the view that the Guru Granth Sahib is sacrosanct and that any attempt to examine it amounts to blasphemy. For these scholars, textual analysis can elicit only outraged indignation. Nevertheless such questions should be honestly faced, always heeding, of course, the obligation to tread exceedingly softly and always communicating one's findings with the utmost courtesy. To leave these subjects inviolable and untouched may be necessary in some parts of the world, but if that is to be our response everywhere, and Sikhs do nothing about it, we necessarily condemn them to stagnation while the world rushes on. An unquestioning attitude may suit those whose understanding has already been definitively formed, but it certainly will not accommodate a growing generation who will insist on comparing their faith with the world which they find around them. As the world changes, they will find their inherited faith further and yet further out of harmony with it, and that is assuredly a guarantee that many at least will be compelled to relinquish the substance of their belief. Some will remain and lend credence to the voices of those who insist upon no change. They will, however, be a dwindling band.

The Dasam Granth

For the Sikhs of the later eighteenth century there was no problem about the Dasam Granth. When the Granth was invoked it meant that an appeal was made to both the Adi Granth and the Dasam Granth. Both were present at meetings of the Khalsa and both received the same reverence. Now, however, it is different. Portions of the Dasam Granth are as familiar as any passages in Sikh literature, but the scripture as a whole raises serious questions. These have been settled by placing the Dasam Granth on one side. Although it still counts as scripture, there is usually only one volume present to signify the Guru, and that volume is the Adi Granth.

The origins of this second scripture of the Sikhs are obscure. The traditional explanation attributes it to the famous Sikh martyr Mani Singh, who, during his tenure in charge of Harimandir Sahib in Amritsar (1721–34), is believed to have compiled a miscellany known as *Dasven Pātśhāh kā Granth*, 'The Granth of the Tenth Master'. Following his death in 1734, the Khalsa debated whether it should be preserved as a single volume or whether the works reputed to be by Guru Gobind Singh should be held separately. In 1740 a Sikh called Matab Singh, who was on his way to slay the sacrilegious Massa Ranghar for desecrating Harimandir Sahib in Amritsar, proposed that the volume should be divided if he was killed. If, however, he was successful, it should remain intact. The plan was accepted, Matab Singh returned victorious, and so there survives this substantial collection of heterogeneous works associated with Guru Gobind Singh.

Mani Singh's collection, however, was not the only one. An independent collection is said to have been gathered by the martyr Dip Singh and a third collection is attributed to Sukkha Singh of Patna. The greater part of the three collections is the same, but there were some differences. In 1885 a committee was set up by the Sanatan Sikhs of the Amritsar Singh Sabha and in 1902 it published an authorized version, giving it the name 'Dasam Granth' for the first time. This title, 'The Book of the Tenth [Guru]', evidently served to distinguish it from the Adi ('Original') Granth. An alternative theory (much less likely) is that it means one tenth of a longer collection.

The Tat Khalsa faction was less happy with its publication. Some of the works contained in it seemed obviously to be by Guru Gobind Singh and these certainly met with their warmest support. Many of the ideals incorporated in its other works, however, are plainly Hindu. This means that they can be interpreted as at variance with the Tat Khalsa claim that the Sikhs are not to be regarded as Hindus.

The Dasam Granth presents considerable problems and very little is being done to solve any of them. One reason is apparently this general uneasiness on the part of orthodox scholars at much of the content of the volume. Approximately 80 per cent of the collection comprises largely a retelling of Hindu myths. Given the strong emphasis of Tat Khalsa reformers on the fact that Sikhs are not Hindus, it is scarcely surprising that they should have viewed the contents of a major portion of the Dasam Granth with less than enthusiasm.

A more solid reason is that, whereas the script of the Dasam Granth is Gurmukhi (the script in which Punjabi is written and that virtually all literate Sikhs know), the language is predominantly Braj (which few understand in any detail). Braj is the language which is spoken around Mathura and Brindaban, and was used for the important cycle of Krishna legends. In the late seventeenth and early eighteenth centuries, its coverage was much wider, taking the Punjab into its sphere of influence. Very few people who know the Braj language well also know the Gurmukhi script. There are accordingly few who possess the linguistic credentials to study the Dasam Granth effectively, and as a result it continues to be largely ignored.

In its approved and published form, the Dasam Granth is a substantial work comprising 1,428 pages. Four varieties of composition may be distinguished in it. The first group comprises two works normally regarded as autobiographical (or at least as biographical), both attributed to Guru Gobind Singh. These are *Bachitar Nāṭak* ('Wondrous Drama') and *Zafar-nāmā* ('Letter of Victory'). The second cluster consists of four devotional works, also attributed to the Guru (*Jāp*, *Akāl Ustat*, *Giān Prabodh*, and *Śhabad Hazāre*). The third comprises two miscellaneous works (*Savayye* and *Śhastar Nām-mālā*). And the fourth is a collection of mythical narratives and popular anecdotes (*Chaṇḍī Charitra*, *Chaṇḍī kī Vār*, the *Chaubīs Avatār* and the *Trīā Charitra* or *Pakhyān Charitra*).

Bachitar Nāṭak describes the Guru's pre-birth meditation in his previous incarnation and the early battles of his career in the Shivalik hills. It concludes before the founding of the Khalsa. *Zafar-nāmā*, which is in Persian verse, is addressed to the Mughal emperor Aurangzeb and was composed after the Guru's withdrawal from Anandpur. After detailing infamous deeds by the Mughal, it declares that the Eternal One is just and that justice requires the sword to be drawn when order is threatened. Although the *Zafar-nāmā* is now in the Dasam Granth, its inclusion was only fixed towards the end of the nineteenth century. Sikhs generally regard it as unquestionably authentic, which may be correct but is certainly not established. The lengthy period of transmission may well have produced changes both in language and content.[8]

Jāp Sāhib is a poem of 199 short verses containing numerous terse descriptions of Akal Purakh, many only a single word.[9] *Jāp* should not be confused with Guru Nanak's *Japjī*. In the unfinished *Akāl Ustat* ('Praise to the Timeless One') the Timeless One is addressed as *Sarab Loh*, the 'All Steel', and is described in militant terms as absolutely supreme. *Giān Prabodh* perhaps belongs rather to the fourth group as it consists partly of tales from the Hindu work, the *Mahābhārat*. It also includes, however, salutations to the Eternal One of a kind reminiscent of *Akāl Ustat*. *Śhabad Hazāre* is a series of short compositions covering such subjects as yoga and austerity, designed to elicit a fervent response from the reader or hearer.

The *Savaiyye* are panegyrics in the metre known as *savaiyyā*; and the *Śhastar Nām-mālā* is, as its title indicates, 'an inventory of weapons'. Seven weapons are listed and the deeds of some who used them are related. The seven names are cryptically expressed as puzzles.

Finally and by far the most prolific are the mythical narratives and popular anecdotes. It is this fourth group which constitutes the bulk of the collection, comprising more than 80 per cent of the total. Three of them graphically depict the goddess Durga or Devi (the two lengthy versions of *Chaṇḍī Charitra* and *Chaṇḍī kī Vār*), and during the eighteenth century virtually every Sikh source makes mention of Guru Gobind Singh's encounter with her. Her appearance in the Dasam Granth, as in these other eighteenth-century sources, created a problem for Tat Khalsa scholars. The question was settled by concluding that in the form of Bhagauti (one of the names taken by Durga, the name she assumes in *Chaṇḍī kī Vār*) she symbolizes the Eternal One as the Divine Sword and as such she (or rather it) is addressed in the invocation to *Ardās*.

The *Chaubīs Avatār* are tales of twenty-four incarnations of the god Vishnu. They comprise 4,371 verses, of which 864 concern Ram and 2,492 deal with Krishna. The *Trīā Charitra* are cautionary tales of the wiles of women, and in several cases their inclusion in a sacred scripture is somewhat difficult to justify. They were, however, very popular among their originators and occupy 580 pages in the printed edition.

Is the Dasam Granth all the work of the tenth Guru? There are at least four theories concerning its authorship. The traditional and popular view, current among the great majority of the Panth and based largely on ignorance of the contents of the Dasam Granth, is that the entire collection is the work of Guru Gobind Singh. A second theory, this one favoured by a majority of the Panth's scholars, is that only the first three clusters should be attributed to Guru Gobind Singh, with *Chaṇḍī kī Vār* also added. The remainder must have been the work of writers who belonged to his retinue. A third theory (a more radical view) maintains that only *Ẓafar-nāmā* can be attributed to Guru Gobind Singh, the entire remainder being by his followers and expressing a reflection of their ideas and attitudes. And an extreme view holds that *Ẓafar-nāmā* is merely based upon the letter dispatched by Guru Gobind Singh and that the first three clusters represent his thought without actually being by him. According to this view, the strict authenticity of *Ẓafar-nāmā* is open to doubt, partly as a result of its late appearance.

These four theories have been given hesitant currency, but it would be quite wrong to suggest that any dramatic controversy has resulted from them. That must await an uncertain future, at a time when scholars with the linguistic and historical credentials are available. In the meantime, those portions of the Dasam Granth which are already well known will continue to give inspiration to devout Sikhs. *Jāp Sāhib* and the *Ten Savayyās* are already a part of the regular pattern of daily devotions; *Akāl Ustat* offers poetry of rare quality; *Bachitar Nāṭak* provides a view of the early life of Guru Gobind Singh; and *Zafar-nāmā* portrays his defiance.

Clearly these works will continue to have a significant influence within the Panth, with the greater part of the remainder set aside for the foreseeable future. We must hope, however, that the delay will not be too long. It is a great mystery, yet it is an important source of Sikh history, or could be if its true character were understood. To the Panth of the late nineteenth century, and even more the twentieth, the Dasam Granth has received a much lower status than the Adi Granth, excepting only those works which are generally held to be unquestionably those of Guru Gobind Singh. Only the Nihangs, the blue-garmented steel-bedecked remnant of the eighteenth-century Khalsa, still give it a place of honour in their gurdwaras.[10]

The works of Bhai Gurdas and Nand Lal Goya

Gurdas Bhalla was a faithful disciple of several of the Gurus, notably the fifth and the sixth. In his long lifetime, which ended around 1633, he wrote two kinds of poetry (the *kabitt* and the *vār*). The 675 short *kabitt*s are in Braj and this (as with the Dasam Granth) explains their chronic neglect. The thirty-nine *vār*s are, however, accessible. Their language is Punjabi, an annotated Punjabi commentary exists, and as 'the key to the Guru Granth Sahib' they occupy a place of considerable importance in Sikh tradition. Although their poetic quality varies, several are of a high order and they include material of considerable interest. Some of them are narrative works that relate episodes from the lives of the earlier Gurus or incidents which occurred during the author's own lifetime. Many more are doctrinal or exegetical.[11]

Little research has been done on the works of Bhai Gurdas in recent years, and work on the compositions of Nand Lal Goya (1633–1715) is even more restricted. Nand Lal was a disciple of Guru Gobind Singh and for several years held a position in the Guru's retinue. Two of his collections, his *Dīvān* (a collection of sixty-one *ghazals* or odes) and the *Zindagī-nāmā* (a series of 510 couplets), merit special attention. Like most other Khatris he declined to take initiation into the Khalsa, and his poetry reads more like the devotional works of the early Gurus. Unfortunately it is little heard nowadays and has seldom been heard for a long time, a result of being composed in Persian. Here too facility with the language is nowadays comparatively rare within the Panth, though certainly it is more common than a knowledge of Braj.[12]

The works of Bhai Gurdas and Nand Lal Goya are the only compositions that *Sikh Rahit Maryādā* mentions as suitable for singing in gurdwaras, other than those contained in the sacred scriptures. They do not occupy the same pre-eminent position as the compositions of either the Adi Granth or the Dasam Granth, but they are certainly placed higher than any other composition in Sikh literature. As such they can be treated as within the bounds of canonical writings.

Other traditional writings

The janam-sakhis have already been covered while dealing with the sources for Nanak's life.[13] The *rahit-nāmās*, or manuals containing the Rahit, have also been considered.[14] Of the traditional writings of the Sikhs, this leaves only the *gur-bilās* literature awaiting description.

Gur-bilās means literally 'pleasure of the Guru' and works composed in this style concentrate on the mighty deeds of two Gurus, Hargobind and particularly Gobind Singh. These were the two Gurus renowned for their deeds of military valour and it is upon these gallant deeds that the *gur-bilās* writers typically concentrate. The piety represented by the *gur-bilās* literature is of a distinctively different quality from that of the janam-sakhis, emphasizing as it does the heroic deeds of the warrior Gurus.

The beginnings can be traced to *Bachitar Nāṭak*, recorded in the Dasam Granth, and following Guru Gobind Singh's death in 1708 comes the first clear example of the style, Sainapati's *Gur Sobhā*. Late in the eighteenth century Sukkha Singh produced his *Gur-bilās Dasvīn Pātśhāhī* (1791) and during the mid nineteenth century there followed *Gur-bilās Pātśhāhī 10* by Koer Singh and *Gur-bilās Chhevīn Pātśhāhī* attributed to a poet called Sohan. In the same period Rattan Singh Bhangu completed his *Prachīn Panth Prakāśh* (1841), the climax of the *gur-bilās* style.

In 1844 Santokh Singh issued his *Gur Pratāp Sūray*, popularly known as the *Sūraj Prakāśh*. This marked a reversion to the janam-sakhi style of presentation earlier represented by the author's *Nānak Prakāśh*, a work which is strictly in the janam-sakhi style. The *gur-bilās* mode was still alive, however, and later in the century was present in the works of Gian Singh. In 1880 Gian Singh published his *Panth Prakāśh*, and between 1891 and 1919 he progressively issued the several parts of his substantial *Tavarīkh Gurū Khālsā*. This, like its predecessors, represents the history of the Khalsa in terms that emphasize the heroism of the Gurus.

Unlike the works of Bhai Gurdas and Nand Lal, these three varieties of literature – the janam-sakhis, the *rahit-nāmā*s, and works in the *gur-bilās* style – are definitely outside the bounds of canonical scripture. They do not constitute writing that is treated as sacred and accordingly they occupy a lower level in the estimation of the Sikhs. It is, however, a higher level than any modern treatment of the Sikh religion. They deal as primary sources directly with elements of the faith which are viewed by Sikhs as absolutely fundamental and as such they assuredly come within any definition of distinctively Sikh literature.

9

SIKH SECTS

How does one define a sect? The existence of sects presupposes an orthodox form from which they differ, and accordingly one can only speak of sects when that orthodox form has been identified. As far as this book is concerned, the orthodox form of Sikhism is unquestionably the Khalsa mode. This was not always the case. Prior to the rise of the Singh Sabha, variety was tolerated in the Panth, and during the early years of the Singh Sabhas the Sanatan Sikhs strove to uphold the pattern of diversity. The Khalsa interpretation, however, was firmly established as orthodox by the activities of the Tat Khalsa reformers in the early decades of the twentieth century, and ever since it has dominated the Panth. Sects are sects because they differ from the Khalsa mode as spelt out by the Tat Khalsa.

Is it the right word to use for the different varieties of belief and practice that one finds in the Panth? 'Sect' has a pejorative meaning which, strictly speaking, one is not entitled to attach to Sikh variants from the orthodox. The difficulty is, though, that there is no other word available. If we were using Punjabi or Hindi, the meaning would more accurately conveyed by *sampraday*, a word that carries a similar meaning and can be used for 'sect' but which lacks any derogatory sense. *Sampraday* would indeed be closer than 'sect' to the meaning we seek, but the word is too alien to most eyes and ears. We are left, unfortunately, with 'sect'.

The fact that certain groups are clearly labelled as sects does not mean that in orthodox eyes they are necessarily excluded from the Panth. Most Sikhs would, for example, acknowledge that the Namdharis (otherwise known as Kukas) are truly Sikhs. They may be sadly astray (in the view of the orthodox Sikh) in one or two fundamental points of belief, but this does not block them from panthic membership. The same would be said of the Nirmalas, and (rather more hesitantly) the claims of the tiny remnant of Udasis might perhaps be acknowledged. It seems to be generally agreed within the orthodox Panth that acceptance should be withheld in the case of any group that draws a substantial body of support from Hindu society or adopts practices which orthodox Sikhs find offensive. This would account for the marked degree of hesitation in the case of the Udasis, and likewise the difficulty many Sikhs have in assessing suggestions that the Radhasoami Satsang of Beas is Sikh as well as Hindu.

The Udasis

The earliest of these sects is unquestionably that of the Udasis, though nowadays its importance is historic rather than contemporary. Modern Sikhism is generally opposed to asceticism and for that reason alone it has little place for the Udasis. This was not always the case. Prior to the period of the Singh Sabha movement (the late nineteenth and early twentieth centuries), the Udasi way enjoyed considerable prestige, and under the Sikh rulers of the Punjab its practitioners were recipients of substantial land grants. The eclipse of asceticism in general and of the Udasis in particular reflects the convictions of the Tat Khalsa. Today one finds few Udasi centres, the yogis of the Udasi way being banished to the outer fringes of the Sikh Panth. Many Sikhs refuse to accept them as their co-religionists.

The Udasis were an ascetic group, claiming descent from Siri Chand (one of Guru Nanak's two sons) and following the path of renunciation (*udās*). Their austerities, their celibacy and their refusal to acknowledge such practices as keeping their hair uncut made them very different from the Khalsa, but they nevertheless maintained they were Sikhs. Although they recognized the line of ten Gurus from Nanak to Gobind Singh, the Udasis were much more interested in the chain of succession which descended from Siri Chand down to the reigning Mahant ('Superior') of the branch they followed. They revered the Adi Granth, imparting to its teachings a distinctly Hindu twist. Like other Sikhs they wrote commentaries on particular portions of the Sikh scripture, together with janam-sakhis and *gur-bilās* works.

Never uniform in terms of organization or doctrine, the Udasis numbered more than a dozen orders by the end of Sikh rule in 1849.

By this time they had more than 250 *akhāṛās* or centres. They were respected by the early Panth, particularly as Gurditta (the eldest son of Guru Hargobind) evidently favoured them. During the eighteenth century they were not targeted by the rulers, as were the orthodox Khalsa, with the result that many gurdwaras evidently passed into their care. Certainly the *mahants* of the late nineteenth century frequently claimed an Udasi descent, though their lifestyle was by this time very different from that of the traditional Udasis.

Khalsa Sikhs, as we have seen, became increasingly uneasy about Udasi authority over gurdwaras, and during the Gurdwara Reform Movement of the early 1920s all the so-called Udasis were summarily ejected from positions of control.[1] The turning-point of the campaign came in 1921 when the Mahant of Nankana Sahib (who had declared himself to be an Udasi) caused the massacre of a large group of Akalis, an event that branded all Udasis as the enemies of the true Khalsa. During Singh Sabha days they had been targeted by the Tat Khalsa as prime examples of Hindu influence and are now but the palest shadow of their earlier wealth and power.

The Seva-panthis

A second sect which merits a fleeting mention is that of the Seva-panthis or Fellowship of Service. The Seva-panthis are principally Sindhi Sikhs, celibate and very few. Their one reason for inclusion is that they were founded by a disciple of the celebrated Bhai Ghahnaiya. Bhai Ghahnaiya was a disciple of Guru Gobind Singh, and during the siege of Anandpur he toured the battlefield carrying water to wounded friend and foe alike. Sikhs are very proud of Bhai Ghahnaiya. The Seva-panthis, however, are of no importance.

The Nirmala Sikhs

The third sect comprises the Nirmala Sikhs. Like the Udasis, the Nirmalas commanded considerable influence under the Sikh rulers of the Punjab, but unlike them they have been able to preserve at least a measure of that earlier respect. By tradition the Nirmala order was founded by Guru Gobind Singh, who dispatched five Sikhs to Banaras to learn Sanskrit. This is highly improbable, and the Nirmala order is scarcely mentioned in Sikh literature until the late eighteenth century. At that time the references rapidly multiply, largely in land grants and religious endowments made by Sikh rulers.

During the first four decades of the nineteenth century, the Nirmalas continued to prosper under Maharaja Ranjit Singh. As with the Udasis their centres were known as *akhāṛās*, each headed by a *mahant*. Each *akhāṛā* would accommodate varying numbers of celibate Nirmalas, initiated by the *mahant*. Within it their time would be occupied in meditation, yoga and scriptural study. The books they were required to study would obviously include the Adi Granth, but they also spent much time on such Hindu works as the Vedas, the Shastras, the Puranas and the Epics.

Although the Nirmalas are accepted as a part of the Panth, ascetic discipline and the strongly Hindu nature of their study deviate sharply from the teachings of the Tat Khalsa. Members of the order wear saffron robes and observe celibacy, and the teachings they receive and impart are strongly Vedantic. As itinerant preachers, they did much to commend Sikh teachings beyond the Punjab (particularly in such centres of Hindu pilgrimage as Hardwar and Allahabad), and although some of their doctrines met with strong disapproval from the Tat Khalsa, they were regarded cordially by Sanatan Sikhs. In the controversies that enlivened Singh Sabha days, their fortunes declined with those of the Sanatan Sikhs, but never to the point of being totally eclipsed. They still exercise some influence within the Panth, particularly in the Patiala area.

The Nirankari Sikhs

The first and oldest of the two Nirankari groups to be considered as sects are the so-called Asali Nirankaris (the 'true' Nirankaris), thus called to distinguish them from the Nakali Nirankaris or 'spurious' variety with whom the Khalsa fell out so spectacularly during the late 1970s and 1980s. The true Nirankaris trace their beginnings to Baba

Dayal (1783–1855), who endeavoured to reclaim the Sikhs of the Rawalpindi area from the temptations associated with military triumphs under Maharaja Ranjit Singh. Because the movement was confined to the Rawalpindi area, its followers were mainly Khatris and Aroras by caste. At the partition of India in 1947, the Nirankaris abandoned their centre in Rawalpindi and established themselves on the Indian side of the border in Chandigarh, from where their activities are administered to the present day.

The name 'Nirankari' arose because of the stress that Baba Dayal laid on the formless quality of Akal Purakh (*nir-ākār* or *niraṅkār*). According to him, the Sikhs were increasingly being seduced by the military glories and economic opportunities of Ranjit Singh's time, and were neglecting their duty to remember Akal Purakh through the practice of *nām simaraṇ*. His duty was therefore to preach the message of liberation through the divine Name and to insist upon *nām simaraṇ* as the one effective means. External aids to worship were, as Guru Nanak had so clearly taught, a positive obstruction to meditation. Worship should be strictly within the mind and *nām simaraṇ* was the method to follow.

Baba Dayal left his Nirankaris with a brief manual of instruction. Understandably this is not called a *rahit-nāmā* as most members of the sect were not Khalsa Sikhs and so not bound to observe any Rahit. The manual is, somewhat confusingly, called a *hukam-nāmā* in that its format and contents are modelled on a *rahit-nāmā* and do not resemble what Sikhs refer to as a *hukam-nāmā*. Its content is strictly Nanak-panthi, by which is meant that it upholds the teachings of Guru Nanak without mentioning the Khalsa of Guru Gobind Singh. The essence of the Nirankari Hukam-nama is contained in the words which every adherent is commanded to utter again and again: *dhan dhan niraṅkār*, 'Glory, glory be to Nirankar.'[2]

Baba Dayal was himself a Sahaj-dhari Sikh, as were most (though not all) of his followers, and the important thing was to dedicate one's life to the practice of *nām simaraṇ*. This did not mean, though, that his followers were expected to give up their occupations and retreat into a life of renunciation. Nirankaris were typically traders and shopkeepers, and these occupations they were expected to continue while focusing their attention on remembrance of the divine Name.

Later, under the influence of the Singh Sabha movement, many of them adopted the Khalsa insignia, but the Nirankari philosophy retained its Nanak-panthi character, still attracting a substantial number of adherents who identified as Sahaj-dhari Sikhs, as Hindus or as both. In the Singh Sabha controversies, the movement was clearly aligned with the Sanatan Sikhs rather than with the Tat Khalsa.

The stress that the Nirankaris lay upon *nām simaraṇ* certainly does not qualify them to be regarded as heretics, nor does their reverence for the Sikh scripture. Their most serious fault in the eyes of the orthodox Khalsa lies in their acknowledgement of a continuing line of Gurus descending from Baba Dayal. In this respect the Nirankaris do not question the historic line of Gurus from Nanak to Gobind Singh, and they do not claim any connection with it beyond the beliefs they share with all Sikhs. Baba Dayal preached renewal, and it is for constant renewal in their Sikh faith that the adherents of the movement maintain their faith in the line of Gurus descending from him.

Confronted by this doctrine, an orthodox Sikh of the Khalsa would have to conclude that the Nirankaris were strictly heretical, and some might well have difficulty in regarding them as fellow-Sikhs. Such patent heresy is, however, accompanied by a conspicuous dedication to other features of the Sikh tradition and many more would give them the benefit of the doubt. Principal Teja Singh was clearly speaking for the Tat Khalsa when he declared that the differences were 'already obliterated almost completely'.[3] During the Singh Sabha controversies, the Nirankaris were actually of considerable assistance to the Tat Khalsa in that they provided by their example the Anand marriage ceremony which the reformers adopted. The extent of their heretical behaviour can be judged from the fact that Jodh Singh, a prominent Tat Khalsa reformer, married his son to a daughter of the Nirankari Guru. Clearly their message was not far out of line with that of the true Khalsa.

The Namdhari Sikhs (the Kukas)

The Namdhari Sikhs have proceeded rather further down this heretical path than the Nirankaris, yet they too are accepted as Sikhs by all but the strictest of the Khalsa. Commonly they are known as the Kuka

Sikhs, *kūk* or 'shriek' being a name earned for them by the ecstatic cries uttered during their rituals. The major emphasis of the Namdhari or Kuka Sikhs actually differs from that of the Nirankaris in that they preach a purified Khalsa as opposed to Baba Dayal's Sahaj-dhari message. Emphatically it is the Khalsa that they proclaim, not the Nanak-panthi professions of the early Nirankaris.

The origins of the Namdharis were very similar to those of the Nirankaris, with regard to both geographical setting and the solution for humanity's problems. Up in the north-west corner of the kingdom, in Hazro and the Peshawar region, Balak Singh (1797–1862) also preached the doctrine of *nām simaraṇ* as a remedy for the ills of Maharaja Ranjit Singh's time. He was succeeded by the most famous of all Namdhari Gurus, Ram Singh (1816–85), renowned because he was believed by the Kukas to be the actual reincarnation of Guru Gobind Singh. Ram Singh's succession produced a radical change in the Namdharis. Stressing the paramount need for a restored Khalsa, in 1862 he moved the centre of the group's activities down the Punjab to Bhaini (or Bhaini Raian) in Ludhiana District. The sect's high standing travelled with him and Bhaini exercised for some years a considerable influence. From there (with an important second centre at Sirsa in Haryana) the movement still continues to function.

Balak Singh had been an Arora by caste, but Ram Singh himself was a Tarkhan. This was the carpenter caste (later to form, in the case of the Sikhs, the Ramgarhia caste[4]), and most of his followers were Sikhs drawn from the same comparatively low caste or from the ranks of the poorer Jats. It was, in other words, a sect with a distinct class constituency, one which set them in potential conflict with wealthier Sikhs and with the British rulers who at the time were governing the Punjab. Certainly it was a caste and occupational constituency that set them well apart from the Khatris and Aroras of the Nirankari movement. The Nirankaris sought a return to Nanak-panthi principles. The Namdharis, by contrast, preached a restored and regenerated Khalsa.

Ram Singh was never happy with the British rulers and instructions were issued to the Namdharis to exercise a boycott of all that the British had brought. They were to use only locally made goods and to avoid such services as the post offices or courts of law. In response the government subjected the Namdharis to close surveillance and placed restraints on their activities. Trouble arose when in 1870 Namdharis (who deeply venerated the cow) attacked butchers' stalls in Lahore and Raikot. In 1872 a group of them set off from Bhaini to break into the armoury at Malerkotla and seize weapons. When they arrived they were arrested, and Cowan, the Deputy Commissioner of Ludhiana, proceeded to execute fifty of them by blowing them away from guns.

The incident created embarrassment for the British administration and Cowan was dismissed. The government, however, was convinced that Ram Singh was too dangerous to be left at large. Clearly no court would convict him, but under the provisions of the Bengal Regulation III of 1818 he could be and was detained indefinitely. He was sent to Rangoon and then to Mergui in southern Burma, where he remained until his death in 1885. Thereafter the Kukas gave no serious trouble to the British authorities, the sect settling into a peaceable condition which they continue to maintain to the present day.

The Namdhari Sikhs are strict vegetarians and, as we have seen, vigorous protectors of the cow. They attach equal importance to the Adi Granth and the Dasam Granth and they include the Dasam Granth composition *Chaṇḍī kī Vār* in their daily *Nit-nem*. All Namdharis are at least Kes-dharis. They wear only white homespun clothing, and the men are easily recognized by their method of tying their turbans horizontally across the forehead. Around their necks they wear a white woollen cord, woven as a series of 108 knots and serving as a rosary. Ram Singh left them with their own Rahit-nama and also with a Namdhari version of *Ardās*.[5] Their distinctive rituals include a fire ceremony, a *jag* or *havan jag* designed to cleanse all evil thoughts from the minds of participants, to be replaced with the spirit of true piety. The format is described in the following terms by their Rahit-nama:

> When a *jag* (*yajnā*) is to be performed purify the place where it is held [i.e. the *jag* square] by plastering it. Bring earthen vessels which have not previously been used and wash your feet before entering the *jag* square.[6] There perform the *havan* or *hom* [ritual fire ceremony]. Use wood from either the *patās* or the *ber* tree. Do not [fan the fire by] blowing it with human breath. During the course of the ritual fire service [five officiants] should read the following from

copies of the scripture: *Chaupaī*, *Japjī*, *Jāp*, *Chaṇḍī Charitra* and *Akāl Ustat*.[7] A sixth officiant should meanwhile pour incense [on the fire] and a seventh should [intermittently] sprinkle a few drops of water on it.[8]

Fire is also used in marriage celebrations, the couple circumambulating it instead of the Guru Granth Sahib during the course of the ceremony. This was the form current in the Panth before the introduction of the Anand marriage order. The Namdharis normally conduct these ceremonies with many couples being married at the same time. This is to give conspicuous publicity to the fact that marriages do not need to be expensive and also to guard against the provision of dowries.

The Namdharis' Rahit-nama continues in a thoroughly practical vein, communicating some very explicit instructions from Ram Singh to his followers:

> Always wear the approved breeches (*kachh*). When taking off a *kachh* withdraw one leg and put it in the leg-hole of another pair before withdrawing the second leg. Never conceal an evil deed committed by another person. Do not sell or barter a daughter or a sister. Constantly repeat the Guru's name. Never eat meat or drink alcoholic liquor. Fear the Guru always.[9]

Loyal Kukas obey these commandments, as indeed they obey all the words of scripture (both the Adi Granth and the Dasam Granth) that are amenable to belief or behaviour. These they obey literally. Others may disagree with some of their interpretations, but nobody seems inclined to question their sincerity.

The Namdharis are more overtly heretical than the Nirankaris as they claim that their line of Gurus continues without any break the sequence begun by Guru Nanak. Guru Gobind Singh, they believe, lived his later life in secret as Baba Ajapal Singh and personally passed the office of Guru on to Balak Singh before dying in 1812 at the age of 146. This is the crucial difference between the Namdharis and the orthodox Khalsa, although such practices as the use of fire in marriages are also important. Their loyalty to Khalsa traditions as they understand them is, however, altogether too obvious to be ignored and only the strictly orthodox would be prepared to place them outside the circle of Sikhs. Faced by their devotion, the Tat Khalsa in general and Principal Teja Singh in particular concluded that even if they were astray on one vital point they were at least potentially aligned with the Panth.[10] Ganda Singh (another historian with sound Tat Khalsa credentials) declares the story of Ajapal Singh to be 'pure fiction of recent creation', but does little else to dispute the claims of the Namdharis to be regarded as Sikhs.[11] The battles over Nirankari and Namdhari membership were fought many decades ago and the issue of panthic membership has in their cases been conceded.

The Radhasoamis of Beas

It is not so evidently conceded, though, in the case of the Radhasoami Satsang of Beas, a movement which the Panth is finding much more difficult to digest. A serious objection to accepting the Beas Satsang is the nature of their teachings and their substantial Hindu membership. If there is a place for Hindus in the Radhasoami Satsang of Beas, its doctrines will be regarded by many Khalsa Sikhs at least with considerable suspicion and probably with outright condemnation. This much is true, yet Sikhs must acknowledge that some conspicuous members of the Panth have actually been members of the Radhasoami Satsang.

The Radhasoami Satsang is a Sant movement which traces its origins to its foundation in Agra by Swami Shiv Dayal in 1861. During the movement's second generation the two principal disciples of Shiv Dayal organized separate branches, one of them on the banks of the Beas river in Amritsar District. This was the group led by Jaimal Singh, a Jat Sikh and a Kes-dhari. In 1903 he died and was succeeded by Sawan Singh, 'the Great Master', who was also a Kes-dhari Sikh. A line of Gurus was thereby established, each of the incumbents always a Sikh. The Beas Satsang teaches a three-fold message comprising *simaraṇ* (by which is meant repetition of the Lord's many Names until attention is focused on the Third Eye that lies within), *dhiān* (contemplation of the immortal form of the Master) and *bhajan* (listening to the celestial music within us).

Not surprisingly, the Satsang attracted many Hindus, adding to the offence it had caused by acknowledging a succession of Gurus. Equally unsurprising is the difficulty most Khalsa Sikhs have in accommodating its teachings within the Panth. As a result, its Sikh members are viewed by most other Sikhs as marginal to say the least. The Beas Satsang is, however, thriving (both inside India and beyond) and it includes in its membership many Sikhs. Can it be regarded as a sect of Sikhism? Most Sikhs would be uneasy at the question and many would answer it with an outright negative. Have its principles, then, any significant parallels with Sikh teachings? In this case Sikh scholars would give an affirmative answer, but then the mere existence of parallels does not add up to a genuine relationship. The connection is regarded as slim at the very most.[12]

Sahaj-dhari Sikhs

The founding of the Beas Radhasoami Satsang carries us into the period of the Singh Sabha controversies and raises the question of whether Sahaj-dhari Sikhs are to be considered a sect. Sahaj-dharis are Sikhs who cut their hair and do not recognize the Rahit.[13] The answer to whether they should be regarded as a sect of Sikhism depends, as usual, on what is to be considered orthodox. If the Khalsa constitutes the orthodox form of Sikhism, it follows that the Sahaj-dharis must be regarded as a sect, though in fact this is rarely conceded. They themselves would certainly reject any such label, for do they not honour the Gurus and reverence the Adi Granth? The fact remains, however, that they do not adhere to the Khalsa nor observe its Rahit. They assuredly were not always a sect, but with assertion of Khalsa supremacy within the Panth they have been effectively placed in that situation.

In caste terms those who acknowledge Sahaj-dhari status are almost all Khatris and Aroras, with some Ahluwalias also joining them. The teachings of Nanak are revered, the gurdwara venerated and the Adi Granth adored. Certain parts of the Adi Granth are held in particular affection, most notably Guru Arjan's *Sukhmanī*. It is this sect (if sect they be) which has adopted as a common feature the practice of having the eldest son initiated as an Amrit-dhari, honouring the Khalsa Rahit, while the remainder of the family remain Sahaj-dhari.[14] The problems associated with describing them as a sect will be at once apparent.

If the Sahaj-dharis are to be described as a sect, why should the Khalsa be spared the label? The Tat Khalsa Sikhs, contending on behalf of a religion which placed the Khalsa squarely at the centre, were (after all) merely the more successful in the disputes with their opponents, the Sanatan Sikhs. That may be so, but we must return as usual to our definition of a sect and base it firmly on divergence from the orthodox. The Tat Khalsa succeeded in establishing their variety of religious belief as the most successful one, and for that reason their version has come to be inescapably seen as orthodox.

The Nihangs

One group which is certainly different from the Tat Khalsa ideal, yet which prides itself on being the only true Khalsa, is that of the Nihangs. Today the Nihangs form only a remnant of their initial strength of the eighteenth and early nineteenth centuries. At that time they were known as Akalis (not to be confused with the twentieth-century political party and its followers) and were greatly feared as determined warriors. The origins of the Akalis or Nihangs are not known, although they claim to be the true representatives of Guru Gobind Singh and in consequence the true Khalsa. In the time of the *misl*s they usually fought for the Shahid *misl.*[15] Under Ranjit Singh, they were renowned both for their intrepid bravery and their total lack of discipline, except when controlled by other Akalis. After the death of their famous leader Phula Singh in 1823, their importance dwindled and they survive today only as a historic relic.

The Nihangs are seen by others as having two main vices, namely their fondness for *bhaṅg* (cannabis) and their habit of not paying for anything they require. In general, however, they are rigorous in observing the Rahit as they understand it. The name Nihang ('free from care' or 'free from worldly concerns') was probably taken from the pre-initiation name of Akali Phula Singh. Before he was initiated a member of the Khalsa, his name was Nihang Singh.

The Nihangs are divided into four 'armies' (*dal*), each under its own *jathedār* or commander. Most are unmarried, believing that as true soldiers of the Khalsa they must remain unencumbered by family ties. For part of each year they remain in their 'camps' (*ḍerā*), attending to cultivation. At other times they roam around the Punjab and adjacent states on horseback, conspicuously visible in their blue garments and for the range of steel weapons they carry. On their heads they wear a high turban known as a *damālā*, surmounted by a piece of cloth called a *pharaharā* ('standard' or 'flag'). For the festival of Hola Mahalla they converge on Anandpur to participate in mock battles.

In recent years a section of the Nihangs has earned some unpopularity in the Panth as its leader Santa Singh agreed to supervise the rebuilding of Akal Takhat by the government of India following its virtual demolition in the assault on the Golden Temple in 1984. This action met with the severe disapproval of the Panth, which, following the rebuilding, demolished the restored construction and proceeded to rebuild it again, this time with Khalsa hands unsullied by the attack on the Golden Temple.

Followers of various Sants

The Nihangs are generally consistent in their extreme beliefs and militaristic way of life. This is not the case with the next sectarian form to be considered, one which adopts a wide variety of patterns. It is the form associated with the ideas or practices of particular religious teachers, and predictably no pattern will be precisely the same as another. In varying degrees all differ one from another and it is consequently impossible to speak of them as a separate sect. They are rather a collection of differing views, united by the allegiance to particular teachers.

The term used for such teachers is Sant. At once there is the danger of misunderstanding, for the word Sant has already been used on many occasions in this book to designate a movement and its adherents, which is clearly different from the meaning attached to these religious teachers. The Sant Movement of northern India was the tradition that provided Nanak with the components of his religious thought and teachings. It was something quite distinct from these Sants whom one finds in such abundance today.

The use of the term in its modern meaning obviously derives from the need many Sikhs feel for personal instructors combined with the fact that they find it impossible to call them gurus. 'Guru', without doubt, would be the traditional term that would be applied to such preceptors in the Indian situation, but for the majority of Sikhs the word cannot possibly be applied to human beings other than the ten historic Gurus of the Sikh faith. A few sectarians, such as the Nirankaris or the Kukas, may encounter no such problem, but most ordinary Sikhs are confronted with insuperable objections to calling such teachers 'Guru'. A word must, however, be found and the word which has been chosen is Sant.

Sants have a lengthy history in the Sikh Panth, almost as long as the entire post-Guru period. In the eighteenth and nineteenth centuries they were not actually called sants. Such figures as Bir Singh and Maharaj Singh (two prominent religious leaders in the time of Ranjit Singh and his successors) were obviously filling the need for many Sikhs for preceptors. They were, at that time, called simply Bhai or 'Brother', a title which in this context was a highly honoured one. During the latter years of the nineteenth century and throughout the twentieth the designation has become 'Sant' and the individuals who have acquired it have greatly increased.

Not all of these sants have earned the title simply by reason of the religious instruction they give. A person such as Sant Attar Singh of Mastuana (1866–1927) would certainly have earned it in this way and his considerable fame throughout the Punjab would have rested entirely upon his religious teachings. Others, however, were more like Bir Singh and Maharaj Singh, acquiring the title for political reasons as well as for religious. Sant Fateh Singh, the political leader under whom Punjabi Suba[16] was secured, was one of the political variety, though one should add that before he became politically involved he earned the title for reasons which can be called religious. Another was Sant Harchand Singh Longowal, leader of the Akali Dal during the confrontation with the government of India and assassinated in 1985. Perhaps the most celebrated in recent years has been Sant Jarnail Singh Bhindranvale, the ardent Khalsa preacher who met his death when the Indian Army invaded the precincts of the Golden Temple in 1984.

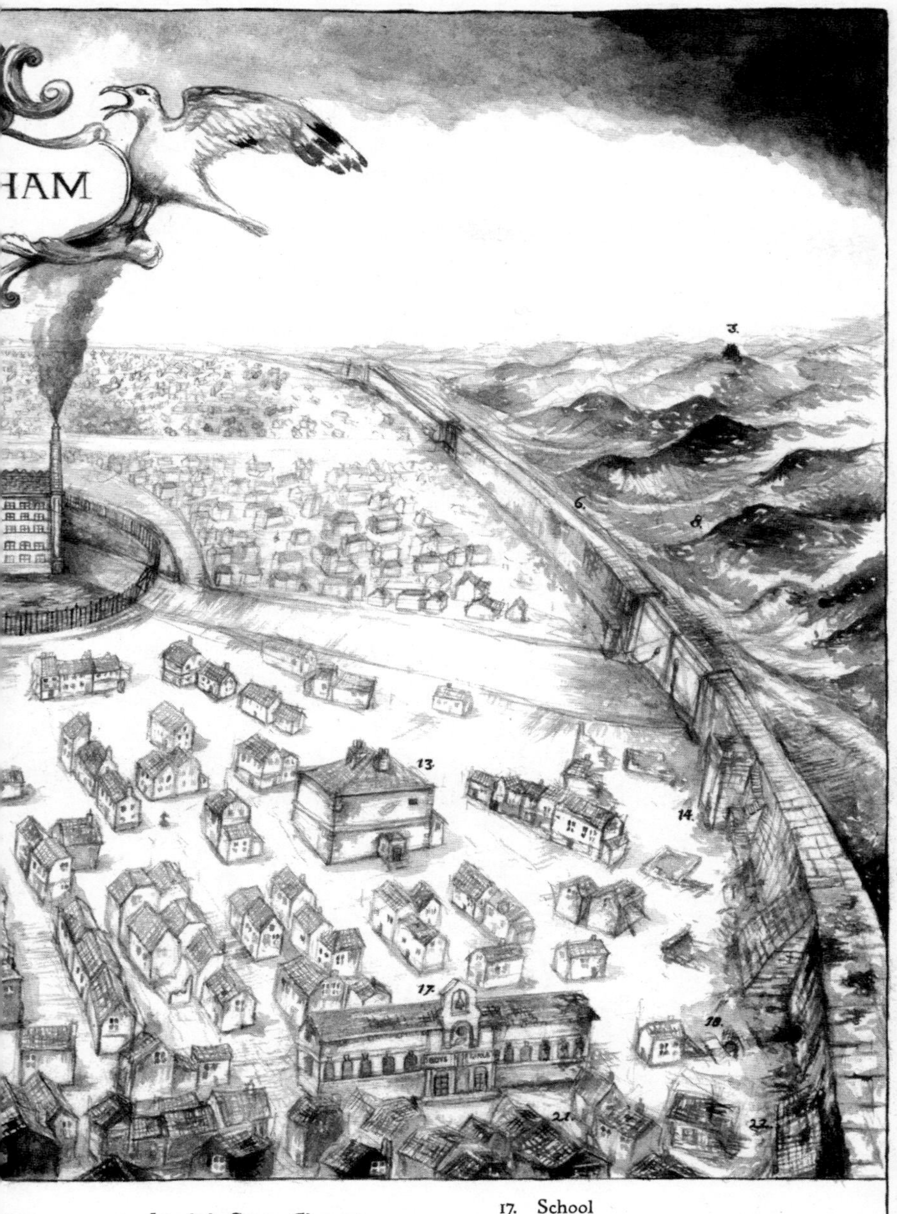

12. Jebediah Griggs, Chemist
13. Policing Station
14. Turret of the Heap Wall Officers
15. Lambeth Barracks
16. The Heap's Rest
17. School
18. Here Sarah Jane Hayward hid
19. House of Rats
20. Foulsham Pie Shop
21. Here the Tailor hid
22. Orphanage

First published in Great Britain in 2014 by Hot Key Books
Northburgh House, 10 Northburgh Street, London EC1V 0AT

This paperback edition published 2015

A CIP catalogue record for this book is available from the British Library.

PB ISBN: 978-1-4714-0163-3

1

This book is typeset in 10.5 Berling LT Std using Atomik ePublisher

Printed and bound by Clays Ltd, St Ives Plc

www.hotkeybooks.com
Hot Key Books is part of the Bonnier Publishing Group
www.bonnierpublishing.com

For Gus

FOR
SALE
FOULSHAM
PIESHOP

Part One

Foulsham Streets

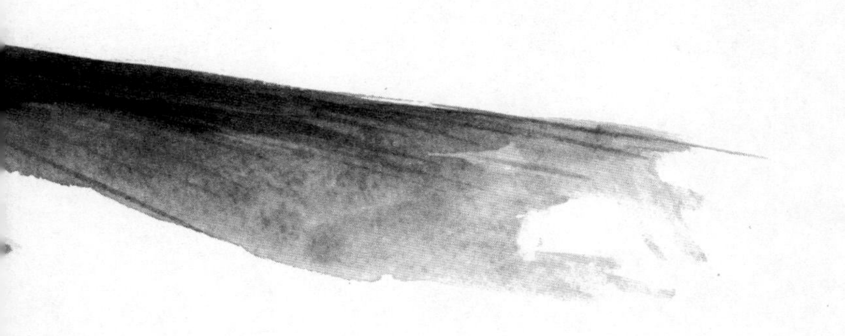

James Henry Hayward
and his Governess Ada Cruickshanks

I

OBSERVATIONS FROM A NURSERY

The narrative of James Henry Hayward, property of Bayleaf House Factory, Forlichingham, London

They told me I was the only child in the whole great building, but I wasn't. I knew I wasn't. I heard them sometimes, the other children. I heard them calling out somewhere down below.

I lived in a mean room with my governess. Ada Cruickshanks was her name. 'Miss Cruickshanks' I had to call her. She gave me physic very often from a tablespoon, it had a strange enough smell to it, but it felt very warming inside, as if it took away winter. I was given sweet things to eat, I had pound cake and tea cake, I had Forlichingham Pie too, which, in truth, was not my absolute favourite, the top of it being somewhat burnt according to tradition and the insides rather a swill bucket of left-overs all covered over in sweet black treacle to disguise the taste. Miss Cruickshanks said that I must eat it all up, she would be cross with me if I didn't. So then I ate it.

She would tell me odd stories, Miss Cruickshanks would, not from a book, but from her head, she should sit by me and looking sternly she should begin, 'Now listen, child, this is the truth of it.

'There are two types of people, those that know about objects and those others that don't. And I'm one of the former grouping, and so I can tell you. I can tell you that once there was a place where the objects didn't do what they were told. In that place, I shan't tell you its name, I shall not be so bold, in that place people had got so thick and muddled about with things that things may have appeared a human and a human likewise be struck down a thing. In that place you must have been very careful with whatever you picked up, for you may have thought it just a common teacup when in fact it was someone called Frederick Smith who'd been turned into a cup. And amongst that place there were high lords of things, terrible bailiffs, who may turn a person into a thing without ever much caring about it. What do you think about that?'

'I hardly know what to think about it, Miss Cruickshanks.'

'Well then, consider it until you do.'

Often she would ask me, 'Do you still have it? Show me now! Show me!' I would take the golden half sovereign out of my pocket and show it her. I always had to keep this particular coin with me, my own sov it was. What a fuss they made over it. If I took it out in public the people around in the big old place gasped at it, and then Miss Cruickshanks shrieked,

'Put it away! Put it out of sight! It isn't safe! It's not safe!

You never know who's looking!'

Once in a while I would be summoned out of the nursery rooms to visit an old man. I should be sent into his grand room with all its shelves, and he would let me look at the things on the shelves, but not to touch them. Such odd things there were, some of it just rubbish, bits of old pipes, or a roof tile, an old tin mug, but others that shone and were silver or golden. I did not know why he kept them all. I supposed they were his special collection. I thought I would like to have a collection of my own someday.

The first business I had always to do when visiting the old man was show him my sov. I brought it to him and I dropped it into his large wrinkled hands. He studied it and turned it over and over. He was very content to do this for some time. At last he would return it to me and watch me place it deep in my pocket.

'I am pleased with you, young James Henry. You do good work.'

'Thank you, sir. I should very much like to work, sir, if it is with you.'

'Owner Umbitt is a very busy man,' said Miss Cruickshanks.

'You must never spend that sovereign, James Henry,' the old man told me.

'I know, sir. I do know that,' I said, because he reminded me of it each visit.

'Say it to me, James Henry.' Very serious now.

'I am never to spend my sovereign.'

Where ever should I spend it anyway? There was certainly

nowhere in the factory, and I was never allowed out into town. How they went on about it, over and over. Do not spend. Never to spend.

'Good child,' the old man said. 'Mrs Groom shall bake you something. She is a most excellent cook, the best in all Forlichingham. How lucky we are that she sends us food here to Bayleaf House.' And then I should have to make a small bow to him and be taken back to the nursery.

Bayleaf House, my home, was the tallest, grandest place in all the whole borough. Built like a great weight it was, like an anchor. It was a certain place. It wasn't going anywhere. You might sleep easy in such a place, knowing that when you woke up in the morning Bayleaf should still be standing. Yes, what a place it was! How fortunate I was with all the good things to eat!

Actually, it was them that told me how fortunate I was to be there, over and over. I was not sure I felt very fortunate. Bayleaf House was some sort of factory, though what exactly it made I could not tell. It was very hot in places. There were ovens and chimneys that poured out smoke. They smothered the rest of the borough with soot.

There were pipes all over the house, great metal pipes that snaked over the ceilings that columned the walls, sometimes a hundred thick and more. They got everywhere those pipes. I doubt there was a single room in the whole place that didn't have pipes inside it. Some of these pipes were cold to touch, very cold, and some were awful hot and could scald you.

There were so many rooms where I was not permitted.

You're not to go in there, boy, do you hear? That place is not for you. Keep clear of the second floor, of the third. Where are the bells sounding from? I would ask. That is none of your business, they would say. What do all the whistles mean that blow day and night, I wondered. That need not concern you, they replied.

So, all in all, it must be said, I knew very little of Bayleaf House. Sometimes I heard the house about its business. I might hear people calling out, calls that sounded as if someone not very far off was hurting. They were children's voices, I'd swear on it. When I heard the calling I got unsettled. And then Ada Cruickshanks picked up a hammer and banged it upon the pipes. Then, after a moment, the calling would often stop.

'I heard them, Miss Cruickshanks! I heard children!'

'You did not.'

'I know I did.'

'You know nothing.'

Well, and that was true enough.

I knew that my name was James Henry Hayward, that I lived in the London borough of Filching, just by the great waste heaps. I knew that I was born here, in Filching. I have the place in my blood. But it was Miss Cruickshanks who told me all that, it was not something that I remembered. She called me gutter-born.

I tried so hard to remember my family but I could not. What did my mother look like, my father? Did I have any brothers or sisters? Why was I stuck inside with her and not out there with them? How did I come to be in this great house? Why did I live in a factory at all?

'Might I go out?' I asked her, 'Are my family still living there? I can't really remember them. May I go and see them?'

'No, no!' she snapped, 'Dirty! You'll get filthy out there. You'd get yourself lost, out in Forlichingham. It's not safe, there are terrible people, thieves and murderers. Come away from the window, how many times must I tell you!' Then she'd turn on me. 'Do you still have it? Show me! Show me!' And I'd show her the coin.

It was all smallholdings, Filching was. I saw it from the window, little places a bit derelict here and there, smashed windows, holes in roofs, buildings propped up, jerry-built, that sort of thing.

I saw the heap wall that protected Filching from all the mass of dirtheaps, and on the other side of the dirty town was the other wall. The wall that kept Filching from London itself. That wall was taller than the heap wall and more recently built. It had spikes on the top it did, and beyond it was London, true London, so near to us, so close but so far away because that London we should never enter. London was an impossible place to us people of Filching. No Trespassing.

Beneath my window, just beyond the factory railing, was the very nearest part of Filching to Bayleaf House. It was a tall white building, people kept running in and out of it. I liked to watch it. When I looked out from the windows and saw the crooked town I knew I loved it. I knew that I longed to get out into it, to be in those winding dark streets. Somewhere out there was my family.

I got terror headaches, and when I got them, when my poor old top smarted from all my thinking, then Miss Cruickshanks brought me the physic on the tablespoon. You felt so warm inside after eating it and the headache went right away and it all rather fogged over, but in a very nice way. All in all, I'd say, it was always foggy for me. I knew so little, so much was kept from me, that I lived in a smog. And on top of that, or confirming it really, was Miss Cruickshanks who wore a black bonnet that had a veil to it, so that I could not see her face properly. It was kept from me. I saw just hints of it, shadows under the veil. I never saw it properly. I could not say what she actually looked like.

But even after taking the physic, I could not stop thinking about my people out there in Filching.

'Do you know where my parents are?' I asked her.

'There are greater matters at stake.'

'I would like to visit them. If they are there, beyond the gates.'

'Well, you can't, boy. You mustn't.'

'Why may I not?'

'Questions! Questions! Nothing but questions. Your questions peck at me like beaks, they scratch into me and send me into a fury. Let me tell you then, that which others would spare you: the place is dangerous and rickety, full of disease and cruelty. They don't say Filching any more, the common people, they call it Foulsham these days, because it is a stinking, quagmire of a place, thick with pestilence.

'A man they call the Tailor hides in the alleys out there and murders people – and the people out there are of such little worth that no one makes much of a fuss about it. Step out,

James Henry Hayward, and you would not last a minute. You cannot be safe out there. The very air is pestilential. Step out and die, step out and crumble, step out and shatter.'

'But there are people out there. I have seen them in the dark streets.'

'Rat people, roach people. Ill people, dying people.'

I think it must have been the mention of rat people that jogged my memory, for I suddenly found myself remembering something I hadn't before. I remembered a house, I recalled a room in a house with a dirt floor. There was a cupboard there, a door to it. I remembered opening the cupboard door, there was a little girl inside putting her finger to her lips to shush me. I remembered that! I remembered something! I couldn't tell who she was, at first, or where I'd dreamt up such a thing. But I liked the thought of it. I kept trying to picture that face, but each time when I went back to it in my mind, when I opened the cupboard again in my thoughts the girl was not there, and in her place was a rat.

The night after I'd remembered the girl in the cupboard, I heard Miss Cruickshanks muttering away in her side room. I wondered what she was muttering about so furiously. She'd already twice come tiptoeing in to see if I was asleep and to make sure I had the half sovereign beneath my pillow, and so I think she must have felt sure I was finally sleeping. I wasn't though and I quietly, so quietly, got out of my bed, and so, so silently moved across the floor and then looked into her room and there she was, sitting on the side of her bed with a looking glass in her hands, and I saw her lift up her veil. And then I saw her face. Oh, the shock of it!

There was a great crack down the centre of it! A great rent running down the middle! Like she was a bit of pottery and not a person at all!

'Evil child!' she screamed, turning round.

'I'm so sorry, Miss Cruickshanks. I didn't mean to.'

'Horrible little thief!'

'Does it hurt, Miss Cruickshanks? Your cut I mean? I am very sorry for it, I did not know you were hurt. Excuse me, miss.'

'I hate you!'

'Yes, Miss Cruickshanks.'

'I hope you rot!'

'Yes, Miss Cruickshanks.'

'Take your medicine. Now.'

'Yes, Miss Cruickshanks.'

'We are stuck with each other, child.'

'Yes, Miss Cruickshanks.'

'Go to bed!'

Seeing her wounded face made me feel different about her. Poor old Cruickshanks, I resolved to think of her more kindly. Cruickshanks was a person and a woman to boot, with all those woman things around her, all those bits and pieces signifying a female. I didn't like to credit the thought.

I preferred not to take my physic so much afterwards, I didn't want to be so fogged over. I began to pretend to take it. I'd slip it in my pocket. I'd spit it out when I had a chance. All that thick whiteness went away and I could focus again. My head hurt perpetually, but I remembered more. I remembered the girl in a cupboard, I saw her better.

She was hiding there; it was her secret place. She kept her rag doll in there. I began to wonder if the girl was my sister. I began to be certain she was. And with that certainty I remembered more than a cupboard. I saw a whole room and people in it. An old woman coughing, a younger woman and man. There was a boy then as well, all busy about some activity. I could not tell what it was at first. Then forcing myself, I began to see more. I could look over their shoulders. They were making small cages. Cages, cages for what? I looked up, there were cages, any amount of them, hanging from the ceilings, there were birds in some of these cages, scruffy seagulls and dusty pigeons.

And there were other cages on the ground. The ones on the ground had a sort of shutter to them on a spring. Then I knew it! Then I had it! Traps! Rat traps, they were rat traps. That's what they were, they were ratters, these people. They were champion rat catchers. How my heart raced at that. Yes, yes I knew them. I knew them and I loved them. They were my family. My family were great ratters of Filching!

There was my father, strong and burly, scratches all over his hands and face, what a champion rat catcher he was! There, my mother, scratched over a good deal too, fierce and fond. Yes I know you, Mother. My brother, learning to make a mouse trap. My sister and her rag doll, not a rag doll, a rag rat she had, a rat in a dress. My grandmother in the corner, fixing traps, two of her fingers missing from her early hunting days. What stories she used to tell us of those, of grandfather and wharf rats! And there was my grandfather, bent over, but grinning. Oh my family, my family. They all came flooding back to me.

How I loved to be there with all of them.

There was more I saw, there was me amongst them all, going out with father in his leathers to hunt, to lay down the traps. And there was the outside of the house, a one-storey place, fairly rickety, but with a shop sign flapping merrily in the wind, HAYWARD RAT CATCHERS FULLY LICENSED BY APPOINTMENT TO TUNCRID IREMONGER, GENT. Yes, home, what a home it was! And there pasted on the walls, the bill stickers, RATS FOR SALE, and MOUSETRAPS, FLYPAPERS, GULLTRAPS, GULL MEAT, RAT RACKS, TAXIDERMY, WE ARTICULATE!, FEATHERS BY THE SACK, SKINS! What a home it was, what a place! That was it, the House of Rats, that was my place, that was where my people were. I had to find it.

The House of Rats.

Home.

That was the start of it. From then on I needed to learn more. Miss Cruckshanks kept a diary. I had seen her at it often enough, but I never should have thought to look at it, not until after I stopped taking the physic. She went out every day, locking the door behind her, to give her report to the old man. And so I took out her diary, and I read there all the thoughts of my governess, and those words brought even more confusion into my head,

I split. I crack. I am coming apart. Every day a little more.

One day, one day soon, I shall be in pieces.

Do not let me shatter, keep me in one part. I want, I so want to stay whole. But they say that I shall not. They say it is hopeless for me. They say I have the fever and that in time I shall fall to pieces. Shall it be tomorrow, I ask. Shall I be broken tomorrow? They tell me perhaps, though it is not likely. There is some time yet. Probably.

A little further on I read,

Sometimes, in the night, if I am very quiet, I can hear myself splitting. My skin when I tap it lightly makes a noise. It should not make a noise. I should not sound like porcelain. I look at cups and saucers, at plates and bowls with disgust now. Is that what I am? A china thing?

I heard her outside then, and was quick to put the diary back. The next chance I had I read further and longer.

My parents were from Italy, from Napoli, they were cheap performers, they sang and danced a little. They had a dog who did tricks, and they had me too. The theatre they were working in, The Heaving Heap in Filching, always a braced-up building, never a steady place, one day collapsed. So many died that night, the night that I was left alone. I hadn't been performing with them. I was outside the theatre with the sandwich board trying to get people to buy tickets. I was ten then already and so able enough to stand up on my own. My family name was Crenzini and that came with much prejudice; it showed us up as foreign and alien, so I called myself Cruickshanks after Mama and Papa died because I thought it sounded hard and respectful and English. And no nonsense. The Ada I have always had with me.

I found work as an assistant to a Filching schoolmistress. I was very strict. I worked so hard not to sound Italian, and I must have had some of my parents' theatrics because people found me clipped and upright and quite believable. "You're quite a woman already, Ada, aren't you? I suppose you were born grown up," she told me. I learnt from the mistress and soon could teach English myself. A great bully she was, Mistress Winthrop, but so thick with gin that she was ever more gin than human, more bottle than body. It may as well have been that transparent perfumed stuff swilling through her veins and not blood at all. I did more and more of the teaching.

She could not be blamed perhaps; she had been brought low. Her husband who had been the schoolmaster was nowhere to be found. He'd upped and left, and the mistress remembered him often while polishing a small rubber truncheon that she never let out of her sight. This truncheon, it now seems to me, actually was her husband only in his changed state.

And then one morning several of the children had

gone missing, one whole form – my form. There was no one there, but such a chaos of objects that I had never known before: a brass cymbal, a milk jug, a horse whip, a fish hook. I said I did not know how such a thing had happened. I was called forth and given something to eat by a very kind-seeming man and that is the last I remember.

That much, and no more. It is enough. I wish to go forwards not back again. I wish to remain Ada. To make her more solid than she has ever been before, it was a tenuous hold I had on life when I worked in Filching schools. I would like to live. This is the testament of Ada Cruickshanks. I am Ada Cruickshanks.

The last time I read from the diary, I found this passage:

Each person in the Iremonger circle must keep his thing to him, his birth object. You shall not last long without it; the disease shall come upon you. But I have lost mine. It was a clay button I am told, but is lost, lost for ever. And to think I must spend my precious time with the child who takes his birth object, that shining sovereign, and polishes it and plays with it not knowing how he thus mocks me. How he clings to it, and how they make such a fuss of it, for, they tell me so, there's a person trapped inside that half sovereign, an important person.

The person that is trapped in the sovereign has power over objects enough to rival Umbitt. I have been told that he, when he was a person, had somehow – because he had fallen in love with a common servant – sent all the objects into a turmoil. And so, if he could do that, if he could upset all because he had fallen in love – because in those moments he had such feelings – then what else might he be capable of? He was dangerous, I am told, and a wonder. For now, he must be kept as a sovereign where he may do no harm. He may be terminated. Umbitt might murder him, it has not been decided yet. They debate whether to ever let him out again. How could I tell the child that they are waiting to decide if he should live or no?

Sometimes I look at the sovereign and I wonder if it were a person again could it help me? And what then, I wonder, should happen to the poor dumb child? How I should dearly like to warn him, but what good should that do?

We are bound by some dark love. We are its opposite, its reverse. We suppress it, James Henry Hayward and I. We have snuffed it out, that forbidden loving. It is not our choice perhaps. And yet it is so.

And yet, and yet, despite their efforts, I think it is already coming undone.

They who live here around us see it, that old passion finding itself again. The truth of it is in my cracking. I am breaking up.

I could not fully understand the passage, though there was surely that within the diary which terrified me. I resolved that the first ever opportunity I had I should be out of there and run into the Foulsham streets. I should search for my family. I should find my people. All my thoughts were on my escape, on my freedom, all I could think of was breathing air beyond Bayleaf House. I should have to take their precious coin with me, for a half sov was a deal of money and I should need to have that about me.

I waited. I tucked myself up in my bed and waited. I waited for them to make a mistake. I lay blank before them, feeble and compliant, but my head inside me raged and raced!

It happened right enough one morning. One early morning before the sun was quite up, when there were less people about, before the ritual of medicine and prodding and coin lifting.

The mornings should generally begin with Miss Cruickshanks shaking herself up from the room beyond and then coming to talk at me through her veil. But she never came, not that morning.

I crept out then. I looked over. Still nothing. I slipped out of bed. I crept over to the door, even braved myself to look beyond into her room. And she was not there. No Cruickshanks not for love nor money. She had been there though, sure enough. Her bed was unmade. Very unlike Cruickshanks that was. Then I saw that there was something in her bed, something other than sheets and blankets, something in the middle where the Cruickshanks body should generally be. I couldn't see it very clearly. It was still dark, but a grey light was beginning to come. I got closer and even put my hand out towards it. It was a box of matches, an ordinary box of matches. How did that get in there? Perhaps it had fallen from her bedside table, for there was a candle there in a brass holder, and yet there was a lucifer beside it. Bringing the box from the bed up to my face I saw that it said SEALED FOR YOUR CONVENIENCE.

I needed more light, some light to help me, so I tore it off and straight away took out one of the matches. Struck it, it didn't light. Struck it again, and what a sizzling strange flame came off it! A weak, sad flame, barely enough to light the candle before it fizzled out.

'Miss Cruickshanks? Miss Cruickshanks?' I whispered.

Not a sign of her, her clothes were there though. Her black dress laid out on the chair ready for her to put on, lying there like a deflated Cruickshanks, and there too was her terrible bonnet with its black veil, and all them outer things of Cruickshanks, waiting in the place. Waiting for Cruickshanks to tug them on to herself to cover herself up. Had she gone out in her nightdress?

And that was what gave me the idea.

Could I?

Could I do it?

The sun was still not all awake. It was dark yet. It was better to do it now. I'd have a greater chance if I was about it straight away. Yes! I would do it! I would dress myself up in Cruickshanks' clothes. I'd be Cruickshanks with the veil over me and that way I'd get me out of there. What a plan! What recklessness! To wear all them women's things! It wasn't to be countenanced. Well then, show me another plan. Give me another way. There was no other way. It was only this or nothing else.

So then.

I put my own clothes on underneath. I tugged Cruickshanks' dress over me. It was tight, she was such a lean one. It felt horrible, but I must do it. On, on! Hurry yourself James Henry Hayward. You're more James Henry Hayward today than you have been in many a day, whether you wear women's clothes or no. I tied the bonnet on, I pulled the veil down. I picked up Cruickshanks' looking glass and looked through it, well there was a shadowy face beneath the veil, one that was not like Cruickshanks, but maybe, I thought, maybe in the half-light: get you going!

I was in her black lace-up boots, which gave me some extra height. I was all ready by the door. I had the key, it was around her belt. I had the key in the door, ready to head out. Wait though! Wait up! I went back to my bed, lifted my pillow, took up my half sovereign. There then! I plopped it fair and square in Cruickshanks' pocket and then, only then did I turn the key in the lock and open the door.

There was a guard there. I was expecting that, right beside me, upon a high stool. He stood up when he saw me, drowsy he was, napping I think. He stirred himself.

'Sorry, Miss Cruickshanks,' he said, 'I was awake, honest mum.'

I made a Cruickshanks-like snort. That was the advantage of pretending to be such a strict one that grunted so: I did not have to speak.

'Going out are you, Miss Cruickshanks?' the guard asked.

I locked the nursery door, put the key back on the belt.

'Not like you is it, Miss Cruickshanks? Not like you to go

out of a morning. Everything all right is it?'

I gave a single brief nod.

'Anything I could do?' he asked.

A very brief shake of my bonneted head, and I threw in a grunt for good measure, to tell the guard he should not presume. I went down then. I clacked down the stairs in that horrible bootwear. I wobbled a bit I suppose, and nearly fell upon my face.

'Are you sure you are quite all right, Miss Cruickshanks?' the guard called down.

My answer was a furious, 'Sssssshhh!'

I had to hope that had done it. I turned the corner then, the nursery was out of sight. I went down, down Bayleaf House, even to the ground floor. No one had stopped me yet. Every trembling footstep took me closer to victory. I was soon enough in one of the offices below, people readying for the day's business, all the desks there, all the pipes and people running this way and that. I passed through them.

Sometimes people stopped and bowed to me, but on I went, on and on. There was a sudden loud shriek which nearly set me screaming: I've been found out, I've been discovered. But it was only the noise of the black steam-engine coming in from the heaps. The old man would be arriving now, coming up into Bayleaf House for the day's business. In former days I should be made happy by that sound, comforted by it. But not now, not any longer. I walked on, people passed by. Keep going, I told myself, keep going, with purpose. And there, there right ahead was the main door, the entrance way out of this place, and I walked to it, didn't I, and the doorman opened it, didn't he. And I walked on, just me doing that, no one else, I walked to the gate, right up to the gate. I spoke then, clearing my voice,

'Let me out,' I said, as strict as I may.

'You want to go out, miss, into Foulsham?'

'Out,' I said.

'Yes, miss, if you're certain.'

I nodded, and the gate was opened, and I was through. I hurried on down the street, I was outside! Passed the tall white building that I had often watched from the nursery window. I could see the other side of it then, see more of it than I ever managed before. There was writing on the front wall of it, MRS WHITING'S CLEAN HOUSE it said. ROOMS TO LET. There was an odd little man sweeping the steps with a broom who quite glared at me. And so I rushed on then, into Foulsham!

It was so cold out there. Hadn't felt it at first, so cold out from the factory, cold like I'd never be warm again. Steam out of my mouth, like I was an engine. How I missed my physic then, what I should have done for a spoonful. But I was free, I was out. There were tumbled down houses and not many people about, not that early. The sun up now, but only just, doing its best to break through. I could hear the waste heaps in the distance, waves of it smashing against the wall. There was ash in the air, and soot.

I hid behind a gloomy hut. I tugged off the clothes, ripped off all Cruickshanks' things and stood in my own togs, myself again. I had no shoes, I'd forgotten to bring them. It did not matter much. Most of the children of Foulsham I had seen from my window had no shoes or wore rags on their feet. I ripped some of Cruickshanks' dress and tied myself some shoes from them. There I was then, out of it, away from Bayleaf House! All I wanted at first was to get me as far from that great factory as I may, so I just stumbled along, not looking in anyone's face, not daring to, just making progress. I would have to ask questions, get directions. I knew that I must. I had my half sovereign in my pocket. I held onto it. I warmed it. It felt a little like company. Perhaps this sov was a person once after all. Only how could that ever be so, that was some fancy surely? Oh my own sov, whatever and whoever, I'm that glad to have you.

Here I was then, back again in what was Filching and is now Foulsham.

There I was at last.

I plunged in. I told myself, go on, make a meal of it. I turned a corner and entered more populated streets, rough people in dirty clothes sitting in gutters, rag children running around, so different to how I was, so dirty. I walked on, less and less happy. I hadn't thought I'd stick out so. Despite my rag feet, I was too well dressed for them. People everywhere looked up at me. I didn't fit in, I didn't belong there. And yet I could hardly go back.

'Can I help you?' someone said.

And rather than answering I turned and ran.

'What's up with him?'

'Up to no good.'

'What's he done then, to make him run like that?'

People came after me, more of them, calling out, 'Who are you? What's your name? Stop a moment. Stop and have a word with us. Not the Tailor himself, are you? Hey, Nice Togs!

Come and talk to us.'

Children got up and followed me, finding the whole business delightful, running and skipping after me, singing,

Spit spat sputum,
Whither are you walkin',
Forlichingham Mound
You are bound.
Crick crack sternum
You shall fall in.
Slip and trip and smack your head
Foulsham Mound, that's your bed.

I knew that song. I felt in my head that I knew it, that I had sung it myself as a child, no doubt skipping along these same dirt streets. Help me, oh help me. There must have been twenty of them and more coming along after me.

'Leave me alone!' I called, but still they followed. My way was blocked suddenly by a tall gruff man in a battered hat.

'Have you got something?' he said. 'Something I'd want? Do you? Have you? What have you got? We share here in Foulsham, give it me. Hand it over. I mean to have it. Who says it's yorn when it's mine all along.'

A huge ugly hand was put out, and I pretended to search my pockets, but then I bent down and I sprinted for all I could into a different street.

'It's mine!' I heard the man call. 'Whatever he has it's mine! Grab 'im! Take that fat child down!'

There was a house in front of me now with a crooked

chimney pouring smoke from it. There was writing on the window, FOULSHAM PIESHOP. And in there I rushed. People at rickety tables in the half-light of the smoky room. Everyone looked around when I came in. I shut the door behind me. There were the grubby children peering in at the window. I couldn't go out there, I shouldn't go out there. I'd stop here a while. I'd stop here and catch my breath and after a time those children were certain to get bored, then I'd step out, but not a moment before.

A very skinny girl with a filthy apron came up to me.

'Do you know the House of Rats?' I asked.

'What are you havin'?' she asked.

'I'm sorry,' I said, 'truly I am. I don't mean to disturb, but do you –'

'Don't care about your sorriness. No interest in it. What are you havin'?'

'I *am* hungry,' I said, 'and that's the truth. I haven't had breakfast, I've usually had breakfast by now.'

'Quite a regular one, are you then?'

'Yes, I suppose, yes I am.'

'What are you havin'? Can't stay here if you're havin' nought, don't cater for that lot. Got any money have you?'

'Yes, yes I have.'

'So then, sit you down and for the fiftieth time, what are you havin'?'

'What have you got?'

'Pies!' she bellowed as if there were no other way to utter the word, and she followed it with one even louder, 'Buns!'

'Yes,' I said, 'a bun, please, thank you, and a pie.'

'Well then, hand it over, nothink for nothink.'

'What?' I asked.

'Your lolly, you clown. Pay first, pie follows after. That's how it is, if not you'll be back out with your chums there. They look most eager for it.'

'I need to find the House of Rats,' I said, 'I'm looking for my family, for the Haywards, do you know them? Could you give directions? Could you tell me? Hayward. House of Rats. Most urgent.'

'What's the rush? Done something have you?'

'No, no, I haven't. No rush, no rush. It's just . . . do you know the House of Rats?'

'Certainly I do, but sit you down have something to eat first, then I'll tell you anything. That's if you have any money.'

'I do have money.'

'So you says.'

'Though I'd rather not spend it.'

'And that's a common enough sentiment. E'en so, cough up!'

I put my hand in my pocket. I felt my half sovereign there. Held on to it.

'I've no time for this,' she said. 'I'll set Charley on you and he's a brute. Charley! We've one that won't pay here, he needs tossing out. Charley!'

In the background, from a room quite full of steam, a very large shape began to stir.

'No,' I said, 'please, miss, not to be so hasty. I said I have money and here it is indeed. Here.' I took it out, out in the open. The wretched girl looked down at it, she lay her hand out flat.

'This is my money,' I said.

'That'll cover it,' she said. 'More than cover it several times over.'

'It's a half sovereign,' I said.

'So I see,' she said.

'It's my half sovereign,' I said. 'My particular half sovereign.'

'Is it though?'

'I'm to look after it.'

'Loyalty's first to your stomach, I always say.'

'I'm never to spend it.'

'Shan't do nothing for you if you don't.'

'It's mine you see.'

'No,' she said, 'you're wrong there. Mine now.'

She had it in her own filthy hand then.

She was walking away with it.

My sovereign!

Why did I feel so sad of a sudden? Why was I crying, the tears coming so fast?

My own sov!

My bloody sov!

Binadit

2

DEEPDOWNSIDE

The narrative of the Former Ward of the Borough of Forlichingham, no longer resident at that address, disposed, thrown out into the heapland

I found it and so it is mine. Takes one such as me to find such a thing as that. I scrambled upwards. Hadn't been on top for many a day. The weather had been so miserable that it wasn't safe to go up, so I lived under, in the dark. I sees in the dark and am comfortable enough there. I live under, in the deeps. I knows it, knows it well. Sometimes, when I get the fancy, I surface. I find me a spot, a place to perch, and I sing out. I cry out. I groan and whoop and make my big noise.

'Binadit!' I screams. 'Binadit! Binadit!'

That's what I sound most. That's much of my vocabulary. They threw me out here in the Heaps, sent me out over a mile in distance and left me here to drown. But you can't sink me.

I'm made of such stuff I am. I survive. I live out in the Heaps and have grown big on it. I'm twice the size I was before who was already much. They're frightened of me, those indoor dwellers, terrified of me. Whenever they catch sight of me they run inside for cover. I'm the outdoors, I am.

I made a deal with the objects. We're one. We're of a piece, me and the wastelands. We're familiar. Intimate. The people from over the wall don't spot me mostly, lumbering in their distance. I'm invisible to them. I'm every piece of rubbish. I can be big. I can be monstrous as a mountain when I call all the rubbish to me, and it plays and throws around me and we are BIG BIG!

I'm everywhere all about.

You can't see me.

Here I am.

But where was I? I move in my mind about from bit to bit. I'm no constant thinker, I tell a bit of this a bit a that. I'm as varied as the Heaps, which to the unfamiliar observer is only brown and greyish, but to me is a kaleidoscope of experience. I move from object to object and with it shifts my mind, roll me over, lift a cover, drag out a bone: I'll tell you another story. Binadit am I. 'Tis home. 'Tis mine. I found it! There we are again! That was it. I found it! And so it's mine. Wot is it? Nothing much you might say, but I knows it. I feel it's good. I take it, I grab at it and hold it to me safe, and quick down I take it, deep deep under where I sleep in the deeps. Drowned dead. I am rubbish. Yes, yes, but wot is it? The new thing?

Wot?

I didn't say again?

No, I never.

Dumb old Binadit, foolish old Binadit, wobbly old Binadit, forever moving on, living heap, man of filth, heaphead, idiot, idiot. Meant to say. Well, I'll tell you then, I mean to.

Didn't say again.

Wot again?

No, you never.

Well then, here it is:

A clay botton.

My clay botton.

I found it.

I've a nose for it, always have had. I know your fresh filth from your old filth, I knows new stinks from ancient stunk. I can smell a mile off. I knows it, I feels it. I hop about upon the surface rummaging here and there finding my grubbing. I love it, I love it, it's all my living. Picking it up, putting it in, swallowing, sometimes sicking it back up, not often. I do digest most things. Rubber, cloth, rich pickings for me they are, metal sometimes. I like the slice of it, like blood it is.

But so, there I was up above after the big winter storm and out in the sunlight, and moving me here and there seeing wot's come up, wot's new, a bit of this a bit a that. Have a bite of seagull. That I will, thank you very much. Maybe I'll catch me a rat, alive or dead doesn't much signify. Iron gut, that's wot I am. Mister Eat All, ever have been. And there it was, very near the top. I picked it up, a botton, a clay botton, so wot? So very much. I like bottons. I keep bottons, shiny or dull. I'll have the lot. I've got me a tin Deepdownside and in that tin

I keep my bottons. I smelt the clay botton, put it to my old nozzle, those sniffing tunnels of mine. Where'd you come from? And I looks up and I sees the House way over yonder and I says, you're from there, from that ugly heap, the foul heap, the big blood heap, the spit heap, the dung heap, that heap of heaps where the real filth is, that's where you've been, ain't you? You've been tossed out. Why did they? Wot did you do? You're a botton, you are. Why do they hate you so? Well, I'll have you, little thing. Come under. Come down. Come deep down into the darks. My botton. Come along.

Past. Future. Present. Wot's that to me? Every day for me is like the one before it, just as much the one after it. They tumble in on each other. I can't tell any from the other. It may as well be a Tuesday as a Friday. I see times of the year only when I come up. Sometimes I'm down so long the season's shifted while I've been in the dark places eating my fill of the ooze at the bottom, where the black rivers run, and I hadn't noticed the spring come till I saw the flowering weeds growing out of the dirts. We do got flowers here, even here they shall grow. There's beauty for you. Tenacious, beauty is, you can't blot it out.

Deep down where I live with me, there's no summer and no winter. There's no Mondays or Sundays. We don't do Christmas or Michaelmas or Candlemas or Martinmas, never no Lent, never was an Easter to speak of. All's the same down deep in the dark, all year, day and night, all the same, and down here, down below in the thick black of it, it's always the same temperature, never varies. Down here, at this depth, down here in Deepdownside (my address, that is, my castle, my shed, my lean-to, my kingdom, my box, my place), in the thick black, deep black, pitch black, black black.

Down here the creatures alongside me, the deep ones, are all blind. Little white eyes. There are rats deep down here and white things which once upon a time were perhaps seagulls but now are closer to fish than birds, all blind. There's no use in seeing this deep under, no future in it. Sometimes I think I might go blind, and that didn't use to worry me much, but every now and then I have a fancy to see a thing and then I clamber up, gets harder to go all the way up there. I heaves and pushes and eats my way up and then how the light stings. After a while all that terrible light spooks me, the great height of sky, the cold bigness of it, and back down I go into the darkness. It's constant, it's peace, it's forgetting: it's home.

Home is a big metal room, was a huge safe room from a banking house that went bust and was thrown out, the whole jimmy of it. That's where I keep me deep under, with drawers and treasures, sharp and soft and crackling and spiking and dead and forgot and rescued and remembered and this and that I have for my liking, to stroke or to eat or to have for company. My home.

Was home.

Not no more.

Not the same after, was it? It was home but home was taken from me, different afterwards, suddenly very different. After I found the clay botton time came back to my life. I began to remember. I thought of things I hadn't thought of for years in the dark. I joined candlestubs collected and made me light below, hadn't had light down there for so long.

They called me 'It'.

I am It.

It of the Heaps.

Wot thoughts! All because of that newest botton. And then I seem to know streets and leaning buildings. I remember people just over the wall, people on the edge of Lundin, and another wall keeping them in in their turn. For they are not loved either. The Lundin ones think them horrible and build a wall 'tween them, and they think the Heaps horrible and build a wall to keep Heaps away. So much walling there is. Filchin', the place is called. Filchin', the town between the walls. One wall keeps Lundin away, the other keeps the Heaps out. Heaps! Heaps! How they fear them! And something else I know: I was born out here in the Heaps. It was my own mother, the Heapland was, a loving mother to me. That other mother, she that bore me, flesh mother, she that tried to poison me inside her, she left me out here in the Heaps, hoping I'd never be seen by anyone. Didn't happen, did it? She left a little token, a scratch on scrap tin. BINADIT read the wobbly hand. She must a done it after I was born, made the name with some hair claps or shard of glass or rusting nail. Put it there, my own name in faint hand, BINADIT. And beneath that, RIP. Only I didn't rip, no, no I didn't. Why did you not want me, Mother? Why did you leave me there? I wasn't alone though. Heaps, heaps all about me, the Heaps they protected me, they fed me. I don't like to remember.

Didn't think of it till the botton.

Why does that botton make me remember so?

I curse that botton then. I hate it and want it gone. I want to forget! It hurts me so to remember. I'll smash it, I tell myself. I'll stamp upon it, I'll crush it. I'll eat it, I'll crunch it and then it shan't come again ever more.

Oh a botton, a botton! A botton's a thing!

I have such other lovely bottons. Bottons that never did me no harm. Brass bottons with anchors, brass bottons with crowns, mother-a-pearl bottons, tin bottons, embordered bottons. Bottons, pretty bottons. Not that clay botton, not pretty one bit.

'Orrid botton.

Wot it has done to me? I was happy enough before now.

'Binadit!' I shout at it in my darkness. 'Binadit!'

I put my fist out. I mean to thump it. I want to see it broken and rubbed into dust. I want to see it hurting. I strike a flint against a wall. I fire up my candlemess. Not enough. Spluttering sun. There too I have a little paraffin salvaged, but once in a rare while I flint it alight. There, how the flame makes the botton looks like it's dancing, makes it looks like it's shifting from side to side. I'll crush it!

'Binadit!' I howl. I screams at it. I shake the light at it.

That thing dances, that 'orrible botton thing. It shifts and flips, and makes a dance all of its own. It's just the light upon it, it's only the flames that are wobbling so. I hold the light still. The light steadies but the botton doesn't. It flips and turns and makes a general nuisance of itself.

A botton dancing in the dark.

Hold you now! Stop that!

But it don't, not a bit. It flips and spins on, spins faster and faster and seems in fact to grow. A great botton. Wot will you do, shall you do damage unto me? I am the one to doubt it. I hate the botton then, I'm frightened of it. It stretches and twists and moves until it is no longer botton shape at all, and there in my dim light is something else.

Not botton no more.

It's a great rat.

No, it isn't.

'Tis.

Is not.

It's a person-thing. It's a person, an unleathered person. When did I last see a person out of leathers? This one in a thin black dress. So much pink! Then I think, then I have it: I'll eat it. Yes, I'll eat it. It's very fresh. But then that thing, that person-thing, it shifts in its place and looks out and then it makes a noise. It says some sounds that I cannot make any sense of. It says the same sound over and over and then at last I think I have it. I seem to have it in my head, a new sound sitting beside my Binadit. This is the call it makes, here it is, very fast,

'Loosypinnnnott.'

Eh wot?

'Loooseee Pennnint.'

Eh?

'Lucy Pennant.'

A Serving Girl, a Thief, a Chemist

3

ODYSSEY OF A HALF SOVEREIGN

Beginning the narrative of Clod Iremonger, formerly of Forlichingham Park, London, moved to Bayleaf House, Forlichingham, stolen from that place

Bound and Round

Am I dead now? I think I may be dead. I am not a person, that much is certain, though I do so remember being one. I think I am a thing. I think I have been stuck in this thing-prison for some time, I cannot tell how long. Yet suddenly I can think more. I can feel more. I can hear, such new hearing, not the small and vague whispering of before, now I catch real sounds, all about me. I have been dropped in a dark place, there are many other things beside me, some of them make little noises.

'Elsie Protherow.'

'Teddy Newbolt.'

'Joseph Turner.'

'Ida Goldenbaum.'

'How do?'

'Welcome.'

'Morning to you.'

Little lost voices trembling in the dark. I was huddled next to other things, heaped among them. I heard their mutterings.

'Who's there?'

'Someone new?'

'Is newness? Some new story?'

'Tell us, tell us!'

'We'll tell you ours.'

'It's only friendliness.'

'If you tell us yorn.'

'Just being social.'

'Who first?'

'I'll go. I was a boy once. Was a good boy I was, was useful,' came a small voice. 'I was needed. I slunk about with the sifting lads in the heaps, top wave, that was me, but then I slipped and got a cut and then the Iremonger foreman he came for me. He pulled me from the line. Took me down a back way. He says, show me your cut and I shows it. And he says, "Well then, what are you worth? Eat this, it will make you useful." And then, suddenly I am on the floor, not Jos Turner that I was before but now only this ha'penny bit.'

'Tha's as nothing,' came another. 'My own brother Porky – so named cos he was but skin and bone – he wot used to work one of the sump pumps. A cold came into his lungs and took up permanent lodging there. No matter how he tries to persuade it out, it stays on. So my bro Porky, getting thinner all the while, though you shouldn't think it possible, he coughed and hacked and spat red poor boy he does, and then an Iremonger he comes along and says, "Well, Pork, I reckons you needs a rest, don't ye?" And I never saw Porky again but that Iremonger when he came by he had some lead piping with him that was never there before. For myself, they just asked me my age and looked at my teeth. Eat this they say, and then all of a suddenly here I am, coin of the realm. Penny am I, though once I was Phil Bishop, please to remember.'

'Tuppence, am I called,' a different voice began. 'Though once was counted little Jenny Northam. My mam and dad they turned over one morning into glazed tiles. Cannot say how it had happened, yet I knows it was them. I called out, screaming through the district. "Look what's come of them, my own mam and dad!" and an Iremonger he sidles up and says, "Poor girl, let me help you now, give over the tiles. Have this to suck on, it shall make you good and useful." And I don't know if I'd given the tiles before I turned tuppence. I don't know, and if I didn't, did I then drop Mam and Dad? Did I shatter them?'

Such stories, stories in the darkness.

'And you, you new round, what have you to say?'

There was a silence.

'Come now, Shiner, cough it up. Let's hear from you.'

Only silence.

'I thought as much. Stuck up, that one, all shut up.'

Then something occurred to me.

'Excuse me,' I said.

'Oh, but now he speaks!'

'I can speak!' I cried.

''Course you can. Whatever did you think?'

'And you can hear me!'

'Not fast, not a very quick one, are you?'

'Hello, hello!' I said. 'Hello one and all!'

'Morning.'

'Morning. How do you do?' I cried.

'Polite for a half sov, ain't you?'

'All the half sovs and sovs I ever knewed before, they'd never talk.'

'Not to such as us.'

'We haven't had such as you in here afore. I've seen sovs, but when I was in the counting house. Not 'ere, though, not in such a place as this.'

'Excuse me,' I added, 'and forgive me if I am but slow as you say – am I to understand, am I to believe, that I am here among you all, in a drawer perhaps, and that we are all, to think of it, we are all coins?'

Laughter from the coins then, grim laughter.

'Excuse me,' I continued, 'could you tell me then, if you shouldn't mind overly much, if you might inform me how one, well . . . stops being a coin.'

No laughter then.

'You are green, aren't you,' came a voice at last. 'You're a coin now, and you stay a coin, for always till you run down, that's how it is. I'm Willy Mead that was, a penny now. One minute here one minute there, in a pocket out a pocket, through and through, I've been all over Foulsham I have. I was once out

Kentish way, nearly had me up to Scotland, but I was back here again. Foulsham once more, got dented, so I'll likely keep here now. I'm good for a half pie in this shop, equal to a bun, am I. I'm the poor person's friend. I hungered once, when I was a boy, thought I'd run for it, out of Foulsham, took my chances. I got over the London wall, with rope, that was all. Heaved me up in the night, and then dropped me down the other side, and run in. Out of Foulsham and into London itself.'

'What a thing!'

'What a story!'

'I come down hard enough the other side,' the coin continued, 'but they didn't catch me, not at first. They heard me though, came running after. They caught up with me down the Old Kent Road. They found me soon enough, they knew I was from Foulsham, could tell in an instant. Didn't want our type there. Gave me a beating so's I knew it. Thought I shouldn't survive it but I did. Sent me back.'

'They'd shoot you for that now.'

'And that's the truth. There are soldiers the other side of the London wall, and if you so much as put your head over, then they pop you off. Only last week someone was shot trying. Only the carts of rubbish can come in and out, and how they're searched when they leave empty. No, there's no use in trying, can't get over.

'I was but ten years old when the London constabulary returned me to Foulsham,' concluded the coin. 'Some Iremonger, he took charge and pennied me. Not so much to worry over is there now. I'd rather be a penny. I been about now well enough! I've been beyond!'

'Oh! Oh!' I cried. 'What you have known and felt!'

'Don't pity us, do you?'

'Do you?'

'He pities us!'

'Who's he to pity?'

'No, no,' I said, 'I'm just . . . I'm just so new to this. You know so much and, in truth, I so very little. I should very much like to learn. Are we lost then, quite lost?'

'What a baby you are! Fresh minted I'd say. You don't know nothing of anything, do you?'

'Not much I suppose,' I said.

'I've seen the Tailor, the Tailor himself! I was in his pocket awhile.'

'No!'

'You don't say!'

'Oh, but I do say!'

'The Tailor?' I asked. 'Who is the Tailor, if you please?'

All gasped at me as if I'd said something quite unfathomable. Something of quite considerable ignorance.

'You are dumb, ain't you? Been sitting in silk pockets I shouldn't wonder. You spent so long amongst worsted and tweed that you don't know nothing of the real world, you're that cushioned. Well, buck up, lad! You're in Foulsham now, prepare to get dirty. I don't know how you made it here, but now you're here amongst us you'll get good and scratched.'

'I'm sure I shall,' I said, 'and I'm glad of your teaching. Who, please to tell, is the Tailor?'

'WANTED FOR MURDER. That's who. Him who the posters are all about, all of them with his name on it. He's the spanner in the machine. He goes to a person with sharp scissors and he cuts at them and they all spill out. He's here in Filching. Around us e'en now. Thick among us. He's in every corner, and yet no one ever catches him.'

'Is he really true, this Tailor?' I asked.

'Certainly! Who asked you anyway, you great shiny bit? Who's talking to you? Who are you to interrupt our meeting?'

'How you do talk on so,' I said. 'I've never heard such talking from objects before.'

'Money's always talking, you yella lump. We're always moving here and there, ever being spent, going from hand to hand, from place to place. We know more than anyone, we do. We see far more. We get about, we rootless ones. Everyone needs us, everyone wants us. But how comes you don't know that? What were you anyway before you spruced up a sovereign?'

'Yes, come on. We'll have your story. What were you?'

'Just a moment ago,' I said, 'I began to understand that I was in James Henry Hayward's pocket. He was supposed to look after me. I've always been with James Henry, all my life, but now, it seems, we have become separated.'

'You've been spent,' some coin said.

'I've been spent?' I asked.

'Yes, yes, you've been spent, you have.'

'But why? Whatever for?'

'For buns, I shouldn't wonder, and for pies.'

'He's spent me for a bun, for a pie?' I asked. 'Why would he do such a thing?'

'You're worth many pies and buns you are. You're all of a feast you are, with trimmings on the side. Because of you we lost half the drawer in change. There was a shilling giving us an excellent story before he was pulled out on a cause a you. So then, make up for it why don't you. What's your name? We like a story we do; we'll spread it yonder all about here and there, sow it we shall. Come on then, give over. Your tale, your bit of property.'

'Before I was a sovereign?' I asked.

'A half sovereign!' called a penny. 'Don't get above yourself.'

'Yes, quite right thank you. Before I was a half sovereign I was called Clod.'

'Clod? What sort of a name is that. Clod? That don't have the making of a half sovereign if you ask me.'

'I lived in a big house with my family. I could see Filching.'

'Foulsham we call it now, Foulsham since all the stinking black smoke came to us. Falling over the town.'

'I could see Foulsham as you call it,' I resumed, 'in the distance, though I'd never been there, not actually. I wanted to . . .'

'Well you're here now, ain't you, chicken.'

'In the thick of it, ain't you.'

'Clod? That's not a name. What was your real name?'

'Clodius,' I said. 'Clodius Iremonger.'

That stopped them. They all suddenly clammed up. Not another murmur from any of them. Silent coins, as if that's all they were, just coins, nothing more than coins, not coins made of turned people.

'Hallo,' I said. 'Hallo, talk with me won't you? I knew someone from Filching. She was called Lucy Pennant. Have any of you heard of her? Come along, please. I do implore you.

Lucy Pennant. She has red hair and is freckled all over. Do you know her? Might you help me? Please talk to me, please don't shut up so.'

But they never made another sound.

The drawer was opened now and then and light was amongst us a moment, but I was not taken out. Other coins were and different ones plopped down in their place, and whenever a new one arrived, there was a quick warning call from the coins,

'Iremonger! Among us!'

And then afterwards only silence.

I don't know how long I was in the drawer but at last dark fingers plucked me out. I was rubbed on an apron and taken away.

The Thief

I was shoved in a pocket and taken from what I understood was a pieshop, out I supposed into Forlichingham, or Foulsham as they seemed to call it now.

I was happy to be away from all those grim coins, though I supposed it must mean I was further away from James Henry. How far away from each other must we be before we both begin to suffer? I remembered then – everything rushing back to me – the poor wretch Alice Higgs, and Aunt Rosamud's agony at losing her. There must be so many people lost from each other all over London, all those broken people, half people, missing their object, or lonely people not knowing why they feel so incomplete. And then, on top, all those people not people any more, all those people tumbling into things, and then no one to love them any more, no one to know who they are.

There were such noises, such noises on the way! I heard them all, louder, ever louder: the cries of all the objects. Such calling from the things of Foulsham.

'I was Georgie Brown afore now, here I am a boot scraper.'

'Can you hear me? I'm a wicker basket!'

'Me, me, I'm a flat cap.'

'On the ground, over yonder, you hear me, I am a milk churn. Was Eve Bullen before time.'

'Wheelbarrow, wheelbarrow, I was Edvard Pedersen.'

'Am a sandwich board. I boast ALLBRIGHT'S ARTIFICIAL TEETH but before I was known Archie Stannard.'

'I am a tooth! Am a false tooth what once was Annie Pugh.'

'Oh, I'm a shoe now!'

'A belt! A belt!'

'Here I am Hamilton Foote but you shall not recognise me, I'm string only.'

'I hear you!' I cried. 'I hear you all, poor devils that you are!'

'He hears us!'

'He hears us!'

In a moment there were less voices, we'd moved somewhere more remote. I was suddenly out in the open again – the bakery girl, she can't have been more than fifteen, her black fingers were holding me up to someone else. Such light, I could see, I could see out and see clear. But now I was out and seeing and remembering more it seemed to me I heard in some new and strange way that I hadn't before. Was it, perhaps, being an object that made me hear all the greater? There was a noise of something wailing somewhere, not words, just sounds, sounds like a new language, like something I'd never heard before. A naked strange sound, coming, I thought, from the girl, from deep within. How to explain it? There was a sound inside her wailing, so I understood it, that made the noise, 'Thimble.'

This girl was showing me to some shaven headed man in thick dirty leathers, he had that other sound about him too, but deeper and quieter. I heard it though, it said, 'Steaming iron.'

'I brought it,' she said.

'Give it up then,' said the brute.

'First you must give me back the candlestick you stole, the one that I think my mother became. You said you should, for a half sovereign, well I have it now. But I want the candlestick. You must return it, it's my ma I think.'

'I see the coin, but I don't feel it. Hand over.'

'The candlestick, I'll have the candlestick first.'

'The half sov.'

I was passed over to thick crude hands, fingers sausage thick, and scarred and scuffed.

'Now the candlestick,' she said. 'I must have it.'

'Where'd you come by this anyhow, so great a sum? Did you steal it?'

'It's from a customer.'

'Likely story. Who've you been entertaining in your slophouse?'

'Please, please, the candlestick.'

'Thimble,' came the noise from within her again, though

louder this time.

'Who did you steal this from? You've lifted it from the till, I reckon. But hold on a minute now, hold back. Something is coming to me, yes it is. It looks familiar it does, now it seems I recollect it, I reckon it was mine all along and you filched it from me.'

'Please, no, please, give me that candlestick, it's all I want.'

'You little thief.'

'I did not steal it! Please, I'm begging you.'

'Don't you touch me, you cutpurse. I'll call an Iremonger on you, just you see if I don't.'

'Where's the candlestick? WHERE?'

'Oh, let off! It's gone, hasn't it! Such a fuss over a candlestick. I sold it on a week ago. Now get off me or I swear I'll hit you so hard you won't wake till next week.'

'Who did you sell it to? Where?'

'I'm bored on this now, get lost.'

'Thimble,' came the under voice.

'Ma! Ma! My own ma!'

'Shut it, or I'll strike.'

'Give me my money back.'

'Money, what money are you talking about? Never was none that I recall.'

'My half sov!'

'Don't know what you mean.'

'Please! Don't do this! Please!'

'Thimble.'

'Help! Help me!'

'Thimble!'

'I'm not touching you.'

'Help, oh help me!'

'I tell you I'm not touching you!'

It took but a moment and on the ground just where the girl had been standing before was a mere thimble. The poor little object let off a little steam on the ground, as if it were quite hot. Then I heard it whisper,

'Annie, I'm Annie Nelson. Help me. Please help me.'

'God 'ave mercy,' the thief said, shaking himself as if he had a sudden ague, he ground the thimble in the mud with his boot, pushed me deep down into his leather pocket and rushed off.

The Chemist

The next I knew, I was being taken out again, out into the light and passed on to another hand. I was in a different shop. There were jars of strange things all around and, hanging from hooks in the ceiling, many dried herbs. There were new voices from objects calling out, they seemed to start shouting from every corner.

'Chas Butler.'

'Josef Singer.'

'Anushka Dugal.'

'Olive English.'

'Francis Sullivan.'

'Help me, I'm a bell jar!'

'Over here! I'm Patrick Leary the tongue compressor. Help us, you can help us!'

'Please! Please help! I'm a bleeding pan!'

Those unhappy sounds were drowned by the thief addressing the chemist, 'I need me some grinding for my pipe. I've ever such a headache.'

The thief seemed very distracted and the noise inside him, 'Steaming iron', that much more confident.

'Yes, sir,' said the man behind the dusty counter. 'Seven and six, or ha'p'orth.'

'Ha'p'orth.'

'I'll make the measure.'

'Don't you fix it mind. I know your scales. Be generous, will you?'

'Steaming iron.'

'I shall be exact, sir. Your money first.'

'Here.'

I was upon the counter.

'So much?'

'Come on. I've paid you ain't I?'

'Where did you get that?'

'What's that to you?'

'Steaming iron, steaming iron.'

'A little moment, sir.'

The chemist picked me up then, looked at me hard, and next I know I am between his yellow teeth and he is biting me for proof that I'm real.

'It's proper,' the thief said.

'Yes, it does seem so. Only thing is it isn't legal.'

'Not legal, what are you saying? You're trying to thieve me.'

'No, indeed sir, you may see the posters all about the streets, fresh glued it's true, but all stating that half sovereigns are no longer legal tender in Filching.'

'I need some grinding; I've such an ache for it!'

'I'm sure we can come to some accommodation.'

'I've such a pain of a sudden. A gnawing pain.'

'Steaming iron, steaming iron.'

'Yes, yes, of course sir. I don't mean to cast aspersions, but you never can be too sure, can you?' said the chemist.

'Come now, oh my head, my head!'

'Are you quite well, sir?' the chemist asked, standing back from the thief.

'Quick with the medicine! I've never known such pain.'

'Steaming iron, steaming iron.'

'I must be careful, the right amount,' said the chemist, looking at the thief most particularly and standing further back.

'Help me now, help me can't you?'

'Can I?'

'STEAMING IRON, STEAMING IRON.'

'Any moment now, I think, sir,' said the chemist to the thief, 'and you'll be off.'

'Any minute what? What are you saying? Off I go where? My head!'

'STEAMINGIRONSTEAMINGIRON!'

'Goodbye, sir, I thank you for your custom,' said the chemist.

'My h—' but the thief could not finish his sentence, his face suddenly stiffened and in a terrible instant grew grey and shrivelled up solid and landed with a loud and unsettling clang upon the floor. Thief no more.

'Well, well,' said the chemist, leaning over his counter. 'What have we here? Is it of any use?'

With the aid of a pair of fire tongs from his hearth he lifted this new hot object – formerly a thief – beside me on the counter. It gave off heat and whispered very faintly, 'Billy Stimpson.'

'Sir,' said the chemist, 'you are now a steaming iron. I daresay I may sell you to the Iremonger washers themselves. You'll be losing the creases off their starched shirts no doubt. A quality item you are, most useful. Most grateful. I may get a bargain for you, and besides, here is this to boot: a half sovereign. Most kind, most generous. Thank you, Mr Iron, you are most excellent for business.'

I was pushed into the chemist's pocket. I heard a door open and shut. I was outside again. Objects calling out up and down the street.

'A tin spoon now, was William Wilson.'

'I was Janet Bolton once.'

'Joanna Thompson, I was, I was.'

A Family by the Fire

When I was taken out once more, I was in a very different place. There were cages all about, busy people making things. Cages hung from the ceiling, cages all about the floor. And basins and sinks, and troughs. Objects called out again,

'I'm here a cage, I used to be Mabel Taylor.'

'I was Cyril Cronin. I don't want to be a gluepot. Can anyone help me?'

I was handed over.

'I can't take the half sovereign,' someone was saying. 'It isn't safe.'

'You may have it in exchange for a tanner's worth of rat. Now there's a deal you don't see every day.'

'Not such a deal if I'm found with such a coin upon me.'

'Then hide it, keep it safe until the search is over.'

'I've a family to think of.'

'You have indeed. When did you last see such money?'

'I cannot deny it has been a while.'

'Hasn't it! Hasn't it! Do look at the coin, Herbert Arthur! Look at it shining. Think what you may buy for that.'

'Nothing now, half sovereigns are not allowed in Foulsham. They are to be turned over.'

'Nothing now perhaps, but so much later.'

'Come, come, two pound of rat is all I'm asking.'

'For an illegal coin, it's not much of a bargain.'

'Oh look, Father,' said a young woman. 'A whole half sovereign! May I hold it?'

'No, Sarah Jane, you're not to touch it. It isn't safe.'

'Oh look,' said an older woman. 'Will you look at that, a half sovereign!'

'Please to look,' said the chemist. 'Please to. Have a feel, do.'

I was then handed around all the people in that small factory. A young man had me, he passed me to the youngest, Sarah Jane, and she in her turn handed me to the wife and thence I was held by a very old woman lacking several of her fingers. And what fingers they all had, these people. They were so gnawn at, so bullied and scarred.

'Come, come,' said the chemist, 'have you ever seen such

a coin? You may consider yourself rich. You could buy things, purchase new tools, put something by. We have such little to hold onto, we people of Foulsham. We must make do with what we have; we must grab at chances when they come our way. We are under Iremonger tenancy, all of us. What are we to do, Umbitt owns us. We are his property after all. We must only be cunning and fight for our crust of bread, and when help is offered, then we must take it, and be grateful of it. Now, tell me, how is business? Does it thrive?'

'Indeed, I must say it does not.'

'The truth, justly spoken. So then, my offer is a blessing on this house. Come now, what do you say?'

'I say we should, Father,' said Sarah Jane.

'We must all be agreed on this,' said the father. 'Everyone must agree. We'd be hiding it. If it were found there'd be no mercy.'

'Oh, Herbert Arthur, it might save us,' said the wife. 'We'll keep it.'

'It may also, my dear Agnes Nancy, be our death.'

'Well, Pa,' said the young man, 'I think we should chance it. We've known Mr Griggs these many years. He shan't rat on us, so to speak.'

'No, indeed,' said the chemist, Griggs by name as I now understood, 'not I. You know me. Young William Henry speaks true.'

It was then that I heard the undervoice of the chemist calling. It came up like a wind from deep within him, 'Hairnet.'

'There's a reward for anyone who correctly informs on those who are shielding half sovereigns,' said the father.

'What's that to me? Why should I do such a thing? The very mention of it is insulting. I need rats. Rats are necessary for my work. How often have I come to you for the buying of rats?'

'In truth, not much of late.'

'Come now, I came to do you a favour.'

'Or to collect a reward.'

'I am an honest professional. I'll take the coin back and be gone!'

'Wait!' said the mother. 'Not so fast, Mr Griggs. We'll take your coin; we'll give you the weight of varmint you require.'

'At last some sense! I've half a mind to rescind the offer.'

'Only first off,' said the mother, 'we'll have you sign a piece of writing, something that says that we come by the coin from you and the date and the time.'

'You don't trust me!'

'No,' said the father, 'that's about the size of it.'

'But I came out of kindness!'

'So then, be kind. Be kind and sign.'

'Hairnet.'

'I cannot believe you people.'

'Here we are then, Mr Griggs, please to sign.'

'I'm not certain that I shall. What's in it for me?'

'Your rats, Mr Griggs. Didn't you say you were in great need of rats?'

Mr Griggs let out an almighty belch which coincided to my hearing a loud exclamation of 'Hairnet!'

'Are you quite well, Mr Griggs?' asked Sarah Jane. 'Can we get you something?'

Again Mr Griggs exuded a mouthful of air, again with the sound 'Hairnet! Hairnet!'

'You look unwell, sir.'

'Hairnet!'

Mr Griggs was put in a chair.

'Thankee, I feel powerfully gaseous. Some trapped air I think, please to excuse. Oh, my stomach, the sharpness!'

'Hairnet!'

Mr Griggs doubled over suddenly. He tossed about on the chair like he was some small black cloud of weather. He spun and circled like black wool in a tempest, out of that mass sometime a hand appeared like it was drowning in the sea, clutching for land, and then, finally, there was no more movement and the lank black stringy thing lay docile at last upon the chair. Inevitably, a hairnet.

'I'm Jebediah Griggs. I'm not at my best, please to help.'

'The disease!' cried Sarah Jane. 'The disease has come to this house!'

'Quick, Herbert Arthur,' cried the mother, 'the tongs. In the fire with it.'

The father picked up the hairnet with a pair of rusted firetongs and pushed it into the fire. All that was left of Mr Griggs, chemist of Foulsham, sizzled mournfully, sparked a little, and was quickly consumed. The last of him a dissipating cloud of black smoke, that, judging by the reaction of the family, stank something chronic.

'What do we do now?' asked the young man. 'What do we do with the coin?'

'We hide it,' said Sarah Jane.

'We throw it away,' said the mother.
'That coin is dirt,' said the grandmother.
'Fetch the crucible,' said the father. 'We must destroy it.'

Binadit

4

MAN OF FILTH

Beginning the narrative of Lucy Pennant, of no fixed abode

'Lucy Pennant.'

I was in a fight. I was trying to get out. I was with Clod. He couldn't hear. There was this thing, huge it was, made of many things and an old man and a teacup that the old man danced upon it until it was crushed to dust. I called out for the teacup and the old man had me launched off the ground and spinning in the air. And then nothing. Nothing at all. Then suddenly back again.

I was in the dark, very dark, huge stink. Couldn't see anything, shut in with a pig, at first I thought. I'm in a piggery. I did not know how I got there, wherever I was. I didn't know even if I was still alive at first. But I could talk. In fact I couldn't stop talking. And all I could say over and over was,

'Lucy Pennant. Lucy Pennant. Lucy Pennant.'

Couldn't stop myself, over and over.

But then in the darkness, there was that something else. Something big and dark. The pig? And it, this thing, it said,

'Binadit.'

Whatever that meant.

And I said,

'Lucy Pennant.'

And it said,

'Binadit.'

'Lucy Pennant.'

'Binadit.'

'Lucy Pennant.'

I couldn't see what was making the noise, only that it was huge and each time I said my name the thing in the dark responded 'Binadit.' It was quite close. I had no idea where I was or how I had come there.

'Binadit!'

It was getting angry, each 'Binadit' was louder than the one preceding. It was shifting in the darkness, getting closer. Well, I thought, I don't know what you are or what you want but you don't sound exactly contented, and if you shout at me then I shall shout back. No doubt you're quite a thing, no doubt you are. Well good luck to you, I thought, because I'm quite a thing and all. I shan't go without a good fight. I've seen too much already; there's not much that frightens me any more. I have not come all this way to be dinner for a great pig. In truth, this thing before me was large and unpleasant and it did frighten me, but whatever is the use of being frightened? How will that get you anywhere? So then, when next it shouted,

'Binadit!'

I bellowed back,

'Lucy Pennant!'

'BINADIT!'

'LUCY PENNANT!'

And so we shouted back and forth, and when this big thing snapped his jaws and made loud grunts well then I did the same. And when the big thing spoke his noise quieter, well then I followed likewise. And so this was our first communication and we went on sounding each other out in the darkness until at last the big thing moved and he struck at something. I pushed myself backwards on all fours waiting for it to hit, but it didn't touch me. It struck into a lamp of some kind, and the light it gave off was a great sharp pain in my eyes, I covered my face over. And when I took my hands away again, I began to see what it was in the darkness with me there. Well what can I say of it? How to picture that, that thing, that dark, looming, breathing creature before me? Never seen the like.

It was such a thing of dirt. It was all got up in rubbish. Bits of things were stuck to it and grew upon it. The hair on top of the great gross head was so matted and thick that it had become a kind of armour. Things, dark crawling insects, crawled about over it and the creature paid them no heed. Bits of different things were stuck upon it, sealed hard upon it as if a welder had smote them there. You couldn't name the things, only that they created odd, jagged shapes so that the creature seemed made head to toe of rubbish and to fit into the landscape of his home so very exactly that if it didn't move and make its sound so often, you'd think it just a mound of filth. It opened its mouth to say its word and I saw that great cavern and the rocks it kept inside it. Black and grey teeth, yellow and green. And when it opened its great head hole the outgoing stench was incredible.

'Whatever are you?' I asked.

'Binadit,' it said.

'Some sort of enormous bear, I suppose, aren't you? Some sort of beast, not one I've seen before. Something strange, grown up in filth. Whatever are you then?'

'Binadit.'

'Are you animal, vegetable or mineral? Or all three perhaps.'

'Binadit.'

'If they put you in a cage they could charge a tanner for you at Filching Fair.'

At the mention of 'cage' it seemed to grow upset, it struck the dirt floor with its paw, it brought its face closer to mine and I winced at the stench of it.

'Binadit!' it growled.

'I'm going to have to be careful with you, whatever you are. Good boy, sit you down.'

'Binadit. Binadit.'

'Is that your name then? Binadit?'

That stopped it. It looked at me most strangely then. It seemed to shake its head from side to side, some itch or pain had bothered it for certain. It must have so many pains about it.

'Binadit!'

'Binadit?' I asked. 'What are you saying? Binadit? *Benedict*! You're saying Benedict, are you? Oh my sweet lord, you're one of us, aren't you, all along? You're a person too!

'Who did this to you?' I asked. 'How long have you been here? Where are we, Benedict? Where?'

'Where?'

'Yes, where, that's it, what is all this place?'

'Under. Binadit.'

'Under, Benedict? Under what?'

'Under.' He twisted his jaw trying to make it work, to move in old, forgotten ways, it was, *he* was, trying to remember. 'Under . . . heap.'

'The heaps? Under the heaps? Buried. The heaps! How, how did we get here? How do we get out?'

'I found it. I found it and so it is mine.'

'Found what? Make sense!'

'Botton. My botton.'

'What botton? Do you mean button? What are you talking about?'

'You!' he shouted. 'You were a botton before now. I found you up top. I brought you down here, to my home, to here, my place. Deepdownside. You were a botton. But now you're not a botton. Now you're a person thing. Better a botton. Like bottons. Have bottons, box of. Want to see? My bottons? Be a botton again will you? Go on. Please. Put you in my tin I will.'

'I am not a button, Benedict. I'm Lucy Pennant. Lucy Pennant, do you hear?'

'Be a botton, please to be a botton again.'

'No, I won't. I shan't!'

'Binadit!' he snapped, a warning.

'Lucy Pennant!'

'No room for you. Not now, not like this. No tin big enough. No box that large. Don't collect what you are, no collection of . . . of girls.'

'I am not part of your collection.'

'I found you!'

'I do not belong to you!'

'But I found you!'

'I am a person!'

'Be a botton.'

'I will not!'

'You were a nice botton.'

'I need to get out of here. I need to find Clod.'

'A nice botton, but a nasty girl.'

'I'm going now. If you'll tell me how.'

'Nasty girl. Taking up all my place. Not invited! Binadit!'

'I'll go happily enough and then all will be as it was.'

'No, won't! You owe me my botton. I *found* it!'

'Please, Benedict, please, I'll find you buttons. I promise, hundreds of them. Just show me out of here, get me to Filching, then I'll –'

'Not leaving. I found you. You're mine.'

'No, no, I'm not.'

'Binadit! Binadit!'

'What do you want with me?'

'Hongry. I'm hongry.'

'You won't eat me.'

'Won't I? You're fresh. Why wouldn't I?'

'I'm a person!'

'You were a *botton*!'

'*You* are a person, Benedict. People don't eat people.'

'Rats eats rats.'

'And they are vermin. We are human, we talk.'

'Rats make noise when I eat them, I used to talking food.'

'But you don't talk rat.'

'Do talk rat. Talk rat well.'

And he made a noise then, very like a rat it was.

'Benedict, talk sense, be sensible. I'll find you wonderful food. You wouldn't want to eat me, you wouldn't. I'd taste terrible . . . I'm poisonous.'

'Then I'll sick up. I don't mind.'

'Now, I've had just about . . .'

But I stopped then, there was a sudden sharp pain in my stomach, as if all my insides were being compressed. I thought I was being turned inside out, a strange violent spasm. And then it was gone again.

'What was that?' I said. 'I felt something. It hurt!'

'Was what?'

And then there it was again.

'A pain in me, a tugging, a tearing. There it is again. Help, help me, Benedict. What's happening? Help. Help! HELP!'

Unry Iremonger

Unry Iremonger

Unry Iremonger

Unry Iremonger

Unry Iremonger

Otta Iremonger

Otta Iremonger

Otta Iremonger

Otta Iremonger

Otta Iremonger

5

PUBLIC NOTICE!!!

STOLEN:
1 HALF SOVEREIGN

All half sovereigns are to be handed over to Iremonger Officers without delay.
Any half sovereigns found in the personal possession of individuals or businesses beyond 14:00 hrs this day January 12th 1876 to be considered an act of law breaking and subject to the severest penalty.

By Order
Umbitt Iremonger, owner

In service thereof Unry Iremonger, the faceless.
In service thereof Otta Iremonger, the shifter.

Unry

I, Unry Iremonger, secreted about the people. I, Unry, the one they do not know that from young age was sent out into Filching-Foulsham to be a general spy unto them all. I, Unry, person-shifter, person of little face, born in sweat and agony with a malady most peculiar. I lost my features. I was born bald like so many but my hair never grew, not a wisp of it. When I was but five my nose came off when I was a-blowing it. It dropped clean off. Likewise my ears were gone from me by ten. First the left, then the right. I keep my eyes, which I'm uncommonly grateful for. My face is a blank. It is a canvas waiting to be drawn upon, so that faces, any faces, may be set upon mine own and that I may be, as is my choosing, any number of people.

I have noses!

I have ears for any occasion.

Wigs!

I can be anyone.

I, Unry, he in the crowd, the man sitting next to you, your old workmate, the old man coughing in the coffee house, the young boy playing with the hoop. I, Unry, am set a new task. I am on the sniff for half sovereigns and all that carry them. I'm the one to do the labour. I play all roles, and have none of mine own. I'm family; I'm Iremonger every drop. But who of my family knows me? So few, so few.

They've lost something from Bayleaf and I'm to find it. They've had Governor Idwid, blind and brilliant, move his clever ears all around. They propel him through the streets in a wheelbarrow, ordering all to be silent as they rush through, and he listens. He hangs his ears out. But he does not hear it, not yet. They move him into rooms all over the borough, shoving him in here and there at random, they say,

'Quiet! Silence! Let the Governor listen! There's something lost, something lost that must be found.'

If they have half sovereigns, these people, they've hidden them long before the hearing blindman appears. They are cunning, the people of Foulsham, cunning and numerous as rats. But I, Unry, have laid in their sweat manys the night. I know their stench; I stink of them in truth. I'll find it out; I'll have them. Unry's the one to do it.

And sure enough I, I was the one that found him.

And sure enough, and sure enough, I, Unry, I was the one that caught him up.

Plump boy in the street, crumbs down his front.

Had to be him didn't it? We don't do plump here. Maybe in Bayleaf House but not here. Here the children have ribs. So I came up to him with one of my kindest noses on, and a most pleasant set of ears and such a wig of generosity to match, some welcoming, and I says,

'Well, son, what's the trouble? I'm a friend, you look as if you need one.'

'Can you help me, please, may you?'

'Yes, yes,' I says. 'Surely I can. Tell me your troubling.'

'I've . . . I've . . . I've –' what a stammering he gives – 'I've lost my sov.'

'Poor chap,' I says. 'What a thing.'

'I spent it in the pieshop and they won't let me have it back. But I must have it; it's mine you see.'

'Of course it is,' I say. 'Come along a me.'

And he follows, the sad thing, like I was a magnet. No argument, no protest, meek I'd say, and I wander him round the corner, and there at the end of the road is the Policing Station just where it should be.

'What's that?' he says.

'It's a place,' I says. 'Keep up, lad.'

'I don't like the look of it.'

'A fine place,' I say. 'They have everything there, what are you after? Are you hungry?'

'No, no I'm not. I don't ever want to eat again.'

'Thirsty then?'

'All I want, all I need is my sov, and that is in the pieshop. Then after I have it, then I'll look for my mum and dad. Have you seen them?'

''Course I have.'

'I haven't told you their names yet.'

'I know everyone.'

'Who are you anyway?'

'And I know everywhere, keep you coming.'

'Was it you, were you the one that called me? Back then, years ago. I seem to remember it now, were you the one? I was playing truant from school. Was it you? I think it was. I think it was you. You gave me the boiled sweet, was it you who took me away?'

'Come along a me, up these stairs now, nearly there.'

'It was you, wasn't, wasn't it? Why did you do that to me?

Why did you?'

'Just a couple more, up you go.'

'Why did you do it, oh why did you?'

'Through this door then, good my lad, good boy.'

'Please, you're not to do it again, do you hear?'

'Let me show you the way.'

'You shan't do it again, shall you?'

'Let me tell you your way; I know the very route.'

What a greenhorn!

I've seen it all: Foulsham love stories in dark corners, rubbish moving when it shouldn't, a whole sweatshop catch the disease of a moment, all two hundred come tumbling down. I've even seen the Tailor's long length running through the shadows. Nearly had him. I'll have him next time. I'm getting closer. I knows my way about. I'm sitting next to you. I'm everywhere all about. You'll never know me. I'm everyone.

Only thing that may signal me out, only way you might know me, the one part of my guise that is always the same and cannot alter. I always carry with me my umbrella. My birth object it is; can't go anywhere without it.

I forgot to mention, the boy, the soft-edged boy, crumbs down his side. I took him in, gave him shelter. He's safe now. Very.

Otta

My bro, my big bro. He's a lovedove; he's special. Though it may take me a minute to recognise him, my own flesh, still I'm the one that will know him, only me, just me. Guaranteed. Poor Mother, poor Father, what a shock we must have been to them. The noseless, earless bald boy and his sister, the little Thing. Father, Ulung Iremonger and Mother, Moyball Iremonger, worked and met and loved one another out in Security, in the Policing Station. They were ever such clever ones for detecting things. They were ever such sharp ones for sticking their hands down throats and getting the words to come out of people. It was even there, in the hard Station, that Unry was born and then later, to their shock and worry, me, Unryotta, though I'm generally known as Otta, merely Otta. In part I think on 'cause of my having quite sharp teeth, which as a child – and if I be honest even as a grown one – I find do snap on things from time to time. They've a grip, my crushing gnashers.

I came out of Mother in the form of a shapeless hunk of flesh, but they found a mouth on me, screaming. Later I was a bottle, a cup, a pan, a chair, a pole, a box, a book, a pig, a rat, a cat, a gull, a dog, a pump, a pillow, a pot, a doorstop, a bell pull, a floorboard, a sack, a hat, a pen, a brush, a wig, and, on occasions, when I must, oh they said I must at times, a little girl. They never knew where I was; they never knew what I was. That's what comes with working with such filth, says Mama, hard to wash off after. Oh, the terror when they thought they'd thrown me out with the rubbish. How I loved to play hide and seek with them! How it made them tug their own hair out in distress. To see Mother taking hold of a kettle and saying, 'Otta! Otta, stop that this instant. You're not a baby. You're not a kettle. You're six years old now, and should know better. One day the wind will change and you'll be stuck a kettle!' Oh, the games, Unry pretending he was any number of people ('Who are you there?' says Mama. 'Ulung, there's a strange man in the Station, come quick!' Or this classic, 'Owner Umbitt, how good of you to call! Excuse me, sir, but you seem just a little shrunk.') and me being any number of things. They were better days they were, before we were of use out of doors, before we were put out in Foulsham, learning the place, noticing, shifting, finding out all sorts. But we must never declare ourselves, for if we did, they'd know us ever afterwards.

We're secret people, Unry and I. Sssh.

He's all of twenty now.

And I eighteen am.

When I'm myself, I mean really myself, which is not usual, on occasion only when I get together with Unry at the Station for a bit of a flop, or when I need to report, or when I'm called in (a certain whistle is blown) such as today. Then I'm a young woman, big of bust. I have nice legs, tall too. Maybe one day I shall find me someone to take up shop with, maybe I'll retire out in Heap House. I'd like that I think.

Today I'm told there's a half sovereign gone missing, only it's not just a half sovereign. It's an Iremonger called Clod, a very gifted Iremonger but one with a flare for disobedience, and I'm to find him, and I'm to bring him in. 'Can he shift?' I ask. 'No,' they says, 'not yet. He hasn't learnt but he has great natural knowledge of things. He must be caught.'

Well then, off I scuttle.

A door is opened, a rat runs out the door down the steps of the Station. Notice that rat, it runs faster than all the others. Notice that rat, it has round its neck or its hips, or caught up in its tail depending, a ring, a curtain ring. Know that curtain ring, that brass curtain ring, it's always upon me. I never lose it. I fix it to myself, here or there, so that it doesn't fall off. I have it somewhere about. Off I go, rat and ring. See it there! Into and under and deep within. I've been everywhere. I've been everything.

There runs a rat, over your feet maybe.

That was me.

That was I.

Otta.

Gone a-hunting.

The Hayward Family –

Rat Catchers of Foulsham

6

HAVE YOU SEEN THIS BOY?

Continuing the narrative of Clod Iremonger

Notice, Missing Boy

They sat about me, waiting and waiting. In the background the father, Herbert Arthur, was stoking up the fire. The son, William Henry, had got out the crucible and was heating it up. The room was terribly hot. The people were sweating so. All the objects all about were quieter now, whispering to each other. I did not like that, it seemed to bode no good.

'Soon,' the father said, 'soon it shall be hot enough.'

'Don't touch the coin,' said the old grandmother, 'it shouldn't do to touch. Wear thick gloves when you drop it in the pan, Bertle, don't let anyone else. It's dirty, that thing is. It's filth.'

'It doesn't look dirty,' said Sarah Jane. 'It looks golden and pretty, I like it. I cannot help it, I like it. I feel a fondness for it.'

'Don't look into it, Sarah Jane. It isn't safe,' said the mother.

'I cannot help it, Ma. It is such an object. It would be a pity to harm it, I feel that in my heart. I feel I've dreamt of this coin before, as if I somehow know it.'

'It's calling her,' the grandmother cried. 'It will get to a young 'un easy, the disease, those of weak constitution, the over-innocent, the stupid. It'll bring them down. Bertle, will you hurry now!'

The fire grew hotter and the pan on top of it shifted from black to red. The family sweated over me. I tried calling out to them, but no matter how I cried, they could not hear. Only Sarah Jane seemed to want to keep me. These were superstitious people, poor people, living on the edge. I looked about their small room where they all crammed in everything that was theirs, where they worked and where they slept in rickety bunks leant against the walls. There were no pictures on the walls such as there had been back at home in Heap House. There was a single, framed bit of needlepoint, such as probably Sarah Jane had made at school, in neat, sewed lettering with flowers surrounding it, the needlework said:

TAKE THE BABY FROM THE HEAPS
AND THE WALL SHALL FALL

The only other decoration in the whole place were bill posters pasted on here and there, I supposed, to stop up cracks. Old tattered advertisements for theatre acts:

COME FEED THE IT OF THE HEAPS!
BRING ANYTHING, HE EATS ANYTHING:

GLASS, METAL, CHINA, WOOD
MR EAT-ALL! FEED HIM YOURSELF – 2D A SPOONFULL

But most of the bill posters were all the same, the same one over and over:

NOTICE, LOST PROPERTY: MISSING BOY
LAST SEEN NEAR HEAPWALL MAY 14TH 1860,
5 FEET 2 INCHES, BROWN HAIR, BROWN EYES.
ANSWERS TO THE NAME

JAMES HENRY HAYWARD

JAMES HENRY, IF YOU READ THIS PLEASE COME HOME.

HAVE YOU SEEN THIS BOY? Please contact
Herbert Arthur Hayward,
HOUSE OF RATS, Old Salvage Street, Forlichingham

James Henry! James Henry! My James Henry! My plug, oh my plug James Henry Hayward! This, this was where he came from, this, even this, was his home! I was in James Henry's home! Here were his beloved people! Hallo, hallo, to you! I know James Henry, I've been with him all this time! Sixteen years ago he was lost to these people, sixteen years since I've been born and he's been with me. Sixteen years! Sixteen years has James Henry been stalled, sixteen years asleep as a plug, his sister and brother were just small children then. Now quite grown up. But James Henry's still alive, I called out to them. He's not dead, though missing these long sixteen years. Help, oh help!

Listen, Haywards, listen to me!

I've seen him, even today was I with him. He's alive and well.

I tried to tell them. I thought as loudly as I could. I screamed in my mind: just a few hours ago! You may find him yet, you may find him before anyone else does. Go, and find him, now, run to him. He's in the pieshop, at least he was there this day. Run to him quick, for I need to be with him, and he with me.

But the people couldn't hear. And those people, those sacred, dear people of James Henry's, were set upon destroying me, which would harm their missing son. They'd suffer their own boy.

Help me, oh help me.

The only person who seemed to understand anything was Sarah Jane, who sat in front of me and began to weep.

'Why ever are you crying, Sarey?' asked the mother. 'It's just a coin.'

'Is it, Ma, is it? How can you be so sure? What should have happened had James Henry been turned into a coin such as this? He may have been for all we know. And now you want to hurt him!'

'One thing I do know, my girl,' said the father sadly, 'if our James Henry should have fallen into something, it's very unlike he'd turn up a sovereign. It's not like a Hayward to be a sovereign, is it. Look on the mantelpiece at your dear grandfather, look at that beloved rubber glove and tell me that that sovereign is related in any way to that rubber glove.'

'Oh, my George Henry,' wailed the old woman of a sudden, reflecting no doubt on happier days. 'Oh my rubbery glove!'

'Oh my old love,' whispered the glove.

'I know, Father, I know,' said Sarah Jane in tears – somehow my thoughts were getting to her. They must be. 'I do know, and yet there's something in this sovereign here, something more to it. I do know it! Oh, why am I thinking of James Henry so? Why does he flood back to me, it's as if I see him now in the cupboard there where we used to hide. Why can I not get him from my head?'

'You're upsetting yourself, Sarah Jane,' said her brother, 'and you're upsetting Mother too. It isn't right. You oughtn't to.'

'I cannot let you destroy it!' cried Sarah Jane.

'Just you try and stop me, my girl!' said the father, holding long tongs now and coming forward with purpose.

'No, Father, you mustn't!' she cried and scooped me up.

And just at that moment there came a quiet knock at the door.

For the Heapsick

The family stopped dead. They looked at one another in a panic, but Sarah Jane held on to me and when the father put out his hand, she shook her head.

Another quiet knock at the door.

'Sarah Jane,' whispered the mother, 'give it over to your father. Now.'

'Hello,' called Sarah Jane, 'who is it out there? Who's at the door?'

''Tis old Percy Howlett,' came the voice beyond. 'May I step in?'

'It's only Percy,' said the grandmother. 'I've known him since I was but a girl in new leathers. Let him in, he shan't do any harm.'

'Sarah Jane,' said the father in determined whispers, 'will you give that to me this instant?'

'No, Father, I do not think that I shall,' said Sarah Jane as she opened the door. 'Dear Mr Howlett, won't you come in? So sorry to have kept you.'

'Evening all,' said an old, thin voice. 'Not disturbing anything, am I?'

The Haywards, every one of them, were quick to say not.

'Only,' said the old man, 'I heard raised voices. Did I call at the wrong time?'

'No, no, Percy, don't talk rot,' said the grandmother. 'Come now, sit by me.'

I heard shuffling and wheezing.

'Your cold's no better then, Percy?'

'No, no, not much it isn't. My dancing days are spent, I reckon. Hot in here, isn't it? Hot as hell I reckon!'

'Is it, Percy?' said the father. 'Doesn't feel so hot to me.'

'Nor me, nor me,' echoed various Haywards.

'That pan's red hot!' the old man exclaimed.

'So it is!' said the mother. 'I'd quite forgotten it. William Henry, take it off the stove.'

'What's new, Percy?'

'Fearful flap about, ain't there. Looking for sovereigns!' said the old man, laughing. 'They can search me right enough, how many sovereigns do I have upon me? Don't you hear me rattling with sovereigns? Idiots, what idiots! How many of us in Filching should have sovereigns now, I ask you. But I come this eveningtide with a tin, I'm afraid. I'm collecting for the heapsick. There's awful fever about. I know a family all dependent on their eldest son but he collapsed into a boathook Friday last and now the family sit about the unhappy object, starving. I hate to ask, but do you have anything? Anything at all?'

'Oh, Percy, we've not been doing well, you know,' said the mother.

'We have something surely,' said the grandmother. 'A ha'penny bit, surely, for Percy and his heapsick. We can manage that can't we? I shan't have it said the Haywards give nothing!'

'Go on then, Sarah Jane,' said the mother, 'give over a ha'penny, but don't call again soon Percy. We're not Iremongers you know, we're not made a money.'

'I shan't, I promise. I hate to do it.'

Sarah Jane, still holding me, fetched a coin from a cup on a shelf with her other hand and gave it over. The old man quickly clasped his withered hands over Sarah Jane's and so over me. He held on to her. I could feel Sarah Jane struggling, beginning to panic.

'Bless you child, bless you.'

'Percy, Percy Howlitt,' exclaimed the grandmother, 'is that a new umbrella you have there?'

'It is, it is,' said the old man, 'to keep the weather and me a distance from each other.'

'How ever did you afford it?'

'It was gifted to me, most generous.'

I heard the umbrella then, it was whispering, 'Barnaby Macmillan, a brolley, his brolley, would that I wasn't.'

'Well, dear Haywards,' said the old man, 'I must be on now, I've my tin to rattle elsewhere alas, and it does feel to me fearsome warm in here.'

'What's the rush, Percy? Have a bite with us.'

'No, thank you, thank you, I must on, really I must.'

'It's not like you to turn down a meal. You're skin and bones, Percy, come now, take a bite. When did you last eat? I won't have it said the Haywards are a mean people.'

'No, no, honest, I must get on. Please detain me no further.'

'Don't be rude, Percy, it doesn't suit.'

'Please stay, Percy, you've got to eat.'

'No!' the old man shrieked. 'I've got to get on! Urgent!'

'Why, Percy Howlett, what a way to behave, how cruel you are.'

'You're not yourself, Percy, to snap at us so.'

The old man was panting and rushing about in the room.

'Well, well,' the old man gasped at last, 'the truth is, I can't keep food in me. It won't stay down.'

'Oh, Percy, poor dear man, have some grinding will you then, have some physic. Smoke a pipe.'

'Thankee, thankee, dear friends,' the old man wheezed, 'but I've already had some, thankee kindly. I've just been to chemist Griggs and he set me up.'

'What Griggs have you, Percy? When was that?'

'Just five minutes ago.'

'Five minutes ago you were at Griggses?'

'Yes indeed, just a few moments before seeing you, he set me up.'

'Well goodnight then, Percy,' said the father, 'mind how you go.'

'Goodnight, all!'

The door was closed, the family silent a moment and then,

'Why did the old man lie to us, why did he say that?'

'Something's up, Herbert Arthur,' said the mother. 'I don't like it.'

'To think I've known him since I was a girl,' said the grandmother, 'and have trusted him all these years.'

'We must get it out! We must get it out quick. We have to lose it!'

'Sarah Jane! Sarah Jane! Where are you going!'

'Come back! Come back!'

But Sarah Jane was already out the door, still holding me tight, out the door and running.

Under the Bridge

Sarah Jane was running, running, running for all her life.

'Stop! Stop there!' someone called out.

But Sarah Jane didn't stop, she rushed on. There was a whistle blown somewhere behind us. On she ran, on and on. She stopped suddenly, I could just see through her fingers a man before us with a wooden barrel. He had a rag covering over his face. He was pouring whatever was in the barrel down a coal chute, into an old house. He looked about, most perturbed.

'Who are you?' asked Sarah Jane.

But the man stopped, he looked at her a moment, such a cleanliness about him, as if he was not a Foulsham creature at all.

'Who are you?' she asked again. 'You're not from here are you?'

The whistle sounded again, the clean man ran off into the darkness, and Sarah Jane ran too, in a different direction. She slid a little, but was up again. Noises of people behind us. She slowed at last. She stopped. She was panting so. We were crouched down under a bridge of some sort. There was an upturned bucket down there, dented, with a brass ring about its handle. Sarah Jane knocked it over, it rolled under the bridge.

'I think we're safe, safe here a while.'

She brought me up to her eyes.

'There you are then,' she said. 'I wonder if you're not James Henry, I think you might be. Oh, you're definitely someone, I know you are. Are you James Henry, are you? To think at last you come home and we nearly murder you. I'll keep you safe, James Henry. I'll hide you somewhere, yes, that's it! Somewhere that no one can ever find you, but somewhere where I can still get to you. But where is that? Where is that place? Who's there?' She suddenly stood up. 'Who is it?'

There was a movement in the shadows beneath the bridge. From the darkness a rat scuttled forwards. It did not run from a human in fear but rather sauntered closely, as if we were disturbing it and it had a mind to tell us off.

'Oh, a rat,' said Sarah Jane, 'only a rat. You gave me quite a scare. I'd trap you, you're huge. We'd get a good price for you. Go on now, get out of it, before I put an end on you with my boot. Get on! Get out!'

But the rat, rather than rushing away, sat down now, scratched its face with a forepaw, and just stayed there, looking up at Sarah Jane.

'Go on!' she cried. 'Get!'

But the rat sat on.

'Go! Get away!'

The rat's head moved a little to the side, as if it were purposefully looking at Sarah Jane from a new angle.

'I said *get*!' She was up now, and stepped towards it.

But the rat stayed where it was, looking at her. Then it hissed.

'You great bully, you foul filthy thing! I hate you! I'm going to squash you under my boot!'

The rat hissed.

'You don't frighten me,' she said. 'I'm not going to be frightened by some rat. My family have killed rats for generations, that's what we do, we Haywards. We've a license for it. I know rats, I know what they look like inside and out. I've skinned hundreds on them. I've a mind to make you into part of a hat. I'll use your tail to tie up my boots. I'll boil your bones up for glue, see if I don't.'

Hiss, went the rat.

'I'm going to pop out your eyes, I am. I'm going to hear your bones snap!'

Hiss, went the rat.

'You're dead, rat! You are dead!'

Hiss, went the rat.

'What's that on you, rat? An old ring, quite caught round your waist, you dirt thing, you, I'll catch you!'

I listened out. I heard the big brass ring. It barely murmured, 'Agatha Peel.'

'Hiss!'

'Come on then! Come on!'

Hiss, went the rat.

Hiss, went the rat, and then it lunged.

'Ow!' cried Sarah Jane, for the rodent had bit into her hand, and she had dropped me upon the ground. 'You, rat, you shall pay for that! I'm cut! I'm bleeding!'

The rat was running about on the floor, sniffing at me dreadfully.

'Where's it gone, where's my sov?'

The body around me seemed to grow larger of a sudden.

'What are you? You're a cat! You weren't a cat afore! How did you do that?'

What only a moment ago had been a rat was now a large, fat, scarred, bristling, hissing tortoiseshell cat, rabid with disease, fleas and flies thick about it. The old brass ring, Agatha Peel, fixed high upon one leg.

'Give it back! Give it back!'

The cat hissed. It dropped its whole body over me, and I could see nothing.

'I'll have it, I'll have it now! Get gone you filthy beast!'

It hissed, it screamed; how it screamed, an awful human scream.

And Sarah Jane was stumbling.

'You're not natural!' screamed Sarah Jane.

The foul cat screeched to make your blood freeze over.

And Sarah Jane slipped on the ground as she tried to kick the thing, but the foul cat was rushing towards her, on the attack.

Help! Oh help her!

There was a frightful bellow then and the cat went flying. Someone else had kicked the beast, someone else was there. Who was it? Someone tall, some thin new figure, in a dark coat.

'You know me, girl,' he said.

'No,' she said, her face white in terror, 'I never . . .'

'You *do* know me.'

'I know you,' trembled Sarah Jane. 'Oh, please, please! Don't murder me! HELP!'

'Rrrrrun!' said the terrible emaciated man. 'While you're still able!'

That got her shifting, screaming for all she was able, poor Sarah Jane scrabbled up and was away from the bridge and screaming yet.

The cat shrieked, and was very suddenly a seagull, a grim looking piece, a very red tip to its beak.

'Ark!' it screamed.

'Come here, Feathers. I need to unbutton you.'

'Ark! Ark!' it screamed and up it went, labouring hard to climb high, screaming all the while, 'Ark, ark!' A warning, it was screaming a warning, this creature, a call, an alert.

The thin man picked me up from the dirt, wiped me off. 'What have we here?'

He held a pair of scissors, pinking shears they were.

The Tailor, here was the Tailor.

And then came the pain.

7

THE HEAPS ARE KNOCKING

Continuing the narrative of Lucy Pennant

Acid. Acid inside me. Burning. Like someone had lit a fire. Like I was on fire, burning up, that I'd be no more than a mound of ash in a second. Don't know how long it went on like that, the pain something terrible. I was drowning in it, couldn't do anything but hurt. I wondered if I was dying, if that was what it felt like. I wondered if this was the end of it, that I should die here, deep in the darkness with this cruel abused thing beside me. No doubt he'd eat me. What a way to end it.

But I didn't die, not yet, not then anyways.

I was dark under the pain, suffocated by it, and there were terrible dreams about buttons and clay and I thought I should be a clay thing, baked of mud, in the earth where it's all dark and cold. But I was fighting it, striking back, biting my own illness. Clawing at it. I shall not be a button. I shall not do it, get off me. Dreams of matches striking me, of being buried in a box of matches and a thin strict woman with a veil over her face, looking at me straight and saying, 'Me! Me! Me!'

'Me! Me! Me!' I called back, and as I called back I came back, back, back to me, I'd fought the thing off.

'Binadit.'

I was back there in the dark deep. The thing, Benedict I must call him, was beside me. Couldn't see him, just heard him, and, Lord knows, smelt the fellow.

'Binadit.'

'Get away!' I cried, kicking out. 'Get away from me!'

'Binadit,' he said, but further away.

'Were you trying to eat me, Benedict, were you?'

'Hongry.'

'Don't you dare.'

'Hongry?'

'I'm not on the menu!'

'No! Hongry?'

'Do you mean, am *I* hungry? Are you trying to feed me?'

'Have fed you, you've been sickening, I've been feeding and drinking. Went up. Got new! You ate, you ate it all.'

'You've been feeding me?'

'Yes, yes, Binadit! I thought you'd be a botton. I thought you might. I wanted a botton, but you said you'd get me more bottons. So then get me, get me.'

'How long have I been ill?'

'Long?'

'How many hours, or days?'

'No day down here. No clocks. I went up twice, light the first, dark the second. Space inbetween. Your skin was getting stiff, you started getting small, but I shouted at you and you come back big again.'

'I think I must thank you, Benedict. I think I must, I'm being fought. There's someone somewhere who has been made a box of matches and I don't think she likes it. She's fighting me, Benedict, she'll keep fighting me. She's quiet now, she's just matches now somewhere, but she's still thinking. I know it. She's gathering her strength; she longs to be human again.'

'Don't let her!'

'She's tough, I felt her. She so wants to live.'

'I want my bottons!'

'And you shall have them. You have earnt them all right.'

'Like bottons. Do like bottons.'

'Benedict, is there any light? I think a little light might help me.'

'No, no, no more light, all light spent.'

'I need light. Can we go up? I want to go up. I must get out!'

The fear of being trapped down in the darkness was too great for me. I felt all the heaps breathing all about me. I felt so lost deep within it, that I was drowning, drowning.

'Get me out of here!'

'Do you hurt? Is it the match woman coming for you?'

'No, no, it's the heaps. The feel of them, the weight of them!'

'Don't fight it. Mustn't.'

'Please, I must get out!'

'It'll know if you're frightened. It'll know it. It'll come for you if you're frightened. It'll get you.'

'Please, please, which way? I must have light!'

'No, no! Lucy Pennant, listen.'

'Help me! Help me, please!'

'You'll crush us. It won't let us be if you hate it!'

Just then there was a fearsome smash against the metal walls of Benedict's hovel, things knocking against it from the outside, things scraping against the metal walls, making terrible screeching, screaming noises.

'It heard you,' said Benedict. 'It heard your fear and now is come.'

'We have to get out! Right now!'

'No, no, mustn't. Can't go now. 'Tisn't safe. Must stay.'

'I can't stay! I'm suffocating!'

'Binadit, Binadit,' he said quietly, stroking my hair.

'Don't touch me!'

'You're frightened, not to be, not to be.'

The noise of things smacking and shifting against the metal room grew louder and louder, a drumming against the walls, huge things trying to crush us.

'We're going to die! I'm going to die here.'

'No, no, we're not.'

'Help me!'

'Trying to help you. Am trying.'

'What then . . . What was that? Oh God!' Something was drilling against the walls, the whole room was shuddering, then the boom, boom, boom, we were shaken in our cage, our vault, our trap, our tomb. 'Tell me, oh please tell me. What will make it stop?'

'You must be stiller, you must not be scared. It knows you're scared, and that's what scared it, and when it gets scared it gets fretful and then it pounds and crushes and is a big terrible thing. So, so, Lucy Pennant, not to frighten it.'

'I frighten it?'

'You do,' he shouted above the noise of all those things come to crush us. 'Tell me, Lucy Pennant, a nice story. Tell me a story of Lucy Pennant, so to keep us all calm and put away the storming.'

And so, gasping and shaking, I stammered out the story of my childhood, of the boarding house where I lived, of Father and of Mother, of running up and down that house, of finding things, of stealing a bit here and there, of looking in on the homes of all those different people, and of the man upstairs at the top of the house whose door was always closed, who never came out at all, but we could hear him, me and my friends, moving about inside. I told all of Filching, and of the orphanage and of the red-haired girl Mary Staggs and of coming to Heap House, and of being a serving girl, and of Clod, of my Clod and his plug and of kissing him, and of promising him, no matter what, that I should find him again.

When I had finished it was a shock to learn that all was calm, that nothing was tapping against the walls, the storm in the deeps had stopped. I was not frightened and, now I must believe, it, the great thing beyond, was not frightened either.

'Lucy Pennant,' said Benedict quietly, 'she has talked to the Heaps, and they have listened.'

And I said, smiling, despite of all, because I could but help it, and it seemed the only possible way to mark the occasion, 'Binadit!'

We stayed in the darkness, listening to the heaps growing

quieter. The tapping on the walls ever less frequent and fainter.

'Is it going away?' I asked.

'It is always here, it don't ever go,' said Benedict, 'but sometime it is angry and sometime it is not. Not now. Calm now. What a thing it is!'

'Is it safe to go up?'

'Safe for me.'

'I must get out, I cannot stay here.'

Something banged against the walls.

'It hears you,' he said.

'I don't mind it,' I said. 'It may do as it pleases, but I shall not stay in here the rest of my days. I mean to go out and I mean for it to let me. It bloody shall.'

I listened then, listened for its banging, but no sound came.

'Will it let me go?' I asked.

'Is your decision,' said Benedict. 'Is for you to be calm and unfrit.'

'Well then, I am,' I said. 'Well then let us go, I must find Clod. He'll be waiting for me. He won't be able to do anything without me. Never could, the booby. I quite miss him. Ow!'

My leg hurt so when I moved it, as if it had been crushed, as if a part of it had been torn off, and there was a crust of blood there, a scab.

'When you was sleeping,' he said, 'of a sudden your leg was bleeding. Wasn't me that done, it just sprung a leak, most strange.'

'All on its own.'

'Yes, yes, of its own.'

'Benedict,' I said, 'you help me and I'll help you. What do

I want: to get out of here and to find Clod and to stop that woman of matches. What do you want: buttons. Very good then, I'll show you to buttons. We'll go into Filching for buttons, oh they have buttons there.'

'Filching?'

'That's right, is it far?'

'Depends on the weather. Up to the Heaps.'

'Well, Benedict, the sooner we start the sooner we arrive. I'll find my friends there, and I'll gather my strength up. Yes, that's it. In Filching I'll work out just what to do.'

'They put you in a cage there and show you off to crowds. They gives you all sorts to eat and they beat you and laugh at you. That's Filchin'.'

'They did that to you?'

'Big crowds! All looking in at me. I was in a cage! Different, they says a me, so different you are, as always, not actually a mun, nor either a thing. Want to be wanted. Want to be! Don't want to be in a cage. Things not mun, things it was that chose me, welcomed me. Free now, free to run and eat as I likes!'

'Over in Filching I've friends, Benedict, and they shall be your friends too.'

'I was born out in the Heaps, Heaps is my home. I'd be all at sea anyplace other.'

'Will you help me, Benedict?'

'It's not Benedict, it's Binadit. That's my proper name. That or It, they called me. Binadit, Binadit!'

'Steady now, Benedict, don't get so excited.'

'Binadit! Is Binadit to call!'

'What sort of a name is that, Binadit? I shall call you Benedict, which at least is a proper name.'

'Binadit, is Binadit!'

'We'll see.'

'I'll eat you.'

'No, no, you shan't. We will need money.'

'Money!' spat Benedict. 'Have money!'

Benedict rattled around in one of his dirty cupboards and came out clinking all about him, and rustling. Coins, coins and even paper money. How much finding in the heaps he had done himself, how much he'd kept away from the Iremonger sorters. He was a rich man living in squalor.

'Well!' I cried, feeling all them notes. 'Behold the Bank of England!'

'You laugh at me! Don't like it!'

'Happily, Benedict, you're a rich fellow from what I feel all about us, you're rolling in it. What a person you are!'

'Am I?'

'Yes,' I said, 'yes, I truly think you are.'

He grunted at that, I think it was a happy grunt.

'Well then, Benedict, gather up your money and let us go up to the surface and into Filching.'

'Up? It's not up for Filchin'. Is down, down for Filchin', along the pipes, get in the pipes, go along, bit wet as maybe, but is the quickest way. No, it's down, down is best for Filchin'. Sometimes I sit there, on the edge, and watch them, watch them people peopling. No, no, down, must down for Filch.'

'What pipes, Benedict?'

'Them pipes, the tunnel. The Effra!'

'What's the Effra?'

'Don't know?'

'Never heard of.'

''Tis the lost river, the Effra is! Was once on ground in Roman days they told me, now under the ground. Still flows the Effra does, but underneath, been bricked over and used now much for swidge and such, under it is, flowing still. Is still alive, only buried, still flowing, only out of sight. Flows all the way to the Thames it does, so they says. I ain't never seen the Thames.'

'Well then, Benedict, let us find this lost river.'

'And catch a lift on it. It'll take us, the Effra will.'

8

TO BREATHE AGAIN

Continuing the narrative of Clod Iremonger

I Fall Out to Myself

The emaciated man picked me up from the dirt, scissors in his hands.

A seagull cried overhead, 'Ark! Ark!'

Then the pain came, like I was splitting and shifting inside, like I should rupture myself.

'Not yet, mustn't yet,' the Tailor hissed. 'It's too open, keep small, you devil! It's not safe!'

But I was struggling and shifting, hurting so, I couldn't calm, wouldn't calm, I should burst.

'Curse you!' he cried.

Then, holding me hard in his fist, he ran. For a while I was only aware of moving fast and turning, dashing, onwards and onwards, and then we would stop suddenly, wait a moment, and then on, sometimes I heard cries behind us, then he hastened on further and faster. He hid in the entryway to a house, stood in the shadows, panting in a porch. People rushed by, people with lanterns, and some pushing some sort of wheelbarrow, and in that wheelbarrow, I heard a voice that I was shocked to understand I knew, because behind it a metal instrument sounded its sharp noise,

'Geraldine Whitehead.'

'Wait, wait, hold you there my lovelies!' My Uncle Idwid, the Governor of Birth Objects, was very close to me, listening in the street, his ears out on high alert. 'I hear something, silence all. Not a sound. Hush, hush. I do hear! Come now, a little louder, a little more yet. I'm certain I heard.

'Come to me, oh come, come to me. Don't be shy now. It is your own uncle calling. You can hear me. I know you can. You are in terrible danger. Let me help you. Just whisper, whisper your name. Let me hear that little syllable: Clod. Come, Clod. Come, come, Clod to me, sing Clod to me.'

All the people were still around him as the little man in the wheelbarrow listened out. The Tailor pushed me deep down in his pocket, and I in my agony tried so hard to think of nothing, I tried to be nothing, nothing at all, to forget the pain.

'I heard 'Iremonger'! I heard at least one thing call 'Iremonger!' Where are you, love? Speak to me!'

Silence. Silence but the distant noise of the heaps and the drip dripping of Foulsham Town.

'You're here. I know you're here somewhere!' sang Uncle Idwid. 'I can almost hear you. Whisper, just whisper and I'll come to thee.'

Such an itching, such an agony to call out, to scream out my name, as if Idwid in all his cleverness was tickling me with his words.

'You've grown strong. You've grown cunning, little Clod, but you cannot hide from me. You cannot fool such ears as mine. I can hear you, I can hear your very soul, Clod, I hear it breathing!'

And I should have screamed, I should have called out there and then and surrendered myself to the sharpness of Geraldine Whitehead were it not for the sudden noise of heavy boots breaking the irresistible call of Idwid's will.

'Idiot!' he cried. 'I should have had him but for thee! Manlump, thick of ears, deaf of mind! Fool, noise-murderer!'

'Please sir, please governor!'

'What, what is it, you thug?'

'There's been a half sovereign spotted, sir. In a ratcatcher's house!'

'All the cacophony of Foulsham streets: it's enough to make a fellow mad. Who saw the coin? When?'

'There's a man over yonder, sir, under that umbrella there. He's the one that saw it, swears he did.'

'Well then, that's different, we may hear *him* a little.'

The whole brood, noisy now, rushed away, and I felt at last I might breathe a little. In a moment the Tailor was on the move too, putting streets between him and Uncle Idwid's party. But there were watchmen everywhere; it seemed from every corner I heard voices calling out.

'Not yet, not yet!' he said. He took me out, held me in his hands, nearly dropped me. 'So hot! We shall not make it back in time. Curse you. We must do it here; we must find a place!'

He ran on for a while longer, stopped in somewhere and, with the aid of a handkerchief, he placed me on the ground. The Tailor was looming over me. I saw him clear then for the first time. He was a very tall, shabbily dressed man in a long coat of patched leathers, unhappily tall, like he'd been pulled and stretched, with a white, livid face, with eyebrows that joined in the centre, very lean and underfed almost to the point of being a skeleton. He swallowed; he looked at me.

'You have caused much trouble this night!'

He came close and tapped me with one of his emaciated fingers.

'I shall not hang for thee!'

He pulled at his own lank black hair.

'I shall not be put out on account of you,' he cried. 'But come now, come! Will you not come out, you're hot enough. Come, before it is too light and we are trapped here. It must be now. Now! Come out!'

And then –

And then –

And then.

The pain! The burning pain.

And then, breathing, breathing as if I'd never breathed before. How my arms seemed to tug from me, my legs to rip out of me, my head, my boiling brain seemed to bubble up in agony. Spreading out, filling up, back, back.

Alive.

There I was.

Clod.

I was me again. I was flesh once more.

Flesh again in some dingy, abandoned place.

And I said the only words I could at first say,

'Clod Iremonger, Clod Iremonger, Clod Iremonger!'

'Shut it! Shut it, Clod Iremonger,' said the Tailor, 'or you'll have the whole town down upon me. Shut it, or you'll give us all away.'

'Clod,' I whispered.

'Careful,' he said, raising a fist.

'Iremonger,' I involuntarily finished.

'Not a sound, Clod Iremonger,' he said, his long scissors in his hands now, 'or they'll hear you. Not a murmur. There's someone in the alley. Another squeak and I swear I'll gut you here and now.'

Binadit

9

THE EFFRA AND AFTER

Continuing the narrative of Lucy Pennant

I cannot say what it was that we passed through in the darkness, only sometimes it cut me and sometimes it wetted me, sometimes it moved as I touched it. Once it bit, once it was soft and even warm, and all of it passed alongside me as Benedict, pulling on a length of rope he had tied about my waist, pulled me down and down after him.

You don't feel you're falling so much if there are objects all around you, pressing against you, trying not to let you have your bit of space. Down through his little passages, moving bits before me out of the way, and when I was stuck he did not try to carefully win my freedom. His answer was only to tug me down and down by force, to muscle the objects out of the way. There are holes in the heaps, deep lanes, tunnels like the flues of the chimneys of Heap House and like them with hot and cold breaths, and with other creatures, rats as big as cats, forcing their own way along them, unhappy at the company.

At last we came to the bottom, or rather to a shelf in all that rotting land. I tried to call to him but there was no sound to come out of you that deep, and breathing was the hardest thing all on its own, the air so thick and soiled it felt liquid.

We forced our way along on top of a huge brick ceiling. At last there was some kind of hatch, for which Benedict found the thick cover and lifted it up and he pushed me through first and there were winding stone steps but no light, and the going was very wet and I slipped and soon enough the steps came to an end and there was only the sound of water then, rushing by.

'What now?' I asked. 'There's no more steps.'

'Jump,' he said.

'How far is it?' I asked. 'Stop, Benedict, I'll fall to my death I think.'

In response he shoved me and I fell in and he came after.

Icy, icy water. Quite took my breath from me.

We were in the buried river called the Effra, being swept along. I thought I should freeze to death. I'd be ice any moment. The place was alive with dripping sounds, with the plonk, plonk, of water dropping down, and then of waves, of things moving in the dark flow. Like being inside the organs of a massive whale, swimming along its colon.

'Is low tide,' he said.

'What luck,' I panted. The river was slowing and I could stand now, shivering and miserable, the foulness reaching quite up to my waist.

What a place it was, long ago, so long ago ancient Britons must have fished this river, and Romans had marched beside it, where I was now. Only then, back then, back then the river was on the surface, there'd be ground and sunlight beside us. The past, our past is buried deep beneath us, dig down and there is ancient land. Alfred the Great might have bathed where we waded.

'And here's our stopping,' called Benedict. 'Here's Filchin' steps now.'

He could see in the damp darkness, I could not. He had us winding up different slipping steps, not so many, and after a moment Benedict had found the manhole cover, and there was a circle of light.

Filching!

It was early evening. The sky was darkening which was never best bright in Filching, but bright brightness did it seem after that dank darkness. Like I was newly bathed in life, more beautiful than I ever knew possible.

'Filchin' foul,' said Benedict. 'I know the smell on it.'

'You showed me the way back there in those different darks, now I'll show you. I'll be your candle, Benedict, allow me.'

I saw him properly then, in Filching light. To think I'd taken up with such a one as that. You're braver that I thought, Lucy Pennant. He really did not seem a human being exactly, more a great mound of rubbish joined together into something almost human-shaped. There were eyes but they were so dark and yellowed they were hard to notice. The mouth more a rip than anything else. The hair was a wiry threadbare growth of weed. The clothing he wore was not to be described in any way like other people wore clothes, no recognisable garments there, just different things grown together. Bits of rat stuck upon him like fur in patches. If he wasn't moving you'd take him for just a pile of stuff, not living, just raked up. Like a mountain all of his own. But this, even this, was a person, this giant beside me.

'Don't like it,' he said, and he had begun a-trembling. 'Don't like it here. Don't want no cage.'

'It's all right, Benedict. I promise you.'

'You got no power to promise. Who are you to promise anything? You don't know, you're as nothing. You're a little bit with a bright red top. What protection can that be? No, no I shan't. Go home!'

'But what is home, Benedict? What is there for you? It's just rubbish and filth. I shall show you new things, new things and new people. You'll find a home here, here among the lodgings of Filching.'

We had come out close to the heap wall, it was very cracked the wall was, it never used to be so cracked, there were metal girders propping it up and huge buttresses made of brick. I wondered how long it should hold. I thought then it surely shall come down one day.

In the distance I saw the long slipway leading up to the wall. It was lined thick with carts piled high with London dirt. There were carts back as far as the eye could see, a great queue of wastedroppers. It was always so, it was a familiar enough sight. The carts came and went with their heavy loads through the day and into the night. They never stopped coming, there never was an end on it. More and more and more. Seagulls were thick about it all and on the other side, I knew, there would be a whole great army of Filching sorters, all of them married to the heaps, thousands of them, with their forks and pikes and shovels and bags, and the rats working their own work between them.

Has always been so. Would seem most strange for that road to have no carts on it, not to see the full ones lining up, not to see the empty ones going back. The horses pulled the loads and were whipped to keep them at it. They pulled and were pulled, until, giving up, buckling under the hopeless endlessness of it all, they slumped to the ground, were opened up and skinned on the spot, or if there were already too many gulls and rats about the carcass, they were shovelled over the wall and into it with all the rest. It was a grand and harrowing sight. Something Bible about it all.

'My home,' I said. 'Here I am.'

Binadit grunted.

'Well then,' I said, my teeth chattering, my whole body shaking with the cold. 'We'd best get in before we freeze to death.'

'Am fearful.'

'No need.'

'Your hair,' he said.

'What of it?'

'Most red.'

'Yes,' I said, 'always has been. Can't help it.'

'Like it,' he said. 'Fond on it.'

'I'm going home,' I said. 'I'm going to where I grew up, to where I lived with Mother and Father before they got the sickness and died. I'm going back there, to my old boarding house!'

'On then,' he said, grinning I think, I couldn't be sure. 'Show us! Bottons!'

'Here we go!'

'Lucy Pennant,' he said and the clarity of it was a bit alarming, 'don't be a botton. Stay as now ever.'

'I'll do my best,' I said. 'Come on!'

Alexander Erkmann,
The Tailor of Foulsham

10

THE TAILOR OF FOULSHAM

Continuing the narrative of Clod Iremonger

My Companion

'Clod Iremonger,' I said, though I'd rather have said something else. 'Help' should be more justified. 'Help', screamed out, may have been the most sensible.

In response the long jaws of his scissors snapped once. And came closer, and snapped again.

I think I should rather have been any place, than in a mean hovel with a man so lean and stretched. I think I may rather have been back with the Hayward family, or even with the coins of the pieshop. But I was in this dismal, dark place, hopeless and lightless, abandoned by all other people, fit for nothing, fit for no person, for no thing. How was it that I felt less free now than I did when coined. I was myself, but how long may I stay so?

'Clod,' I whispered, 'Iremonger?'

'Yes,' said the Tailor and the scissors snapped once to his syllable, he leant in very close to me. I saw then that his very skeleton was stretched and thinned out, that his own skull beneath the limited pelt of his horrible skin was most elongated. 'Yes, you are Clod Iremonger,' he whispered. 'Do you know me, Iremonger? Do you remember me?'

'Clo— no, sir,' I managed now. 'I think I should recall you if ever we had met before. You are rather singular, sir. I mean no offence, but, excuse me sir, are you quite well?'

'You do not know me?'

'Please to excuse, I've not been myself of late, which brings me to wonder, sir, if you yourself were not exactly as you are now. That you have, perchance, over the time since our last acquaintance, if indeed there were ever such a thing, if you might have – a suggestion only, you understand – have added some to your height while perhaps simultaneously mislaying a fraction of your width?'

How I cursed myself. No matter how I struggled against it, whenever I was in position of worry and terror I come over with a fit of talkativeness, and spouted out and could not stop myself from filling the room, perhaps in the hope of taking away a portion of the fear with words. Tummis, my dear late cousin, was much the same. And this was perhaps one of the causes of our intimacy.

'You wonder if I have changed?' he said, his painful face come close again.

'Am I very much mistook?' I said, though I'd hoped to make a simple 'yes'.

'Indeed, Clod Iremonger, I am changed, indeed I am. Last you saw me, I was but nine inches long!'

'Then indeed, sir, you have made quite a progress! Indeed you have!'

The Tailor pulled from a deep pocket a bundle wrapped in thick cloth, he unravelled the material to reveal a very dented and abused hip flask. 'Recognise this?' he asked.

I had never seen the object before and was about to admit as much but then I heard its particular noise, a strained, shrunken calling out.

'Rippit Iremonger, Rippit Iremonger!'

And then I listened and heard within that stretched, bony form of the Tailor the sound leaking out, 'Letter opener. Letter opener.'

'Excuse me sir, but would it be relevant for me to wonder if that is not my cousin Rippit who was taken from us so many years ago?'

'Very like, Clod Iremonger, very like. Though how you know so quick, I cannot say.'

'And, excuse me then, sir, if I may wonder, is your name, your real name, might it be, Alexander Erkmann?'

'Why yes, you devil!'

My Cousin Rippit, Now a Hip Flask

'I do remember Cousin Rippit,' I said.

There was never any forgetting of my cousin Rippit. Cousin Rippit had been Grandfather's favourite. Dangerous Cousin

Rippit who could set someone's hair alight just for the fun of it, just by thinking of it. Cousin Rippit who bent metal just by pointing at it. Cousin Rippit whose calls of pain in the night upset the whole house.

He was always ill, was Cousin Rippit, ill and dangerous. You might try to help him, you'd put your hand out to help him, and suddenly your hand would grow numb and have blisters upon it, because Rippit had somehow bewitched it. We steered clear of Rippit, we younger cousins, and I think the older ones too, and because of that he had a look of terrible loneliness about him, even as he was being cruel.

I did not know him very well. Once he attempted to drop a book on my head from a great height, he nearly brained me. Once he got hold of one Tummis's seagulls and plucked it without killing it. It was a very unhappy thing, that naked bird, until the rats got to it. And then, one day, he was gone, and later, much later, on that terrible evening when Lucy fell before me into a button, Grandfather told me that Rippit, most gifted and strangest of all Iremongers, had been subdued and stolen by his own birth object, a letter opener that I had heard calling 'Alexander Erkmann'. And here was Alexander Erkmann in the flesh, my companion in this cruel shed.

'He doesn't like to be made so small,' said the Tailor. 'How he struggles and twists himself over it. We've so stretched and pulled and hurt the shape of each other, we've corrupted and deformed ourselves. We're bent out of all order and shall not come back right again.'

'Poor Cousin Rippit!'

'You see how we have changed over these five years, how I

have stretched and tugged and how he has shrunk and dented and rusted. How we have hurt one another. I am not as strong as once I was and sometimes, particularly of late, I fear he may get the better of me. But he has not yet, though he pulls me so hard!' The Tailor wrapped and returned the flask to his pocket. 'Back at Heap House, your cousin had a certain way with objects. He summoned up people every now and then, pulled them briefly from the objects they had become. He stalked the house upsetting things, bullying them, bringing them for the briefest moments back to themselves, only for them to be drowned once more back into object form. There was pain all over the House, the things were hurting.'

'Yes, there is truth in this. The objects do hurt so!'

'One day your cousin called upon the object nearest him, to bring it out, just for a moment he hoped, and then to close it back in the form of a letter opener knife. Thus did I stretch and stand once more, and thus did I pounce and keep him there, that twisted metal soul: your cousin the hip flask!'

'Poor Cousin, though he was never kind to me, still I say it, poor Cousin.'

'Rippit Iremonger,' said the abused metal from deep within the pocket.

'Begging your pardon, sir,' I said, 'but what shall you do to me? Shall you tailor me?'

'I have been tracking you, Clod Iremonger. I have read the bill posters, seen the policing doubled, seen the Iremongers come out from their gates because of you. That's not normal, that's not like them. They keep their distance in general, from all the filth. I've been after you since I understood how much they wanted you. I told myself, if they want you so much, then *I* should be the one to have you. Why are they after you, Clod Iremonger, why do they want you so?'

'I cannot say, sir.'

'Well they shall have you again, true enough, once I have emptied you out. Once you shall cause no harm.'

'I do no harm, sir. I do not indeed.'

'Listen to me, Clod Iremonger, listen well – ever since I stole to Foulsham I've had but one purpose in my life, one solid purpose that never have I stirred from though it stretch me and pull me so I snap. I do not waver, it gives me reason. My life: to go about me in these foul streets and to poke at Iremongers with something sharp, to find me some lonely Iremonger down a lonely street and to send him off, as his kind has to so many others. But rarely, no I shall admit it, *never* have I had a full Iremonger in my reaching. I am Revenge, Clod Iremonger. That is my title!'

'You won't hurt me, shall you, sir, Mr Erkmann?'

'Shan't I? I think I might.'

'Please not to. I never hurt anyone so much as ever I was aware of.'

'Your name is enough hurt right there, your name's done a thousand, thousand murderings!'

'I cannot help my name!'

'No more can I,' said he, lifting the scissors above his head. 'Say your prayers now.'

I closed my eyes. I waited for the sharpness to come.

In the hovel I heard the sounds of things calling out in darkness. I had not heard them before, but now as I concentrated the voices declared themselves loudly.

'Elsa Howard, now a nail.'

'Horace Bentley, wooden plank.'

'Wilfred Pilcher, under the straw, a child's left glove long forgot.'

'Mr Sandford, a pillow cover, rag now.'

'Hello, hello to you all, I hear you,' I whispered.

'What's that?' cried the Tailor. 'Who do you talk to? Be quiet, shall you!'

'He hears us!' the things cried.'He hears us well!'

'Goodbye, dear things, goodbye to you all,' I whispered.

'Who are you talking to, Clod Iremonger? There's no one there. You and your family were ever such mad ones. But not for long I do swear it!'

'He says goodbye,' said the pillow case. 'Do you hark at that? He thinks of us before he dies. Shall we let it happen, shall we allow it?'

Their voices were a comfort to me.

'I seem to hear you all,' I said, 'in the darkness there. Can you, do you think, can you come forward perhaps? I should so like to see you now.'

It was the pain of it, the horror of my place. It must surely have been that that did it, because as I stood there now so close to my own ending, I saw Grandfather in all his high misery, moving the things about. If only I could do that, I thought, if only ever I could.

Why not? I thought. Why not, after all you're an Iremonger, you are.

'I should like, I should so like you, Wilfred,' I whispered, 'if you may, should you jump into a mouth for me?'

'Yes, sir, I think I shall, if you wish it true.'

'Elsa? Elsa, are you there still?'

'Oh, he calls my name! He calls it!'

'Elsa!' I whispered in my mounting excitement. 'Elsa, have at a hand now, shall you strike a hand that holds some scissors?'

'Stop this!' said the Tailor. 'Enough of your talking! Keep still shall you?'

'Oh, for the life of it, I shall!' called Elsa.

'And Horace, Horace, shall you strike a back?'

'I shall, with all my love!'

'Mr Sandford, I shall need you. I shall be wanting you most particular!'

'Here, I am! What service? Give the word!'

'Mr Sandford, cover a head shall you?'

'Sir, sir! Sandford's the man!'

'Now, all,' I said, 'now should be best. He comes on so close to me!'

'Now, Clod Iremonger,' called the Tailor.

Movement in the hay, sudden rustling and shifting, *things* with life and purpose, all at the rush. The Tailor turned around in a terror himself now, his scissors snapping uselessly in the dark. The nail rushed up and cut at the hand that held the scissors and the scissors dropped to the floor, the Tailor made a yelp. The plank lifted up then and struck the back, the Tailor cried out. The moment his mouth opened the glove filled the mouth, then came the pillow case over the head. And so! And so the Tailor was on the floor! In the dirt. And I stood over him.

How had I? How had I done it? I'd knocked the Tailor down,

unscissored him and had him in the dirt.

'I'm Clod Iremonger,' I said.

The Tailor made a muffled cry from beneath Mr Sandford.

'I'm Clod Iremonger,' I said, 'and I can do such things. I am Clod Iremonger, the friend of things!'

The Governor Extraordinary
of Birth Objects
Idwid Iremonger

II

IN FOULSHAM STREETS

Continuing the narrative of Lucy Pennant

We scrambled down the hill into town. It felt different to me, how to say exactly? It felt darker and damper. There was black smoke around the town that I couldn't remember being there before. It seemed to stick, that dark smoke, like it was permanent weather. The walls too, was it my imagination or did they seem to drip now? Everything was dank. Yes, it dripped, Filching Town did, never stopped dripping though there was no rain. The streets were thick with mud and waste, that was always true, but it was harder going than I recall, like we was wading back in that river again. Benedict shook a little, he trembled to be out there among the old houses, at each distant figure moving through the filthy streets he stiffened and seemed about to flee, and had often to be encouraged on.

Round a corner we surprised two men moving a great barrel. Their faces covered by rags, they were tying the barrel hard to a building. Seeing us they ran off. Something wrong about that. What was that about? But I soon enough forgot them, because there before us was clothes for the picking, clothes to warm and change us.

People as often kept their heap leathers outside as in, on account of the stench of them, especially if the weather had been rough. I grabbed at some sorry looking forms, they were hanging up on a line, trying to run away with the wind it looked like, the smoke and wind of Filching getting up the trouser legs and down the arms so that the abused leathers seemed to live by the weather. I caught up a couple and tugged them down. Someone tomorrow should howl for my thieving, but I couldn't help that. Trying to get Benedict into leathers was no easy business and he cried to have himself so constricted, he split them a bit, but at least was mostly covered now.

A march of Iremonger police came rushing by, men in brass helmets, all in a worry. We'd go the other way to them, shouldn't like to find them face to face.

'If anyone asks you anything, Benedict,' I said, 'say you've just come in from the sorting and your leathers have been that ripped up. It's not too far now, the boarding house is the far edge of town, close to Bayleaf House.'

We passed into another street. Police whistles were going off in the distance, not for us though, nothing for us to worry over.

'Go home,' Benedict said.

'I'm trying,' I said. 'I am so turned around.'

'Go home,' he said again.

'Hold on a while, Benedict, everything shall come right, I think it shall.'

'No, no. Go home!'

I turned to him then, looked hard at him. He wasn't talking about me or even himself, he was talking to a trail of rubbish that seemed to be following him.

'Go home!' he cried and kicked out at it, and the things seemed to disperse, only to gather up again a small while later, to do it on the sly, when Benedict had turned around.

'Is following me,' he said.

'What is?' I asked.

'It misses me. It calls me back.'

'What is, Benedict?'

'The Heap is, is crying for me.'

'It's just rats, isn't it? They will follow a person if they get a fancy.'

'No, it's rubbish,' he said sadly. 'Likes me, always has.'

'Bits from the heaps you mean?'

'Yes, yes, Heaps bits.'

'Tell them to go away.'

'Am trying! Go home!' he called and for a moment the trail dispersed, only to begin forming itself, and to grow larger this time, just around the corner.

'Let us move faster, Benedict, let us run a little.'

'Is begging me,' he said.

We began to pick up our pace but the trail of rubbish followed after, growing, but always, for now, some little way behind us, but growing in size and, I suppose, in confidence. What a welcome home this is, I thought.

We were back near the Corn Exchange then, the old place where the heaps bits used to be weighed and counted up, long disused that was, even when I was a girl. There was a wheelbarrow in front of it. Someone had just left a wheelbarrow there. As we came a little closer I saw that something was in the wheelbarrow. Some pile of clothing, I thought at first, only then that pile moved, slumped forward a bit, and then I understood it was a person, leaning forward, a person with a balding head who seemed to be in communication with a seagull. Yes, a fat seagull padded around the wheelbarrow, cawing and screeching. At last the man in the wheelbarrow waved his hand and the seagull ran down the street and heaved itself into the air.

The man sat up, looked about him, east and west, what a shiny moon face it was, grinning it was, then I saw the eyes. I'd know him any day. I'd know him by his eyes. He was a cruel one from the House, nearly had me before, on account of the doorknob I took a shine to. Didn't have anything with me much then did I? Oh no, nothing much to speak of, just some pilfered leathers and some man with half the dirt heaps stuck to him and the other half in pursuit. Nothing to declare, no, sir, no, nothing at all.

How he sat up, the blind one in his wheelbarrow.

'Who's there?'

I came no further forwards, pushed Benedict back a bit. But behind him the heaps came on, through the street we'd just quit, tumbling on in after us.

'Who's there? Who's new there?' He put his head out at an angle so the ear could hear the better. 'Such Foulsham calling. Can't hear right, but was there, a moment, did I catch: Iremonger?'

He sat still amongst all the clattering, all that smashing. 'Dunnult?' he cried. 'Where are you, Dunnult?'

There was an officer come running.

'Where've you been?'

'Just patrolling, sir, as you said, giving you some space.'

'There's something wrong here, something very unnatural. Something disturbed and hurt. I never like being out in these streets, would much rather stay indoors. I couldn't catch its name, but there's something very wrong with it, terrible pain and anger. No, no, come, come Dunnult, wheel me on, this town's gone all to hell!'

The wheelbarrow squeaked off into the night, and we could on ourselves. The pursuing dirt had reached our feet by then, was tangling around them, was over us, was lapping there, we only just kicked it off, I reckon, and ran on before it grew any bolder.

Our feet too noisy down the streets. And after it the tumble-crash of objects.

A small blue-glass bottle dislodged itself from the pile and flew at my head.

'Ow!' I cried, picking up the bottle, an old poison one it was, it had marked upon its side NOT TO BE TAKEN. I threw it down again, it rolled away with a greater speed than it should have. 'That hurt!'

'It don't like you,' said Benedict.

'I don't like it,' I said.

'It hates you,' he said.

'Thanks, thanks a lot.'

'Is jealous.'

'What on earth for?'

'It blames you.'

'Blames me for what?'

'For stealing me.'

'I didn't steal you.'

'It thinks you did, maybe you did.'

Round the corner there was noise in the street, such a different sound, the noise of people all bunched up together. How I cheered to hear it! Yes! We might try that, I thought, some company to hide in. I grabbed hold of one of Benedict's arms and quickly pulled him along the way and then ducked quick inside a building, slamming the door behind me, instantly there was a thumping on the door. But it could not break through. We were in a public house. I'd been inside this place when I was a child, sitting with my father: THE HEAP'S REST.

An Iremonger Counterfeit

12

IN WHICH A PROMISE IS MADE AND SOMETHING COMES UNDONE

Continuing the narrative of Clod Iremonger

The Tailor Strikes a Bargain

How he was crumpled upon the floor, the Tailor of Foulsham, his scissors kicked far from his hands.

'Wilfred Pilcher,' I said to the glove that had thrown itself into the Tailor's mouth, 'Wilfred, you may come out now, I thank you. Let the fellow breathe.'

A small and dirty glove fell down, crawled out from under the pillow case and scuttled back into the straw.

'Devil! You very devil!' called the Tailor from underneath Mr Sandford, the old pillow cover.

'I am a friend of things,' I said. 'I do thank you Mr Sandford,

Horace, Elsa, Wilfred, I thank you most awfully!'

'You are that welcome, sir.'

'Glad to be of service.'

'Most gratifying.'

'Please,' called the Tailor, 'call them off, call off your things, get them from me!'

'They've never done that before,' I said. 'I've heard them, I've always heard them, but I've never had them move before, not on my account. The truth is, Mr Erkmann, I'm that astounded. I'm quite impressed!'

'Take them off, call them off!'

'You did provoke me, sir, you must admit to it.'

'You're an Iremonger!'

'I am, sir, it seems even more certain now. In truth, sir, I run from my family. I do not love them very much.'

'Get them off!'

'You must promise, Mr Erkmann, to behave, then they may stand down.'

'I promise,' came his cracked voice.

'Very well then, Mr Sandford, if you wouldn't mind overly.'

'I like to do it,' said Mr Sandford. 'I could quite take his breath from him.'

'Better not, I think, Mr Sandford, on the whole. Do come away now.'

The pillow case blew upwards of a sudden as if by a sharp wind and floated down upon the floor, quiet and still again, a pillow case. The Tailor sat up then, coughed and heaved, his very body rattling. Looking about him much disturbed, 'Indeed,' he said at last, 'you are an Iremonger. I know your family and their business. There are of you ones that can move glass, and them that have a way with metal, or porcelain, and some that can only summon newspaper. I have seen one of your family walk the grounds within the railings of Bayleaf House with ten and more footstools lapping at her feet, and one solemn man who seemed to go a-wandering with a hatstand. You are not a proper people, I think. You oughtn't to be let alone. You should be done away with.'

'We are not all of us, I think,' I said, 'not all so bad. My Cousin Tummis was a very decent fellow, only he was drowned, you see. Ormily, she's a good sort . . .'

'Listen hard, use those precious ears of yours,' said Alexander Erkmann. 'I'll tell you a family story. One to warm your illbred heart.'

'Oh dear, I do not think I shall like it much.'

'Those people that I kill, Clod Iremonger, they are not real people. Your family made them in Bayleaf House. They put them together out of rubbish, they made them from the heaps, to do their bidding. They are among us, these non-people, walking among us, everywhere about us. Slowly, slowly they have been populating Foulsham. They are very like us, indeed they are very clever now, at first they were not, at first they might catch a part of themselves upon a nail, for example, sticking unseen out of a wall and that nail should snag their shirt and then the thing should simply come apart, their insides should pool out of them, sawdust or stones or old cracks of glass, all that they are comes out and spews upon the floor and there is their clothing before us, quite deflated, a person who only a moment ago was sitting beside you. But he has grown better since then, your grandfather. He has found another way. Listen now, Clod Iremonger, harken to this.'

'I do hear, sir, your unhappy history.'

'There are pipes, pipes all over Bayleaf House. Umbitt suffers the children to come unto him, and the children are instructed to breathe into those pipes, that is all, just to breathe, and as they breathe into those pipes, at the other end is a dummy, a thing of human shape but with no life to it, no life at all, but that child he breathes through the pipe, and the child's breath is pumped into the dummy and slowly the dummy inflates, with each breath it has more life, and begins after a time to breathe all of its own, and to take the breath out of the child. One child may have breath enough to make several dummies. Until that child, that child at the other end has had the childhood sucked right out of it.'

'He murders them!'

'No, I cannot say that, it should be a kindness to murder them perhaps. He pulls all the youth out of them, he sucks it out and takes it from them so that after they are left older and deader. Good for working perhaps, but of such small intelligence, they are content to be pushed back and forth. Their eyes are grey and their souls broken, they do not complain. They go on and on until they fall down, and never know why. They often fall to the diseases of Foulsham, they do not last so very long. They tumble into objects within months more often than not. And that is the other terrible prospect about the false people, they spread the disease, their breathing spreads it.'

Very quietly I whispered, 'My family does this?' In the darkness of that hovel, the glove, the plank, the nail, the pillow cover crept into the depths.

'In Bayleaf House, they do it,' said the Tailor. 'And since the children have breathed into the counterfeit people, the counterfeit people are so much the greater, they are almost impossible to spot. Those strange people are much stronger now. They have leather skin many of them, but I knock them down, I unstitch them. Their breath, when they breathe, comes out a slight smoke, like a small fire. It's a little dark smoke their breathing is, but often so small as not to be seen. But I find them, I know them well enough. I was a murderer in my day, from Germany, town of Gelnhausen, I slit a man's throat in an argument grown out of hand, and fleeing to London I stayed awhile, but being traced, I ran to Filching and there I was found by the Iremonger gatherers, and straightway made a letter opener. But, Clod Iremonger, I mean to make amends, and I have done my best, Clod Iremonger, but I am losing this battle. I cannot forever fight that troublesome flask.'

'I shun them, Mr Erkmann, my family. I'll leave here, I'll find Lucy, my friend Lucy, I don't know how. I'll find her and then we'll get out of here somehow and then never see them again, never hear of them, we'll go so far . . .'

'You'll leave them, while they hurt people so?'

'It is terrible. I do see . . .'

'Though they stamp upon lives, and build up a great army of unnatural people, though they spread their foulness all about? They shan't stop, Clod Iremonger, though they are out of your sight. They mean to go on at it, to go on and get strong at it, and then on they'll move into London with all their soulless tribe and on they'll go all over the country, all through Europe, and at last, they'll find you, they'll come to you sudden!'

'My family.'

'Your *family.*'

'I think then, I think they must be stopped. You must do it, sir, you're certainly the fellow.'

'I've not the strength any more.'

'Then whoever shall, if not you?'

'Who indeed, Clod Iremonger?'

'Your look,' I said, feeling a horror mounting inside me, 'your look seems to say . . . that I must.'

'Yes, Clod Iremonger, I think you must. You have your Iremonger talents to you, of that there is no doubt. Put them to better use.'

'Oh,' I said, 'I'm not your general heroic stuff.'

'No, you are not.'

'I'm not one to wield the scissors.'

'No, you are not.'

'Not fierce, you see.'

'I do see that.'

'Not particular brave.'

'No, not particular.'

'It is terrible what they do . . .'

'It is.'

'If it is the absolute truth.'

'It is, and you know it.'

'I suspect it.'

'You do.'

'I do, I do.'

'Well then.'

'Well then, well then . . .'

'Well then?'

'Well then, I suppose I must.'

'Then we're of a mind, you and I.'

I looked up at the taut man and thought what strange bedfellows war gives a person. I shook his hand then, long and thin and cold and absolutely upsetting to the touch.

Well, Clod, here's a murderer beside you. What a daguerreotype that should be, and what's at the end of this long trail for you, I wonder, the hangman's rope?

Boots in the mud broke up our shaking, men marching by and a young voice calling out.

The Tailor had one long finger to his lips.

'You cloth soldiers,' called an officer beyond our hovel. 'March now, hurry, vermin. How I hate you! That I should have to have you for my companions. Look smart, will you? We're after a gloomy boy, you maggots, dark hair, we've got his plug back at the factory, so he'll be turning soon enough if he hasn't already. That and the Tailor, do you hear, he's here somewhereabouts. Come on, leatherbags, you find him or you'll answer to me. Spread out, I want every bit of this turd-town searched.'

My cousin Moorcus, I should know him anywhere.

'I've a new gun here,' Moorcus continued. 'I'm very fond of this here pistol. It's so new and I've such an itch to use it. I'll call it my new birth object.'

'But, sir.'

'Shut up, Toastrack, or I'll brain you! Listen, sackmen, I'm that fond of this pistol. Here, what a thing it is. It's a

Beaumont-Adams it is, smuggled in from London. Give me a chance. Give me a reason to be upset with you, any one of you, and this shall make a nice hole in your face!'

A brief silence after that.

'You there, what's your name?' Moorcus called.

'Giles Clompton, sir.'

'Got your whistle about you?'

'Sir.'

'Search the huts along here, any trouble blow you, call out, man. Go, maggot, slug, earthworm, go on! The rest of you, follow me I say! Come along, Toastrack! Keep close will you?'

Boots going off, and then one man marching about, swinging the neighbouring doors open, looking inside.

'It'll be my turn to show you something in just a minute, Clod Iremonger,' the Tailor whispered. 'Quiet, quiet.'

The door of our hut swung open, an Iremonger officer was there with a lantern, shining it about. I heard no sound coming from him, no noise at all. He stepped in, kicked some of the straw on the ground. And the Tailor ventured forward.

It didn't take long.

It was all over in a horrible moment.

A sudden flashing of something bright and metallic. The scissors snapped hard on the officer, they made a quick puncture through the coat. And the officer, he just stood there, looking so confused, not hurt, only very confused, and a terrible smell came off him, like that of rubbish trapped inside a metal bin for ages and suddenly lifting the lid, the stale air escaping out into the night. From that hole began to pour out bits of old ash and burnt-up wood, much rotten paper and material, some chips of old crockery, all tumbling out on the floor.

'Whatever have you done?' said the officer, his voice perturbed. 'I seem to be, how now, I seem to be emptying . . .'

The Tailor stepped up and with one swift and thorough gesture took hold of the cut and made a huge rip of it, now all tumbled out and the officer grew less and less.

'Oh,' he said, 'oh, I seem to be coming undone!'

The black gas was coming off the fellow, the bad stink. He looked up at the man who had ripped him.

'You're, you're . . .' but his voice was getting weaker, 'you're . . .'

'Your tailor,' said the Tailor.

But as the officer collapsed upon the floor, a wisp of black gas from his nose, like a slug, and it crawled its way rapidly along his collapsed chest, and it found its way into the whistle that hung on a chain around his neck and that gas, it somehow blew upon the whistle, it blew hard, and with that final awful excursion the whole body of the thing slumped down lifeless.

'Come, Clod, they shall be upon us in a moment!'

The Heap's Rest –

A Foulsham Public House

13

BEER AND BED

Continuing the narrative of Lucy Pennant

Sawdust thick on the floor, hunched people propped over tin mugs, some red in the face, some yellow, women sweating by their men, a lone child being given sips to keep him quiet. The publican, the same publican I had seen when I lived with my parents, a familiar face amongst all those faces, there he was! A bit older perhaps, a bit larger maybe, a bit more bowed but the same man, and his wife, where was she? I remember her too; a thinner woman, her hair was falling out even then – her face resembled a chamber pot. We used to laugh about it, me and my school friends, I shouldn't now. I couldn't see her anywhere. But on the bar rested a large enamel pot.

It was noisy inside in that dim place, else our entrance should perhaps have caused more upset. There was a man singing out one of the heap ballads and all were listening or singing with him.

Deep in the dirtland, I was a-shifting,
When in the darkness, I found a-trickling,
A beautiful maiden, all dressed in white linen,
She smiles at me lovely and calls me to come in.
I'll never go picking, no more, no more.
I'll never go picking no more.

Such people, my people, all huddled together, banging on the table, clinking tankards,

She walks further out in the darkness and deep.
She walks on such light skipping feet.
And I follow her stumbling,
While the weather is rumbling.
I'll never go picking no more, no more.
I'll never go picking no more.

Some people had hung their old hats and coats up by the door, the raining heap weather collected in puddles beneath them, soot, bits of old papers (love letters, newspapers) got up in the heap winds, shards of glass, old rusted nails, bones, scraps of cloth. It was like home. How it warmed me to see such things.

I took an old cap off a peg. I slapped the hat on Benedict's head to disguise him a bit, to at least cover up the beetles that still crawled about his face.

I follow on after each clumsy step,
And further and further out of my depth.
She calls me, she calls me, my darling my dear,

And on do I follow though the heaplands I fear.
I'll never go picking, no more, no more.
I'll never go picking no more.

I went in among them and pulled Benedict after, shuffling by, smiling at them and saying 'How do' like I'd never been away. All the while the song went on and for the moment the knocking on the door was not heard above it. I tugged Benedict on, he was shivering under the coat, quite in a terror.

There was a way out the back, I'd used it as a child. I was making my way towards it when the publican called out, 'Now then, what's your measure?'

'Two jars,' said I, turning back.

He filled the drinks. I looked hard into his face. Recognise me, I thought. Please, please recognise me. But his bloodshot eyes barely seemed to notice anything.

'Thruppence,' he said.

'Thruppence,' I repeated to Benedict. 'You must pay the man.'

For hours we walked on, through bog and through creek,
When finally she stopped, we were out there so deep.
She turned around then, and I saw her so close,
She was all a skeleton, a dead person, a ghost.
I'll never go picking, no more, no more.
I'll never go picking no more.

What a shambles that caused from poor Benedict. His claws dug into the pockets beneath his leathers, pulled out bits of china, a few shining buttons, some earth, a portion of a seagull, a charred puppet's head.

She grabbed at me fast, I felt her embrace,
And I screamed as I stared at her own bony face.
She took all my breathing, she took all my breath,
And alone then she left me, alone with my death.
I'll never go picking, no more, no more,
I'll never go picking no more.

Then came out Benedict's money, a torrent of it, clanging upon the table, and then all stopped and then all did watch.

'Only thruppence,' I said, passing the coins over. 'The rest may go back in the pocket.' I shoved the coins away. 'He's newly arrived,' I tried to explain, 'from Russia originally. Very new to Filching, very new indeed.'

'Filching?' said the publican. 'We don't say that no more. It's Foulsham called, where've you been?'

'Do you know me? I was here with my father.'

'Could be,' he said. 'Could be yes, could be no. Wait up, wait up a minute, was that a half sovereign I saw in that pile? There's to be no half sovereigns in this house!'

At the mention of the coin they all set to murmuring, eyes flashing in the shadows, and then a young spotty man with an umbrella got up from a table and moved hurriedly towards the door.

Someone called to us, 'Hey, wait a minute, that's my hat that is. He's stole my hat!'

Just then the umbrella man reached the door and took the handle and pulled it open and then what a mound poured in over him.

There were screams of, 'A Gathering! A Gathering!'

'Quick! This way!' I cried, grabbing hold of Benedict and pulling him to the other door, away, away from the heap that was pouring in. Through a side door we ran, certain to shut it firm behind us, and we were in the street, and there at the far end, up the steep hill, was the boarding house. Home! There was the lettering, much patched up, much added to, upon the building,

MRS WHITING'S CLEAN HOUSE
ROOMS TO LET
MOST REASONABLE RATES
APPLY WITHIN
PORTER ON DUTY AT ALL TIMES
CLEAN!
NO DISEASE
ONLY THE HEALTHY NEED APPLY

'Come now, Benedict, before those things find us. Onwards!'

The side door opened behind us.

'Come on! Come on!' I cried.

A man stumbled out. 'My hat!' he called. 'You got my hat!'

'Let him have it,' I said. 'Give him the sodding hat.

'Our mistake,' I said. 'It's so like his. Beg pardon.'

I gave it over.

'Who's that with you?' he asked. 'Who's your fella? I think I know him . . . there's something familiar . . .'

'Mind your own,' I said. 'Good night.'

'Wait up,' the man said, jogging alongside us. 'There's something wrong with him and all. What's happened to you, mate? What happened?'

'He's ill, isn't he. He's turning you fool,' I said. 'I shouldn't come close.'

Well, that stopped the chap, he even handed the hat back to me – 'Maybe's not my hat after all. You're welcome to it so ever it were mine.' – and went rushing the other way.

'Here we are then,' I said. 'Tug that hat down.'

I pulled on the bell. Nothing. The wind was picking up all around us, blowing objects about the street, clanging, and clattering against the buildings, just a little way away there came a large crashing of glass. I pulled on the bell. Sheets of newspapers were dancing in the wind, pages were somersaulting down the street, but more and more of them, as if it were snowing. I pulled on the bell again.

'They're coming, they're coming!' cried Benedict.

'Come on, answer! Why won't you answer?'

There was a shadow amassing around the corner, something was coming, something very large.

'Come on, oh come on!' I cried, pulling on the door.

The shadow was coming closer, a whole great clot of things gathering up and rushing forwards I pulled on the bell.

And then at last there was someone the other side, an old voice, 'Who's there that's not weather? What do you want?'

'Is that Mrs Whiting? Is it?'

'Who's asking? I've a great gun in my hands, my husband's blunderbuss. Be off with you!'

'It's Lucy Pennant.'

'Lucy Pennant? No, no, she's dead. Dead and buried and out the game!'

'No, Mrs Whiting, at least not quite yet. Will you open the door please?'

'I'm full up.'

'We have money, Mrs Whiting, lots of money.'

The door opened and we tumbled in. The old lady shut it behind her, and I helped her to push the bolts true.

'Lucy Pennant! It *is* Lucy Pennant! Only you're . . . well, well . . . you stink. You'll smell my house down.'

There she was. She seemed barely to have aged. The old woman in her finery, quite the best dressed woman in the whole town. Quite the shock to see her, to be recognised again.

'Been travelling, Mrs Whiting, but home now. Need a room.'

'Need a bath,' she said.

There was knocking on the door, light this time, like pebbles. Oh, it's cunning, that heap, I thought. It knows a thing.

'Don't answer,' I said. 'Please don't.'

I took some money from Benedict. I counted a deal out, almost half a quid.

'So much currency!' the old woman muttered.

'There's more,' I said, 'much more.'

'Well, Lucy, well, pet, let's situate you, shall we?' she said, shuffling on.

'Thank you, thank you kindly.'

'I'll give you old Mr Heighton's rooms. They need an airing but you'll not grumble over that.'

'Dear Mr Heighton, what happened to him?'

'He turned to a brass fender last spring. Saw it coming.'

'Poor Mr Heighton.'

'Who's to say? Better out of it, I think. There's a new porter, pet, name of Rawling. No doubt you'll see him in the morning. He went out drinking before the sun gave up and no doubt he can't find his way home. He always does in the end though, comes back to me of a morning, bad tempered and sorrowful, and swears he'll never be at it again, but he is of course after a week or two. Lucy, I am sorry about your parents, such a shock. Such good workers, such clean people too.'

'Thank you, Mrs Whiting, that's very kind of you.'

'I said to my Mr Whiting, I said,' she said, 'never were ones for portering as those Pennants, never were such as them.'

'That's kind.'

'Good people.'

'Thank you.'

'Who's he then, under the cap? Don't say much, do he?'

'This is Mr . . . Mr Tipp,' I said. 'He's very shy.'

She turned the corner. 'Well then, here we are.'

'You're very kind, Mrs Whiting. I'm glad to be back.'

'Welcome home, Lucy Pennant. Welcome home, Mr Tipp. Perhaps we shall have some order in this place now you're back inside it.'

I closed the door. All Mr Heighton's things were still in the room and all very dusty. We both had the same worry, and both looked a little through the faded curtains. A gathering had amassed outside, that thing of things was swirling on the street beneath us. For a moment it seemed to me to take the shape and look of Benedict, as if in its misery it were imitating him, showing him beating his fists in agony against his head and then no sooner had it assumed its vague human shape than, with a sorrowful groan, it spat apart as if detonating, making a terrible crashing sound all along the street.

'Go to sleep!' cried Mrs Whiting out into the night. 'It isn't decent!'

Rippit Iremonger, found at last

14

BEFORE THE SUN RISES

Continuing the narrative of Clod Iremonger

The Last Post

'Come, Clod Iremonger, come,' the Tailor called. 'They shall be upon us in a moment!'

I went with the Tailor then, back out through the lane, people running, officers there.

Lights behind and more whistles blowing and calls of, 'Stop! Murderer! Stop! Stop or I shoot!'

Behind us guns now, guns at us exploding. Chips and dust coming off the wall from where the bullets hit. They'll murder us this night, they shall do it.

He knew his way, the great length of Tailor, and how I must rush to keep up with his long strides.

'Hurry! Hurry! If we can but reach the house, come, Clod!'

But as we ran along through obscure ways, stepping over

sleeping bodies, even into grim buildings with families huddled by a small fire, or holding in their filthy arms some object that had once been a loved one of theirs, I became more and more certain that it was not I that needed to hurry up, but the Tailor who was beginning to slow.

Ever since we were on the chase my cousin's voice had grown stronger and louder and was calling out now, as if to give us away, 'Rippit Iremonger! Rippit Iremonger! Rippit Iremonger!'

And beneath the tall man, rattling through his ribs as he panted on, came, as if in unhappy answer, 'Letter opener, Letter opener, Letter opener.'

Those two voices in terrible conversation with each other.

We were in a tenement house of some kind then, smashing by people who one and all screamed to see the Tailor. But always behind us the wails of Foulsham beggars and the calling of Moorcus and his officers on the hunt. There was a great tall cupboard before us that I heard moaning its name: 'Sergeant Clark.'

I stopped before it.

'Please Sergeant, if you could, I should be ever most obliged if you could lay yourself flat and so block the way.'

'Sir, do you bid me?'

'I do, Sergeant, if you shall.'

'Sir, I shall,' came the instant response and when we had just cleared him he came crashing down the way, and now none might follow us on this route.

We came out of the tenement through a back door and then a wide street. How naked we were, running across such a street and the day coming on, the sun beginning to strain through the dirty air of Foulsham, sending its yellow light down upon us like a massive torch pointing us out, saying here they are, get them, look how they progress up the hill!

'Rippit Iremonger! Rippit Iremonger!'

'Letter opener! Letter opener!'

'Rippit Iremonger! RIPPIT IREMONGER!'

'Rippit, Rippit!' I cried. 'Be quiet, I command you to be quiet.'

But in response there was a louder wailing, 'RIPPITIREMONGER!'

Police whistles behind us calling out, police on their tramp, 'Which way? Which way?' they called and the people answered them with awful speed, 'There they go! There! There!'

Our shadows, our shadows such long shadows up the hill, up the wide street, climbing the high ground towards the factory. Alexander's shadow so long and thin stretching almost the length of the hill as if it had arrived at the place already, so far before us, but that shadow was suddenly wavering now, growing weaker. Was it the sun on that shadow or was it Rippit biting at it?

'See, Clod Iremonger, see far up there near the top, a tall white house at the back of the square? Do you see it?'

'Yes, sir. Yes I do.'

'There I live, there I hide, in the attic at the top.'

'Come on, sir,' I cried. 'Do but come on, they are fast behind!'

'I weary, I do weary now.'

'RIPPITIREMONGER! RIPPITIREMONGER!'

'Letter opener! Letter opener!'

'Clod Iremonger, Clod fellow, run now. There is a hatch, it

looks like a coal chute leading down the building, but it is not, it is a thin passageway between walls where you can climb up and come out unseen in the attic, my place, my hiding place these five years.'

'I understand, sir, but please come on!'

'I am out of breath!'

'RIPPITIREMONGER! RIPPITIREMONGER!'

From below in the town, the sun coming up, a great calling out, and then a terrible echoing of that inner noise, the same words spoken out, out in the open. Someone calling out to us in response,

'Rippit! Rippit Iremonger! I hear Rippit calling!'

'It's Uncle Idwid!' I cried. 'He has heard Rippit!'

'I am going, Clod, I am going now.'

'No, sir, please, please do not leave me.'

'Run now, run fast, find the place.'

'Please sir!'

'RIPPITIREMONGERRIPPITIREMONGER!'

'You must stop them, Clod.'

'Rippit Iremonger, I heard you now!' came Idwid from down the way. 'I am coming! I come to you!'

'LETTEROPENER! LETTEROPENER!'

'RIPPITIREMONGERRIPPITIREONGER!'

'Run, Clod, for all your life. I am going back down the hill.'

He turned then, the Tailor of Foulsham, and began his descent, his scissors out, raised before him. I ran on, I ran higher, tears down my face.

Such noises, such calling out behind me, all the police running from the small streets all gathering up at him, snapping at his heels, and people at their windows screaming, all around him. All calling, all calling, all calling,

'The Tailor! The Tailor! The Tailor! There he is! Get him! Bring him down!'

One last look back. I saw the Tailor, tall amongst them all. His head went back, there was a terrible snapping sound, more snaps and cracks going off as if someone were breaking sticks, one after the other snapping his bones, and with each snap the lean man twisted and lurched and fell down so that he was ever smaller, ever less himself, the snapping creating a blur of tearing clothes and flesh, moving so fast that I could no longer see him, he was only fast, toppling weather, and when the weather had stopped, he was no longer there. He had clattered to the ground.

And then, in all that shrieking and clamouring, one piercing cry of 'Alexander Erkmann!'

He had tumbled out of himself, he was a knife again. And out of that cry came a voice from a relative of mine, a small, wide man, strangely small and strangely wide, not a person you had ever seen the like of before, saying over,

'Rippit Iremonger. Rippit Iremonger.'

'Nephew!' called Idwid. 'My nephew! Back again!'

I was at the top of the hill, along the square. The white house.

MRS WHITING'S CLEAN HOUSE
ROOMS TO LET

So much filth and dirt all about it, I picked my way through. They'd be up, the Iremonger police in their hunt, up in a moment after me. I found it at last, the coal hatch. I was in then, inside, so black, so dark. I crawled through, there was a ladder just as he said, up I went, up and up, feeling the walls should give way and squash me any moment. But then the ladder stopped, I found the tunnelling and fell out into a fireplace, into an attic room.

MRS. WHITTING's
CLEAN HOME
ROOMS TO LET

Part Two

The Boarding House

Binadit

15

HOME AGAIN, HOME AGAIN

Continuing the narrative of Lucy Pennant

It didn't feel any more certain in the morning. I hadn't supposed it would really. The day, when it came, was grey and windy. The house shook with the wind, the windows rattled. It rained and it rained. Only after a bit did I realise it wasn't water that was knocking against the windows, not raindrops, it was heapbits. Old scraps of clothing, glass, nails, shattered bits clinked against the windows. All felt miserable and unwelcome. And familiar too, sounds from my childhood.

I was home. Home at last and after such a journey. I lay on Mr Heighton's bed and looked up at the ceiling, trying to find some meaning, some pattern in the cracks there. I hadn't known idleness like this for so long. I thought that perhaps if I was really still, if I kept absolutely still then maybe none of it would ever have happened.

Then maybe Mother and Father would come up the stairs

and scold me for being in Mr Heighton's room, then maybe Mr Heighton would come back too and no longer be a brass fender, then I should never have gone to the orphanage and Cusper Iremonger should never have picked me for a servant instead of Mary Staggs, that spiteful auburn creature, then I should never have gone serving out in that twisted mansion, then I should never have met Florence Balcombe, who was my friend, and likely she should have been better off without me, that there had never been a moustache cup, that there had never been a storm, such a terrible storm, that never poor Tummis should have drowned out there, sucked down into the deeps and smashed by them, that none of it had ever happened, that I had remained only and forever here, with my mother and my father and all was safe and ever as it had been and none of it, none of it, had ever happened.

I wondered if that could ever be, if it might all be cancelled out, if only I kept very still. Perhaps if I lay still, then it might all go away again. Only if it did, if none of it was ever true, if objects weren't people, if all was safe and true and trustful, then, oh then, oh, then, I should never, never have met him.

'Clod!' I cried, as if he was actually somewhere near, and then I fell out of bed.

It had all happened. Every horror moment of it, 'course it had. I'd never have been with him otherwise. No going back, no scrabbling backwards for safety, only forwards from this black spot, from this bad space – there had been worse, I knew that, darker wheres than this one. I made this promise. Clod. Clod, we've tumbled into this together, and must venture to untangle ourselves from it.

I must find him; I promised I would. My leg hurt, ached like it was dying. Painful to stand on it. So what, I thought, may that hurting be a reminder to you, keep you going, got to keep on going.

'Ow!' came a wild voice, quite shocking me.

Oh. Yes. Certainly all true then. Every last bit of it was true, because there upon the floor was a mound of rubble rubbish, and that unhappy collection was alive, was breathing. Indeed I had just stepped upon it.

'Ow!'

'Mr Tipp, I presume,' I said to him. 'Morning to you.'

'Where?'

'Home,' I said. 'We've come home.'

I looked out of the window onto the street, the people shuffling about in the early day one man, an official type, at the corner, looking up at the house as if he was watching it. I looked across up the hill, through the gates of Bayleaf House, at the great building there spewing black smoke, thick with its own weather. I looked down. There was stuff around the boarding house, more around it than any other building, twice as much maybe, like they were coming gradually, those heap bits, sneaking their way there. I looked back at Benedict. I'd need to disguise him better. Couldn't do anything with him like that. I'd give him the best disguise possible: I'd clean him.

'I mean to civilise you, Benedict.'

'Not to do it.'

'Oh yes, I mean to clip you and snip you and scrub you clean.'

'Shall hurt?'

'Yes, I believe it shall.'

'I'll eat you.'

'We'll see about that.'

'I'm hongry.'

'This is 1876, my man. Time to get modern.'

A fat beetle perambulating upon Benedict's person came to his attention, and he pinched the thing in his claws and proceeded to eat it. Not an auspicious beginning.

'I shall need help,' I said.

I bade Benedict keep himself quiet in the back room and positioned myself at Mr Heighton's door. I was waiting to see who I might spy upon the stairs, who else lived there, who was new and who was remembered. This was my turf. I knew it, every part of it, every corner, every flea almost, you could say.

Sat there at the keyhole upon a stool, I saw old Mrs Walker with her pet rat Solomon passing by. God, how that thing had grown bald and shabby since I last saw it. Snappy little thing that rat was, been at my heels, hadn't it. I could almost remember the feel of its teeth even now.

She used to pay me in sugar cubes to take the thing out and walk it around the block. She did love it so, poor thing limping along. There's many of the lonely people of Filching seek a pet for company, the cats of Filching are too dangerous to befriend, and the last Filching dog died its death before I was born, all of them eaten by the cats or the rats, or the people too, but the rats could be tamed up to a point, they were all right.

Off she went, Mrs Walker and her rat, wheezing up the stairway, both of them sounding like they had the same wrecked lungs. Well they couldn't help it, I'd leave them be. Good to see you, someone else from before. 'Good morning,' I whispered, so quiet that I should never be heard.

Not long after I saw Mr and Mrs Harding on the stairs, all buckled up in their leathers they were, off to the morning shift, both of them coughing and looking grim. Never liked them much, they ticketed both their children. And thereafter everyone in the block blanked them. Others in leathers followed, all off sorting. Didn't know them, new people, at least the ones with faces on show. Many were already hidden beneath buckled leather masks to keep them from getting cut. All must sort unless they had a pass. Children too most days, when there wasn't school.

Wouldn't do to stop anyone if they were off sorting. Get reported for holding someone up, there was a heavy fine for that. No, no, leave them be. Soon enough the house would be emptied and only the old and the young would be left inside, the old women and men telling the young unlikely stories of old Filching, of bygone ogres and the like, of the Iremonger family and what they did to things in their dark properties.

After a bit there were more lively feet on the stairs, and a girl about my own age came into view, tugging her younger brother behind her. It was Jenny Ryall and her little brother Dick, who everyone always called Bug because he used to catch roaches and race them. Earned quite a bit doing that, used to collect bets from all of the boarding house, till it was stopped by a policing Iremonger after the new rule about no gatherings of people being allowed, no more than three persons together at a time. Still he was called Bug, even after, it had stuck.

'Oy!' I whispered through the keyhole. 'Oy! Jen! Over here.'

That stopped her, what a frown on her dear old face, and Bug's too.

'Who's there?' she asked.

'Who do you think?' I asked.

'Wait a minute,' she said. 'It can't be.'

'What is it, Jen?' said Bug. 'You said we'd be late.'

'There's someone behind the door there,' said Jen.

'Is it Heighton's ghost?' asked Bug.

'But it can't be,' said Jen.

'Yes,' I said, 'it bloody is.'

'Who bloody is it?' asked Bug.

'It's only bloody Lucy Pennant!' said Jen.

'Bloody Moory! I thought she'd been dead by now,' said Bug.

'Well, I'm not,' I said. 'Not yet any rate. Come in. Quickly!'

In they rushed and the door closed after.

'God, do you stink,' said Bug.

'Thanks,' I said. 'Nice to see you and all.'

'What happened to you, Lucy?' asked Jenny. 'Your hair's wilder than ever it used to be.'

'That,' I said, 'is the very least of it.'

'What happened to you? How did you get like that?'

'Is quite a tale I admit.'

'You haven't run away, have you? They'll come for you if you have. What are you wearing, that's a maid's dress isn't it? What are you doing in that? Come along, spill it.'

And I told her, well, some of it, but then Bug called out,

'OH MY BLESSED HEAP! What ever is that?'

Bug, snooping about, had found Benedict.

'Who's there?' screamed Jenny. 'Oh Bug! Come away, run!'

'No, no,' I cried, 'it's all right, please.'

'A Gathering! A Gathering!' screamed Bug.

And then, frightened by the sudden people and their noise, Benedict started screaming too, and all three were at it, until I, screaming over the top of them to shut it quick, managed at last a little peace, but anyone in the house could have heard that, or anyone outside watching it.

'He's with me. He's all right, I promise. He won't hurt you. They won't hurt you, Benedict. Calm please, and quiet.'

'Wherever did you find that?' whispered Bug.

'*Him,*' I said. 'He's called Benedict.'

'You call *that* Benedict? Odd name for it,' said Bug.

'I found him,' I said, 'or at least he found me, out in the heaps. I need to tidy him up. He might startle people as he is.'

'Well, I never,' said Bug. 'I'm Bug, by the by, how do?'

He put his hand out for Benedict to shake and Benedict, opening his mouth, nearly bit it off.

'No, Benedict, no!'

'He nearly eat me, he was that bloody close!'

'Now, Bug, don't go on so,' I said. 'There are things he's not used to. He's to be schooled, he's been neglected, but he's all right. Though I do need to clean him up. That's the first thing, and I need soap and a tub, and brushes, and scissors, I think, clippers. Can you help?'

Jenny said she would, Bug thought he might.

'Hang on,' said Jenny. 'Have you papers? Has he?'

'Well,' I said, 'no, not as such.'

'You need papers to be in Foulsham, Lucy. Oh, where've you

been? You can't go anywhere without papers. They're always asking for papers, anyone in the street, not just Iremongers either. Any neighbour may come to any neighbour's house any time of day or night and ask for papers, it's seen as a person's duty. And Rawling, the porter, he's a particular one for doing it, sits at his desk by the door and he sees people's papers as they come in or out. What ever are you going to do?'

And I admit I felt a bit defeated then, and sat down to wonder a little. What was I after all, just Lucy Pennant, nothing more, Lucy Pennant with a strange giant for company. Both of us illegal, both of us apt to be picked up in a moment.

'Well,' I said, after a moment, just to keep going, just so something could be spoken, 'well, what's new, Jenny? What's new in the house? Anything much? I see Mrs Walker's rat's gone bald.'

And Jenny, she sits beside me, and she tells me about those that had turned, about Rawling and his prowling. When I asked after my old friends Anne Dawson and Bess Whitler and even Tom Jackson and the cross-eyed Arthur Beckett, she told me that they had all been ticketed. That their parents had sold them off, every last one of them.

'How ever could they? It's disgusting!' I said.

'Wait a moment, Lucy, not so fast, don't you go judging no one. Not until you know. They put the price of tickets up. It's a lot of money you get for a ticket now, a whole lot, and for some families it's the only choice they have. And besides, when you're ticketed they say you're looked after, you're well fed and educated. And so it's not so easy to argue with, not really. I may get ticketed. I may yet, Bug too, and sometimes I think

I don't mind the idea of it. No, I'll tell you, sometimes I love the idea of it, for then I'll be somewhere other than here. The days will be different, I'll no longer have to go sorting, I'll do things, I'll have a uniform maybe, I'll count, I'll have *meaning*. It will be something at least, something other than day after day in this dreary boarding house, with precious little money and with no space. No, I think, after all, maybe it's not so bad. I'd find Bess. I'd see Anne again.'

'What a business,' I said, and very quietly, because she'd quite broken my heart with her little speech. The house and all of Foulsham were quite going rotten. Poor Jenny was nearly lost to it all. I'd have to bring her back, reel her in, poor doll.

'What about the man at the top?' I said. 'The one who never came out. Is he still there? Remember how we used to creep up and listen out for him, and look through his keyhole, remember that?'

'Mam said it was just the house creaking,' cackled Jenny. 'That no one lived there. That we were just being silly. But no one goes up there, not any more. I shouldn't, not likely. Mrs Walker's rat hisses on the stairs but won't go up. Porter Rawling won't clean there, so it's got worse and worse.'

'Look at the fellow,' Bug said, pointing at Benedict with admiration. 'He's got creepy-crawlies all over him.'

'Yes,' I said, 'they do tend to nest in him. About that soap . . .'

Jenny and Bug went upstairs to their place and fetched some washing things, they said they'd have to take them back when they returned from school in case their parents should notice them gone.

'I'm glad you're back, Lucy,' Jenny said before leaving. 'I'd keep yourself quiet if I were you. Rawling's always snooping and he has the key to this room, has keys to all of them, goes in and out of anywhere without bothering to knock. He's got so rude of late. The tenants complain to Mrs Whiting all the time, but it don't do no good. He's an Iremonger man through and through. I think he may have been behind some of the ticketing if I'm honest. Were hardly any tickets in this house before he came, only the Hardings and they're awful Iremonger in their doings too.'

'Jenny, have you seen any of the children after they went into Bayleaf House, after they were ticketed?'

'No, of course not, they never come out. They've no need to.'

'And do you think, Jenny, that it's a good life stuck inside those walls?'

'Couldn't say, could I? Reckon it is.'

'But what if it isn't?'

'It must be, Lucy, it has to be. There's got to be something for us other than the heaps. There has to be and it's there, through them gates.'

'But what if it isn't?'

'They say it is!'

'But you've never seen anyone after, so how could you know?'

'But then there'd be nothing for us, would there, nothing at all! We can't go out into London. The London wall is guarded and they shoot anyone if he so much as peeps over it. The dirt carts are searched thorough, and all there is, is the heaps for us. So if it isn't better being ticketed, then . . .' Her voice was so quiet now. 'Then there's nothing, is there . . . then it's all hopeless.'

'I know a boy out there in Heap House,' I said, 'one of their own. He believed in them at first, but he found things out, terrible things, and they tried to hunt him down, to shut him up.'

'You met an Iremonger?'

'Yes, I did.'

'I don't believe it.'

'It's true, and we got lost from each other, and I need to find him again.'

'You need to find an Iremonger?'

'He's in trouble, I think, terrible trouble. They'll crush him if they can, though he's of their blood. Maybe they have already. 'Cause he knows things and he can help us. Listen, Jenny, will you do something for me?'

'Depends, doesn't it?'

'Do you think you could get everyone together from school, could we meet somewhere and talk?'

'It's not allowed. There'd be trouble, sure to be.'

'Everyone's so frightened,' I said. 'If we could just somehow get everyone together and talk, we could make things seem clearer, if only we could do that, then maybe we'd start to fight them, to get our people back, to ask, Jenny, at least to ask to see all those children who've been ticketed. Only let us see them, let them come to the gates, then we'd know.'

'They wouldn't like that.'

'No, no they bloody wouldn't, but if no one ever stands up then we'll slowly, one by one, be trampled under, miserable and quiet and broken forever!'

'Well . . .'

'Just to talk, Jenny. Let me talk . . .'

'All right, I'll see,' she said, then, 'I'm frightened, to be honest, Lucy. I'm that frightened.'

'Good. I'm glad you are because then you're realising that they like to scare, don't they? And why would they scare if they hadn't something terrible to hide?'

'All right, Luce,' she whispered. 'I'll do me best.'

Bug and Jenny went off to the schoolhouse. Well, I thought, it's a start. It's got to start somewhere. I was even quite proud of myself. We'll form an army, I shouldn't wonder. What a thought! I turned to Benedict sitting on the floor.

'Well then,' I said. 'Are you ready?'

'Wot?'

'Off with them . . . things.'

'They're mine, they live here.'

'They're evicted.'

No sign of that porter yet, so I risked treading out with a couple of buckets, out to the old well in the square. I had them purloined leathers over my old rags, so I looked the part: by which I mean I looked ordinary enough. I left Benedict in the rooms, told him to keep there and still and all, and not look out the window. So.

I pushed the front door open, wouldn't come at first, that much stuff loaded around it, but I heaved the door to, and the stuff fell away. I kicked it and swung the buckets at it. It moved like it was only rubbish blown there, like I was making it all up in my head, only then why was all the rubbish at the boarding house door and none nowhere else? I shoved the door shut behind me, and ploughed over to the well.

I saw the watching man close up. He wasn't looking at me, only at the houses around. He wasn't alone, I noticed then, there were several of them, one at each corner, all looking up, one puffing on a pipe, one eating a Forlichingham bun, the dark treacle of it down his front, but you could tell they weren't proper people, not our lot at all, you could tell by the sheen of them. There was something put on about them, something not of our Foulsham at all, something very Iremonger, I should say. I wondered then if our old boarding house wasn't a deathtrap.

I marched along to the well looking so innocent, my steam coming out of my mouth in the cold morning air, and then I noticed their breath seemed to be coming out black, not white like mine, very queer that. Wasn't natural, was it? What had happened here, since I'd been away?

I got the buckets home, heaved them back. Sure enough, all those things, all them heap bits had got back in front of the door while I wasn't looking, covering over the steps, though I'd kicked them off not two minutes ago. I shoved them along again, though I hated even my old clogs to touch them. I shoved them along, Lord knows I'd scrub myself after touching that. I slammed the door behind me and was up the stairs, and there in Heighton's rooms was Benedict, shaking.

'Gone so long!'

'I'm back now, don't fuss!'

'Worried!'

'I can look after myself.'

I made a good fire and heated the water. I washed myself

first for I certainly I had a need to, and so that seeing me wash, Benedict should know it was all right. I tugged my dress off, what was left of it, and threw it in the fire. I pulled my drawers off, threw them in too. Well then, there I was, naked as the day I was born.

Benedict was staring at me.

'Hongry,' he said. He picked a spider from his hair and nonchalantly chewed on it. 'White and red, aren't you. Not much to you. Not much meat.'

'Will you stop your staring?'

'Like to.'

Well, I got on and washed then, wasn't going to spend any energy on being modest, gone well past that sort of sentiment. I needed to scrub him good and that meant getting him stripped so it seemed stupid to fuss over myself like some modest princess. We're all of us only animals anyway, no good pretending we're not. There's a body under every suit and dress wandering the streets, no matter that they pretend there isn't. Even Victoria herself has a body under all that black bombazine; even queens got bodies, got blood and skin and all of it. Good to be naked, after the prisoning of clothing, after all. I'm not ashamed of me, not one little bit.

I pulled on one of Jenny's dresses she had brought for me and felt much better, human even. I heated the other bucket, poured it in and then I turned to him.

'Mr Tipp,' I said, 'now then, what are you under all that? Take it off, take it all off.'

But Mr Tipp didn't like to, not one bit. The problem was working out what was him and what was . . . not. The water was black very quickly, and the longer he soaked the more things floated around him. Some bits of things sticking to him came off quite quickly, unglued by the water, but much of it was stuck firm and no amount of scrubbing seemed to help. I do not know how many insects I drowned that day, but there were many and as Benedict lay there splashing about, so splashed the creatures too, some managing to find their way to the bath's edge and, clambering up, won their freedom.

It couldn't be done in one go, he needed a fireman's cannon I think, he needed a surgeon's knife. I couldn't bring him back human, not all at once. I should have to reclaim him very slowly. Bit by bit. Taking it all off in one go might kill the poor thing, be like flaying him. He'd grown into all that, stuff stuck to him and him into stuff, so that they were of a piece. Coaxing the person back had to be done carefully. I knew it wasn't just about the outside of him either, I knew there was the inside too, and that was hurt and strange.

The best cause was to get at his face and hands, the parts of him that would be on display. I took up the scissors. What first I had assumed was his hair at the top of him was actually bits of old wicker mat, I also found about him an embroidered cushion, a lady's hat (remains of), two paintbrushes, a book of Psalms, an advertisement for A NEW SERIAL ROMANCE ENTITLED *NEVER FORGOTTEN* BY THE AUTHOR OF *BELLA DONNA*, some of a bicycle, the blackened head of a puppet (Punch, I think), a darning mushroom, some wild garlic (actually growing on him), parts of two kites (maybe three), the remains of a cat, the bones of a rabbit, many layers of old newspaper, some of a horse, two crucifixes, a length of rubber tubing and part of a door knocker. There were many other things besides, but they had passed beyond recognition. Whatever they were they weren't it any longer.

With each part pulled off, he was growing smaller.

'How do you feel, Mr Tipp?'

'Wrong,' he said, then, 'Wronged.'

I found, how strange the discovery, a patch of skin upon his forehead. I thought it was something else at first, a white tile, something stuck upon him, a bit of rubber. 'Whatever is this?' I asked. 'It won't give!'

'Ow!' he cried.

At last I saw I'd come to the bottom of him, that this was his head, it was not a foreign object. It was his skin, a little patch of it. I leant forward and kissed it. Poor old fellow.

From that patch I went further and scrubbed more, the circle of skin getting bigger. I pulled off a layer or two of old glued bill poster from his face and then some wallpaper (I think) from his nose, there was some stuck tar too, and something that once had teeth, and then it was as if his face was still huge but half the size and there was a person there, frowning back at me, the shock of it. It quite unsettled me, as if now he was wearing the mask, not before. This was someone new, I hadn't known this one earlier.

'Benedict, I think I've found you.'

'Lucy Pennant, I'm lost.'

He leant his mug close to mine and his bruised lips touched mine. Shouldn't call it a kiss exactly. Poor fellow, what ever was that for? He came close again.

'Maybe we shall stop there for now,' I said.

He came forward again, his mouth on mine. That was a kiss, that one. I gave it back a bit, then stopped.

'Well,' I said, confused and in a sudden panic. 'Well, well.'

'Lucy Pennant, Lucy Pennant, what am I?'

'Why, what do you think, you're a man.'

'Am frit.'

'And that's all right.'

'Big frit.'

'Well it's nothing to boast of.'

I put him in some of Mr Heighton's old things, grey trousers, collarless shirt, patched black jacket. There was a pipe in the pocket, that was sad. Poor old Heighton, he wasn't a bad sort, all his poor orphaned objects were still everywhere about the rooms, though by now lacking some of their buttons that Benedict had sought fit to collect. There were boots too, which I struggled to get on him. When he was done he wandered around in the clothing, looking very miserable and only cheered himself up by placing some of the things that had come off him into the jacket pockets, with each added thing weighing him down he seemed a little calmer, a little quieter.

'Well, Mr Tipp, I think it's time we brought you out into society. We're going calling,' I said. 'Mrs Whiting, she's safe, safe as houses. I've known her that long.'

'Don't please not to.'

'You needn't speak much, just say hello and such. I'll do the rest of it, now then, best foot forward.'

He shuffled about, his every footstep bringing noise from the house as it complained under his weight. No one on the stairs, on the landing, very well then and off we went, unto the public. Quite coming out in society.

Up the stairs we went to Mrs Whiting's place. I had been taken on just such a journey as a child, with my parents beside me, exhibiting me to the woman that gave them their jobs. I'd know the place with my eyes out. It had been to me over my life a place of terror, of wonder, of strangeness and possibilities, so full of things as was to me a great delight and caution. Whatever it was I'd be glad enough to see it now. Whatever else it was ever the largest and proudest dwelling in all the house, it was to be found upon the third floor. She had lived there all her life, she had been born there, it was her home. In it she kept mementoes of every stage of her living. She had some of her late parents' hair (carefully embroidered into a pattern and framed), she had her parents' shoes and letters, all her parents' objects. She never threw anything of theirs away.

She was a great respecter of things, Mrs Whiting. She was very proud of her collection. For Mrs Whiting, every object was proof of her living; here was her past all before her, things that confirmed she had been. All sorts of things. The floor of Mrs Whiting's rooms bowed under their weight, indeed her sitting room was a sunken place. Rather than lose any of the weight of her rooms (she would never part with a single object, all was far too precious) she had the Mortons who lived in the flat below turned out and had great steel girders fill their old home to prop hers up.

'Welcome, welcome, Lucy, I so hoped you'd come!' she looked most particularly at Benedict, not trusting him at all.

'Tell me again, Lucy, what is that with you there?'

'Mr Tipp, Mrs Whiting. Mr Tipp, you see.'

'Well, if you insist, though he shouldn't be my choice of a husband.'

'We are not married, Mrs Whiting. He is a friend.'

'Oh, my dear! I am much relieved. Your dear parents should never have allowed it, and now they are gone, and you are back, I see that I shall have to be your parenting figure. I feel I must collect you, Lucy, though I am not sure about Mr Tipp, indeed I am not. Mr Tipp, do you like things?'

'Do yes,' he managed.

'How very sensible, may I show you some of my things, may I?'

'Do yes,' he repeated.

'You are good. Well then we're quite coming along, aren't we? Perhaps there's more to you than first I thought . . . what a man you are! What muscles! Come, come, sit down, I'll bring them to you.'

I had suspected that this might happen, and was in fact hoping for it, so that as Mrs Whiting introduced so many of her things to Benedict, I might, in helping pass this or that to her, I might find some papers of former tenants and keep them for us.

'Please to pass me that vase over there, shall you, Lucy dear?'

I obliged.

'Most kind,' she said. 'Mr Tipp, this vase is my late husband, Arthur Giddings. Arthur was such a sweet man, very gentle with me, but quite weak of chest. He inhaled a child's milk tooth while sorting out in the heaps one day, he came back most wiggy and within a week was a vase as you see before you. Lucy, Mr Shanks, if you would be so kind.'

The old lady was growing quite tearful with her reminiscing and was now full tilt at it. I handed as requested the heavy-cast iron paper slicer from the dresser.

'Here is Mr Shanks, Mr Tipp, a very sharp one was Mr Shanks, not always gentlemanly, and very heavy when on top of one. Mr Shanks proved to have a most provoking temper under his great oiled moustache. He had hopes to be rather more than he was and when melancholy with gin he should become most foul of mouth and should set me screaming as he went about all my things, all my people here, all my dear dead departed friends and tenants, and, do you know, Mr Tipp, he even trampled upon a couple? Of course I called murder and some of my better tenants came rushing to my aid. I have been aided a great deal in my life, I am not ashamed to admit it. I like to be propped up, I do. You, Mr Tipp, have muscles, don't you? Well then, I was talking of Mr Shanks, he made great dents in my mattress – a dear mattress, formerly my great aunt Grace, a most commodious lady in her day – and then one morning, just a night after one of his awful seizures, I wake and there beside me, was that heavy thing! Mr Shanks turned paper slicer. He's dreadful sharp, careful how you handle him!'

Without invitation I next brought to the gabbing old dear Mr Whiting, her pride and joy.

'But Mr Whiting – quite right, Lucy, how I've missed you – was a very different sort of case indeed. I cannot help but grow melancholy when I think of him. Despite all my friends so thick about me, I have felt loneliness since Mr Whiting became a handbell. He was the gentlest of men, not talkative, perhaps. But so few words that are spoken are actually worth the effort, don't you find? Whiting, dear Whiting, he was a whisperer. He used to be one of my tenants, as did Giddings and Shanks before him. He would come and whisper at my door there, and he should slip little things under, so that I should come to wait for them, little missives, a fried plant of some kind, bits of his own dear hair, anything. He knew how I loved it all, his nail clippings, the sweet fellow, and of course I should collect them up. I have a huge collection of all the old bits of Mr Whiting, I may show you if you like. There was much to Mr Whiting until, one day, I could not find him anywhere, nowhere, not throughout my house, for days and weeks I went looking for him. I listened out for his quiet whispering but he was not to be heard. Oh, dear, where could he be and then, there he was, behind the door where I had not thought to look. There! A handbell! A handbell that I had never seen in my life and yet I knew instantly and intimately. Poor, poor Mr Whiting. First Giddings, then Shanks, finally Whiting. What a luckless lady I am.'

I had found them! Pages of them in a drawer, the papers of her expired tenants, many of whom I used to know, the names were all crossed out in pencil, and written in Mrs Whiting's own spidery hand were the things the poor people had fallen into. I put a couple into my pocket and, returning to the overcrowded sitting room, I heard Mrs Whiting addressing Benedict.

'Dear man,' she said, in conspiratorial tones. 'I know when it is coming. I have never yet been wrong in that. Over years I have watched the faces of my husbands, of my tenants, and

I can see the very first play of the disease upon a face. I know when it is near. Let me tell you, Mr Tipp, let me favour you this, it is coming for Lucy, I see it already about her face. She shall turn. I know she shall. I am sorry for it, most sorry. But tell me, Mr Tipp, may we make a deal, when she turns, as surely she must, when she turns, might I have her please?'

Benedict looked at her, uncomprehending.

'You see, if I could have her,' she continued, 'if I could keep her for myself, I mean to look after her. I even – I knew the moment I saw her – I have the perfect place for her, may I tell you?'

Benedict leant forward.

'When she goes, I shall put her over there, between the soup pot and the candle scissors. That's where she'll go. And may I tell you why? Because those two over there are all that remains of her parents.'

Was that them? Was she telling the truth? Was that poor Mother and Father there? I thought that it might be just as she said. I thought they might very well be them. Oh my mother, oh my father. There was something then, after all, something that belonged to me in the world. There they were. Father. Mother. A soup pot. A pair of candle scissors. They belonged to me.

'If you should let me have Lucy when she was turned then I should have, so to speak, the full set. Indeed, those two look very melancholy without her, don't you think? Let me keep Lucy, and understand I'd polish her nicely, she'd never know dust.'

I'd take them, I'd take them now, yet if I did the old woman would surely call for Rawlings and we should be done with instantly. I could not take them, not yet. I shall come back for you, Mother, Father, I promised myself.

'I hope she shan't be very big,' the old woman was saying. 'Lucy is such a slight thing, but you never can tell, can you? There was a child, a baby, barely a few days old, and she suddenly turned. Now you'd think a baby should be something small and delicate, something very tiny and precious, but no, when this baby turned it turned into that great cooking range over there. It is the very devil of a thing, but still I should never part with it, not for anything. I wonder what she shall be when she turns. In truth, I do not think the wait shall be very long at all.'

'Be a botton,' said Benedict.

'Think so?' she said. 'Who can tell? Now, Mr Tipp, here's what I say, I am not a fool, and know when I may crush a person or not, I have not survived this long time without my clevernesses. Now, my dear man – such muscles – if you do not give me Lucy when she's turned then I shall tell Rawlings of your presence here and Rawlings, you know, he shall do for you.'

'Do for me?'

'Yes, indeed, you see, he doesn't like strange people in the house, he won't have them. He knows all the faces of the house, and yours is not one of them. He had a neighbour arrested just for stepping over the threshold last week. She's been taken in, to the station, no one has seen her since, no one's heard a word. There is to be no rule breaking, you understand, Mr Tipp, none whatsoever, but perhaps I'll take a chance with you, and have Lucy on account. Besides, muscles! And yet . . . and yet . . . I seem to recall something suddenly, Mr Tipp, have we met before?'

'No, mum, no, not.'

'Are you certain? I do feel I know you, I feel I've seen you. Your face is not unknown to me, and yet where can it have been? I seem to remember seeing your face everywhere. On a wall! Yes, that's it, a bill poster! Oh, heavens, oh heapness, oh my things! It cannot be!'

'Whatever is it, Mrs Whiting?' I said, stepping forward.

'You've gone and done it, Lucy, haven't you, you've gone and done it!'

'Done what, Mrs Whiting? Please be calm.'

'You've took him from the heaps, haven't you?'

'Please, Mrs Whiting, you are loud.'

'You've gone and done it!'

'Please.'

'Gone and done it.'

'Done what?'

'It, that's what. It!'

'It?'

'That, that thing, the It!'

'His name is Tipp, Benedict Tipp.'

'Binadit! You let him out!'

'Please now.'

'Let him out and brought him here!'

'You must quieten, Mrs Whiting.'

'To my house, little bitch, my house!'

'You'll bring the police in.'

'How could you, how could you?'

'He's a nice man, Mrs W.,' I said. 'Very wronged.' And as I said that I felt Benedict standing next to me, I felt his great hand reaching out for mine. I held it, that big old hand, I'd not let it go, not for anything.

'You don't understand!' the widow shrieked.

'He's done no harm.'

'He was banished . . . thrown out . . . cast away.'

'And there was no right to do it!'

'Idiot child, foolish, foolish girl. He was thrown out, why was he, why was he, tell me that?'

'I cannot say, for some dumb reason.'

'He was born out there. No one knows who his mother was, no one knows where he came from, not from us I think, but they took him in, here to the town, they should never have done that. Children died, all over, but not him, never him, he gets fatter and fatter. My own child died! My own daughter taken from me! There she is on my mantel, that soap dish was once my child, Nicolette Rose! But he goes on, that pig thing, and eats, they give him foul food not fit for rats and still he eats, he eats and thrives. He's not proper, there's nothing proper about him!'

'He is proper,' I cried. 'He's as proper as any of us!'

'No! No, he's not! The filth always stayed over the wall till he came, but after he came, it got out! It fell over, it lurched like it was an ocean. It came after him, wherever he was put the filth followed him. It would fill houses, the stuff that came after him, one old man drowned on it. So they brought him to Town Square, didn't they, they set him down in the centre and stood back, and in a half hour there blew in a mountain of heap, all after him. So that was that then, they threw him over the wall where he belonged where he should ever have stayed! He was ten years of age then, that should make all of about twenty now. And look at that, that thing may as well be twenty as any age! He'll drown us, don't you see? He'll drown us all! He must go back before all Foulsham is drowned!' She began screaming then. 'Get him out! Get him out! Get him out of my home!'

There was noise below, a bell ringing, someone had entered the front door.

'That shall be Rawling,' the old woman said in her panic, 'come home at last. He must not see you, he must not find the It here. What shall happen if he finds the It here, what will they do to me? Hide, hide, both of you! And the moment, the moment it's safe, I want you out! Both!'

The stairs were creaking as heavy feet came up, and a loud, grating voice sung out,

'I've been sifting! I've been sorting!
Over in the rubbish ground,
I've been sifting! I've been sorting!
Come and see what I have found!

'I've been sifting! I've been sorting!
I have found there much for thee,
I've been sifting! I've been sorting!
Let me in now, come and see!'

'Rawling is coming, coming fast,' cried the old woman. 'We shall all be arrested!'

'Mrs Whiting, please listen,' I said, 'where can we hide?'

'Into the hulk cooking range with you both, and close the door hard and fast, you in one door Lucy, hurry yourself, and that It thing into the other, larger one, hurry now, hurry, he'll be here in a moment.'

It was a very large cooker and even Benedict, bent over and squeezed, could fit inside it. He looked very desperate, and I could just about feel him trembling in the other oven beside of me. There was a tiny hatch in the door where a cook may look in and see how his business was proceeding. I could see through it, I could look out.

There was a knock at the door.

'Come in, Rawling,' said Mrs Whiting, 'where ever have you been?'

Mr Rawling was a white faced, balding man, his head slightly misshapen as if he may have been in an accident at some time, he was dressed in a dark grey boilersuit, the lower half of the legs were covered in dirt.

'What's been doing here?'

'What muscles you have, Mr Rawling, what muscles.'

'There's a deal of filth around the house.'

'Indeed your feet are most uncomfortable,' she said.

'And up the stairs, I see someone's been in Heighton's rooms, what's the cause of that? What's afoot, you sneaking old pomfrit? What's going on here while I'm out? There's villainy here, I know it. And why is all the rubbish all around the entrance of the house? What's it doing there? And who's the one to tidy it? It's me. Me and no one else. No one else to do it. And I don't like it! Someone shall have to pay for it, it shan't be me. Why should I?'

'They've found me,' Benedict whispered. 'Oh, Heaps, Heaps have found me.'

'I had to dig my way in to get here,' Rawling was saying, 'and it seems to be collecting up, to be growing around it, as if the heaps themselves were coming here, deliberate like, were forming a place of gathering. And Gatherings, as you know, aren't legal. I'll have to chop it up before it gets too sure of itself. If it gets big then it'll smack at the house and do it great mischief. It's not allowed. Strictly not. Things and people are not to congregate, the rule is very clear on that. I can't think why it's happening when it's against the law. Speaking of law, now, let's see your papers.'

'Mr Rawling, do you really think that necessary?'

'Is the law, I am to do it. Come now, how do I know you're legal? Let's see. Come, come, old girl, hand over.'

He walked over to Mrs Whiting to collect the paper but as he did, he stopped short suddenly. 'Hello now,' he said, 'what's this? What's going on?'

Small bits of heap, scraps of paper and little slivers of glass from Mr Rawling's boots had come free and were slowly twisting their way towards Benedict.

'What's this?' he said. 'What's going on here?' he asked. And then he hollered, 'Villainy! Seek it out!'

Officers of the Heap Wall

16

IT SHALL NOT HOLD

Heapwall log

Entry 26th January 1876
7 a.m.

Heaps are up. Level's rising, has been some spillage over the wall. Not much unusual about that perhaps except that all the storm seems to be against the wall side and the heaps appear to be massing, so that, if this continue, which is very unlike surely, there is certain to be a flooding of this part of Foulsham, the warning horns have not yet been sounded, but it's wise for us to keep strict notice.

10 a.m.

There are cracks on the wall now, undeniable cracks. I do not think it shall fall, surely it shall not, but the cracks are palpable certainly. I could fit my little finger through one. Not good, not good. We take measures with us by the cracks and write with chalk next to them how wide they are and come back every half hour to see if they are widening. They are.

Heap dangerously high, more has spilled over the top, but the wall does hold for now. Sky calm, why do the heaps rage so?

11 a.m.

I have advised clearing the houses and streets nearest the Heap Wall, but Churls Iremonger, Wall Governor, will not permit it, he says we are to stand our ground whatever else. There's emptying of the heaps further out, I see it now, in the distance, Heap House looks naked over there, less and less heap around it, as if it were being abandoned.

I can even see some of the pipes under now, never seen them before, not since I was a child, when they were first laid down, and to do that they had to make special barriers first. I can fit my fist through the deepest cracks.

The rats, the rats are leaving!

They're coming everywhere about us now, squeezing through some of the cracks, or over the top, everywhere you look, never seen the like, never seen anything like it. More and more and more of them. When will they ever stop? From the height of my wall office, I can see down into Foulsham and the street that goes into the town has turned black with rats on the run. It's been black for more than a half hour now. They're going, all the rats, they're on the run.

Heap level still rising.

12 p.m.

One of the men says that Hawkins was measuring a split in

the Heap Wall when a section of wall come off on him. He's dead now, Hawkins is. We're bracing the wall with everything we can, but I am not certain any more that we can last. I don't think Octaviam's wall will see this day out. Governor Churls says that it shall calm down again soon enough, that it shall not breach, but he himself has left now.

I shall sound the siren, whether I am punished for it or not.

My men may leave the Heap Wall and go to high ground. There are two parties of sorters still unaccounted for, you cannot see them, the heaps spit so. And far, far out, Heap House in the distance – do I see this? Can it be true? – seems to be splitting up.

Heap level still rising.

It will spill I think.

It will spill.

God keep us.

Tom Goldsmith, Mrs Bailey, Bentley Orford and Helen

17

MY INHERITANCE

Clod Iremonger's narrative continued

The Tailor's Room

This is what a room looks like when the world has forgotten it, the floor thick with dirt and dust. Here hid the Tailor Alexander Erkmann for five long years. I could almost feel him there, as if he were beside me whispering, 'Clod Iremonger, Clod Iremonger, you must stop them, you must. You are the one to do it.'

'I am just Clod,' I said to the room, 'and that's not an awful lot.'

But the Tailor was there no longer, he was lost again in the shape of a letter opener. That room, poor room, was a dead place. I needed to see something else, something other than this room, so thick with Tailor. I opened the filthy curtains. The begrimed windows were impossible to see through. I wiped clean a patch the size of my hand, of clear, clear enough, smudged and smoky glass. I looked out across the grey dullness that was the great smoking factory, a hulk of a place, Bayleaf House. There was no mistaking that place, Bayleaf House itself.

Bayleaf House, where my family was, and not only my family,

'My plug!' I said. 'Oh my plug, my James Henry plug.'

I sat in all the dirt and dust, in all that thick air and wondered what was to become of it all.

How much longer, James Henry? I wondered. What time do we have left, before the creeping illness comes into me? What to do in that time? I must go in, I must go in and find those people and see all that they do. However can I stop Grandfather? I used to think living was a safe thing to do. I shall have to wander over there through those gates of metal, slip in there, just a Clod amount of space, and feel through all that smoke, sniff out Grandfather and my family and stop them. However should they listen to me? They never used to. What's changed that they should now? I've changed, I thought then. I've changed. I shall tell them, it's all gone foul and wrong and must be stopped. I'm Clod, I am, and I mean to stop them.

I sat up, the dust moved around me.

'Battle, old Clod, old fellow?' I whispered.

I sat in the dirt.

'I'd manage better with Lucy beside me, that I know. Battle?'

Just sat there in the dirt.

'Well, I may as well march alone. I am alone after all.'

From somewhere deep in the dust, other voices called through the cobwebs and dirt.

'Someone new,' came a voice.

'Come to help?' asked another.

It was an old broken wicker seat talking to a cracked picture frame.

Other obscure things murmured in the darkness.

'Who's there?'

'Who called?'

'Something new.'

'Oh, how he shines!'

'What life he has.'

'Help us, will you,' something called. 'I was Bentley Orford once, am old split bellows now.'

'I was Helen before ever I was this old crib.'

'Oh, hullo,' I said. 'I do hear you. I am most glad of it.'

'Now, that's proper of him,' said the bellows.

'That's breeding, that is.'

'I'm of bad blood, actually,' I said. 'Though I'm awfully glad of your company.'

'No, come now, you're a bright young man, and kind to talk to old broken bits such as us.'

'What shall we call you?'

'Clod,' I said hopelessly. 'Clod the warrior!'

'Clod the warrior, is it? What's your true name?'

'Tummis had some Coldstream Guards,' I muttered. 'I'll be a soldier in my turn, just you see if I'm not.'

'Clan of Orford am I,' said the proud thing. 'My old dad, dear old fellow, lost in the heaps.'

'I am most sorry to hear it,' I said. 'It is awful dangerous out there.'

'That it is, no doubting.'

'I used to watch it from another attic window,' I said. 'Nearly got heap blindness from watching it so often, back at Heap House.'

'Heap House, says you? Heap House?'

'Yes, I did live there, you know.'

'Did you? Why ever should you do that?'

'I was born there, you see.'

'Not Iremonger are you? Not an Iremonger, we had one of them an old dented flask how we hated him and liked to shout at him and make all a misery for him. But suddenly that flask's here no more. Not an Iremonger, are you, surely not. Not with manners like that.'

'I am, yes, I must say I am, through and through.'

'But you sound so different.'

'Do I? I thank you for that at least.'

'We haven't had new company, not for so long.'

'You may come to me,' I said, 'if you like.'

And out of the dirt and dust, making their own timid tracks, broken bits from the attic came and sat beside me. And so we sat together a while, and felt each of us the better for it. Remembering our histories to one another.

We may have continued happily for some time, but then came a noise from somewhere within the house. I had so completely forgotten that there must be more to this place, I'd thought it only a room, but there were surely rooms and rooms beneath me. That was a cheering thought. What went on in those other places? Were there people down there? Were there lives? And I must admit, tears in my eyes, such happiness, that there was! There was life below, because then

I heard a man singing,

'I've been sifting! I've been sorting!
Over in the rubbish ground,
I've been sifting! I've been sorting!
Come and see what I have found!

'I've been sifting! I've been sorting!
I have found there much for thee,
I've been sifting! I've been sorting!
Let me in now, come and see!'

But on hearing this man's singing all the heap bits around me, and on my lap, began to stir again and to retreat into the soft corners, to lose themselves in cobwebs.

'Come back,' I said. 'Please come back.' But they would not, as if they were afraid.

Mrs Whiting and her late husdbands
Mr Giddings, Mr Shanks and Mr Whiting

18

IN A COOKER LOCKED

Lucy Pennant's narrative continued

'Binadit,' said Benedict from his place in the cooker.

Please, please, I thought, you must be quiet, Benedict. But the heap bits falling from the cuffs and feet of the new porter were rushing across the floor towards him, and pinging against the door of the cooker, eager to get in.

'What's going on?' asked Porter Rawling. 'What's the size of it?'

The bits stuck fast to the cooker door, like magnets.

'What's the meaning on it, Whiting?' asked Rawling of the old woman, coming closer. 'What have you done, you old sack of bones? You've no license for such a business, this I know. That shouldn't happen, it's against the rules. Why do them things do that? They oughtn't to, I'll have them impounded for less. Hi there, get off that, will you?'

He poked at the things, but the bits stuck fast to the cooker.

'Why would they do that, isn't natural, is it?'

'I cannot tell what you are making such a fuss about,' said the widow. 'Do you not have duties, Rawling? Do not let me detain you further.'

'Is there someone in there, Mrs Whiting, is there now?'

'Rawling, are you insinuating that I am hiding someone in my apartment?'

'That's about the size of it.'

'I am shocked and I am hurt and I am disappointed.'

'Well, well, I can live with that, that's as nothing.'

'I've a headache. I need to be left alone.'

'I've a headache, name on it: Leonora Whiting.'

The porter had his hand on the cooker latch then. 'Who's in there? Come out, shall you?'

Benedict was silent inside.

'You see, Rawling, it is quite empty. How could it be otherwise?'

But Rawling, he lifted the latch, he lifted the latch and he opened the door. He sprung back of a sudden and screamed,

'Well then, look what's for dinner!'

'Binadit!' cried Benedict. 'Binadit! Binadit!'

'What's your name then?' asked Rawling.

'Help! Murder!' cried Mrs Whiting. 'There's a man in my room! Muscles!'

'Come you out,' said Rawling. 'Come you out now, come, come!'

'I stuck,' said poor Benedict.

'Papers!' snapped Rawlings. 'I'll have papers, I will! Papers for being in this house, papers for hiding in that there cooker.

Is it legal, is it right? Get out, get out will you!'

'I stuck cannot!'

'No, no! I'll not sanction it,' the porter went on. 'This is wrong, this is most wrong and I do hate it! I will have order in this house. I am the rule book on these premises, and you, you there, big fellow in the stove, I'm taking you down. You're cooked!'

Saying that, Rawling, in one excited leap, took hold of Mr Whiting and rung him like his life depended on it. That set Mrs Whiting screaming for her husband the handbell and Benedict screaming as loud as he might for 'Lucy Pennant! Lucy Pennant!'

I struggled to get from my portion of the cooker. I struggled to free me. I pushed on the door with my feet but it would not come open. Mrs Whiting had closed the latch and I couldn't get out. I thought we had a chance of getting him, I thought together we could surely overpower the porter, but I could not get free. I could not shift to tell Benedict. He was too confused, the great big man, he needed instruction. And still the porter rang his bell, not stopping for a moment, as if he was not a man at all, only a machine built for the single purpose of ringing a handbell. It all happened so fast. It all went wrong so quick. And then there were other people in the room, men in policing leathers and with truncheons and pikes.

'What is the meaning of it?' called one officer. 'Who are you to disturb the day in this manner? There had better be call for it, better be good call or there'll be such an answering.'

'You,' said another officer to the porter, 'have even interrupted Umbitt with your noising!'

'Umbitt!' cried the porter, most terrified, 'Not Umbitt! Surely not!'

'Umbitt himself!' repeated the officer.

'Oh Umbitt, Owner,' cowered the porter.

'Silence! You little dirtpile!'

'Oh my Maker!' Rawling added involuntarily. 'Didn't mean it.'

'You're making foul noise with that brass instrument.'

'Poor Mr Whiting, dear Mr Whiting!' wept the widow.

'Will you turn that noise off!' said the officer, meaning the widow.

'Shut it, Whiting,' said Rawling, 'or I reckon I'll bash you.'

'What's that then?' said an other officer pointing at Benedict.

'That's what the noise is for,' said Rawling. 'That's a varmint, a walloping great varmint, I reckon. Something huge and unsavoury.'

'Not peculiar to these premises?'

'Most peculiar, but not our peculiar,' said the porter.

'Name, Peculiar, what 'tis?'

'Binadit,' he stammered.

'Name, Binadit? Binadit, did you say?'

'No, no,' poor Benedict stammered, ''tis . . . Benedict Tipp.'

'Why mention Binadit, Mr Tipp? Why would you say that name?'

'No, no, not to mention.'

'How came you here, Mr Tipp?' asked an officer.

'That's the question, let him answer that,' added the porter.

'Shut it, you, stand down, or I'll clock you good and hard.'

'Sir,' nodded the porter, 'sir.'

'Now then, Mr Tipp, explain yourself.'

I kicked at the door.

Benedict stood in front of it.

'I am Mr Tipp,' he said, 'very new here, no home, no lodging.'

'Very like,' said the officer, 'and so you come here of your own volition?'

'I come,' continued poor, poor Benedict, 'for shelter, I come for light, I come for company, I come for the red company that I like so, the red heat, I mean, the warmth, I mean, and I come on my own.'

'Where've you been then, afore you was here?'

'Lost in darkness, Heap! Heap!'

'On the heaps?'

I kicked the door.

'What was that?'

'Was me!' cried Benedict. 'Was my fault, things follow me, things noise for me, I cannot help it. I came here to escape the Heaps, the Heaps were following me.'

'That is true,' said Rawling, 'that's true enough, certainly. I seen it.'

'If I hear you ever once more, Porter, you'll be portering out where no one shall ever hear you and there you may talk till you're blue all over, or any other colour!'

'Sir, sir.'

'Now then,' the officer said to Benedict, 'show me.'

I kicked the door as hard as I could.

'I made the noise,' said Benedict. 'I would like to say, I shall step away and the noise shall not start again, for there's no point in both drowning when one may be safe to help the other later, is there.'

'What are you talking about?'

'I'm telling the stove to be quiet, or I'll be hurt by it, I mean I'll hurt it, I mean it'll be hurt.'

'I'm not following.'

'You see,' said Benedict, leaving me, though it was my fault, all my fault, 'I've been most looked after, I'm happy for it. Now, I shall step away from this thing and when I does it shall be silent, and then, all them heap bits yonder, shall in a moment come along a me.'

I did not kick, I did not call out. I'd raise an army, I bloody would.

'Look, after me,' he said, 'things, oh things, here, come to me.'

I heard one or two of the heap bits following him. 'See how they come after,' he called. 'Come, come, here I be!'

More followed him, more joined into him, covering him over again.

'Come! Come!' he cried and as he wailed, with laughter and horror, the filth from the heaps dragged after him, but he was at the door already, he was out of Mrs Whiting's room and thundering down the stairs before the officers knew what was happening.

'Good God!'

'Did you see that, the things rushing?'

'It's . . . it's It, the Baby, it's out of the heaps.'

'I thought it a story. One to scare the dumb people.'

'Does that look like a story?' the other replied. 'Does the house wobble on account of a story?'

'Must get him!'

'Get him fast, trap him!'

'Call every man! Now, quick, before the walls fall!'

'After him!'

'After him!'

And all ran after, even the porter. What sounds down the boarding house stairs, what calls and hollering. Benedict would outrun them, surely he would, he had a chance, he had a head start.

I called out to the widow then, she was sitting, panting in her armchair with a doily at its headrest, she had her handbell in her lap.

'Mrs Whiting, Mrs Whiting,' I whispered, 'you can let me out now. It's safe I think.'

But she sat on in her chair, stroking her handbell.

'Mrs Whiting,' I said, 'do you hear me?'

'My heart,' she said, 'old organ. Old muscle.'

'Will you let me out?'

'Will I?'

'Yes, will you, please, Mrs Whiting.'

'Oh, Lucy, dear Lucy, I do not think I can.'

'Yes, you can, Mrs Whiting, yes you will.'

'No, no I cannot, you see, dear Lucy, I know that you are about to turn, I've seen it in your face. I do know when such things are about to happen. I've never yet been wrong.'

'Please, Mrs Whiting, I'm begging you.'

'I don't think it'll be very long, dear. Not long at all.'

'I need to get out, please, please Mrs Whiting, poor Benedict!'

'And then all will be done.'

'I have money.'

'Yes dear, but it's not really money I care for.'

'I'll find you such things, better things, the best.'

'I'm so sorry, Lucy, believe me, I am, but I mean to collect you. Do you see? I mean to put you upon the shelf there. I would like that, I'll look after you, have no fear of that. I mean to polish you, and dust you. I shall not ever forget you. I'll cherish you, I promise. You'll never be neglected, but loved, dear, only loved.'

I sat hunched in the darkness, sometimes looking at the old woman through the hatch slit, she dozed with the handbell in her lap. I saw her get up after a while and move her things about, admiring her collection, making much fuss of it, I believe she was readying it for a new member. She was waiting for me. Did I feel like I was turning, did I feel it, that buckling, shrinking, sickening feel? I wasn't certain. The pain in my limbs may just be from my old wounds, or because I was so buckled over in there, the bad feeling in my stomach, that hollow yearning, was surely because I was hungry, because I needed to eat.

Or was it that other pain? Was I beginning . . . No, no, Lucy, you cannot think like that, you mustn't. You've got things to do. You must help Benedict before he's harmed. You cannot turn to a button when he needs you, that'd be no good, how can you help anyone when you're a button . . . a button . . . a clay button. And having these thoughts, round and rounding in my tired head, I seemed to be nodding off. I seemed to be sleeping a while and in that sleep, all of a sudden, there she was. The woman. The matchstick woman, she was very close to me, I knew it. She somehow knew where I was. She sensed it, she sniffed me.

'Me,' she said, 'me, me! I come!'

In my dream I tried to run from her, but suddenly there was smoke rising all about and I was choking and there were flames. I dreamt round and round, and felt myself spinning and clattering, growing so small again, and that face, the face of the other woman, long and thin and crying out for her life, trying to take mine from me, to scrabble back. But then suddenly pushing her away was Clod, Clod in a room, in a dark grey room, and the matchwoman was very frightened of him and then she was gone again, the flame was out, the smoke disappeared.

I opened my eyes.

I was still there, locked up in the old woman's cooking stove, still doubled up in the dark, Mrs Whiting was shuffling nearby.

'You're done, I reckon,' she said, 'poor dear. I heard the turning, the fuss, the swift movement, you cannot stop it. I knew you were mine from the moment I saw you at the door. I knew I'd collect you. But you'll be hot yet, I'll leave you to cool a moment. I'm glad it's over; I never like the wait. My poor heart.'

She had a pair of fire tongs with her, she leant them against the cooker.

There was a knock at the door.

'I'm busy,' she said, then she whispered to me, 'This is our moment, isn't it, no one else's?'

She lifted the latch but did not open it.

'Let it cool, best to let it cool.'

I readied myself, put my feet to the door meaning to slam it hard and knock the old bat over.

But instead the door to her apartment was opened.

Hold on, Lucy, not yet, not yet.

'I said I was busy,' said the widow.

There were official Iremonger men walking into the room.

'Good evening, masters,' she said. 'I did not know it was you, I'm very glad to receive you. May I help you, poor old thing that I am, in any way?'

'Your house is in front of ours.'

'I know,' she said, 'that has always been true.'

'It is directly in front of Bayleaf House, the nearest habitation.'

'I have ever been grateful for the view.'

'The heaps are shifting, they are brewing bad.'

'They will get agitated, but if you have put the It back, and I'm sure you have, such capability – muscles! – then it shall calm soon enough. (I know nothing about it, you understand, nothing to do with me.) For myself, I'm an old woman only, thrice widowed with all her small property about her. Little keepsakes, mementoes, of no monetary value, but valued highly, on an emotional plane.'

'Never seen the heaps so upset. And your home so close to ours.'

'We shall, we residents here,' she said, 'under my guidance, keep ourselves most quiet and discreet, a nice house on a nice street.'

'No'

'No?'

'This house is too close by half.'

'It has ever been here, masters, why does it offend you now?'

'There are other movements, movements of people not

houses, there are changes coming, great and fearful changes, changes in which small people, little people, minor creatures, such as yourself . . .'

'Father was tall, I remember.'

'Will likely be brushed aside, trodden on, it cannot be helped. It is the nature of the times. The Heap Wall is buckling.'

'Buckling?'

'It may break.'

'Oh my weak heart.'

'Here we are on high ground, on the highest ground of Foulsham.'

'Are we? *Are* we? Yes, I suppose we are.'

'The great house, Heap House, is uncertain in this weather, and it has been made necessary for some of its residents to be repatriated.'

'Oh yes?'

'To be in a safer place, you understand.'

'Oh yes?'

'They have been moved.'

'Oh yes?'

'The family shall stay in Bayleaf House.'

'Oh yes?'

'And the servants.'

'Yes?'

'They are here.'

'Here in Foulsham?'

'Here in this boarding house.'

'But there are no rooms.'

'There are many rooms.'

'But the paying guests?'

'Are requested to find alternative accommodations.'

'Oh. Oh?'

'You have a question?'

'And I myself?'

'Are to leave.'

'To leave!'

What a scream followed, a scream of a terrible hurt beast, a soul's scream.

'Leave, I cannot leave! Cruel!' she cried. 'This is my home! These are my things! How can I leave them? No, no, it's unthinkable!'

'It was your home, and now it is requisitioned. Take what you can manage and be a history.'

'No! *No!*' she shrieked. 'I cannot! My home! My things! They are *mine*!'

The widow ran around in a panic until she was picked up and carried out, how she cried, the poor old thing, how she scratched at the strong arms taking her away. 'Muscles!' It was enough to make you pity her. I should even perhaps have thought of helping her, only then the new resident of that busy room marched in and I felt all my hope fading away. For I knew her, oh I knew her all right, her in her corset, her with her sharp looks. When she smiled the teeth were quite worn away, I knew that, I remembered that.

Mrs Piggott, housekeeper.

'This,' she said, 'this is my parlour?'

'Yes, Mrs Piggott, until the House has been declared safe.'

'I shall have these ugly things removed, thrown from the

windows, that shall be the quickest way. Let us make short work of it. Iremongers!' she called. Various serving girls ran forward. I knew their uniform, didn't I. Hadn't I worn it myself? 'I'll have a bed set up here, and I want all of this rubbish, every last bit, removed. Do it, please, we'll have this temporary house in order!'

'Yes, Mrs Piggott,' they chorused, they tugged down the windows and let the Foulsham smog in, very thick it was, I could hear the Heaps bubbling and cracking in the background. The servants started throwing out all the precious belongings of Mrs Whiting, they hurled them out into the street below, I could hear them shattering, and along with them, a part of that rash removal, was a soup pot and a pair of candle scissors, my own dear mother and father, and I could not cry out to stop them. And then I saw the faces of those serving girls, many of them I could remember so clearly. I had slept in the same dormitory as them, told them my story, and all of them, to my head were only ever called Iremonger.

But, hang on a moment, that wasn't exactly true either, was it? Not all of them, I knew a name of one of them. Wasn't likely to forget that. There she was, the auburn creature, Mary Staggs herself. I could of spat. How I should like to toss *her* from a high window. With what diligence did she throw the stuff from the old woman's home.

'Wait!' Piggott called. 'Leave that.' She was pointing at Mr Whiting. 'That shall have a use.'

And she put old Mr Whiting to immediate use, her bony wrist flapped back and forth and set the maids all over the house come running to her.

'Listen now, listen good, my dear ones! My Lady Ommaball Oliff is this moment on the train heading towards Bayleaf House, her marble mantelpiece, at great labour, has been uprooted and is in the car beside her. She is apt to be very put out and disturbed. She has never yet spent a day outside of Heap House, nor even out of her own fine apartment. She may be a little short of temper, and we must calm her and be a cushion for her pain, we must provide her with every comfort. There shall be plenty of time to get our quarters ready, right now it is my lady who we must attend to. I want every one of you to be immaculate and lined up upon the station platform ready to receive her. Do you hear me, Iremongers?'

And the resulting resounding, 'Yes, Mrs Piggot!' might have swung chandeliers, had the boarding house any such thing.

Then the serving girls were busy about their business. I saw the unfortunate spectacle of Piggott regarding herself in a small looking glass and picking at her stubby teeth, before at last she smoothed down the corset over her dress and marched out, closing the door behind her.

This was my chance, maybe there shouldn't be another. I'd get out of this house and fast as I could before those Iremongers found me. This house was indeed a deathtrap now.

I pushed open the cooker, it creaked somewhat but no one came. I moved over to the door and looked through the keyhole, no one there, noise down below, no doubt the serving maids were rushing across the way to old Bayleaf House. I'd been in there once myself, before the whole terror began. Well then, give them a moment, clattering on the stairs. No doubt all Sturridge's men were there as well. Wait, wait, don't mess it up, take your time. Listen out. Nothing there? Nothing, all gone out.

So I opened the door slowly, slowly. Come on, Lucy Pennant, out you go, back out, steady, steady.

I was on the landing, no one there at first, not a person, but then suddenly at the bottom, there was Rawling the porter and before him came the heavy thudding of Mr Sturridge and many men in leathers too, their faces quite concealed, all hurrying up, coming my way.

There was nowhere to go, couldn't go back, must go up, up higher, up to the top if needs be, to the very attic. I went up a flight, terrified to see someone on my way, no one yet, a door opened and there was Mr Briggs, the shining underbutler, his door wide open, carefully positioning what looked like a load of pin cushions.

'Briggs! Briggs, man!' called Sturridge.

Briggs dropped a pin cushion in surprise and the moment he bent down to pick it up I rushed past his door and went further upwards, more noise more people in this house, how ever many were there now, up and up, round the corner.

Here, where the carpet was a different colour, grey because of all the dust and dirt, all the cobwebs and dead things, further up, further up, the stairs creaking, shouldn't go up there, wrong to do, my mother said I never should, but I did then, I must, was at the top even, very dark, more noises below, there was a door before me, there was a door handle, I turned it. It wasn't locked, I opened the door, hard to open, pushed hard against, I heard a ripping, a tumbling of stuff, but it gave way at last and I stepped in. Shoved the door closed behind me.

Couldn't see anything, nothing at all, dark, dark.

There's no one here at all, never has been.

But wait.

I felt a coldness against my face.

'Who's there?' I asked.

No answer.

Nothing, no one, spooking myself. That's all.

Was I?

Hang on, hang on just a minute. Go, Lucy, get out, get out of there fast, go down the stairs, run screaming down the stairs, better be out of there, better be anywhere than here, I've been frightened of this place all my life. It's horrid, horrible, something foul's in here, something very nasty.

What was that? Something moved.

I heard it then, I definitely did, something breathing, something in the corner there, something creeping something ghastly. What ever is this foul thing? Whatever it is, it's done bad things. It's all bad, black dripping bad, surely even Piggott had some kindness in her, some little, little good somewhere about? Something breathing there, oh God.

'Who's there?' I whispered.

I heard the breathing more clearly, someone breathing. Someone shifting, in the darkness, coming closer.

'I'm not frightened, come close and I'll give you such a wallop.'

But it came on and it kept on coming.

I wasn't going to let it just chew me up. I wasn't going to walk down its mouth. No, I was going to smack it hard just as it was going to eat me up. I was going to hurt it back, hurt it for all it was worth. I'm Lucy Bloody Pennant I am and I'm that done with hiding.

I let out a gasp and rushed at the thing. I swung a hard thump at its head, what a wallop, and the thing fell to the ground. I'd smacked it good and proper. Hah! What a one you are, Lucy! I'd pulverise the very devil. Come on again, you thing of dark. I'll have at you again. Come closer, I order you, come on up, come another. I'm ready. But the thing, that thing in the corner, it gives out a groan. Kick it, Lucy, kick it, kick it, kick it until it stops, but then it groaned,

'Lucy?'

'Come again?'

'Lucy.'

'What?'

'Lucy.'

'Eh? What?'

'Lucy!'

Clod bloody Clod bloody Clod bloody Clod!

The Porter Rawling

19

OH MY RED

Clod Iremonger's narrative continued

Oh my Red

She hit me. She hit me so hard across the face that truly I thought I might crack like an egg. She hit me, of course she did. How should I know it was her if she hadn't hit me? What a hurt she was, Lucy Pennant, the very best hurt that ever there was.

'Clod? Bloody Clod?'

'Ow!'

'Clod, Clod, say something. Say something this instant.'

'That hurt!'

'Oh Clod, I done it again, ain't I?'

And she was laughing and crying all at once. Lucy was, Lucy again, could she be, could it, how to believe such a thing. Lucy. Lucy. She was kissing me then all over my face, even where it hurt so, kissing and kissing. Her lips found mine. My heavens.

Salty. The warmth of her and the taste of her, there it was again, I'd never forget that. The gladness of it, the giddiness, the joy. Such joy. That feeling in me, building.

'Lucy?'

'Yes it bloody is.'

'I never thought I'd see you again.'

'And there's faith for you, right there.'

'And Lucy you're not a button.'

'Can a button do this?' she said, kissing me. 'And this?'

'I do not believe so. Perhaps you may try again?'

'I've been a button,' she said. 'I was nearly a button not long ago, and she means me to be a button again. Ada Cruickshanks does.'

'And I've been thinged, Lucy. I've been a golden half sovereign in my time since last I saw you,' I said.

'Have you?' she laughed. 'Isn't that just like you. I have to be a clay button and you get to be a sov. Where's your plug then?'

'I've lost him. And your matches are still with them?'

'They're somewhere close by, that's for certain, I can feel her, very near she is. Looking for me, you might say. Sniffing for me.'

'Then we're both likely to be very ill, I think.'

'Well, I shan't be a button again. I shan't let her. I'll get her goat.'

'Lucy, Lucy Pennant, it's you and your considerable red hair and all your freckles.'

'Every one of them!'

'I am right glad.'

"Right glad' are you? I'd forgotten how posh you are.'

'Oh Lucy, there's much to do, and terrible business it is.'

'Know where we are, Clod? This minute?'

'Foulsham . . . and out of the window, I saw just through the curtains, is Bayleaf House.'

'And what are we in? Name on this particular location?'

'I do not know it, a poor place of some sort.'

'Careful now, I'll knock the other side of you. It's my home, isn't it, where I grew up.'

'Is it? How strange. I should like to see it, could you show me?'

'Not just yet, there's people below with dreadful bad manners. They'd like to have us, no doubt, be most grateful to know that we're up here all along.'

I told her of my run through Foulsham and of the Tailor. But most of all of the business of Bayleaf House, of the breathing in of childhoods.

''Tis monstrous. I'll kill them Iremongers! 'Tisn't right! To do that!'

'I'm an Iremonger, I'll always be an Iremonger.'

'And I'm a Pennant, last there is. Can't help your family, they say, can chose your friends. You, you're my friend, I chose you. There, live with it! I've been searching for you, I made a promise, you're stuck with me, Clod Iremonger, I'm your thing. Like it, lump it, don't make much difference, you're in my heart and there's an end on it.'

'Lucy, I must stop all this.'

'Not without me. I won't let you.'

'This is all Iremonger doing.'

'I'll give you such a knock.'

'Oh, Lucy, I am so happy to see you, at least there's you for all the pain. When did you come to yourself again, however did you manage it?'

And she told me all that had happened until the moment she opened the attic door and found me with a thump. And there was something terrible in that story, something to break my heart and stop anything from coming right ever again.

'You kissed him?' I asked.

'Well, he was the one that done it really,' she said. 'I was just there.'

'But you didn't push him away.'

'Well,' she said, 'no.'

'Oh.'

'Come on, Clod, don't go quiet on me. You're the talker you are, you never stop talking.'

But I did not feel like talking then. I felt my Iremonger heart shrivelling up, growing smaller and harder.

'Come, Clod, it didn't mean anything.'

Smaller, smaller.

'Clod, talk to me.'

'Do you love him?'

'Oh, Clod!'

'If you love him,' I said, 'I shan't stand in your way.'

'What a child you are!'

'No doubt.'

'Clod, dear Clod. I shouldn't have told you. I just wanted to tell you everything . . . Clod, Clod!'

'I'm going now,' I said, getting up. 'I've business to attend to.'

'Clod!'

'What's that?'

We both were suddenly very quiet then, we both had heard it. There was someone on the stairs.

What are Little Men Made of?

Whoever it was was coming slowly up the attic stairs, whoever it was didn't stop but came on. We both kept very still. A scratching voice quietly sung out,

'I've been sifting! I've been sorting!
I've been gone so very long,
I've been sifting! I've been sorting!
Come and harken to my song!'

The singing stopped. Started again.

'I've been sifting! I've been sorting!
I am coming now to you,
I've been sifting! I've been sorting!
I am here now! Here now! Boo!'

'Who's there?' the someone the other side of the door asked. 'Whoever is it there? I do know there's someone. I heard voices. I've not heard voices before, not until this day. Is it one of the new servants, don't be afrit if it is. There's nothing to be frit of. It's only me, Rawling the porter. I'm going to open this door now; I'm a-coming in.'

The doorhandle turned, the door was heaved open. There was a dark figure there, stumbling blindly in the half-light.

'Who's there?' he called. 'I'll know you if you please.'

I listened to him, listened for his inner voice, but there wasn't one, nothing at all. He was absolutely silent. There was no noise, no sound, no mutter from within him, just an emptiness there, a hollowness, nothing, no one, no man.

'Who's there?' he called once more, but his voice was breathless now, like he was frightened. 'I know you're in here. Come out will you? I'll not be angry.'

I heard the things of the attic creeping away, trying to get away from him.

It was the opposite of the gathering that pursued me across the Forest of the Roof of Heap House, that thing made more noise almost than the heaps, but this thing was silence itself, no sound came out of it. I'd never heard such empty silence.

'Come now, let's be having you.'

He was close to Lucy, edging in her direction. He had no right to do that, not this thing, not this no-noise, this quietness. I would not let him touch her, I would not let him.

'You're not anyone,' I said.

'Who said that?' cried the man-thing Rawling, turning in my direction. 'Come here now. I'll have you now. I know where you are.'

'You're no one, are you?' I said.

'Papers, I'll have papers.'

'But what about *your* papers?' I said. 'Whatever name they have on them is a lie, you're not real.'

'I am,' he said, offended, put out, as if I'd stung him. 'I'll show you how real I am. Come here, you varmint!'

'You're no one, Mr Rawling.' This was from Lucy, in another part of the room, following on from what I was saying, playing my game. Rawling spun around. Lucy said, 'You're not anyone at all.'

'There's two on them!'

'Here I am,' I said.

'Here I am,' said Lucy.

'Here I am,' I said.

'Here I am,' said Lucy.

He swung for Lucy and had hold of her by a wrist.

'Well then, I got one of you, haven't I?'

I rushed over, I felt in the half-light for the buttons around Rawling's thick suit. I found one, two, I pulled them open, ripped them off.

'Here!' he cried. 'What's happening? What are you doing?'

He thrashed out, he struck me and I fell.

'Lucy,' I said, and I prayed I was right. 'I've undone two of his jacket buttons. Listen to me, you must rip him open. He's not real, he just seems it. He's not an actual person; he's just made of bits. Feel for the stitching.'

The man Rawling snapped his jaw like a dog, snapped it closer and closer to Lucy's face.

I called then, to the broken bellows, the old picture frame, to the crib.

'Now, I do beg you, Bentley Orford, Helen, Mrs Bailey, I do beg you now. I hear you over there, Tom Goldsmith. I do hear you. You're a wicker chair, I know. I do beg you, come at him, come at it, or he'll so pull the life out of everything.'

Nothing, no movement, and Lucy struggling.

'I do command thee!' I cried.

'Clod!' cried Lucy.

'Varmint!' cried the porter.

'NOW!' I bellowed.

And then they swooped, and then they came raining in.

'Lucy, down, get down!'

The chair came behind him and kicked him like a horse he fell into it, and it, dear Tom Goldsmith, lacking any wicker seating, caused the porter to sit down trapped. Then the old crib flew from the corner and smacked his head, so that it knocked right back, and should have stopped any true man, but the head swung back and the face, though horribly squashed, was still there and re-forming.

'Here!' he cried. 'What are you doing? 'Tisn't legal, is it?'

Then swooping down like some albatross came Bentley Orford the split bellows and it dived into the trapped stomach of the porter and it punctured a good hole, and then up it climbed, flying round to come at him again.

Once there was an opening the rest was easier, I ran forward then and pulled at it, made a great huge rent, such a tearing. It was as if someone had ripped a bit of the world.

'What?' he said, quite stunned. 'What have you done to me?'

I opened the curtain, let in the light. There was this man Rawling sat in the middle of the room, Lucy in shock, backing away from him. There was a great hole in his shirt, only it wasn't a him, and pebbles and bits of old glass and sand were pouring out of it onto the floor.

'You didn't ought to do that,' he said, as it tumbled out. He tried to stop it, he caught some in his hands, but the rest poured on.

'You're not anyone,' I said to him, calmly as I could.

'I'm Rawling,' he said, but even as he said it his head was sinking in like a sack being emptied.

'You're not a person,' I said. 'You're not. I'm sorry.'

'Oh,' he, *it* is more correct, it muttered.

'Oh . . . oh . . . oh I didn't know,' it managed.

The rest of it fell down just then, an old leather thing, tipping out. Out came the stench again and a small cloud of black air, fading on the attic ceiling. Not human, how ever had we thought it was? And then it had stopped, it was just a pile of emptied stuff, a burst something or other.

'What was that?' said Lucy.

'It was just things put together and stitched up and given a little warmth,' I said. 'It didn't have a noise within it, there was no sound. I couldn't hear anything coming out of it, nothing at all. Just silence. Awful silence.'

We looked down at the strange puddle that was Rawling, his leather skin all hollowed out.

'How, Clod, how did you do that, move all those things about?'

'Yes, Lucy, I had almost forgot. Go now, go quick, Tom and Bentley, Mrs Bailey and Helen, quick now, up the chimney and out of the attic, to newer homes. I do thank. I thank you.'

Some tumbled down the stairs, the bellows smashed right through a window.

'What a business,' Lucy said. 'To do that! Clod, little Clod, what a thing! What a person you are!' she said, but she looked shocked at me, disturbed, I might say.

'Yes,' I said, after a moment, 'I think it was well done.'

'That took some doing, opening him up like that.'

'Oh Lucy, he was so silent.'

'Wouldn't do to make a mistake, would it? To undo a man ... who wasn't made of muck.'

'No, no indeed I do not think it should.'

'Clod?'

'Lucy?'

'Clod?'

'Lucy?'

'Clod, I'm sorry, Clod. Oh Clod, it is you, whatever it is that you can do, still is after all only you. Oh Clod, listen, it was nothing, that bloody kiss. You should see the poor creature, he's been in such trouble. And I don't know where he is now, or if he's safe. I think he must go back to the heaps. But only if he wants to, only then. He's so helpless, though so big a fellow. Perhaps we could help him, you and me, we should. Then you'll see him, you'll understand then.'

'Lucy,' I said, 'I think for my part that I must go into Bayleaf House.'

'We can help one another, can't we? We're all we've got, aren't we?'

'I've got to stop Grandfather.'

'Well then, I shall come along too.'

'It is Iremonger business.'

'Is it? Oh, is it? And I've got a box of matches over there through those gates and I mean to have them. So we'll be moving in the same direction I reckon.'

'It's a free world.'

'Not much it isn't.'

'But it *should* be,' I said, 'and that's the point.'

'Perhaps I shall need your particular hearing, Clod, in the search of my matches, perhaps you'd oblige. Maybe you'd set a dinner service on them for me.'

'I hear the undervoice, Lucy, inside everyone,' I said. 'I hear it getting louder when it's going to turn, till it's almost shrieking in my ear. The object sort of calls out, it's not English, but I seem to hear it. It gets louder and stronger and then it sort of gallops in speed and then there's no stopping it, then it flips the person. Past a certain point there's no stopping it, I think.'

'Do you hear it, Clod?' she said, stepping towards me, 'Do you hear it in me? It's not shrieking now is it?'

'No, no, it's not, not now.'

'What an awful queer fellow you are,' she said, stepping closer.

'I'm sorry for it.'

'Not your fault I suppose.'

'Very kind of you.'

'Glad to see you.'

'Yes,' I said, 'most awfully.'

She opened her arms and I went to her, we held each other tight, so tight against everything that surrounded and threatened to bring us down.

'What do you hear?' she said.

'"Clay button",' I said, '"clay button" to the rhythm of your heart.'

Her Royal Highness Victoria
by the Grace of God

20

AN INSTRUCTION TO TERMINATE

Being the official and final proclamation concerning the Borough of Forlichingham, London
Highly Secret

WESTMINSTER, LONDON

ON THIS DAY, the 26th January in the year of our Lord 1876, it has been declared by unanimous vote that the borough district of the great city of London, Capital of the British Isles and of the British Empire, that is called by the name FORLICHINGHAM, is deemed a place of HIGH TOXICITY and is DANGEROUS UNTO THE HEALTH OF THE NATION.

Daily reports of deaths by noxious gas escaping from that region and of a most gross and disturbing build up of *FILTH* has brought into danger the very existence of London. Two hundred and twelve (212) pensioners of the neighbouring borough of Lambeth have been found stiff and discoloured and dead in their homes. An increase of RICKETS has been noted in INFANCY throughout the CITY. BLACKLUNG is increasing. The infection *VIBRIO CHOLERAE* more commonly termed BLUE DISEASE, believed to have been tamed under the labour of JOSEPH WILLIAM BAZALGETTE, is once more in the INCREASE. Daily the winds shed POLLUTANTS from *FORLICHINGHAM* into the city, and that there is a general air of SWEET FOUL STENCH from the top of HIGHGATE unto the bottom of SHOREDITCH. That this FOUL AIR is POISONING and REDUCES LIFE, and that in the market of COVENT GARDEN it has been shown as PROOF that milk arrived in that place SPOILS WITHIN A HALF HOUR due to the PUTRIFYING STENCH of *FORLICHINGHAM*.

THEREFORE, after great discussion and debate, having sought advice of the great officers of HYGIENE, and of those of understanding of the DISPOSAL OF REFUSE that the place *FORLICHINGHAM*, previously given license unto the family known as *IREMONGER* to take from LONDON all that LONDON discards, is a license that is now, under immediate notice, REVOKED PERPETUALLY. And that, this family *IREMONGER*, no longer to any satisfaction policing the EXPULSIONS of LONDON, that the region *FORLICHINGHAM* is a HORRID and DANGEROUS region, known for FILTH, VICE and MURDERINGS COMMON, that therefore it is deemed MOST necessary that the place *FORLICHINGHAM* be TAMED or REMOVED from LONDON. And that therefore, it is understood that there being no chance of BRINGING CLEAN and CALM such a POISONOUS and POISONING location, that the place *FORLICHINGHAM* be in a most thorough and complete way REMOVED, DESTROYED, BROUGHT DOWN, ERASED, from LONDON, and that LOSS OF LIFE therein of the inhabitants of the (FORMER) borough of *FORLICHINGHAM*, be deemed regrettable but ESSENTIAL for the SURVIVAL of the SOVEREIGN city LONDON.

Therefore in SOLEMNITY do we the below signed agree this day, that the place *FORLICHINGHAM* be in a most SWIFT, THOROUGH, ABSOLUTE and TERRIBLE way, **BURNT UNTO THE GROUND** until the HEAT of FIRE has in COMPLETE STERILITY destroyed all GERMS that there abide.

The actions (being all complete in readiness and preparedness in desperate advance of this bill) to ACHIEVE all the above NECESSITIES be carried out with due SPEED and DILIGENCE.

And that as such, it shall become, in the name of Her Majesty, Victoria, by the Grace of God, of the United Kingdom of Great Britain and Ireland, Queen, Defender of the Faith, Empress of India, immediate

People of Foulsham

21

TO THE GATES

Lucy Pennant's narrative continued

I called them all leathermen after that, after Porter Rawling had been unstitched and spilled all over the attic floor. That's how we always knew them as after, those people, those things I should say, them leathermen.

Clod told me there were hundreds of them all over Foulsham. I couldn't say if it were true or not, but Rawling seemed so realistic that who's to say, really, when you look about, who's to say who's real and who's not? There are many people over the years I always thought may just have been filled with sawdust for all the sense you got out of them, and others too who had been so cruel and unkind that they may just as well have been sharp metal through and through, deaf to all bargaining and pleading. Well then, who's to say who's a person?

He was. He had life in him; he could command things to move, however should a person do that. Who ever was Clod, that thing-mover? He looked iller, he shook rather with the weight of it all. I should never have told him about that kiss, should never, that was stupid. I just wanted him, of all people, to know everything about me. Clod with his big old head and his worried eyes, thinner, thinner. No plug about him. His white skin, so white like paper, I'd kiss that all over. Why him, I wondered. Why of all of them, him? Not so very much to look at. You might think that if you didn't know him.

Didn't matter what he looked like, he was himself. He was fighting against it all, my Clod, my everyday Clod. Wouldn't be without him now, not for anything, I'd keep him very close. Never felt that before. All of him. All of me. Can't break something like that, can you? That's strong isn't it? How strong is it, I wondered. Others should try to cut it. Couldn't let them.

I prodded the Rawling pile with my foot.

'Well, Clod, he doesn't look very dangerous now, does he?'

'No, no, Lucy, not one bit.'

'He seemed not to know what he was.'

'I don't suppose they do. I don't suppose any of them do. And there are hundreds of them, Rippit said, they're everywhere about. All Grandfather's dolls.'

'What's he want with them, an old man like that, with his toys?'

'He's building an army,' said Clod. 'That's what the Tailor told me, a great army, to take on London itself.'

Army. That word again. Gnawing at me.

'We'll get us an army and all,' I said.

'Lucy Pennant, how should we ever do that?'

'Nothing will ever be right, will it,' I said, 'not if we don't stand up for it. We live our lives cowering in an attic room until our days are spent. Everyone's hiding in the shadows, being knocked down, one by one, being taken by Umbitt and all his kind. How many hundreds have just sat there and let it all happen to them, all the hunger, selling off their own children? It won't do any more; we'll stand up. We'll not let it go on any longer. We'll have an army of our own. We'll go from street to street, from house to house, and we'll get them to come along with us. We'll show them, and every time we stand up to the Iremongers, then that's a victory, isn't it, and if enough of us stand up and keep standing up then they'll be done for, I reckon. There's more of us than them, much more, if we all get up and say "No" and "Shan't" then that'll hurt them, that'll crush them, shan't it? We'll bloody do it, we'll show them!' I cried. I'd worked myself up, like I was standing at a pulpit but there were only me and Clod, children in an attic room. I'd sort of forgotten that bit, that brung me down a little. 'Well, that's what I think.'

'Yes,' he said softly. 'Yes, I think that too.'

'You do?'

'Yes, Lucy, I'm not afraid to die. I was, was very much in truth, when I was a coin, when I couldn't do anything, only just be moved about by other people, that was frightening because I was lost then, but I'm me again now, and I know Grandfather and what he could do, and I'll do anything to stop him.'

'Then we don't care if we die?'

'No, we don't care if we die.'

'Let them kill us.'

'It'd be just like them.'

'Last time it was for you to show me about, Clod. Now we're on my turf. This is my place isn't it? It may not be as big or grand as yours, but it's not stolen and before your family moved in it was filled with good people. Well it was filled with ordinary people at any rate. They weren't doing anyone any harm, not for the most part. If there's any in this house that still knows me, we'll find them. And we'll get my school fellows along too.'

'Lucy, I do like your idea of an army. It sounds wonderful indeed, and I think of all the people I know you'd be the person to do it, but I think that it should take a time, shouldn't it, and I think there may not be so very much time. Perhaps you may find your friends, will you, and meanwhile I shall go to those gates.'

'Well,' I said, terrified of parting from him, 'well, I could come with you . . .'

'If you could find friends, if you could get help, that should be best I think.'

'Do you? Should it?'

'Lucy, I think if I can get to Grandfather, if I can get hold of his personal cuspidor, Jack Pike is its name, that's what I hear it saying, if I could only get hold of Jack Pike, and steal it from him. Or if only I could make Grandfather stop it all, oh perhaps, perhaps I may have to kill him. Perhaps I may call upon all the objects in there, if I could summon them, perhaps they'd come to me, perhaps they might . . . well, there's no good just talking about it, we must get on.'

'Clod? Clod, would you do such a thing?'

'I could get close, you see. I'm an Iremonger. They'd let me through I think. It does make sense. They don't know that I can ask the things to move, they don't know that yet. So perhaps I may do something with that after all. And it's best not to think of it, overly much, but to rush along, right now. Show me down, Lucy. Get me out of this place. Deliver me to the gates, and then get your friends.'

I didn't say anything to that. If I spoke I knew I'd start weeping. And I mustn't do that. Not a baby am I, after all. Time enough for weeping, Clod, when you're out of my sight.

There wasn't anyone on the landing, not straight off. Most of them had gone across the way into Bayleaf. We'd heard the train arriving, the old woman, that dreadful old woman. Made me sick just to think of her. She'll have come now, must have, the train had made its great shriek.

Looking through a downstairs window there was much running about outside the house. There were crates laid out before the place, all busy, them Iremonger ants, all such a rush on.

We'd made it down one floor, two more to go. There was the old crib on the landing now, beside it the wicker chair. And we were making our steady progress, and couldn't hear anyone nearby, even Clod couldn't hear anyone and that was the best proof of all, wasn't it, because there was never a one for lugs than Clod with all his hidden voices, quite mental when you think about, so on we were creeping in our little way when there came a mighty noise, didn't there. It was a long, wailing, trumpeting sound. I knew that, didn't I? Well enough to make me stop dead in my tracks. I'd heard it before, way back in my childhood when a heapgate came crashing down and fifty people were crushed or drowned.

Should never like to hear that noise, even when it was only sounded for practise, to make sure the great horns were still working. It was the flood horn, one of the great flood horns of the Heap Wall. Where that horn stood there was danger and all must flee from that part, but then there came another horn and another yet, and another, yet another, all joining up, all calling out, all of them, all across the wall. All the horns were sounding, I reckoned, from all over the wall.

'What is it, Lucy, why do you look like that?'

'The walls, Clod. It's the siren for the walls, never heard that many going off at once before. I think the wall may come down, and not just in one place but all over. Oh, I think Benedict is still out then, they have not put him back.'

'And what should happen then, Lucy, if the wall comes down?'

'Then it shall flood, shan't it, you dunce, what d'you think? It'll flood the whole place, it'll all come down. And hundreds, hundreds will be drowned!'

'Is there nowhere safe?'

'This is the high ground here. This is where they'll come. Safer here, but not safe, there's nowhere that's safe if the wall comes down.'

'Everyone will come? All here?'

'Yes, Clod, and soon, any moment, I reckon, all will bubble up around us.'

'I shan't hear, Lucy, I shall not be able to hear anything. I'll be so deaf, it'll be worse than the storming in Heap House, a thousand times worse than that. I shan't be able to hear the objects' names, and without hearing their names I never shall be able to command them.'

'Well then, you'd better keep close, hadn't you?'

'But I think perhaps, it may be, in some small way, perhaps it is good news, Lucy. I think it might be.'

'What's good about it?'

'That's when I'll go in and find Grandfather, in all the chaos.'

'Oh, Clod, are you dumb enough?'

'I think I am.'

There was silence then, a strange long silence between the warning horns and all that followed, like grabbing a little bit of air before plunging deep under the waves. Like the intake of breath before screaming. Small silence, but what a pregnant silence, shouldn't last, shouldn't last.

Then there was a sort of mild buzzing sound in the distance like that of an insect humming about, except the insect wasn't rushing about rooms in the still winter cold, bouncing into windowpanes, no, it was outside, and the buzzing didn't stay on a note, that deep humming grew louder and got greater until you could tell what it was. It was the noise of people all together, not knowing what to do other than scream, and all screaming, all roaring together in a panic, all of one mind. It was a great collection it was. I'd heard of all those other collections before, a parliament of rooks, a squabble of seagulls, a mischief of rats, an itch of Iremongers, well here was another one to add to it, a new collective: a panic of people.

'Everyone's coming?' Clod said.

'A whole army,' I said.

'But you can't control them, can you? They're all in a chaos.'

'Might,' I said, 'might just.'

'Who's there?'

People up the stairs then, coming towards us, three of them, big fellows in leathers, all leathers, hood and all, the works. I looked at Clod.

'Lucy,' he whispered, 'I can't hear anything, except for a button. It's quiet enough now. They're Rawling's sort.'

'What you doing here? This place is requisitioned!'

'Is it?' I said. 'Well no one told us.'

'You're not to be here!'

'Why, who says so?' I asked.

'Umbitt, owner.'

'This is my home. I was born here.'

'Taken over, requisitioned.'

'Oh yes?'

'Most certainly!' the leatherman said.

'Do you hear that noise?' I asked. 'That rising rumbling?'

'We hear it,' they said.

'Know what it is?' I asked.

'Heaps,' they said. 'Heaps is upset.'

'No,' I said, 'it's not the heaps. It's not the heaps at all. It's Foulsham that noise is, all the people of Foulsham, and do you know what they're doing? They're coming up this way, and I think they're unhappy and, you know what, I think they'd all like to come inside, come and live in this high-ground home. They'll break the door down, I reckon.'

Well it wasn't brilliant but it was a start. It was practise, wasn't it, the leathers, dumb creatures, looked at one another and in a mumble hurried away down the stairs in a rush, gone to see for themselves.

Shouldn't be long now, certainly shouldn't, that great noise was smashing around the old buildings of Filching, strange noise to my ears, bouncing off here and there, ugly, distorted, misshapen, that's what it was to my ears, Lord knows what it was to Clod's. We went down after the leathers.

'Where are you going?' they said.

'Out,' I said. 'You told us we weren't to stay here.'

'That's right. Very good. Sling your hook.'

'Good luck,' I said, 'for you shall surely need it.'

'Hey, what's the matter with him? He looks quite turned he does.'

Poor Clod was very white and trembled all over, there must have been that roaring in his head, like all the people of the world at his earholes and shouting in them, not just the voices of them screaming, but the voices *in* them, all a tumble. Couldn't listen to that very long, I supposed, not for long before you'd go mad with all the noise. I had to get him in, into Bayleaf House before all that racket made his brain turn porridge.

'He's all right,' I said to the leathers, 'just sensitive, he's made of silk he is, unlike you lot.'

'Hop it,' said a leatherman, what a look on his face, panic it was. Couldn't blame him really. You could see the crowds now, rushing up the hill, they'd be here any moment. Don't want to get between them and those leathers, shouldn't give them the pleasure.

On, Clod, on we go.

He looked at me, pointed to his ears, shook his head.

I nodded back at him.

All right then, no more talking, this is it, this is. There it stood, Bayleaf House, its chimneys still spewing, greyer than any grave, hard and cold and unlovely, well then, onwards. Better hurry. That noise behind us was coming on fast.

I tugged us over, up the hill and to the very gate.

Part Three

Bayleaf House Factory

The Grand Officer Moorcus Iremonger
and his Toastrack

22

AT THE GATES

Lucy Pennant's narrative continued

The sentry was closing the factory gate up, locking it.

'Let us in,' I said. 'You must let us in.'

'No entry!' said the sentry. 'Strict orders.'

'Did you not hear the horns sounding?'

'That I did.'

'Know what that means?'

'Likely there'll be a flooding.'

'And people will drown.'

'I can't help that.'

'You'll let people die.'

'I have my orders.'

'Listen, just let us in, before the others come, will you? My friend here, he's not well as you see.'

'No,' he said, 'can't be done.'

'I've some money,' I said.

'I'm not talking to you no more. Disperse.'

'Yes you are talking to me, and you'll keep talking, and you'll let us in. Listen, he's an Iremonger, isn't he. An actual Iremonger. He belongs the other side of the gate.'

'No one's to come through, no exception.'

'He's Clod Iremonger.'

'I don't care who he is.'

'He needs to be let in!'

'No one can pass!'

He stood silent, as other guards ran to the gate, there were more then, ten, twenty of the Iremonger guards with their Bayleaf collars, all running out, a sergeant among them now, wearing a brass helmet, thinking himself very grand no doubt. Then I saw his medal. Something familiar in that. Then I knew him, Moorcus Iremonger, Clod's cousin. He that was the cause of Tummis's drowning. I pushed Clod. What to do? What to do? I saw behind Moorcus then, always nearby, like a dog on a leash, his turned birth object, his Roland Cullis. He'd help if there was ever a chance, surely he would.

Behind us the first Foulsham people were coming, all in their rags and leathers, holding what things they had, never very much, all that they could carry, maybe all that they owned, children on shoulders and in carts, old people in carts, all the worried, hungry, desperate, all up to the gate of Bayleaf House, with the horns blowing again and all the terror that the Heap Wall was going to give, and all would drown in its bursting.

I didn't need to talk then. We stayed at the gate, we'd be the first through I reckoned. Wouldn't lose our place, not if I could help it. I was pushing them off already. I was standing our ground. Poor Clod looked terrified to his soul. He looked down mostly, wincing all the while, all those people in his head, couldn't keep them there long, and more people coming on, the gates around Bayleaf House thick with people, so many people, all Foulsham at the gates. Moorcus marched forward, he called out,

'You will disperse, no congregations of people are permitted. This is private property.'

'Don't you hear the horns?' someone called.

'There is no danger, there is no cause for alarm. Please disperse now, go back to your homes.'

'But the horns,' another person shouted, 'do you not hear them? They're all sounding!'

'The walls shall hold,' Moorcus said, and how white he looked. 'Nothing can break the great Heap Wall. You are all safe. Go home, please, go home. All is well. Grandfather – Umbitt Owner has issued his guarantee. The wall is safe. Go home. Do not be distressed.'

That stopped many of them, some fell to whispering then, perhaps all was well, perhaps it was safe to go home.

'Move along now,' said Moorcus, 'go back to your homes, get back now. You'd do well to go home, see that your homes are safe. There are looters at large, it has been reported, even now your homes are in peril. Why will you not protect your things? What have you left there? It may not be there when you go back, quick now. While you still have time.'

And that did it for some of them. Those sheep, they trembled and trotted off back down the lane though the horns had sounded. How they cowered. They weren't people, they were beasts of burden. They'd do anything you ever told them. Believe anything if it was said official enough. They'd all drown, they were going back now, turning around, heading down, down to their drownings. But these were my people, my people that I'd lived with all my life, my people who'd been tugged down so much it hurt to get up, they had to stand up, they had to stand up or they'd have no chance. An army, an army, hold fast together.

'He's lying!' I shouted. And some even stopped their plodding right then. 'He's lying! He just wants you to get away. He's sending you away to drown. Do you not hear the horns? Are you deaf? Them horns mean danger, the wall's going to give!'

'Shut it, miss,' said the sentry, 'that's enough!'

Clod looked up at me, he couldn't have heard but he had a pained smile on his face, and that was encouragement enough.

'He's sending you down to your deaths,' I called. 'You want to die, off you go then, trot along. But I'm staying here and if we all stay here, then we'll get through this gate and be on the high ground. If we all stay they can't stop us. How many more of us are there than them?'

'Hundreds. Hundreds on us!' Jenny called from the crowding.

There she was, there was Bug and all, and the rest of the kids from school, all together: there's a voice, I reckoned, there's lungs there. Now's the time.

'How long will we let them break us?' I had such a taste for it then. 'How long must they order and bully? They let us drown out there in the heaps. How many of us have been pulled under? They've taken our children from us, how many of our children are in that building now, stolen from us! What have they done with them? Come now, let us see. We will be let in!'

'Let us in!' called Jenny.

'Let us in!' echoed her schoolfellows.

'Your children have been ticketed,' called Moorcus, so white now, Roland in the background behind him, smiling, enjoying Moorcus's misery. 'You have been compensated, heavily compensated. Your relations are all well and all cared for.'

'How do you know?' I cried. 'Have you seen them?'

'We haven't,' someone grumbled.

'No, we haven't,' called Jenny.

'That's right,' from somewhere else, the voices coming from all over now, we'd got them talking.

'Look up, good people of Foulsham,' I shouted, my face as red as my hair, 'look up there at that building, our people are in there and beyond this gate is high ground and safe.' Then I chanted, 'LET US IN! LET US IN! LET US IN!'

'LET US IN!' they went.

'LET US IN!'

'LET US IN!'

What a chorus, what a people, what an army.

'People of Foulsham . . .'

'LET US IN!'

'People of Foulsham . . .'

'LET US IN!'

Jenny and her company came around to me then, all that young of Foulsham, such schoolfellows, so strong of voice, all busy about me, all flared up for the fight. Moorcus's hands were shaking. He held a shining pistol out. He fired it into the air. The people moved back a little, so many hundreds of heads flinching.

'People of Foulsham,' Moorcus cried. 'People, good people, would you be so foolish as to be taken in by the whining of a child? Do you even know who this girl is? She's a criminal, a thief, she is wanted by the Iremonger police.'

'That's a lie!' I cried.

'She has been about your streets, murdering in the night. She's with the Tailor!'

'Is she? Is she?' went the rumbling populace.

'No I am not,' I cried. 'Don't you believe him, he's just trying to let you drown, stand up to him. Do I look like any tailor? You've seen the posters, all of you have, a tall man, long and stretched. I am just a girl, that's all, a girl of Foulsham. He'd have me murdered, this Iremonger, quick as anything. I'm sixteen years old, I've lived here all my life. My own parents were turned. He knows nothing of what it is to live and die in Foulsham. How many raids have you seen, how many people disappeared in the night? Why won't he let you in? Why won't he let you come through? You've heard the horns, that's what really matters, if the walls come down, you'll drown. He'll watch you! Let us in through these gates, Moorcus Iremonger, or you'll find we're strong enough to break them down. Let us in! Let us in!'

'LET US IN! LET US IN!'

'You will disperse!' Moorcus screamed.

'LET US IN! LET US IN!'

'Oh, please let us in!' an old man wailed.

'You must disperse! You have been warned.'

'Moorcus,' I screamed. 'LET US THROUGH!'

He recognised me then I think, he saw who was with me.

Roland Cullis saw us too, Roland was clapping.

'Come again!' yelled Roland. 'Get him again, smack him.'

'Shut it, Toastrack,' yelled Moorcus, and hit at his birth companion with the butt of his pistol, blood coming quickly, before turning again to face us. 'Clod Iremonger,' his lips seemed to pronounce, though it was so loud about now you could not hear those sounds, but then it was certain he was saying over and again, 'Clod, Clod, Clod.'

He wavered his pistol in our direction, trying to aim it at Clod. He'd shoot I reckoned. Such a look of hate on his face. I tried to push Clod behind me, but in all that struggle at the gates, the sentry had a hold of me through the gate, his hand about my mouth, his arm round my neck, and I could not breathe.

'That's quite enough, little miss,' he said. 'We've had just about enough.'

'Look! Look!' Jenny called. 'Look what they're doing to her!'

Clod was about, quickly enough, and while the sentry had hold of me, he pulled at the sentry's uniform, he ripped it open, brass buttons flying (I thought how Benedict would like them, where was he, where was he now?). Clod's hands scrabbled about, Clod's eyes wide with panic, as he sought to tear the man open, then I had breath again, the sentry staggered back, a hole in him, he stood back.

'Soldiers, help that man!' called Moorcus, and many ran over to him. 'You were warned. And now it is too late. This mob has wounded one of my men. This shall not be tolerated.'

The people of Foulsham were silent then, all mumbling and of a panic. But the soldiers gathered around the sentry stood back now, stood away from him in horror.

'Look! Look!' I tried to call out, but my throat was so hoarse, but they had seen right enough. They had noticed.

The sentry had his hand at his opened gut , which was was leaking sand, it gushed out of him, and he wailed at the sight of it, his mouth wide open but no sound coming out, as sand gushed and gushed from him. And all saw.

'Not real! Not real!'

'What was that?'

'He's made of sand.'

'A man can't be made of sand.'

'Not a man, that wasn't a man.'

'If not a man then what?'

But other soldiers had come then and were now running in formation before the gate and the railings, all with rifles. All at aim.

'People of Foulsham, this is your last chance,' shrieked Moorcus, his voice so high and panicked. 'You must disperse. Go to your homes. Go now and there shall be no further trouble.'

What a sight, all them guns pointing at us. They wouldn't would they, shoot a fellow? Oh they would, they'd gun us all down. We meant as nothing to them. They'd kill us, kill us at the gate. They'd murder in plain sight, in cold blood.

'Aim!' called Moorcus.

At least twenty of the guns aimed particularly at us, at the gate. Oh, Clod, oh Clod, it was a small stand, ours was, it didn't amount to much. People were screaming down the hill, but others were shouting at the soldiers, screaming at them, and the sky was turning black.

Black?

Black already?

A boom then, a great explosion.

That's when I saw, that's when I understood the new screaming. We'd all been looking at the soldiers in front of Bayleaf, or over towards the Heap Wall waiting for it to tumble. We'd none of us been looking towards London, in the other direction, none of us had, but now we could see it.

The blackness. The blackness. It wasn't night. It wasn't night at all, it was fire. Fire! Foulsham was on fire. Whole streets of it must have gone up by then, great gusts of black smoke, not from the chimneys of Bayleaf but from the fire spreading all around us.

'Let us in, oh let us in!' people cried.

'We shall be burnt, burnt to death!'

'Help us! Oh help!'

The soldiers weren't aiming any longer, their guns were pointing down now. They were all staring at the great flames.

Half of Foulsham must be gone, and in such speed. Buildings were falling. People were dying now, the heat was spreading up the hill, smoke was coming and suddenly the rats were with us.

Rats!

Rats everywhere!

Rats, thick about our heels, rats screaming and screeching. They were through the gates in a moment, all screaming, such a carpet of them, whole black fields.

'Get inside!' cried Moorcus to his soldiers. 'Run for cover!'

They went, all those uniformed Iremongers all sprinting inwards, some tripping over the rats, falling to the ground and the rats pouring over them. What a thing, what a thing to be drowned in rat, a hand rising briefly among the horrible moving ground, but then back down again. But the gates, the hot gates, had not been unlocked.

They pushed then the people did, they pushed and crushed and heaved against the railings, threw themselves at them, and all behind likewise, pushing for all their worth as the flames climbed higher from Foulsham. How many people were trampled to death that horror evening, the pushing and coughing, the smoke, the darkness, we shall be trampled on, we shall go under. People climbed over people in their panic, regardless of what was beneath them and what harm it did, the flames coming closer encouraged them so.

But that was what gave me the idea, that was what did it, I shoved Clod up then. I was stronger than him. I heaved him high, shunted him up aside the railings. He was screaming at me, no doubt it was not anything pleasant that he was screaming, but I pushed him up, till my hands were on his heels and then his feet and then I shoved him up again and he was at the spikes by then, so I shoved further, and, I admit it, I climbed on someone myself to get him over. How he shook and screamed but so did so many others. Why should his panic be paid any heed?

Up and up, I had his feet in my hands, pushing him over, couldn't see him any more. There were so many shoving hard against me that I could see nothing for the squashing of all Foulsham people. Up up and then, then, then his feet weren't in my hands any longer. I wasn't holding anything any more. I wasn't with Clod any longer. He'd gone tumbling over, he'd gone, he'd quite gone and I'd lost him all over again. I couldn't move for all the people, smashing against me. Did he make it over, wherever was he?

Go on, Clod man, go on. It hurts to see you go. I hate to see you go.

I'll catch you up, you go ahead, my own dear man. This gate cannot hold forever now, can it? That's logic that is, sure to give.

How the breath was squeezed out of me, shoved out of me.

I thought they'd have me through these bars in pieces the rate they were going, for it really did seem the bars were so up to me that they were actually in me. I tried to cover my face over, I hunched, braced myself as much as ever I could, I closed my eyes and waited for it to happen.

And there she was.

She'd been waiting.

The matchstick woman, the me-me-me thing.

23

BEYOND THE GATES

Clod Iremonger's narrative continued

Within the grounds

I couldn't see her. I couldn't see her at all. There was such a crowding, so many hundreds of people, all the people of Foulsham up against the gates, and the gates leaning in places against the weight of so many, but not giving over. Oh, the people, the trapped people. Where was Lucy? I couldn't see her in all that great thronging.

Just me in so much space, on the path up to Bayleaf House, and behind me such a crushing-crowding, such breathlessness, and the noise, the awful noise behind me, noise of objects calling out from inside so many hundreds of people, how should I ever hear a clay button calling in such confusion? I had to get on, I must get on. I'd stop them. I should stop them, such cries behind me. If only a key, if only there was a key to the gates.

People get lost in wars, trampled over, I see that, there's no individuals only masses, masses being crushed. But I should do it, stop it all. I had the strength for it then. I'd end this horror, maybe. I'd call on all the things that had voice, they'd come to me, I'd command them.

Everything I love I leave behind me this day, the other side of that horror gate, and I shall tumble in, and I mean to do what I can. Behind me the gate was coming down, was leaning over, and more and more people climbing on, other people adding more weight to it, until it bowed ever more, they'd come through, they'd be through in a minute. Quick, Clod, quick, my deafness, before they crush you in their terror and you never find Grandfather.

'Lucy!' I cried, stuck there in the middle.

I turned back a moment, towards the gate, and as I did a seagull swooped down, it flew right at me. It clawed at my hair but I ran on towards the gate. The gull swerved round and came in again, clawing at me, snapping with its beak, screaming at me as if I'd done it some personal wrong. No matter the seagull, it may scream for all it likes. It may snap at me, and bleed me, let it, I'd had worse. I could not see her anywhere, where was she? Quick. Clod, quick, I told myself, get inside or you may never have your chance.

'I am sorry, Lucy. I am sorry. I can think of no other way!'

One last look back, if only I could see her, I should never hope to see her again after. One last look. The railings of Bayleaf House were bending so, they should not hold, all those hands reaching out through them, such screams, and such blackness too and terrible soot, a screen of black darkness, black and thick, as I rushed on towards Bayleaf House, I could barely see it then for all the smoking.

The gull was screaming, screaming. Must get away from it.

The doors were open. The soldiers must have left them like that in their hurrying or couldn't close them for all the rats. Well then, in, in I went, into it, into the cruel lanes of Bayleaf House along all those pipes and pipes and pipes of it, on to find Grandfather, on to an end.

I'm wearing grey flannel trousers. What a man, Clod Iremonger; you're quite coming into yourself. I've aged this day. God keep her, little heart, who knows what shall happen. Who is there that ever knows?

Deaf, so deaf, I couldn't hear anything but bounded on, some bleeding in my ears, all swollen and numbed, poor things, the sounding in my head like a bell, so loud and plain and on a constant shrill note that it was as if all sounds had been removed from the world, as if there was but one sound so complete and plain that it had drowned all others out. But it began ring-ing-ing again, the further I was away from Foulsham people the more the note broke up, and with that shift came more pain as sound began to return, so that I could distinguish distant voices, so many voices, so many names, calling out in agony. As if each was trying to be heard by me, calling, begging, pleading to be heard.

Doors all opened, things all spilled out on the floor, the whole place had been turned inside out, panic was here in these rooms, panic everywhere, panic up and down the House, panic had been there but panic seemed to have fled, for there was no one about, no one at all.

'Halloo!' I cried. 'Hallo! I'm back! 'Tis Clod, Clod himself, who's there that knows me? You sought me I know, well here I am, Clod, I say. 'Tis Clod! Clod! Clod himself!'

That seagull was behind me again, screaming. I ran along, away from it.

I felt there was someone about me, someone very dark, like a shadow creeping along the wall, tickling the surface, yet when I turned there was no one, just empty passageway, and thick black smoke that crawled its way like a dark vein across the ceiling. Yet I felt someone, I was certain that I had. My ears, my ears would know. Give them time, then they'd hear again. They'd separate those names out, then I'd know. Ever less names calling now, ever less.

Where was everyone?

Oh big and abandoned place, where are your people?

There! I walked straight in to them, a great long line of them, hundreds and more, all shuffling out, all in clothing black and dull, old ones and young ones, his and hers, people, people walking through the smoking house, ordinary looking people, not panicked but calm, out into the borough, they had sticks with them and truncheons, they were all headed out, every one of them, and all of their mouths opened just a little and black smoke coming from them and all were not people, they were all guts of dirt, these ones were, souls of sawdust, some of Grandfather's great army, out and out into Foulsham, going in to meet the real people who they imitated, Grandfather's army of defence, into flames and soot. Dummies.

They blocked so much space, Grandfather's army did, they quite choked the corridors, but they were all of a mind, and went out to meet the running hordes who must surely have trampled the gates down. I found a way past them and so down I went down, and down away from them, for there was nowhere else to go but down and down. There was that black smoke again, trailing across the ceiling, it was dripping, I noticed. It dripped tar, the smoke did. It seemed poisonous, somehow very deadly, so down, yes down and down I went to get away from that coiling black smoke that seemed to draw itself along with me, an insubstantial worm, snake more like, growing thicker.

'Grandfather! Grandfather!' I called.

Down, Clod, down and down, calling out for Grandfather, calling for him to come. And then at last there was someone in the distance, further down the curling iron stairway, someone calling back. Someone calling me, calling my name.

My Cousin

I recognised the figure long before I was close. I'd know that figure anywhere, it was part of the heart of me, part of the blood of me, stuff of my bones, was that young man. Back again, come back again to me.

'Tummis! Tummis Iremonger himself!' I cried, for there, down the stairs at the end of a corridor, wandering in confusion, was my tall and my lanky, wearing some long leather coat, there he was with his faint hair that did not persuade and, true to his very form, a seagull flying nearby.

'Oh Tummis, oh my Tummis!' I cried, for I had thought the

dear sweet fellow dead and dead and lost and gone.

'What ho! Clodius, my plug.' I could hear him, my ears were coming back. I could hear him. To hear that voice again that I thought had been silenced forevermore. The sheer wonder of it. 'How do you do these long days of darkness and sooting, and fleeing and flowing, it is ever a pleasure to set eyes on you.'

'Drip! Drip, my drip!' I cried.

'Old plug!'

'Old drip!'

'I got a little lost,' he said. 'I thought I'd gone under in the heaps, did for a bit. It went black for a moment, dirt in my mouth. I tasted that dirt, it was the dirt of death I think, but, in truth, old Clod, old man, old mucker, old joker, old thing of things, I didn't fancy the taste overmuch. I spat it out, and here am I, so to speak, back on dry land, if you'll have it so, if this be solid which I'm not entirely positive, well then here I am, if you see me so, well then I must be me.'

It wasn't a seagull with him, I'd been wrong in that. It was a cat, I saw now, similar colouring to a seagull, but a cat nevertheless. I'd not seen him with a cat before, though he did ever love all animals.

'Come, Clod, my dearest,' he called. He was still a little distance away. 'Come, Clod, ever closer, Clod closer closer Clod, let me hold you. Clod, let me touch you. Clod, come on now. Clod, do come, come up, come here. Clod, come to your old drip. Clod, Clod.'

But that, that was not quite Tummis, was it now, that was not sounding all him, not entirely, not exactly. Something was a little wrong, what was it, what could it be? If I could only hear better. Then I saw it, I saw there was no snot about him, there was no drip from his nose. Perhaps it was just that he'd lost a little of his dripping, that being separated so long from his tap he'd dried up some. And how could he then, I wondered, how could he have survived without his tap, without his Hilary Evelyn? And hadn't you, Clod, hadn't you listened to that old tap on the dreadful night hadn't you heard it, I asked myself. Yes, yes, I certainly had heard it. And what did it say? It said nothing. Dead it was. Dead all over. Oh, come on Clod, don't be cruel, know a friend, know a love when you see one, don't abandon after all that he must have been through.

'Tummis,' I said quietly.

'Here I am!' he said, his arms opened wide, ready to take me in. 'Come, why procrastinate, plunge, plug, in.'

There was a slight panic in his face, but it was not, I think, a Tummis look of panic, and his arms, I thought now, they were not quite the long heron arms of my departed schooldays, they seemed a little shorter to me, and what was that dangling from the end of one? Some sort of huge bat, some great dark thing he'd found fallen from Heap House's attic, but no, that wasn't it, it was an umbrella. Just an umbrella. A plain umbrella. What did he want with that?

'Come here, Clod!' he said. 'Come along. Hurry up, move now, move.'

That didn't sound like Tummis, not at all Tummis that wasn't.

No, Clod. Stop, Clod. I didn't think it was Tummis, not Tummis after all. It was someone else, wasn't it? It was someone trying to be Tummis. But only Tummis could be Tummis. There was only ever one Tummis that I ever knew and that

Tummis, that poor lost never-to-be-forgotten Tummis was a dead Tummis, was *the* dead Tummis, and so this one, this other Tummis, this was a counterfeit. What a thing to do, what new cruelty was this, why would they? How could they? Why fake a Tummis? He must have been waiting for me, he must have been put here just to catch me, and when he'd caught me, what then, what should he do with me?

'Come, Clod! Come on! Here!'

Then I saw I was wrong again, quite wrong, not about Untummis, for certainly it was a very vague Tummis now, Untummis it was for definite. I was wrong about the animal. It wasn't a cat, wasn't after all. I hadn't seen somehow through all that smoke, so much smoke now, thickening the corridor, that black smoke again, that black, black smoke that dripped. Had the fire reached the building then? Was it running inside, up and down corridors, eating its way in and out, growing bigger and braver and blacker and hotter? But that cat, that cat that I thought a cat previously, was a dog now, a great white and grey dog. How had I never noticed that, a great big beautiful thing? What a head it had upon it and what teeth there were to it! How could I have failed to notice such a hound before? Wagging its tail, it was wagging its tail for me. Nice doggy.

'Please come, Clod, old plug, hurry along now, won't you? Don't give up on a chum. Don't throw me over. It's me, *Tummis*!'

Something in the smoky light glinted upon the dog, something small and something metal. I saw it then, all of a sudden, all of a very sudden, suddenly I knew what that was. I had seen it before plain enough. A copper ring it was, I'd known it on a different dark evening. Listen, listen, Clod. I could just hear the copper ring,

'Still am I Agatha Peel, still with her.'

And from the Untummis's arm,

'I am Barnaby Macmillan, oh let me free!'

It wasn't safe, Clod, it wasn't at all safe there. It wasn't right, no, no, it was very wrong. These two, Untummis and his dog, they were wrong, those two; wrong they were, very very wrong. Get out, Clod, get out of there as fast as you may, they'll murder you those two, they mean to unclod Clod.

'Hey!' Untummis called. 'Clod fellow, be a friend to me, won't you?'

I saw something else then, saw it clear, there was a line on Untummis's nose, a growing line, a nose, a glue-on, stuck-on, a made-up moulded nose, a borrowed nose coming off, a pretend Tummis nose, his shape, yes by God it was, his very loving undripping stolen shape, but not his, no-no, never his, they lie these two, they lie and lie and would kill a fellow.

'Why hang back so? Why do you tarry? Plug! My plug!'

The dog's tail was not wagging now, the dog's hackles had gone up, it was growling now, it was barking, but the bark it let out wasn't like any bark I'd ever heard, it was calling out a name, I heard it then, it was shouting-howling a name,

'Unry! Unry!'

'Otta!' called Untummis in a very un-Tummis like voice. 'Otta! Are we seen?'

And then, my Tummis, that vision of my Tummis, fell off, all that was Tummis fell dead and stripped to the floor, like he'd been killed all over again, that thing, that Untummis,

Wrongtummis, Strangetummis, Stolentummis was coming undone, there was a different someone there, someone I'd not known before, a far from Tummis person with holes in his face where his nose should be, and he, this featureless fellow, was screaming.

'Get out! Get out, get away! Get gone!'

And turning and screaming in reply I fled that horror scene. I tried to run along the landing there but a bat flew out, screaming and screeching and so I turned about and went down again, yet further down into the darkness of Bayleaf House.

I was down and down stairs, down deep into the house, and no nearer to Grandfather than when first I entered. There was luggage all about now, so many things packed up and waiting to go, and above me, as if it was following me all through Bayleaf House, that black smoke dancing on the ceiling. Then I saw that there were two figures, beautiful women rising out of the gloom. Tall and lovely women coming out of the fog. I knew them, I knew those ladies well indeed. I'd known them all my life. They weren't real, they were solid through and through, they were marble, always had been. They propped up a great mantel shelf as they always had, but they had moved, they were on a wooden train car, packed up ready to go.

Augusta Ingrid Ernesta Hoffman.

I knew they must come then, other words from another body.

'Clodius,' the voice said, 'are you come?'

And I replied,

'Hullo, Granny.'